CHapter 8

A Identify parts of a research
paper

A Literature Review, Theory
Development, Hypotheses.

A Research Methods

Results

INVESTING IN PEOPLE

Financial Impact of Human Resource Initiatives

Discution

conclusion.

SO-AZT-105

INVESTING IN PEOPLE

Financial Impact of Human Resource Initiatives
Third Edition

Wayne F. Cascio

John W. Boudreau

Alexis A. Fink

Society for Human Resource Management
Alexandria, Virginia I shrm.org
Society for Human Resource Management, India Office
Mumbai, India I shrmindia.org
Society for Human Resource Management
Haidian District Beijing, China I shrm.org/cn
Society for Human Resource Management, Middle East and Africa Office
Dubai, UAE I shrm.org/pages/mena.aspx

BETTER WORKPLACES
BETTER WORLD™

This publication is designed to provide accurate and authoritative information regarding the subject matter covered. It is sold with the understanding that neither the publisher nor the author is engaged in rendering legal or other professional service. If legal advice or other expert assistance is required, the services of a competent, licensed professional should be sought. The federal and state laws discussed in this book are subject to frequent revision and interpretation by amendments or judicial revisions that may significantly affect employer or employee rights and obligations. Readers are encouraged to seek legal counsel regarding specific policies and practices in their organizations.

This book is published by the Society for Human Resource Management (SHRM). The interpretations, conclusions, and recommendations in this book are those of the author and do not necessarily represent those of the publisher.

SHRM, the Society for Human Resource Management, creates better workplaces where employers and employees thrive together. As the voice of all things work, workers and the workplace, SHRM is the foremost expert, convener and thought leader on issues impacting today's evolving workplaces. With 300,000+ HR and business executive members in 165 countries, SHRM impacts the lives of more than 115 million workers and families globally. Learn more at SHRM.org and on Twitter @SHRM.

Library of Congress Cataloging-in-Publication Data

Names: Cascio, Wayne F., author. | Boudreau, John W., author. | Fink, Alexis A., author.
Title: Investing in people : financial impact of human resource initiatives / Wayne F. Cascio, John W. Boudreau, Alexis A. Fink.
Description: 3rd edition. | Alexandria, VA : Society for Human Resource Management, [2019]
Identifiers: LCCN 2019012961 (print) | LCCN 2019015784 (ebook) | ISBN 9781586446109 (pdf) | ISBN 9781586446116 (ePub) | ISBN 9781586446123 (Mobi) | ISBN 9781586446093 (pbk. : alk. paper)
Subjects: LCSH: Human capital--Accounting. | Labor costs--Accounting. | Employees--Training of. | Personnel management.
Classification: LCC HF5681.H8 (ebook) | LCC HF5681.H8 C37 2019 (print) | DDC 658.3--dc23

Printed in the United States of America, THIRD EDITION

PB Printing 10 9 8 7 6 5 4 3 2 1   61.19305

Dedications

From Wayne F. Cascio:

To my late parents, Frank and Joan Cascio, whose love and devotion to their family were the best investments they ever made.

From John W. Boudreau:

To my family, who continually inspire me to see the wonderful potential in people.

From Alexis A. Fink:

To my parents and my children, for their infinite support in ways large and small.

Table of Contents

Preface

The demand for organizational accountability has never been greater. This is true for all business processes, but perhaps even more so for decisions about people. The future of work, talent, and employment is changing at an unprecedented pace, and organizational decisions about how to invest in people are under increasing scrutiny. Leaders increasingly realize that their decisions about human resources are vital, in an increasingly uncertain and interconnected world. Yet organizational decisions about people remain some of the least systematic and evidence based, compared to decisions about resources such as money and technology. Therefore, a key responsibility of organization leaders, HR professionals, consultants, regulators, and policy-makers is to articulate and improve those decisions. That requires understanding and relying both on logical connections between progressive HR practices and organization performance, and on the data that articulate those connections. This book provides the logical frameworks, analytics, measures, and process elements to illuminate what's inside the metaphorical black box between HR practices and financial/business performance.

Investing in people can and should be as systematic as investing in any vital resource—using evidence-based, logical frameworks that optimize cost, risk, and return—but too often such people investments focus only on reducing costs or mimicking best practices. Too often, organizations adopt a "peanut-butter" approach to talent investments that spreads the same investments (for example, in training or staffing programs) over the entire organization, in an effort to be fair by being equal. It should come as no surprise when such policies are met with skepticism from leaders and employees who are asked to invest in programs or activities because HR—or even the CEO—says that everyone must do it. That approach is in stark contrast to approaches taken with other resources, such as customers and technology, where investments are targeted where they have the greatest effect. Why not make greater talent investments where they matter most? Optimizing investments in people, by investing more where the payoff is highest, is what we call a "decision-science" approach and provides the foundation for the techniques we present here.

Another fundamental principle is that the value of measurement is the extent to which it improves important decisions; that is particularly true for investments in people. It is not enough to build a larger number of or more precise measures. An optimal approach to measuring investments in people will integrate and balance people measures with logic, analytics, and knowledge processes (what we call the LAMP framework). So this book focuses on vital decisions and provides logical decision guides that show the links between HR programs, employee behaviors, and organizational outcomes. Each chapter includes recommendations about process, describing effective ways to communicate results to decision-makers.

In writing this book we drew extensively on our decades of experience assisting senior-level decision-makers to better understand and measure the impact of talent decisions, and also on the best available research that describes the connections between talent and organizational outcomes. We have been fortunate to work with both practicing leaders and academic researchers. This combination is essential for talent measurement and investment decisions to be truly evidence based and to achieve both practical relevance and logical rigor.

Investing in People draws on state-of-the art practice and research in disciplines including psychology, economics, accounting, and finance. Our aim is to provide tools that serve leaders inside and outside the HR profession. The tools help them work together to understand and describe the economic and other outcomes of their investments in people. We focus on HR investments with a rich history of data-based research, including staffing, training, workplace health, employee attitudes, and employee turnover, which also represent some of the most important strategic HR functions. This book provides specific formulas and calculations that you can use to evaluate the impact of your own talent decisions. To make the formulas easier to use, we developed software to accompany the chapters on the following topics: absenteeism, turnover, health and welfare, attitudes and engagement, work-life issues, external employee sourcing, the economic value of job performance, payoffs from selection, and payoffs from training and development.

The Society for Human Resource Management (SHRM) provided generous support for the development of the software, and you can access this software at the SHRM website (http://iip.shrm .org), regardless of whether you are a SHRM member. The software performs the calculations measures, so readers can focus on the logic, analytics, and processes necessary to improve strategic decisions about talent.

In sum, leaders inside and outside the HR profession must use more rigorous, logical, and principles-based frameworks to understand the connections between investments in people, enhanced human capital, and organizational success. We hope that this book serves as a go-to resource for those frameworks.

Acknowledgments

Published books represent more than the words that authors write, for they typically are products of the collective efforts of many people, and this one is no exception. We sincerely appreciate the enthusiastic encouragement and guidance that we received throughout the project from Matt Davis, manager of book publishing with the Society for Human Resource Management (SHRM). We also deeply appreciate the financial support provided by SHRM for the development of the software (accessible at http://iip.shrm.org) that accompanies the book, and we thank our software developers and updaters, Dr. Fred Oswald, Evan Mulfinger, and Leo Alexander III, for the high-quality software that they developed and continue to maintain. Of course, any omissions or errors are the responsibility of the authors alone.

Plan for the Book

Chapter 1, "HR Measurement Makes Investing in People More Strategic," introduces the fundamental principle of this book, that HR measurement is valuable to the extent that it improves vital decisions about talent and how it is organized. This decision-based approach to HR measurement leads to different approaches from the traditional focus on HR services or resource expenditures. It emphasizes that effective HR measures must be part of an investment decision system that recognizes the role of measures in enhancing decisions and organizational effectiveness. The elements of that framework are the guiding logic for each of the chapters that describe specific techniques and measures in selected HR areas.

Chapter 2, "Analytical Foundations of HR Measurement," describes three levels of sophistication in HR analytics, along with fundamental analytical rules and guiding concepts that are used throughout this book. These are similar to foundational principles in finance or marketing, such as risk, return, and economies of scale. New to this edition are discussions of data visualization, natural language processing, structural-equation modeling, and network analysis. Think of Chapter 2 as a primer on the fundamental ideas that all organization leaders should understand about good measurement, not only for investments in people but for all investments as well.

Chapter 3, "Talent Management as a Source of Competitive Advantage," is new to this edition and provides a foundational framework that explains and describes how investments in people enhance talent, and how talent contributes to organizational strategic success. It describes talent management and how to understand "talent segmentation" in the same way that marketing understands "customer segmentation." It shows how to integrate organizational programs aimed at enhancing talent, such as strategic workforce planning, high-potential programs, talent reviews and succession planning, and the role of these common programs in providing measures and frameworks to enhance investments in people.

Chapter 4, "The Hidden Costs of Absenteeism," describes why employee absence is still relevant, even as some work becomes more virtual and project based. Moreover, the chapter provides new research on presenteeism, where employees come to work but are not fully productive because of health problems or other reasons. The chapter shows you how to calculate the costs of employee absence and why those costs are often much higher than leaders realize. Finally, you will find several case studies and recommendations for reducing absence at work.

Chapter 5, "The High Cost of Employee Separations," describes how to calculate the fully loaded costs of employee turnover and how to incorporate them into a complete framework of turnover effects. We show that simple employee turnover rates can easily be misinterpreted, and how to avoid that with better logic and measures. We also discuss the hidden costs of layoffs, a factor often ignored when organizations use layoffs to reduce labor costs.

Chapter 6, "Employee Health, Wellness, and Welfare," presents methods to assess the costs of employee health and wellness problems, and the benefits of reducing those problems by investing in employee assistance and worksite health-promotion programs. It describes evidence-based frameworks for enhancing employee health and wellness, including not only specific programs but also organizational culture and leadership. It illustrates the frameworks using several examples of chronic conditions and successful health-program investments. The chapter also discusses the value of disease-prevention investments and the role of health, wellness, and welfare programs in an age of rising health costs.

Chapter 7, "Employee Attitudes and Engagement," begins by distinguishing three important attitudes from each other: job satisfaction, commitment, and engagement. It focuses on the economics of employee engagement, including research on how engagement and being a "best place to work" connect with customer service and financial results. The chapter pays particular attention to the importance of consistency in the level of analysis when measuring attitudes and outcomes at the individual, team, unit, and organizational levels.

Chapter 8, "Financial Effects of Workplace Flexibility Programs," describes how to evaluate and optimize investments that offer employees flexibility in when and where they work. These techniques are useful as organizations increasingly struggle with deciding how to optimally enhance employee work/life fit in an increasingly competitive work environment. You will find a framework for understanding how workplace flexibility affects organizational outcomes, and examples of organizations that successfully achieve strong returns on such investments.

Chapter 9, "Staffing Utility: The Concept and Its Measurement," introduces utility analysis, an important evidence-based framework for understanding how investments in HR programs, such as recruitment, staffing, training, and compensation, produce financial outcomes, and how to calculate them. Chapter 9 shows how the process of finding and acquiring human talent can be analyzed using tools similar to supply-chain analysis for other resources. That framework helps you optimize investments across the elements of the staffing process (sourcing, selecting, onboarding, etc.) and avoid the mistakes that arise by simply maximizing the payoffs of each element separately. You will discover how to describe and measure one of the most overlooked but vital issues related to talent: the financial value of improved job performance. The chapter provides a framework for understanding where improving performance makes a big difference, where its effects are smaller, and how you can actually estimate the value of improving performance in particular jobs or roles.

Chapter 10, "The Payoff from Improving Employee Selection," takes the utility-analysis framework from Chapter 9 and shows how to use it to calculate the economic value of staffing, including recruitment and selection. The formulas are based on decades of scholarly research and show how you can use statistics such as correlations, base rates, and selection ratios to unlock insights into significant organizational value. The software that accompanies the book simplifies the calculations so that readers can focus on the strategic implications of their findings (available at http://iip.shrm.org).

Chapter 11, "Costs and Benefits of HR Development Programs," addresses one of the most significant organizational enterprises: employee development. Many organizations make massive investments in this area, but specific payoffs are often unknown. This chapter shows you how to evaluate the impact of learning and development, whether delivered through traditional classroom training or through the myriad virtual and social-learning approaches. You will find that research shows that investments in training predict future stock prices. In this chapter you will learn how to use the utility-analysis and performance-value frameworks of Chapters 9 and 10 to estimate payoffs from learning and development within a logical and research-based framework that leaders can actually apply.

Chapter 12, "Talent-Investment Analysis: Catalyst for Change," provides a capstone chapter that integrates the previous material. It's not enough to have solid logic, analysis, and measurements that show the economic effects of talent investments. Key decision-makers must listen and act on them. This chapter describes strategies that we have used to communicate the financial implications of investing in people to employees and leaders outside the HR function. It shows how the HC BRidge framework can help you better connect investments in people to their effects on talent and to their ultimate effects on strategic success. Finally, this chapter also describes opportunities to integrate the decision-science approach to talent with ongoing organizational processes, such as strategy, budgeting, and performance management.

About the Authors

Wayne F. Cascio is a Distinguished University Professor at the University of Colorado, and he holds the Robert H. Reynolds Chair in Global Leadership at the University of Colorado Denver. He is a Fellow of the National Academy of Human Resources, the Academy of Management, the American Psychological Association, and the Australian Human Resources Institute. He has received the Michael R. Losey Human Resources Research Award from the Society for Human Resource Management, the Distinguished Scientific Contributions Award from the Society for Industrial and Organizational Psychology, and the George Petitpas (Lifetime Achievement) Award from the World Federation of People Management Associations. He has consulted with a wide variety of private- and public-sector organizations on six continents, and periodically he testifies as an expert witness in employment discrimination cases. Professor Cascio is an active researcher, writer, and speaker. He has published more than 200 articles and book chapters, has published 33 books, and has delivered more than 750 presentations to professional and business audiences worldwide.

John Boudreau is Research Director at the Center for Effective Organizations and Professor of Management and Organization in the Marshall School of Business at the University of Southern California and was formerly a professor at Cornell University. He is recognized worldwide by both scholars and organizational leaders, for breakthrough research on the bridge between superior human capital, talent, and sustainable competitive advantage. He advises organizations ranging from early stage companies, to government agencies and *Fortune* 100 organizations, to large multinational companies, on strategy, human resource management, work automation, and the future of work. Dr. Boudreau has published more than 100 books and articles, and his work has been featured in professional publications such as *Harvard Business Review*, the *Wall Street Journal*, *Forbes*, *Fast Company*, and *Business Week*. He has won scholarly achievement awards from the Academy of Management. Dr. Boudreau is a fellow of the American Psychological Association, the Society for Industrial and Organizational Psychology, and the National Academy of Human Resources, and the recipient of the Lifetime Achievement Award from the Human Resource Division of the Academy of Management.

Alexis A. Fink, PhD, has spent two decades leading talent analytics, talent management, and large-scale organizational change teams at leading global organizations, most recently Intel and Microsoft. In her practice, she has addressed leadership assessment and succession planning, sophisticated internal research projects, management development, culture and employee value proposition, employee surveys, acquisition integration, process improvement, and major IT implementations. Across multiple organizations and domain spaces, Alexis has brought a powerful focus on driving efficiency, effectiveness, and impact, working collaboratively with other disciplines to achieve business results. An effective and experienced global organizational leader herself, she has been able to practice what she preaches, building high-performance organizations that incorporate professionals from widely diverse backgrounds.

1

HR Measurement Makes Investing in People More Strategic

This book will help you better understand how to analyze, measure, and account for investments in people. However, although data and analysis are important to investing in people, they are really just a means to an end. The ultimate purpose of an investment framework is to improve decisions about those investments. Decisions about talent, human capital, and organizational effectiveness are increasingly central to the strategic success of virtually all organizations.

According to research from the Hay Group, businesses listed in *Fortune* magazine as the world's most admired companies invest in people and see them as assets to be developed, not simply as costs to be cut. Consider how the three most admired companies—firms comparable to UPS, Disney, McDonald's, and Marriott International—managed their people during the Great Recession, compared to their less-admired peers. Those companies were less likely to have laid off any employees (10 percent versus 23 percent, respectively). By even greater margins, they were less likely to have frozen hiring or pay, and by a giant margin (21 points), they were more likely to have invested the money and the effort to brand themselves as employers, not just as marketers to customers. They treated their people as assets, not expenses. Perhaps the most important lesson from these companies is that they did not launch their enlightened human capital philosophies when the recession hit; they'd been following them for years. Once a recession starts, it's too late. "Champions know what their most valuable asset is, and they give it the investment it deserves—through good times and bad."[1]

It is surprising how often companies address vital decisions about talent and how it is organized with limited measures or faulty logic. How would your organization measure the return on investments that retain vital talent? Would the future returns be as clear as the tangible short-term costs to be saved by layoffs? Does your organization have a logical and numbers-based approach to understanding the payoff from improved employee health, improvements in how employees are recruited and selected, reductions in turnover and absenteeism, or improvements in how employees are trained and developed? In most organizations, leaders who encounter such questions approach them with far less rigor and analysis than questions about other resources such as money, customers, and technology. Yet measures have immense potential to improve the decisions of HR and non-HR leaders.

This book is based on a fundamental principle: HR measurement adds value by improving vital decisions about talent and how it is organized.

This perspective was articulated by John Boudreau and Peter Ramstad in their book *Beyond HR.*[2] HR measurements must do more than evaluate the performance of HR programs and practices or prove that HR can be made tangible. Rather, HR measures must reinforce and teach the logical frameworks that support sound strategic decisions about talent.

In this book, we provide logical frameworks and measurement techniques to enhance decisions in several vital talent domains where decisions often lag behind scientific knowledge, and where mistakes frequently reduce strategic success. Those domains are listed here:

» Absenteeism (Chapter 4)
» Employee separations (Chapter 5)

» Employee health and welfare (Chapter 6)
» Employee attitudes and engagement (Chapter 7)
» Workplace flexibility (Chapter 8)
» Employee recruitment and selection (Chapter 9)
» The payoff from improved employee staffing (Chapter 10)
» The payoff from employee training and development (Chapter 11)

Each chapter provides a logical framework that describes the vital key variables that affect cost and value as well as specific measurement techniques and examples, often noting elements that frequently go unexamined or are overlooked in most HR and talent measurement systems. The importance of these topics is evident when you consider how well your organization would address the following questions if your CEO were to pose them:

» Chapter 4: "I know that, on any given day, about 5 percent of our employees are absent. Yet everyone seems to be able to cover for the absent employees, and the work seems to get done. Should we try to reduce this absence rate, and if we did, what would be the benefit to our organization?"

» Chapter 5: "Our total employment costs are higher than those of our competitors, so I need you to lay off 10 percent of our employees. It seems 'fair' to reduce headcount by 10 percent in every unit, but we project different growth in different units. What's the right way to distribute the layoffs?"

» Chapter 5: "Our turnover rate among engineers is 10 percent higher than that of our competitors. Why hasn't HR instituted programs to get it down to the industry levels? What are the costs or benefits of employee turnover?"

» Chapter 6: "In a globally competitive environment, we can't afford to provide high levels of healthcare and health coverage for our employees. Every company is cutting health coverage, and so must we. There are cheaper healthcare and insurance programs that can cut our costs by 15 percent. Why aren't we offering cheaper health benefits?"

» Chapter 7: "I see that there is a high correlation between employee engagement scores and sales revenue across our different regions. Does that mean that if we raise engagement scores, our sales go up?"

» Chapter 7: "I read that companies with high employee satisfaction have high financial returns, so I want you to develop an employee engagement measure and hold our unit managers accountable for raising the average employee engagement in each of their units."

» Chapter 8: "I hear a lot about the increasing demand for workplace flexibility, but my generation found a way to work the long hours and have a family. Is this generation really that different, or should we find folks that are more ambitious? Are there really tangible connections between workplace flexibility and organizational productivity? If there are, how would we measure them and track the benefits of workplace flexibility programs?"

» Chapter 9: "We expect to grow our sales 15 percent per year for the next five years. I need you to hire enough sales candidates to increase the size of our sales force by 15 percent a year and do that without exceeding benchmark costs per hire in our industry. What are those costs?"

» Chapter 10: "What is the value of good versus great performance? Is it necessary to have great performance in every job and on every job element? Where should I push employees to improve their performance, and where is it enough that they meet the required standard?"

» Chapter 11: "I know that we can deliver training much more cheaply if we just outsource our internal training group and rely on off-the-shelf training products to build the skills that we need. We could shut down our corporate university and save millions."

In every case, the question or request reflects assumptions about the relationship between decisions about HR programs and the ultimate costs or benefits of those decisions. Too often, such decisions are made based on very naïve logical frameworks, such as the idea that a proportional increase in sales requires the same proportional increase in the number of employees, or that across-the-board layoffs are logical because they spread the pain equally. In this book, we help you understand that these assumptions are often well meaning but wrong, and we show how better HR measurement can correct them.

Two issues are at work here. First, business leaders inside and outside the HR profession need more rigorous, logical, and principles-based frameworks for understanding the connections between human capital and organization success. Those frameworks constitute a "decision science" for talent and organization, just as finance and marketing comprise decision sciences for money and customer resources.

Second, leaders inside and outside the HR profession are often unaware of existing scientifically supported ways to measure and evaluate the implications of decisions about human resources. An essential pillar of any decision science is a measurement system that improves decisions through sound scientific principles and logical relationships.

The topics covered in this book represent areas where very important decisions are constantly made about talent, decisions that ultimately drive significant shifts in strategic value. Also, they are areas where fundamental measurement principles have been developed, often through decades of scientific study, but where such principles are rarely used by decision-makers. This is not meant to imply that HR and business leaders are not smart and effective executives. However, there are areas where the typical decisions lag behind state-of-the-art knowledge.

The measurement and decision frameworks in these chapters are also grounded in general principles that support measurement systems in all areas of organizational decision-making; such principles include data analysis and research design, the distinction between correlations and causes, the power of break-even analysis, and ways to account for economic effects that occur over time. Those principles are described in Chapter 2, "Analytical Foundations of HR Measurement," and then used throughout this book.

Next, we show how a decision science approach to HR measurement leads to very different approaches from the traditional one, and we introduce the frameworks from this decision-based approach that will become the foundation for the rest of this book.

How a Decision Science Influences HR Measurement and Investments in People

When HR measures are carefully aligned with powerful, logical frameworks, human capital–measurement systems not only track the effectiveness of HR policies and practices; they actually teach the logical connections, as organization leaders use the measurement systems to make decisions. This is what occurs in other business disciplines. For example, the power of a consistent, rigorous logic, combined with measures, makes financial tools such as economic value added and net present value so useful. They elegantly combine both numbers and logic and help business leaders improve in making decisions about financial resources.

Business leaders and employees routinely are expected to understand the logic that explains how decisions about money and customers connect to organization success. Even those outside the finance profession understand principles of cash flow and return on investment. Even those outside the marketing profession understand principles of market segmentation and product life cycle. In the same way, human capital–measurement systems can enhance how well users understand the logic that connects organization success to decisions about their own talent, as well as the talent of those whom they lead or work with. To improve organizational effectiveness, HR processes, such as succession planning, performance management, staffing, and leadership development, must rely much more on improving the competency and engagement of non-HR leaders than on anything that HR typically controls directly.

Why use the term *science*? Because the most successful professions rely on decision systems that follow scientific principles and can quickly incorporate new scientific knowledge into practical applications. Disciplines such as finance, marketing, and operations provide leaders with frameworks that show how those resources affect strategic success, and the frameworks themselves reflect findings from universities, research centers, and scholarly journals. Their decision models and their measurement systems are compatible with the scholarly science that supports them. Yet with talent and human resources, the frameworks that leaders in organizations use often bear distressingly little similarity to the scholarly research in human resources and human behavior at work.[3] The idea of evidence-based HR management requires creating measurement systems that encourage and teach managers how to think more critically and logically about their decisions, and to make decisions that are informed by and consistent with leading research.[4]

A vast array of research focuses on human behavior at work, on labor markets, on how organizations can better compete with and for talent, and on how that talent is organized. Disciplines such as psychology, economics, sociology, organization theory, game theory, and even operations management and human physiology all contain potent research frameworks and findings based on the scientific method. A scientific approach reveals how decisions and decision-based measures can bring the insights of these fields to bear on the practical issues confronting organization leaders and employees. You will learn how to use these research findings as you master the HR measurement techniques described in this book.

Decision Frameworks

A decision framework provides the logical connections between decisions about a resource (for example, financial capital, customers, or talent) and the strategic success of the organization. This is true in HR, as we show in subsequent chapters that describe such connections in various HR domains. It is also true in other, more familiar decision sciences such as finance and marketing. It is instructive to compare HR to these other disciplines. Figure 1.1 shows how a decision framework for talent and HR has a parallel structure to decision frameworks for finance and marketing.

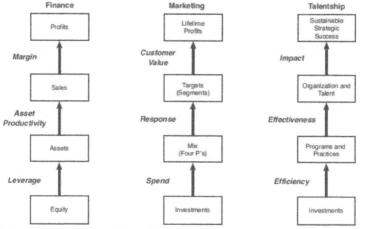

Figure 1.1. Finance, marketing, and talentship decision frameworks.

Finance is a decision science for the resource of money, marketing is the decision science for the resource of customers, and we might use the term "talentship" as the decision science for the resource of talent. In all three decision sciences, the elements combine to show how one factor interacts with others to produce value. *Efficiency* refers to the relationship between what is spent and the programs and practices that are produced. *Effectiveness* refers to the relationship between the programs or practices and their effects on their target audience. *Impact* refers to the relationship between the effects of the practice on the target audience and the ultimate success of the organization.

To illustrate the logic of such a framework, consider marketing as an example. Investments in marketing produce a product, promotion, price, and placement mix. This is efficiency. Those programs and practices produce responses in certain customer segments. This is effectiveness. Finally, the responses of customer segments create changes in the lifetime profits from those customers. This is impact.

Similarly, with regard to talent decisions, *efficiency* describes the connection between investments in people and the talent-related programs and practices they produce (such as cost per training hour). *Effectiveness* describes the connection between the programs or practices and the changes in the talent quality or organizational characteristics (such as whether trainees increase their skill). *Impact* describes the connection between the changes in talent or organization elements and the strategic success of the organization (such as whether increased skill actually enhances the organizational processes or initiatives that are most vital to strategic success).

The chapters in this book show how to measure not just HR efficiency but also elements of effectiveness and impact. In addition, each chapter provides a logical framework for the measures, to enhance decision-making and organizational change. Throughout the book, we attend to measures of efficiency, effectiveness, and impact. The current state of the art in HR management is heavily dominated by efficiency measures, so this book will help you see beyond the most obvious efficiency measures and put them in the context of effectiveness and impact.

Data, Measurement, and Analysis

In a well-developed decision science, the measures and data are deployed through management systems, they are used by leaders who understand the principles, and they are supported by professionals who add insight and expertise. In stark contrast, HR data, information, and measurement face a paradox today. There is increasing sophistication in technology, data availability, and the capacity to report and disseminate HR information, but investments in HR data systems, scorecards, and integrated enterprise resource systems still too-often fail to create the strategic insights needed to drive organizational effectiveness. HR measures exist mostly in areas where the accounting systems require information to control labor costs or monitor functional activity. Efficiency gets a lot of attention, but effectiveness and impact often go unmeasured, and therefore are ignored. In short, many organizations are hitting a wall in HR measurement (see the next section).

You might think this would be corrected by using ever more sophisticated tools such as artificial intelligence and machine learning to gather and analyze vastly more data and deliver a wider array of real-time reports to key decision-makers. However, no amount of additional data and speed will improve decisions if the logic is wrong, such as when the focus is only on efficiency, or when the underlying assumptions and logic are incomplete or faulty. That's why we will emphasize logical frameworks in this book.

Connecting Measures and Organizational Effectiveness

Hitting the Wall in HR Measurement

Type "HR measurement" into a search engine and you will get over two hundred million results.[5] Scorecards, summits, dashboards, data mines, data warehouses, and audits abound. The array of HR measurement technologies is daunting. The paradox is that even when HR measurement systems are well implemented, organizations typically hit a wall. Despite ever more comprehensive databases, and ever more sophisticated HR data analysis and reporting, HR measures only rarely drive true strategic change.[6]

Figure 1.2 shows how, over time, the HR profession has become more elegant and sophisticated, yet the trend line doesn't seem to be leading to the desired result. Victory is typically declared when business leaders approve, are won over, or are held accountable for HR measures. HR organizations often point proudly to the fact that bonuses for top leaders depend in part on the results of an HR scorecard. For example, incentive systems might make bonuses for business unit managers contingent on reducing turnover, raising average engagement scores, or placing their employees into the required distribution of 70 percent in the middle, 10 percent at the bottom, and 20 percent at the top.

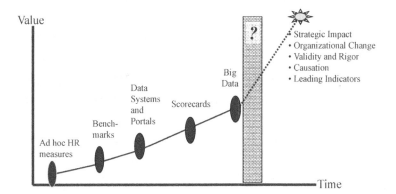

Figure 1.2. Hitting the wall in HR measurement.

Yet using AI, predictive modeling, and big data or having business leader incentives based on HR measures is not the same as creating organizational change. To have impact, HR measures must create a true strategic difference in the organization. Many organizations are frustrated because they seem to be doing all the measurement things right, but there is a large gap between the expectations for the measurement systems and their true effects. HR measurement systems have much to learn from measurement systems in more mature professions such as finance and marketing. In these professions, measures are only one part of the system for creating organizational change through better decisions. Many HR measures originate from a desire to justify the investments in HR processes or programs. Typically, HR seeks to develop measures to increase the respect (and the budgets) for the HR function and its services and activities. Contrast this with financial measurement. Although it is certainly important to measure how well the accounting or finance department operates, the majority of financial measures are not concerned with how finance and accounting services are delivered, or how much money the function spends. Financial measures typically focus on the outcomes—the quality of decisions that leaders make about financial resources. In contrast, typical HR systems focus on how the HR function is using and deploying its resources, and whether those resources are used efficiently. Ultimately, the HR organization should be accountable for improving organizational talent decisions, so HR professionals require a more holistic perspective on how measurements can drive strategic change.

Correcting these limitations requires keeping in mind the basic principle expressed at the beginning of this chapter: human capital metrics are valuable to the extent that they improve impactful decisions about talent and how it is organized. You must embed HR measures within a complete framework for creating organizational change through enhanced decisions. We describe that framework next.

The LAMP Framework
We believe that a paradigm extension toward a talent decision science is key to getting to the other side of the wall. Incremental improvements in the traditional measurement approaches will not address the challenges. HR measurement can move beyond the wall using what we call the LAMP model, shown in Figure 1.3. The letters in LAMP stand for logic, analytics, measures, and process, four critical components of a measurement system that drives strategic

change and organizational effectiveness. Measures represent only one component of this system. Although they are essential, without the other three components, the measures and data are destined to remain isolated from the true purpose of HR measurement systems.

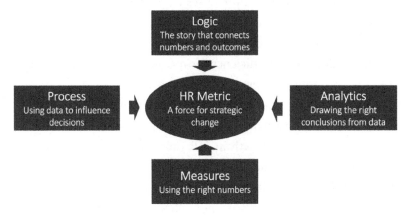

Figure 1.3. Lighting the LAMP.

The LAMP metaphor refers to a story that reflects today's HR measurement dilemma:

> One evening while strolling, a man encountered an inebriated person diligently searching the sidewalk below a street lamp.
>
> "Did you lose something?" he asked.
>
> "My car keys. I've been looking for them for an hour," the person replied.
>
> The man quickly scanned the area, spotting nothing. "Are you sure you lost them here?"
>
> "No, I lost them in that dark alley over there."
>
> "If you lost your keys in the dark alley, why don't you search over there?"
>
> "Because this is where the light is."

In many ways, talent and organization measurement systems are like the person looking for the keys where the light is, not where they are most likely to be found. Advancements in information technology often provide technical capabilities that far surpass the ability of the decision science and processes to use them properly. So it is not uncommon to find organizations that have invested significant resources constructing elegant search and presentation technology around measures of efficiency, or measures that largely emanate from the accounting system.

The paradox is that genuine insights about human resources often exist in the areas where there are no standard accounting measures. The significant growth in HR outsourcing, where efficiency is often the primary value proposition and IT technology is the primary tool, has exacerbated these issues.[7] Even imperfect measures aimed at the right areas may be more illuminating than very elegant measures aimed in the wrong places.

Returning to our story about the person looking for keys under the street lamp, it's been said, "Even a weak penlight in the alley where the keys are is better than a very bright streetlight where the keys are not."

Figure 1.3 shows that HR measurement systems are only as valuable as the decisions they improve and the organizational effectiveness to which they contribute. HR measurement systems create value as a catalyst for strategic change. Let's examine how the four components of the LAMP framework define a more complete measurement system. We present the elements in the following order: logic, measures, analytics, and, finally, process.

Logic: What Are the Vital Connections?
Without a proper logic, it is impossible to know where to look for insights. The logic element of any measurement system provides the "story" behind the connections between the numbers and the effects and outcomes. In this book we provide logic models that help organize the measurements and show how they inform better decisions.

Examples include the connections between health/wellness and employee turnover, performance, and absenteeism in Chapter 6. In Chapter 5, on employee turnover, we propose a logic model that shows how employee turnover is similar to inventory turnover. This simple analogy shows how to think beyond turnover costs, consider performance and quality, and optimize employee shortages and surpluses, instead of always minimizing them. In Chapters 9 and 10, we propose a logic model that shows how selecting employees is similar to optimizing a supply chain for talent; this helps leaders understand how to optimize all elements of employee acquisition, not simply maximize the validity of tests or the quality of recruitment sources. In Chapter 10, we propose a logic model that focuses on where differences in employee performance are most pivotal, borrowing from the common engineering idea that improving the performance of every product component is not equally valuable.

Another prominent logic model is the People Equity, or ACE, model.[8] Research led the creators of this model to conclude that organizations need to do three things right in order to optimize talent: (1) Ensure that all employees and teams are *aligned* with the organization's mission, vision, and values and with other units. (2) Provide the right *competencies*, information, and resources to meet customer or internal stakeholder expectations. (3) Create an *engaged* workforce that is willing to put in discretionary effort and to advocate on behalf of the organization. Application of this framework at Jack in the Box quick-serve restaurants showed strong linkages between each restaurant's People Equity scores and organizational outcomes such as productivity, employee turnover, customer satisfaction and loyalty, quality, internal customer service, and operating and financial performance.

Missing or faulty logic is often the reason well-meaning HR professionals generate measurement systems that are technically sound but make little sense to those who must use them. With well-grounded logic, it is much easier to help leaders outside the HR profession understand and use the measurement systems to enhance their decisions. Moreover, that logic must be constructed so that it is understandable and credible, not only to HR professionals but also to the leaders they seek to educate and influence. Connecting HR measures to traditional business models in this way is described in more detail in the book *Retooling HR*.[9]

Measures: Getting the Numbers Right

The measures part of the LAMP model has received the greatest attention in HR. As discussed in subsequent chapters, virtually every area of HR has many different measures. Much time and attention are paid to enhancing the quality of HR measures, based on criteria such as timeliness, completeness, reliability, and consistency. These are certainly important standards, but, lacking a context, they can be pursued well beyond their optimum levels, or applied to areas where they have little consequence.

Consider the measurement of employee turnover. Much debate centers on the appropriate formulas to use in estimating turnover and its costs, or the precision and frequency with which employee turnover should be calculated. Today's turnover reporting systems can calculate turnover rates for virtually any employee group and business unit. Armed with such systems, managers slice and dice the data in a wide variety of ways (ethnicity, skills, performance, and so on), as each manager pursues his or her own pet theory about turnover and why it matters. Some might be concerned about losing long-tenure employees, others might focus on high-performing employees, and still others might focus on reducing employee turnover where outside demand is greatest. These are all logical ideas, but they are not universally correct. Whether they are useful depends on the context and strategic objectives. Lacking such a context, better turnover measures won't help improve decisions. That's why the logic element of the LAMP model must support good measurement.

Precision is not a panacea. There are many ways to make HR measures more reliable and precise, but focusing only on measurement quality can produce a brighter light shining where the keys are not! Measures require investment, which should be directed where it has the greatest return, not just where improvement is most feasible. Organizations routinely pay greater attention to the elements of their materials inventory that have the greatest effect on costs or productivity. Indeed, a well-known principle is the 80-20 rule, which suggests that 80 percent of the important variation in inventory costs or quality is often driven by 20 percent of the inventory items. Thus, although organizations indeed track 100 percent of their inventory items, they measure the vital 20 percent with greater precision, more frequency, and greater accountability for key decision-makers.

Why not approach HR measurement in the same way? Factors such as employee turnover, performance, engagement, learning, and absence are not equally important everywhere. That means measurements like these should focus precisely on what matters. If turnover is a risk because an organization could lose key capabilities, turnover rates should be stratified according to whether it occurs in key capabilities or in other areas. Where absence has the most effect, such as in call centers with tight schedules, we should be very clear in how we measure absenteeism.

Lacking a common logic about how turnover affects business or strategic success, well-meaning managers draw conclusions that might be misguided or dangerous, such as the assumption that turnover is always bad, or engagement has similar effects across all jobs. This is why every chapter of this book describes HR measures and how to make them more precise and valid. However, each chapter also embeds them in a logic model that explains how the measures work together.

Analytics: Finding Answers in the Data

Even a very rigorous logic with good measures can flounder if the analysis is incorrect. For example, some theories suggest that employees with positive attitudes convey those attitudes to customers, who, in turn, have more positive experiences and purchase more. Suppose an organization has data showing that customer attitudes and purchases are higher in locations with better employee attitudes. This is a positive correlation between attitudes and purchases. Organizations have invested significant resources in improving frontline employee attitudes based precisely on this sort of correlation. But will a decision to improve employee attitudes lead to improved customer purchases?

The problem is that such investments may be misguided. A correlation between employee attitudes and customer purchases does not prove that the first one causes the second. Such a correlation also happens when customer attitudes and purchases actually cause employee attitudes. This can happen because stores with more loyal and committed customers are more pleasant places to work. The correlation can also result from a third, unmeasured factor. Perhaps stores in certain locations (such as near a major private university) attract customers (college students) who buy more merchandise or services and are more enthusiastic, and perhaps these stores also happen to have access to employees (college-age students) that bring a positive attitude to their work, because they can socialize at work with their friends. Store location turns out to cause both store performance and employee satisfaction. The point is that a high correlation between employee attitudes and customer purchases could be due to any or all of these effects. Sound analytics can reveal which way the causal arrow actually is pointing.

Analytics is about drawing the right conclusions from data. It includes statistics and research design, and it then goes beyond them to include skill in identifying and articulating key issues, gathering and using appropriate data within and outside the HR function, setting the appropriate balance between statistical rigor and practical relevance, and building analytical competencies throughout the organization. Analytics transforms HR logic and measures into rigorous, relevant insights.

Analytics often connect the logical framework to the research related to talent and organization, which is an important element of a mature decision science. Frequently, the most appropriate and

(handwritten margin note:) That an employee's nice doesn't mean purchases ↑

advanced analytics are found in scientific studies published in professional journals. In this book, we draw on that scientific knowledge to build the analytical frameworks in each chapter. Analytical principles span virtually every area of HR measurement. In Chapter 2, we describe general analytical principles that form the foundation of good measurement. We also provide a set of economic concepts that form the analytical basis for questions that more rigorously connect business outcomes to organizational phenomena, such as employee turnover and employee quality. In addition to these general frameworks, each chapter contains analytics relevant specifically to the topic of that chapter.

Advanced analytics are often the domain of specialists in statistics, psychology, economics, and other disciplines. To augment their own analytical capability, HR organizations often draw on experts in these fields, as well as internal analytical groups in areas such as marketing and consumer research. Although this can be very useful, it is our strong belief that familiarity with analytical principles is increasingly essential for all HR professionals and for anyone who aspires to use HR data well.

Process: Making Insights Motivating and Actionable

The final element of the LAMP framework is process. Measurement affects decisions and behaviors, and those occur within a complex web of social structures, knowledge frameworks, and organizational cultural norms. Therefore, effective measurement systems must fit within a change management process that reflects principles of learning and knowledge transfer. HR measures and the logic that supports them are part of an influence process.

The initial step in effective measurement is to get managers to accept that HR analysis is possible and informative. The way to make that happen is not necessarily to present the most sophisticated analysis. The best approach may be to present relatively simple measures and analyses that match the mental models that managers already use. Calculating turnover costs can reveal millions of dollars that can be saved with turnover reductions, as discussed in Chapter 5, "The High Cost of Employee Separations." Several leaders outside of HR have told us that a turnover cost analysis was the first time they realized that talent and organization decisions had tangible effects on the economic and accounting processes they were familiar with.

Of course, measuring only the cost of turnover is insufficient for good decision-making. For example, overzealous attempts to cut turnover costs can compromise candidate quality in ways that far outweigh the cost savings. Managers can reduce number and cost of interviews needed to hire a certain number of candidates, by lowering their selection standards. As the standards are lowered, more candidates will pass the interview and be hired, so fewer interviews must be conducted to fill a certain number of vacancies. Lowering standards can create problems that far outweigh the cost savings from doing fewer interviews! Still, the process element of the LAMP framework reminds us that often the best way to start a change process may be to first assess turnover costs, in order to create initial awareness that the same analytical logic used for financial, technological, and marketing investments can apply to human resources. Then the door is open to more sophisticated analyses beyond the costs. Once leaders experience how their human capital decisions have tangible monetary effects, they may be more receptive to greater sophistication, such as considering employee turnover in the same framework as inventory turnover.

Education is also a core element of any change process. The return on investment (ROI) formula from finance is actually a potent tool for educating leaders in the key components of financial decisions. It helps leaders quickly incorporate risk, return, and cost in a simple logical model. In the same way, we believe that HR measurements increasingly will be used to educate constituents and will become embedded within the organization's learning and knowledge frameworks. For example, Valero Energy tracked the performance of both internal and external sources of applicants on factors such as cost, time, quality, efficiency, and dependability. It provided this information to hiring managers and used it to establish an agreement about what managers were willing to invest to receive a certain level of service from internal or external recruiters. Hiring managers learned about the trade-offs between investments in recruiting and its performance.[10] We will return to this idea in Chapters 9 and 10.

In the chapters that follow, we suggest where the HR measures we describe can connect to existing organizational frameworks and systems, offering the opportunity to get attention and enhance decisions. For example, organizational budgeting systems reflect escalating healthcare costs. The measures discussed in Chapter 6, "Employee Health, Wellness, and Welfare," offer added insight and precision for such discussions. By embedding these basic ideas and measures into the existing healthcare cost discussion, HR leaders can gain the needed credibility to extend the discussion to include the logical connections between employee health and other outcomes, such as learning, performance, and profits. What began as a budget exercise becomes a more nuanced discussion about the optimal investments in employee health and how those investments pay off.

Telling a story is well recognized as essential to HR analytics. Too often the story is framed with the language and perspective of HR analysts, which may not engage the audience. HR analysts can do better by using basic storytelling tools. For example, rather than present endless statistical tables describing training and employee turnover, one might start with this assertion: "As a company, we are known as the most effective organization at developing technical talent for our competitors." This demands attention by capturing context and a relevant problem.

You will see the LAMP framework emerge in many of the chapters in this book, to help you organize not only the measures but also your approach to making those measures matter.

Conclusion

HR measures must improve important decisions about talent and how it is organized. This chapter has shown how this simple premise leads to an approach to HR measurement that is very different from those typically followed today; it has also shown how this premise produces several decision-science-based frameworks to help guide HR measurement activities toward greater strategic impact. We have introduced the general principle that decision-based measurement is vital to strategic impact, and we have also introduced the LAMP framework as a useful logical system for understanding how measurements drive decisions, organizational effectiveness, and strategic success. LAMP also provides a diagnostic framework to examine the potential of existing measurement systems to create these results. We return to the LAMP framework frequently in this book.

We also return frequently to the ideas of measuring efficiency, effectiveness, and impact, the three anchor points of the decision framework of Boudreau and Ramstad in *Beyond HR*. Throughout the book, you will see the power and effectiveness of measures in each of these areas, but also the importance of avoiding a fixation on any one of them. As with the well-developed disciplines of finance and marketing, it is important to focus on synergy between the different elements of the measurement and decision frameworks, not fixate exclusively on any single component of them.

We show how to think of your HR measurement systems as teaching rather than telling. We also describe the opportunities you will have to take discussions that might normally be driven exclusively by accounting logic and HR cost cutting, and elevate them with more complete frameworks that are better grounded in the science behind human behavior at work. The challenge will be to embed those frameworks in the key decision processes that already exist in organizations.

Software to Accompany Chapters 3–11

To enhance the accuracy of calculations for the exercises that appear at the end of each chapter, and to make them easier to use, we have developed web-based software to accompany material in Chapters 3 through 11 in this book. The software covers the following topics: employee absenteeism, turnover, health and welfare, attitudes and engagement, work/life issues, external employee sourcing, the economic value of job performance, payoffs from selection, and payoffs from training (HR development).

Developed with support from the Society for Human Resource Management (SHRM), this software is accessible from the SHRM website (http://iip.shrm.org) anywhere in the world, regardless of whether you are a member of SHRM. Of particular note to multinational enterprises, the calculations can be performed using any currency, and conversions from one currency to another are accomplished easily. You can save, print, or download your calculations, and carry forward all existing data to subsequent sessions. Our hope is that by reducing the effort necessary to perform the actual calculations, we will enable our readers to spend more time focusing on the logic, analytics, and processes necessary to improve strategic decisions about talent.

References

1. Geoff Colvin, "How Are Most Admired Companies Different? They Invest in People and Keep Them Employed—Even in a Downturn," *Fortune*, March 22, 2010, 82.
2. John W. Boudreau and Peter M. Ramstad, *Beyond HR: The New Science of Human Capital* (Cambridge, MA: Harvard Business Press, 2007).
3. Sara L. Rynes, Amy E. Colbert, and Kenneth G. Brown, "HR Professionals' Beliefs about Effective Human Resource Practices: Correspondence Between Research and Practice," *Human Resource Management* 41, no. 2 (2002): 149–74. See also Sara L. Rynes, Tamara L. Giluk, and Kenneth G. Brown, "The Very Separate Worlds of Academic and Practitioner Publications

in Human Resource Management: Implications for Evidence-Based Management," *Academy of Management Journal* 50, no. 5 (2007): 987–1008.

4. Rob B. Briner, David Denyer, and Denise. M. Rousseau, "Evidence-Based Management: Concept Cleanup Time?," *Academy of Management Perspectives* 23, no. 4 (2009): 19–32.

5. This section draws material from Chapter 9 in Boudreau and Ramstad, *Beyond HR.*

6. Edward. E. Lawler III, Alec Levenson, and John W. Boudreau, "HR Metrics and Analytics—Uses and Impacts," *Human Resource Planning Journal* 27, no. 4 (2004): 27–35.

7. Mary F. Cook and Scott B. Gildner, *Outsourcing Human Resources Functions,* 2nd ed. (Alexandria, VA: Society for Human Resource Management, 2006). See also Edward E. Lawler III et al., *Human Resources Business Process Outsourcing* (Hoboken, NJ: Jossey-Bass, 2000).

8. William A. Schiemann, *Reinventing Talent Management: How to Maximize Performance in the New Marketplace* (New York: Wiley, 2009). See also William A. Schiemann, Jerry H. Seibert, and Brian S. Morgan, *Hidden Drivers of Success: Leveraging Employee Insights for Strategic Advantage* (Alexandria, VA: Society for Human Resource Management, 2013).

9. John W. Boudreau, *Retooling HR: Using Proven Business Models to Improve Decisions About Talent* (Cambridge, MA: Harvard Business Publishing, 2010).

10. Boudreau, *Retooling HR,* Chapter 5.

2

Analytical Foundations
of HR Measurement

Over the last decade, analytics has emerged as a near-ubiquitous strategic problem-solving approach.[1] The preceding chapter noted the importance of analytics within a broader, decision-based framework of human capital measurement. As you will see in the chapters that follow, each type of HR measurement has its own particular elements of analytics. As computer science and analytic capability rapidly evolve, it becomes much simpler to generate a number. However, that ease of calculation can mean it is more challenging to ensure that the findings of analytics projects are useful, appropriate, and fair.

Nearly every element of human resource management (HRM) relies on one or more supporting analytical concepts. Fortunately, literacy and even proficiency in these concepts does not require advanced training in statistics or data management. The concepts highlighted in this chapter include those that are essential to drawing valid conclusions, as well as those that form the core of economic analysis to ensure that the inferences we draw properly account for important economic factors, such as inflation and risk.

As you read through the various chapters of this book, each of which focuses on a different aspect of HR measurement, you will encounter many of these analytical concepts over and over again. In the interests of efficiency, we present some of the most common ones here so that you can refer back to this chapter as often as necessary for their description and definition. What they have in common is that they are general guidelines for interpreting data-based information. We present them in two broad groups: concepts in data science, statistics and research design, and concepts in economics and finance. Within each category, we address issues in rough order from general to specific.

Traditional versus Contemporary HR Measures

HRM activities—those associated with the attraction, selection, retention, development, and utilization of people in organizations—commonly are evaluated by using measures of individual characteristics, behaviors, traits, or reactions, or by using statistical summaries of those measures. The former include measures of the reactions of various groups (top management, customers, applicants, or trainees), what individuals have learned, or how their behavior has changed on the job. Statistical summaries of individual measures include various ratios (e.g., accident frequency or severity), percentages (e.g., labor turnover), measures of central tendency and variability (e.g., mean and standard deviation of performance measures, such as bank teller shortages and surpluses), and measures of correlation (e.g., validity coefficients for staffing programs, or measures of association between employee satisfaction and turnover).

Measuring individual characteristics, behaviors, traits, or reactions and summarizing them statistically has historically been the hallmark of measurements. Many of these had roots in psychology. Newer statistical techniques provide updated tools to explore and analyze organizational data, and widespread use of analytics across the enterprise has created an expectation that savvy analytics will be used in most, if not all, organizational decision-making, including HR decisions.

Simultaneously, competition for talent has accelerated. In the current climate of intense competition to attract and retain talent domestically and globally, executives demand analyses of costs and benefits of HR programs, expressed in financial terms. They demand measures that are strategically relevant to their organizations and that use defined logic to enhance decisions regarding important organizational outcomes.

Although administrative exercises such as analyzing employee turnover levels for every position in an organization might have previously been busywork for the HR department, today leaders can readily see the importance of analyzing and predicting the business and economic consequences of turnover among high performers ("A players") who are difficult to replace and work in a business unit that is pivotal to strategic success (for example, R&D in a pharmaceutical organization). Developing predictive measures for outcomes such as attrition requires understanding not only its antecedents and consequences but also the appropriate statistical techniques for useful analysis. Translating the probability of employees leaving into a set of consequences for an organization—to support better decisions about whether and how to reduce attrition—requires an interdisciplinary approach that includes information from accounting, finance, economics, and behavioral science. Measures developed in this way can help senior executives assess the extent to which HR programs are consistent with and contribute to the strategic direction of an organization.

Effective Data Management Is Necessary for Analytics

Throughout this volume, we will focus on analytics. It is critical to note, however, that any analysis is only as good as the data on which it is based. Real data in organizations are notoriously siloed and esoteric. Acquisitions, homegrown systems, a sprawling network of third-party tools, and a historic focus on transactions rather than information all conspire to make creating analyzable HR datasets fiendishly difficult for many organizations.

Additionally, in many organizations, the data that are readily available are often only tangentially useful for making HR decisions. When considering promotion, for example, knowing an employee's start date is less useful than having a robust assessment of that employee's capabilities. Yet organizations are more likely to have the first than the second. Finally, the special nature of HR data means that the requirements for data privacy and security are especially important and stringent.

Thus, HR analytics by its very nature will always use imperfect and incomplete data. It is not always feasible or even desirable to gather, improve, or manage data to the highest standards. As you read this book, you may find that the data may not always exist to fully execute some of the analytical models we describe. Or data imperfections may require that your conclusions carry important caveats about the margin of error or limits to generalizability.

Better-quality data is not an end in itself, nor is improved data management always desirable. The frameworks in this book allow leaders to make decisions about data management and quality in a more rational way. In a nutshell, pursue better data management and quality when they are likely to improve decisions with significant, pivotal impacts on an organization. Leaders who pursue more perfect data and data management for its own sake will justifiably be asked to put their efforts into proper context. Sometimes, the best solution is to use imperfect data to make significant improvements in decisions rather than allow the pursuit of perfection to stand in the way of valuable, if imperfect, analytics.

That's one reason that the frameworks in this book are so important. They allow decision-makers to better understand where improving the quality of data and analytics would make a significant difference, and where imperfect data or analytics are likely good enough.

Core Levels of Sophistication in HR Analytics

At its core, HR analytics is fact-based decision-making about people in organizations. Most analytics maturity models outline several levels of sophistication when making those fact-based people decisions. Below, we will describe three different levels of HR data sophistication. It is important to note that all four levels are used in the most sophisticated HR analytic frameworks.

1. **Reporting:** All relevant data about the workforce are tracked, organized, and accessible. Getting this basic step right can be difficult. HR technology solutions, both off the shelf and internally built, can be clunky. The challenges of continually updating the database and ensuring that all end users—from line managers to HR generalists—are getting the data they need are unceasing. Most systems allow users to display headcount, attrition, promotion, and other data, ideally in customizable dashboards. These have the ability to filter the data and to output displays according to hierarchy, employee location, or cost center, for example. Advances in data visualization packages have dramatically increased the ability of report designers to create intuitive, flexible tools for users.[2]

Reporting enables analysts to extrapolate from descriptive data to yield new insights. For example, consider workforce planning. Using basic data on promotions, attrition, headcount by level, and anticipated organizational growth rate makes it possible to project the shape of your organization (i.e., the percentage of employees at each level) at the end of a year, two years, or three-plus years. With the proper formulas in place, users can input anticipated future attrition, promotion, and organizational growth rates to model different scenarios. By assigning salaries to employees at each level, one can see the financial impact of having an organizational shape that looks like a typical pyramid (i.e., fewer employees at each level as one moves up the organization) versus a more uniform distribution across levels, which would occur if the organization is not hiring but employees continue to receive promotions. Currently, reporting is often presented as visualizations, which greatly enhance readability and understanding.

2. **Metrics:** Where reporting captures what has happened in the past, metrics add a component of evaluation. Metrics, ideally based on analytics and strategic priorities, provide a framework for evaluating programs and services. Metrics may gauge efficiency, effectiveness, or impact of HR products and services, and they are often presented as part of a scorecard or dashboard. Strategically relevant metrics provide a baseline against which comparisons can be made to determine whether an intervention is benefiting an organization. Then they can inform strategic actions, such as adjusting programs, expanding services, or discontinuing projects. Metrics are also frequently presented as visualizations.

3. **Insight and Impact:** These analytics differ from reporting or metrics because their focus is on deeper understanding of HR problems, with an eye toward solutions. Typically, they help answer questions about why and what will happen, as part of a larger strategy to drive better decision-making. Analytics projects that might form the bulk of work for an analytics team include exploring relationships among variables, executing statistical comparisons of one group or process to another, or generating prediction of one variable from another. These projects might explore the drivers of key trends affecting your organization or whether a new selection approach is better than the current one. The vast majority of this volume will focus on analytics as a powerful approach to making better organizational decisions.

An essential element of good analytics is determining the best combination of analyses to answer the question at hand. Few analytics projects are entirely linear or constrained to just one type of analytical work. Basic reporting can be an important part of diagnosis, as well as an essential step in validating data sets. Metrics might be useful in evaluating the effectiveness or recommendations coming out of work aimed at insight and impact. Familiarity with each of the levels will help you ensure that you have the right tools for each phase of a research project.

Data Visualization to Facilitate Storytelling with Data

Often the first step in any analysis or exploration of data is visualization. One classic example of the explanatory power of data visualization is Anscombe's quartet.[3] Here, four datasets with the same primary measurement qualities—such as means, standard deviations, and correlation coefficients—are plotted out to show how critical differences that are lost with standard summary statistics become very clear when plotted out visually. Figure 2.1 displays Anscombe's quartet.

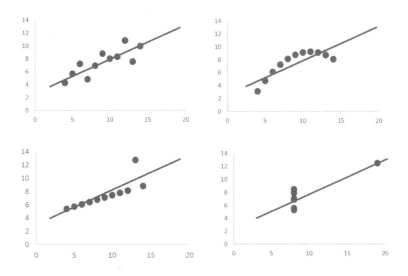

Figure 2.1. Anscombe's quartet.

Advances in analytic packages and overall sophistication with data management have greatly simplified the creation and management of data visualization. Visualized data is more compelling and better understood than tabular data.[4] Data visualization is particularly well suited to tasks such as comparing groups or illuminating things like connections, hierarchy, change over time, or geographies.[5] Thus, while good data visualization can be used to covey complicated statistical information, it can also be thought of as almost "pre-statistical," illuminating patterns in information.

As more organizations seek to use data to inform both strategic and everyday decisions, it becomes increasingly important to convey information in a way that is simple to understand, even where there may be many variables or patterns. Many, if not most, analytical projects begin and end with data visualization, and for many projects, effective visualization is sufficient to inform decisions. Reporting and scorecards are often presented as data visualizations, for example. For more complex projects, initial data exploration often includes techniques such as geographic maps, illustrations of multiple dimensions of proportionality, visualizations of movement from one category to another, or diagrams of relationships among variables or items. Compelling stakeholder presentations generally return to visualization to display complex information simply. These techniques can help the analytical project tell a clear story about the initial problem presented, the logic of the proposed solution, and the outcomes of a change.

The practice of data visualization is actually hundreds of years old and thus has evolved well-established principles. While the specific visualizations best suited to a given dataset or analysis will depend on the nature of the data and the nature of the story you need to tell, there are some common visual features to consider. Position, area, and the use of visual contrast (e.g., hue, saturation, and texture) are all frequently used to convey information. The free companion software to this book incorporates visualizations throughout and shows samples of useful visualizations to illuminate important patterns.

Next, we describe some fundamental concepts from statistics and research design that help ensure that the kind of data gathered, and the calculations used to summarize those data, are best suited to the questions the data should answer. They are general interpretive concepts.

Fundamental Analytical Concepts from Statistics and Research Design

We make no attempt here to present basic statistical or research methods. Many excellent textbooks do that much more effectively than we could in the space available. Rather, we offer guidelines to interpretation and to point out some important cautions in those interpretations. In the following sections, we address four key concepts: generalizing from sample data, correlation and causality, relationships among multiple variables, and experimental controls for extraneous factors.

Generalizing from Sample Data

In general, organizational research is based on samples rather than populations of observations. A population consists of all the people (or more broadly, units) about whom or which a study is meant to generalize, such as employees with fewer than two years' experience, customers who patronize a particular store, or trucks in a company's fleet. In contrast, a sample represents a subset of people (or units) who actually participate in a study. In some cases, organizational researchers will have access to the entire relevant population, but in many others, such as small-scale surveys, pilot tests for new investments, or analysis of social media postings, a sample is the most appropriate path.

If we are to draw reliable (i.e., stable, consistent) and valid (i.e., accurate) conclusions concerning the population, it is imperative that the sample reflect the population—a representative sample. When the sample is like the population, we can be fairly confident that the results we find based on the sample also hold for the population. In other words, we can generalize from the sample to the population.[6]

One way to generate a representative sample is to use random sampling. A random sample is achieved when, through random selection, each member of a population is equally likely to be chosen as part of the sample. Many modern statistical packages can create a random samples automatically. Sometimes a population is made up of members of different groups or categories, such as males and females, or purchasers of a product and nonpurchasers. Assume that among five hundred new hires in a given year, 60 percent are female.

If we want to draw conclusions, based on our sample, about the population of all new hires in a given year, the sample itself must be representative of these important subgroups (or strata) within the population. If the population is composed of 60 percent women and 40 percent men, we need to ensure that the sample is similar. One way to obtain such a sample is to use stratified random sampling. Doing so allows us to take into account the different subgroups of people in the population and helps guarantee that the sample represents the population on specific characteristics. Begin by dividing the population into subsamples or strata. In our example, the strata are based on gender. Then randomly select 60 percent of the sample observations from this stratum (for example, using a computer-generated random sample), and the remaining 40 percent from the other stratum (men). Doing so ensures that the characteristic of gender in the sample represents the population.[7]

Typically, organizations and analysts believe that it is always better to make their samples more representative of a larger population, such as the whole organization or the entire group of applicants. For actual organizational decisions, however, the goal is seldom to generalize to some theoretically large population. Rather, the goal is to improve decisions where it matters most. In that case, the most valuable population is the one where improved decisions will have the most impact.

Somewhat counterintuitively, it is often tempting, and sometimes appropriate, to build a sample that is explicitly *not* representative. For example, it might be useful to conduct a very deep analysis on the reasons that your highest performers or most pivotal populations are leaving the company. In this case, the difference in reasons for leaving between the highest- and average-performing employees are less interesting than the opportunity to prevent undesired exits from your most crucially important population.

Many other types of sampling procedures might be used, but the important point is that it is not possible to generalize reliably and validly from a sample to a population unless the sample itself is representative.[8] Unfortunately, much research that is done in HR and management is based on case studies, samples of convenience, and even anecdotal evidence. Under those circumstances, it is not possible to generalize to a broader population of interest, and it is important to be skeptical of studies that try to do so.

Sometimes one is fortunate to have access to an entire population of interest. In these cases, it can often to useful to create a set of samples from the broader population to allow replication of results across the various samples.

Correlation Does Not Equal Causation

Perhaps one of the most pervasive human tendencies is to assume incorrectly that just because two things increase and decrease together, one must cause the other. The degree of relationship between any two variables (in the employment context, predictor and criterion) is simply the extent to which they vary together (covary) in a systematic fashion. The magnitude or degree to which they are related linearly is indicated by some measure of correlation, the most popular of which is the Pearson product-moment correlation coefficient, r. As a measure of relationship, r varies between -1.00 and $+1.00$. When r is either of these values, the two sets of scores (x and y) are related perfectly and systematically to each other. Knowing a person's status on variable x allows us to predict without error his or her standing on variable y.

In the case of an r of $+1.00$, high (low) predictor scores are matched perfectly by high (low) criterion scores. For example, performance-review scores may relate perfectly to recommendations for salary increases. When r is -1.00, however, the relationship is inverse, and high (low) predictor scores are accompanied by low (high) criterion scores. For example, consider that as driving speed increases, fuel efficiency decreases. In both cases, positive and negative relationships, r indicates the extent to which the two sets of scores are ordered similarly. Given the complexity of variables operating in business settings, correlations of 1.00 exist only in theory. If no relationship exists between the two variables, r is 0, and knowing a person's standing on x tells us nothing about his or her standing on y. If r is moderate (positive or negative), we can predict y from x with a certain degree of accuracy.

Although correlation is useful for assessing the degree of relationship between two variables, by itself it does not allow us to predict one set of scores (criterion scores) from another set of scores (predictor scores). The statistical technique by which this is accomplished is known as regression analysis, and correlation is fundamental to its implementation.[9]

Sometimes people interpret a correlation coefficient as the percentage of variability in y that can be explained by x. This is not correct. Actually, the square of r indicates the percentage of variance in y (the criterion) that can be explained, or accounted for, given knowledge of x (the predictor). Assuming a correlation of $r = .40$, then $r^2 = .16$. This indicates that 16 percent of the variance in the criterion may be determined (or explained), given knowledge of the predictor. The statistic r^2 is known as the coefficient of determination.[10]

A special problem with correlational research is that it is often misinterpreted. People often assume that because two variables are correlated, some sort of causal relationship must exist between them. This is false. *Correlation does not imply causation!* A correlation simply means that the two variables are related in some way. For example, consider the following scenario. An HR researcher observes a correlation of $-.20$ between voluntary employee turnover and the financial performance of a firm (e.g., as measured by return on assets). Does this mean that high voluntary turnover causes poor financial performance of a firm? Perhaps. However, it is equally likely that the poor financial performance of a firm causes voluntary turnover, as some employees scramble to desert a sinking ship. In fact, such a reciprocal relationship between employee turnover and firm performance has now been demonstrated empirically.[11]

Researchers and analysts must also consider two additional possibilities: that some unmeasured third variable is leading to the change in both measured variables, or that the relationship arose entirely by chance. In our example above, it is equally plausible that some other variable (e.g., low unemployment) is causing employees to quit, or that a combination of variables (e.g., low unemployment in country A at the same time as a global economic recession) is causing high voluntary turnover in that country and low overall financial performance in a firm that derives much of its income from other countries. Finally, from time to time, variables move in a coordinated fashion entirely by chance. This is known as spurious correlation, and it is a key reason why repeated measurement is important.[12] The point is that observing a correlation between two variables just means they are related to each other; it does not mean that one causes the other.

There are three necessary conditions to support a conclusion that x causes y.[13] The first is that y did not occur until after x. The second requirement is that x and y are actually shown to be related. The third (and most difficult) requirement is that other explanations of the relationship between x and y can be eliminated as plausible rival hypotheses.

Examining the Relationships among Many Variables

It is often useful to examine or explore the relationships among several variables. Among the most common techniques to do this are regression and machine learning. The fundamental mathematics for these two are the essentially the same, but regression is the more commonly used term in HR, so we will refer to regression here.

Regression is a mathematical technique that examines the relationship between one or more independent, or predictor, variables and a single dependent, or outcome, variable.[14] For example, most analyses seeking to predict workforce attrition will use regression to identify the risk factors for exit. Regression is also useful in analyses such as pay equity; in this case, a good outcome is discovering that gender and ethnicity are unrelated to pay levels.

The recent explosion in data science has yielded many other methods for examining multivariate relationships. A full exploration of these is beyond the scope of this book, but we highlight two below.

Random Forest Analysis

Random forest analysis is a newer technique that examines the relationship between a set of predictor variables and an outcome variable. The output is generally expressed in percentages, much like weather predictions. This technique can be very accurate in predicting outcomes such as attrition.[15]

The simplest way to think about a random forest is to imagine a set of decision trees, where each one is randomly assigned to be sensitive to one variable or feature. This creates a "forest" of trees, each of which has a randomly assigned constraint. This literal random forest essential asks "what if" at each possible intersection and combination. The random forest then aggregates the results of those randomly created decision trees.

Once the what-if questions have been answered with training data, new data can be entered into the model, and very accurate predictions will emerge. For example, a random forest built with past attrition data can make very accurate predictions of attrition risk for existing employees, thus permitting a specific intervention to reduce an individual's attrition risk where necessary or desirable.

Set Analytics

Set analytics is an interesting approach to exploring patterns in data that are not traditionally linear. This approach focuses on finding combinations that are meaningful for a particular audience or segment of the population. For example, research on intersectionality often shows that main effects for a majority group don't translate very well to all audiences. For example, post–high school education might be sufficient to help white men escape poverty, while black women might need to be married without children and complete post–high school education to achieve the same economic progress.

Set analytics are a fundamentally different way of thinking about prediction. Like the combinations of constraints in a random forest, exploring sets requires that researchers examine combinations of factors to identify the outcomes of particular combinations, and especially to identify differences among audiences. Particularly where organizations have unique segments to their populations, it can be fruitful to explore set-analytics strategies. Unique segments might include many different dimensions, such as ensuring effective working conditions for employees with diverse abilities, or effectively nurturing talent pools in multiple countries with significantly different cultures.

Effective set analysis requires thoughtful and careful definition of features as well as exploration of meaningful combinations of those features. This can be accomplished algebraically or, depending on the complexity of the features to be combined, with visualization strategies, such as alluvial diagrams.

This set of techniques can help avoid waste by targeting very specific issues with very precise solutions. Thus, searching for and addressing these intersections can help organizations avoid waste and increase impact. It is important, however, when considering these combinations, to be mindful of the risks of overfitting or underfitting your models. In the simplest terms, underfitted models incorporate too few variables and thus miss some analytical precision. Overfitted models, on the other hand, include too many variables; thus, they work well with one specific training set but do not perform as well when applied to new data.

Eliminating Alternative Explanations through Experiments and Quasi-Experiments

The experimental method is a research method that allows a researcher to control the situation and establish a cause-and-effect relationship by manipulating one or more variables. An experimental design is a plan, an outline for conceptualizing the relations among the variables of a research study. It also implies how to control the research situation and how to analyze the data.[16]

For example, researchers can collect "before" measures on a job—before employees attend training—and collect "after" measures at the conclusion of training (and when employees are back on the job sometime after training). Researchers use experimental designs so that they can make causal inferences. That is, by ruling out alternative plausible explanations for observed changes in the outcome of interest, we want to be able to say that training caused the changes. Many conditions must be met for a study to be experimental in nature. Here we merely outline the minimum requirements needed for an experiment.

The basic assumption is that a researcher controls as many factors as possible to establish a cause-and-effect relationship among the variables being studied. Suppose, for example, that a firm wants to know whether online training is superior to classroom training. To conduct an experiment, researchers manipulate one variable (known as the independent variable; in this case, type of training) and observe its effect on an outcome of interest (a dependent variable; for example, test scores at the conclusion of training). One group will receive classroom training, one group online training, and a third group no training. The last group is known as a control group because it serves as a baseline from which to compare the performance of the other two groups. The groups that receive training are known as experimental or treatment groups because they each receive some treatment or level of the independent variable. That is, they each receive the same number of hours of training, either online or classroom. After the training, we will give a standardized test to the members of the control and experimental groups and compare the results to each other. Scores on the test are the dependent variable in this study. Earlier we said that experimentation involves control. This means that we have to control who is in the study. We want to have a sample that is representative of the broader population of actual and potential trainees. We want to control who is in each group (by assigning participants randomly to one of the three conditions: online, classroom, or no training). We also want to have some control over what participants do while in the study (by designing the training to ensure that the online and classroom versions cover identical concepts and materials). If we observe changes in post-training test scores across conditions, and all other factors are held constant (to the extent it is possible to do this), we can conclude that the independent variable (type of training) caused changes in the dependent variable (test scores derived after training is concluded). If, after completing this study with the proper controls, we find that those in one group (online, classroom, or no training) clearly outperform the others, we have evidence to support a cause-and-effect relationship among the variables.

Many factors can threaten valid inferences, such as outside events, experience on the job, or social-desirability effects in the research situation.[17]

Is it appropriate to accept wholeheartedly a conclusion from only one study? In most cases, the answer is no. This is because researchers may think they have controlled everything that might affect observed outcomes, but perhaps they missed something that does affect the results. That something else may have been the actual cause of the observed changes! A more basic reason for not trusting completely the results of a single study is that a single study cannot tell us everything about a theory.[18] Science is not static, and theories generated through science change. For that reason, there is a method, called meta-analysis, to mathematically combine the findings from many studies to determine whether the patterns across studies support certain conclusions. The power of combining multiple studies provides more reliable conclusions, and this is occurring in many areas of behavioral science.[19] Where full meta-analyses are not feasible, it is still advised to make multiple examinations of the relationship under study to ensure that recommendations are sound.

Researchers approaching organizational issues often believe that conducting a carefully controlled experiment is the ultimate answer to discovering the important answers in data. In fact, there is an important limitation of experiments and the data they provide. Often, they fail to focus on the real goals of an organization. For example, experimental results may indicate that job performance after treatment A is superior to performance after treatment B or C. The really important question, however, may not be whether treatment A is more effective, but rather what levels of performance we can expect from almost all trainees at an acceptable cost, and the extent to which improved performance through training fits the broader strategic thrust of an organization.[20] Therefore, even well-designed experiments must carefully consider the context and logic of the situation in order to ask the right questions in the first place.

Quasi-Experimental Designs

In field settings, major obstacles often interfere with conducting true experiments. True experiments require the manipulation of at least one independent variable, the random assignment of participants to groups, and the random assignment of treatments to groups.[21] However, some less-complete (that is, quasi-experimental) designs still can provide useful data even though a true experiment is not possible. Shadish, Cook, and Campbell offer a number of quasi-experimental designs with the following rationale:

> The central purpose of an experiment is to eliminate alternative hypotheses that also might explain results. If a quasi-experimental design can help eliminate some of these rival hypotheses, it may be worth the effort.[22]

Because full experimental control is lacking in quasi-experiments, it is important to know which specific variables are uncontrolled in a particular design. Investigators should, of course, design the very best experiment possible given their circumstances; but where full control is not possible, they should use the most rigorous design that is possible. For example, suppose you were interested in studying the relationship between layoffs and the subsequent financial performance of firms. Pfeffer recently commented on this very issue:

> It's difficult to study the causal effect of layoffs—you can't do double-blind, placebo-controlled studies as you can for drugs by randomly assigning some companies to shed workers and others not, with people unaware of what "treatment" they are receiving. Companies that downsize are undoubtedly different in many ways (the quality of their management, for one) from those that don't. But you can attempt to control for differences in industry, size, financial condition, and past performance, and then look at a large number of studies to see if they reach the same conclusion.[23]

As a detailed example, consider one type of quasi-experimental design.[24]

This design, which is particularly appropriate for cyclical training programs, is known as the recurrent institutional cycle design. For example, a large sales organization presented a management development program, known as the State Manager Program, every two months to small groups (12–15) of middle managers (state managers). The one-week program focused on all aspects of retail sales (new product development, production, distribution, marketing, merchandising, and so on). The program was scheduled so that all state managers (approximately 110) could be trained over an eighteen-month period.

This is precisely the type of situation for which the recurrent institutional cycle design is appropriate—that is, a large number of persons will be trained, but not all at the same time. Different cohorts are involved. This design is actually a combination of two (or more) before-and-after studies that occur at different points in time. Group I receives a pretest at Time 1, then training, and then a posttest at Time 2. At the same chronological time (Time 2), Group II receives a pretest, then training, and then a posttest at Time 3. At Time 2, therefore, an experimental and a control group have, in effect, been created. One can obtain even more information (and with quasi-experimental designs, it is always wise to collect as much data as possible or to demonstrate the effect of training in several different ways) if it is possible to measure Group I again at Time 3 and to give Group II a pretest at Time 1. This controls the effects of history. Moreover, Time 3 data for Groups I and II and the posttests for all groups trained subsequently provide information as to how the training program is interacting with other organizational events to produce changes in the criterion measure.

Several cross-sectional comparisons are possible with the cycle design:

» Group I posttest scores at Time 2 can be compared with Group II pretest scores at Time 2 (that is, gains in training for Group I compared to gains [or no gains] during the no-training period for Group II).

» Gains made in training for Group I (Time 2 posttest scores) can be compared with gains in training for Group II (Time 3 posttest scores).

» Group II posttest scores at Time 3 can be compared with Group I posttest scores at Time 3 (that is, gains in training versus gains [or no gains] during the no-training period).

To interpret this pattern of outcomes, all three contrasts should have adequate statistical power (that is, at least an 80 percent chance of finding an effect significant if, in fact, the effect exists).[25] A chance elevation of Group II, for example, might lead to gross misinterpretations. Hence, use the design only with reliable measures and sufficiently large samples.[26]

This design controls history and test-retest effects, but not differences in selection. One way to control for possible differences in selection, however, is to split one of the groups (assuming it is large enough) into two equivalent samples, one measured both before and after training and the other measured only after training, as shown in Table 2.1.

Table 2.1. Example of an Institutional Cycle Design

	Time 2	Time 3	Time 4
Group IIa	Measure	Train	Measure
Group IIb		Train	Measure

Comparison of posttest scores in two carefully equated groups (Groups II_a and II_b) is more precise than a similar comparison of posttest scores from two unequated groups (Groups I and II).

A final deficiency in the cycle design is the lack of adequate control for the effects of maturation. This is not a serious limitation if the training program is teaching specialized skills or competencies, but it is a plausible rival hypothesis when the objective of the training program is to change attitudes. Changes in attitudes conceivably could be the result of maturational processes such as job changes, life experiences, or growing older. To control for this effect, give a comparable group of managers (whose age and job experience coincide with those of one of the trained groups at the time of testing) a posttest-only measure. To infer that training had a positive effect, posttest scores of the trained groups should be significantly greater than those of the untrained group receiving the posttest-only measure.

Campbell and Stanley aptly expressed the logic of all this patching and adding:

> One starts out with an inadequate design and then adds specific features to control for one or another of the recurrent sources of invalidity. The result is often an inelegant accumulation of precautionary checks, which lacks the intrinsic symmetry of the "true" experimental designs, but nonetheless approaches experimentation. [27]

Remember, a causal inference from any quasi-experiment must meet the basic requirements for all causal relationships: that cause must precede effect, that cause must covary with effect, and that alternative explanations for the causal relationship are implausible.[28] Patching and adding may help satisfy these requirements.

Some Advanced Concepts in Statistics and Research Methods
The increased availability of both data and the computing power to analyze them has resulted in advanced statistical techniques becoming much more common. Open-source coding libraries like Python and R have greatly increased access for many organizations and professionals. While a deep exploration of the concepts below is beyond the scope of this book, this section will highlight four families of analytical methods that can be particularly useful for HR applications. However, as always, the principle of parsimony applies; the simplest answer is generally best. While these additional tools can provide tremendous power and the ability to discern subtle or complex patterns, recent evidence shows that in many cases, simpler techniques are just as effective—and sometimes better—than advanced techniques.[29]

Natural Language Processing
Many organizations have a great deal of HR-related, text-based information, for example, job postings, résumés, interview notes,

and performance reviews. In addition, many have further access to comments on employee engagement surveys, exit interviews, or award nominations. Natural language processing (NLP) and computational linguistics represent a set of methods to ingest everyday language and make sense of it, adding enormous efficiency and power to HR processes like those mentioned above. For many years, keyword searches and word clouds have represented the extent of text analysis for many researchers in HR. As techniques and computing power have advanced, a host of paid and free tools has emerged to enable more sophisticated analyses based on the content of various pieces of text.

Most NLP approaches require taxonomy, or framework of meaning. For sentiment-analysis tools, such as those that might be used to analyze an engagement survey, the taxonomy is likely to include, at a minimum, words and phrases that suggest negative, neutral, or positive feelings in the comment. Similarly, a library or taxonomy designed for use in exit surveys might be able to interpret the sorts of text that relate to career growth versus text that relates to work/life balance.

Once built, NLP taxonomies can quickly sort through pieces of text to analyze, say, the frequency of comments about effective management in exit interviews versus the frequency of those same sorts of comments in the much larger employee engagement survey. NLP can be used to match candidates to open jobs more quickly and more robustly than a human recruiter can. Similarly, having identified a new risk factor for attrition, researchers can now use NLP of written text to identify what drives one person to leave and another to stay.

Structural Equation Modelling

Statistical methods alone generally cannot establish that one variable caused another. One technique that comes close, however, is structural equation modeling (SEM), a family of statistical models that seeks to explain the relationships among multiple variables. It examines the structure of interrelationships, expressed in a series of equations, similar to a series of multiple regression equations. These equations depict all the relationships among constructs (the dependent and independent variables) involved in the analysis.

Although different methods can be used to test SEM models, all such models share three characteristics:[30]

All SEN models have this 3characteristics

1. Estimation of multiple and interrelated dependence relationships.
2. An ability to represent unobserved concepts in these relationships and to correct for measurement error in the estimation process.
3. A model to explain the entire set of relationships.

SEM alone cannot establish causality. What it does provide are statistical results of the hypothesized relationships in the researcher's model. The researcher can then infer from the results what alternative models are most consistent with theory. The most convincing claims of causal relationships, however, usually are based on experimental research.

Conjoint Analysis

Conjoint analysis (CA) is another technique that researchers in a variety of fields use to study judgment and decision-making.[31] Its purpose is to identify the hidden rules that people use to make trade-offs between different products or services, and the values they place on different features. Consider choices among employee benefits, for example. If a company understands precisely how employees make decisions and what they value in the various benefits offered, then it becomes possible to identify the optimum level of benefits that balance value to employees against cost to the company.

CA researchers generally present a set of choices or options to respondents, who provide their preferences for products or concepts with different attributes (e.g., expected product reliability or color) and different levels of those attributes (e.g., high/medium/low or red/blue/green, respectively). For studies in HR, the choices might compare a tradeoff between days of vacation or compensation. Like other multivariate methods used to investigate dependence relationships, CA derives a linear function of attribute levels that minimizes error between actual and estimated values. Researchers can use several software packages to estimate this function (e.g., SAS or Sawtooth). Whereas many multivariate methods require all independent variables to have the same (e.g., linear) relationship with the dependent variable, CA allows each one to have a different relationship (e.g., linear, quadratic, or stepwise), thereby making it extremely flexible when investigating complex decision-making issues.[32]

We noted earlier that CA researchers specify levels for each attribute (i.e., independent variable) and then present respondents with scenarios having attributes with different combinations of these levels. Because levels are known, researchers need only to collect respondent ratings to use as the dependent variable. In so doing, they can estimate or decompose the importance that respondents assign to each attribute. Hence researchers can learn how important different attributes are to respondents by forcing them to make trade-offs in real time.[33]

Network Analysis

Network analysis is a family of techniques that examine complex relationships in a system. Network analysis is universally displayed in a visualization that clarifies key nodes within the system as well as, say, fragments that may not be well connected. Traditionally, organizational or social network analyses were conducted through paper-and-pencil surveys, perhaps asking participants about their key mentors or advisors or which top experts they might consult. More recently, technologies have emerged to capture and map these relationships from communications platforms within an organization, such as email, instant messaging, and collaborative platforms. Similar approaches can be taken to mapping out connections and behavior in the real world through sociometric badges—devices that capture proximity to others, and the frequency with which different parties speak.

These analyses can be particularly helpful in identifying individuals in organizations that may contribute above and beyond what might be expected as a function of their job. Each of the methods described above can help organizations find their core experts, for example, or identify those individuals who serve as brokers or connectors between different parts of the organization. Network analysis can also help reveal important roles that may be difficult to detect with traditional measures. For example, one particular salesperson may deliver fairly ordinary quarterly results, but network analysis might reveal that new employees who are trained by this person deliver at full productivity in half the time as new employees trained by others. Identifying this pattern might enable organizations to explore this particular pattern and accelerate time to performance for all new employees.

Fundamental Analytical Concepts from Economics and Finance

The analytical concepts previously discussed come largely from psychology and related individual-focused social sciences. However, the fields of economics and finance also provide useful general analytical concepts for measuring HRM programs and consequences. Here, the focus is often on properly acknowledging the implicit sacrifices implied in choices, the behavior of markets, and the nature of risk.

We consider concepts in the following areas:

» Fixed, variable, and opportunity costs/savings.
» The time value of money.
» Estimating the value of employee time using total pay.
» Cost-benefit and cost-effectiveness analyses.
» Utility as a weighted sum of utility attributes.
» Sensitivity and break-even analysis.

Fixed, Variable, and Opportunity Costs/Savings

We can distinguish fixed, variable, and opportunity costs, as well as reductions in those costs, which we call savings. Fixed costs or savings refer to those that remain constant, whose total does not change in proportion to the activity of interest. For example, if an organization is paying rent or mortgage interest on a training facility, the cost does not change with the volume of training activity. If all training is moved to online delivery and the training center is sold, the fixed savings equal the rent or interest that is now avoided.

Variable costs or savings are those that change in direct proportion to changes in some particular activity level.[34] The food and beverage cost of a training program is variable with regard to the number of training participants. If a less-expensive food vendor replaces a more-expensive one, the variable savings represent the difference between the costs of the more-expensive and the less-expensive vendors.

Finally, opportunity costs reflect the opportunities foregone that might have been realized had the resources allocated to one program been directed toward other organizational ends.[35] This is often conceived of as the sacrifice of the value of the next best alternative use of the resources. For example, if we choose to have employees travel to a training program, the opportunity cost might be the value they would produce if they were back at their regular locations working on their regular jobs. Opportunity savings are the next-best uses of resources that we obtain if we alter the opportunity relationships. For example, if we provide employees with laptop computers or handheld devices that allow them to use email to resolve issues at work while they are attending the offsite training program, the opportunity savings represent the difference between the value that would have been sacrificed without the devices and the reduced sacrifice with the devices.

The Time Value of Money: Compounding, Discounting, and Present Value[36]

In general, the time value of money refers to the fact that a dollar in hand today is worth more than a dollar promised sometime in the future. If you were to invest that dollar today at a given interest rate, it would grow over time from its present value (PV) to some future value (FV). If you invest $100 and earn 10 percent on your money per year, you will have $110 at the end of the first year. It is composed of your original principal, $100, plus $10 in interest that you earn. Hence, $110 is the FV of $100 invested for one year at 10 percent. In the second year, you will have a total of $110 + $11 = $121. This $121 has four parts. The first is the $100 original principal. The second is the $10 in interest you earned after the first year, and the third is another $10 you earn in the second year, for a total of $120. The last dollar you earn (the fourth part) is interest you earn in the second year on the interest paid in the first year ($10 × .10 = $1). The general formula is $FV = PV \times (1+r)^t$, where r is the interest rate and t is the number of periods (e.g., years) of the investment.

This principle can be applied broadly, beyond finance. For example, suppose your company currently has 10,000 employees. Senior management estimates that the number of employees will grow at a modest 3 percent per year. How many employees will work for your company in five years? In this example, we begin with 10,000 people rather than dollars, and we don't think of the growth rate as an interest rate, but the calculation is exactly the same:

$$10,000 \times (1.03)^5 = 10,000 \times 1.1593 = 11,593 \text{ employees}$$

There will be about 1,593 net new hires over the coming five years. Thus, the organization must plan to hire, train, and reward not only replacements for those lost through attrition, but also an additional 1,593 over that time period.

Present Value and Discounting

Suppose we ask a slightly different question; namely, how much do we have to invest today at 10 percent to get $1 in one year? We know the FV is $1, but what is its PV? Whatever we invest today will be 1.1 times bigger at the end of the year. Because we need $1 at the end of the year:

$$PV \times 1.1 = \$1$$

Solving for the PV yields $\$1/1.1 = \$0.909$. This PV is the answer to the question, What amount invested today will grow to $1 in one year if the interest rate is 10 percent? Instead of compounding the money forward into the future, we discount it back to the present. The formula $1 / (1+r)^t$ is used to discount a future cash flow. Hence, it is often called a discount factor. Likewise, the rate used in the calculation is often called the discount rate.

The net present value (NPV) of an investment is the difference between the PV of the future cash flows and the cost of the investment. Indeed, the capital budgeting process can be viewed as a search for investments with NPVs that are positive.[37] Similarly, HR investments should not simply "pay for themselves" but rather deliver a higher NPV than other investments could offer.

Estimating the Value of Employee Time
Using Total Compensation

First, a caution. While it is common to calculate the value of employees' time in terms of the cost to the company, this assumption is not generally valid. The more correct concept in estimating the value of employee time is the opportunity cost of the lost value that employees would have been creating if they had not been using their time for whatever activity is currently under study, such as interviewing or training. If the value of what an employee delivers with their time is *not* higher than the direct costs of employing them, they are not delivering value to the business and are unlikely to be employed for long. Thus, the opportunity cost of any activity is necessarily higher than the direct costs of that employee's time. That said, it is so difficult to estimate the opportunity cost of employees' time that it is very common for accounting processes just to recommend multiplying the time by the value of total pay. The important thing to realize is the limits of such calculations, even if they provide a useful, standardized proxy.

However flawed, this total cost approach is the simplest and most straightforward approach, and one with intuitive appeal to many executives. When estimating the cost of an employee to the company, it is important to recognize that the total cost of an employee is much more than the wages received by that employees. Common additional costs include employee benefits, any variable compensation, and overhead costs—those general expenses incurred during the normal course of operating a business, such as facilities and technology. Applying a multiplier, typically in the range of two to three times the salary, is the most straightforward approach to estimating the total cost of employee time.

Cost-Benefit and Cost-Effectiveness Analyses

Cost-benefit and cost-effectiveness analyses are both commonly used methods to evaluate the outcomes of an investment against the investment required. Cost-benefit analysis does this in monetary terms and cost-effectiveness analysis does it in nonmonetary terms, but both answer the same essential question: "Is this a good investment?"

One of the most popular forms of cost-benefit analysis is ROI analysis. The simplest description of ROI is the value of a return in some future time (appropriately discounted to reflect risk and inflation) divided by the resources required by the investment.

ROI has both advantages and disadvantages. Its major advantage is that it is simple and widely accepted, and blends into one number the major ingredients of profitability, permitting relatively even comparisons among investment opportunities. On the other hand, it suffers from two major disadvantages. First, although the logic of ROI analysis appears straightforward, there is much subjectivity in estimating returns and especially in estimating the appropriate discount factors. Second, and more specific to HR, typical ROI calculations focus on one investment at a time and fail to consider how those investments work together as a portfolio. As we noted in the set-analytics section above, often specific combinations are very powerful. Training may produce value beyond its cost, but would that value be even higher if it were combined with proper investments in individual incentives related to the training outcomes?[38]

Cost-effectiveness analysis is similar to cost-benefit analysis, but whereas the costs are still measured in monetary terms, outcomes are measured in units other than money. Cost-effectiveness analysis identifies the cost of producing a unit of effect. For example, to determine the cost-effectiveness of a corporate safety program, one might calculate the cost per accident avoided.

In summary, both cost-benefit and cost-effectiveness analyses can be useful tools for evaluating benefits relative to the costs of programs or investments. Cost-benefit analysis enables us to compare the absolute value of the returns from very different programs or decisions, because they are all calculated in the same units of money. Cost-effectiveness, on the other hand, makes such comparisons somewhat more difficult because the outcomes of the different decisions may be calculated in very different units. How do you decide between a program that promises a cost of $1,000 per avoided accident and a program that promises $300 per unit increase of employee satisfaction? Cost-effectiveness can prove quite useful, however, for comparing programs or decisions that all have the same outcome (for example, which accident reduction program to choose).

It's a dilemma when one must decide among programs that produce very different outcomes (such as accident reduction versus employee satisfaction) and when all outcomes of programs cannot necessarily be expressed in monetary terms. However, many decisions require such comparisons. One answer is to calculate "utilities" (from the word *use*) that attempt to systematically capture the subjective value that decision-makers place on different outcomes when the outcomes are compared directly to each other.

Utility, Sensitivity, and Break-Even Analysis

Utility analysis takes the above processes one step further. Where cost-benefit and cost-effectiveness analyses simply compare inputs to anticipated outputs, utility analysis is designed to aid in decision-making. It is the determination of *institutional* gain or loss anticipated from various courses of action, after taking into account both costs and benefits. For example, in the context of HRM, the decision might be which type of training to offer or which selection procedure to implement. When faced with a choice among alternative options, management should choose the option that maximizes the expected utility for the organization across all possible outcomes.[39]

One important difference between cost-benefit analysis and utility analysis is probability. For example, subjective expected utility theory, a popular means of supporting decision-making under conditions of uncertainty, requires estimation of two key parameters:

» The subjective value, or utility, of an option's outcomes.
» The estimated probability of the outcomes.

By multiplying the utilities with the associated probabilities and summing over all consequences, it is possible to calculate an expected utility. The option with the highest expected utility is then chosen.

Sensitivity and break-even analysis are both approaches designed to overcome the limitations of utility values, specifically the fact that utility values are estimates made under uncertainty. Actual utility values may vary from estimated values, and it is helpful for decision-makers to be able to estimate the effects of such imprecision. One way to do that is through sensitivity analysis.

In sensitivity analysis, each of the utility parameters is varied from the lowest value in its range to the highest, while holding other parameter values constant. Utility estimates that result from each combination of parameter values are then examined to determine which parameter's variability has the greatest effect on the estimate of overall utility.

In the context of evaluating HR programs, sensitivity analyses almost always indicate that utility parameters that reflect changes in the quality of employees caused by improved selection, as well as increases in the number of employees affected, have substantial effects on resulting utility values.[40] Utility parameters that reflect changes in the quality of employees include improvements in the validity of the selection procedure, the average score on the predictor, and dollar-based increases in the variability of performance.

Although sensitivity analyses are valuable in assessing the effects of changes in individual parameters, they provide no information about the effects of simultaneous changes in more than one utility parameter. Break-even analysis overcomes that difficulty.

Instead of estimating the level of expected utility, break-even analysis skips the estimates of utility and moves directly to identifying the smallest value of any given parameter that will generate a positive utility (payoff). For example, suppose we know that a training program conducted for 500 participants raises technical knowledge by 10 percent or more for 90 percent of them. Everyone agrees that the value of the 10 percent increase is greater than $1,000 per trainee, although the true value is estimated to be much higher by many of the stakeholders. Using this minimum threshold of benefit, the total gain is therefore at least $450,000 (500 × .90 × $1,000). Assuming that the cost of the training program is $600 per trainee, the total cost is therefore $300,000 (500 × $600). Researchers and managers could spend lots of time debating the actual economic value of the increase in knowledge, but, in fact, it does not matter because even the minimum agreed-upon value ($1,000) is enough to recoup the costs of the program. More precisely, when the costs of a program are matched exactly by equivalent benefits—no more, no less—the program breaks even. This is the origin of the term break-even analysis.[41]

The major advantages of break-even analysis suggest a mechanism for concisely summarizing the potential impact of uncertainty in one or more utility parameters.[42] It shifts emphasis away from estimating a utility value toward making a decision using imperfect information. It pinpoints areas where controversy is important to decision-making (i.e., where there is doubt about whether the break-even value is exceeded), versus where controversy has little impact (because there is little risk of observing utility values below break-even). In summary, break-even analysis provides a simple expedient that allows utility models to assist in decision-making even when some utility parameters are unknown or uncertain.

Taken together, these concepts can well equip HR practitioners to determine not only the relationships among variables that matter but also the business value of the options being investigated. Effective HR analytics work is at least partially about delivering measurable value to the business; thus a solid understanding of both analytical techniques and fundamental finance and economics concepts will ensure that HR analytics projects are valued by stakeholders and make material impact on their organizations.

Conclusion

As noted at the outset, the purpose of this chapter is to present some general analytical concepts that we will revisit throughout this book. The issues that we discussed fall into two broad areas:

» Fundamental analytical concepts from statistics and research design.
» Fundamental analytical concepts from economics and finance.

In statistics and research design, we considered the following concepts: cautions in generalizing from sample data, correlation and causality, examination of relationships among many variables, and experiments and quasi-experiments. We also considered some advanced statistical and research methods (random forests, set analytics, natural language processing, structural equation modeling, conjoint analysis, and network analysis). We also considered some economic and financial concepts in five broad areas: fixed, variable, and opportunity costs/savings; the time value of money; estimating the value of employee time using total pay; cost-benefit and cost-effectiveness analyses; and utility, sensitivity, and break-even analyses. All these concepts are important to HR measurement, and understanding them will help you to develop reliable, valid metrics. It will be up to you, of course, to determine whether those metrics fit the strategic direction of your organization.

References

1. Thomas H. Davenport, Jeanne Harris, and Jeremy Shapiro, "Competing on Talent Analytics," *Harvard Business Review*, October 2010, 2–6. See also Scott Mondore et al., *Predicting Business Success: Using Smarter Analytics to Drive Results* (Alexandria, VA: Society for Human Resource Management, 2018).

2. Evan F. Sinar, "Data Visualization: Get Visual to Drive HR's Impact and Influence" (SHRM-SIOP Science of HR White Paper, 2018), https://www.shrm.org/hr-today/trends-and-forecasting/special-reports-and-expert-views/Documents/2018%2003_SHRM-SIOP%20White%20Paper_Data%20Visualization.pdf.

3. Francis J. Anscombe, "Graphs in Statistical Analysis," *American Statistician* 27, no. 1 (1973): 17–21.

4. Anshul Vikram Pandey et al., "The Persuasive Power of Data Visualization" (New York University Public Law and Legal Theory Working Papers, no. 474, 2014).

5. Sinar, *Data Visualization*.

6. Sherri L. Jackson, *Research Methods and Statistics: A Critical Thinking Approach* (Belmont, CA: Wadsworth/Thomson Learning, 2003).

7. Jackson, *Research Methods and Statistics*.

8. See, for example, William G. Cochran, *Sampling Techniques*, 3rd ed. (New York: Wiley, 1997); Fred N. Kerlinger and Howard B. Lee, *Foundations of Behavioral Research*, 4th ed. (Stamford, CT: Thomson Learning, 2000).

9. For more on this, see Richard B. Darlington and Andrew F. Hayes, *Regression Analysis and Linear Models* (New York: Guilford, 2017). See also Frank E. Harrell Jr., *Regression Modeling Strategies*, 2nd ed. (New York: Springer, 2015).

10. Joy P. Guilford and Benjamin Fruchter, *Fundamental Statistics in Psychology and Education*, 6th ed. (New York: McGraw-Hill, 1978).

11. Khim Kelly et al., "Employee Turnover and Firm Performance: Modeling Reciprocal Effects" (paper presentation, annual meeting of the Academy of Management, Philadelphia, PA, August 2007).

12. Tyler Vigen, *Spurious Correlations* (New York: Hachette, 2015).

13. Ralph L. Rosnow and Robert Rosenthal, *Understanding Behavioral Science: Research Methods for Consumers* (New York: McGraw-Hill, 1984).

14. Darlington and Hayes, *Regression Analysis and Linear Models*. See also Harrell Jr., *Regression Modeling Strategies*.

15. Tin Kam Ho, "Random Decision Forests," in *Proceedings of the third International Conference on Document Analysis and Recognition: August 14–16, 1995, Montréal, Canada* (Los Alamitos, CA: IEEE Computer Society Press), 278–82.

16. Kerlinger and Lee, *Foundations of Behavioral Research*.

17. For more on this, see William R. Shadish, Thomas D. Cook, and Donald T. Campbell, *Experimental and Quasi-Experimental Designs for Generalized Causal Inference* (Boston: Houghton Mifflin, 2002).

18. Jackson, *Research Methods and Statistics*.

19. Frank L. Schmidt and John Hunter, "History, Development, Evolution, and Impact of Validity Generalization and Meta-Analysis Methods, 1975–2001," in *Validity Generalization: A Critical Review*, ed. Kevin R. Murphy (Mahwah, NJ: Lawrence Erlbaum, 2003), 31–65. See also Frank L. Schmidt and John E. Hunter, "Meta-Analysis," in *Handbook of Psychology: Research Methods in Psychology*, ed. John A. Schinka, Wayne F. Velicer, and Irving B. Weiner (New York: John Wiley and Sons, 2003), 533–54.

20. Wayne F. Cascio and Herman Aguinis, *Applied Psychology in Human Resource Management*, 7th ed. (Upper Saddle River, NJ: Prentice-Hall, 2011).

21. Kerlinger and Lee, *Foundations of Behavioral Research*.

22. Shadish, Cook, and Campbell, *Experimental and Quasi-Experimental Designs*.

23. Jeffrey Pfeffer, "Lay Off the Layoffs," *Newsweek*, February 15, 2010.

24. Cascio and Aguinis, *Applied Psychology in Human Resource Management*.

25. Jacob Cohen, *Statistical Power Analysis for the Behavioral Sciences*, 2nd ed. (Hillsdale, NJ: Lawrence Erlbaum, 1988).

26. Shadish, Cook, and Campbell, *Experimental and Quasi-Experimental Designs*.

27. Donald T. Campbell and Julian C. Stanley, *Experimental and Quasi-Experimental Designs for Research* (Chicago: Rand McNally, 1963).

28. Shadish, Cook, and Campbell, *Experimental and Quasi-Experimental Designs*.
29. Spyros Makridakis, Evangelos Spiliotis, and Vassilios Assimakopoulos, "Statistical and Machine Learning Forecasting Methods: Concerns and Ways Forward," *PLoS ONE* 13, no. 3 (2018): e0194889.
30. Joseph F. Hair Jr. et al., *Multivariate Data Analysis*, 6th ed. (Upper Saddle River, NJ: Prentice Hall, 2006).
31. For more on conjoint analysis, see Hair Jr. et al., *Multivariate Data Analysis*. See also Franz T. Lohrke, Betsy Bugg Holloway, and Thomas W. Woolley, "Conjoint Analysis in Entrepreneurship Research: A Review and Research Agenda," *Organizational Research Methods* 13, no. 1 (2010): 16–30.
32. Hair Jr. et al., *Multivariate Data Analysis*.
33. Hair Jr. et al., *Multivariate Data Analysis*. See also Lohrke, Holloway, and Woolley, "Conjoint Analysis in Entrepreneurship Research."
34. Monte R. Swain et al., *Management Accounting*, 3rd ed. (Mason, OH: Thomson/South-Western, 2005).
35. Swain et al., *Management Accounting*. See also Jerome Rothenberg, "Cost-Benefit Analysis: A Methodological Exposition," in *Handbook of Evaluation Research*, ed. Marcia Guttentag and Elmer Struening (Beverly Hills, CA: Sage, 1975), 75–106.
36. Material in this section is drawn largely from Richard A. Brealey, Stewart C. Myers, and Franklin Allen, *Principles of Corporate Finance*, 12th ed. (New York: McGraw-Hill, 2017); Stephen A. Ross, Randolph Westerfield, and Bradford D. Jordan, *Fundamentals of Corporate Finance*, 9th ed. (Burr Ridge, IL: McGraw-Hill/Irwin, 2010); Denzil Watson and Antony Head, *Corporate Finance: Principles and Practice*, 5th ed. (London: Pearson Education, 2009). This is just a brief introduction to these concepts at a conceptual level and includes only rudimentary calculations.
37. Ross, Westerfield, and Jordan, *Fundamentals of Corporate Finance*.
38. John W. Boudreau and Peter M. Ramstad, *Beyond HR: The New Science of Human Capital* (Cambridge, MA: Harvard Business Press, 2007).
39. Wayne F. Cascio, "Utility Analysis," in Vol. 2, *Encyclopedia of Industrial and Organizational Psychology*, ed. Steven G. Rogelberg (Thousand Oaks, CA: Sage, 2007), 854–58.
40. For more on conjoint analysis, see Hair Jr. et al., *Multivariate Data Analysis*. See also Lohrke, Holloway, and Woolley, "Conjoint Analysis in Entrepreneurship Research."
41. Hair Jr. et al., *Multivariate Data Analysis*.
42. Hair Jr. et al., *Multivariate Data Analysis*. See also Lohrke, Holloway, and Woolley, "Conjoint Analysis in Entrepreneurship Research."

3

Talent Management as a Source of Competitive Advantage

Introduction

The Conference Board's survey of more than one thousand global CEOs revealed failure to attract and retain top talent as the number one concern—higher than disruptive technology, cash flow, or global competition.[1] Ensuring that organizations have the talent they need is a key strategic capability.

However, as Cappelli and Keller note, "good data that describe the actual [talent management] practices of companies are extremely difficult to find, and so we are left with drawing inferences from sources of information that are indirect to learn what is really happening in talent management."[2]

One of the key challenges with talent management in organizations is the level of uncertainty involved. Whereas many of the analytical opportunities highlighted in this book focus on areas where we can be confident the about the outcomes of a chosen path of action, much of talent management is future-looking and by definition uncertain, especially over longer time horizons. However, the purpose of strategy is to place bets about your organization's future, and effective talent management permits organizations to do just that. Thus, investing in talent management is a key opportunity for HR functions to contribute strategically to the success of their organizations.

Developing Strategy

Over the past decade, there has been a groundswell of appreciation for the enormous strategic opportunity in the way organizations approach HR talent management.[3] In this chapter, we will address some of the significant opportunities for talent management to make a strategic impact in organizations. We will also, importantly, address the methods of analysis that can identify opportunities, manage processes, and quantify outcomes to inform effective, strategic decision-making.

A solid understanding of strategy is relevant to the organizational practitioner in at least two ways. First, HR can most effectively support achievement of business goals by clearly aligning to the organization's overall strategy. Second, HR itself should have a clear strategy for its own delivery of products and services.

There is an entire management discipline dedicated to strategy. Although we will not attempt to cover all the complexities here, we will raise a few key points that should be useful to HR practitioners in understanding the organization's strategy and in creating and executing their own strategies within HR.

At the simplest possible level, strategy is about an analysis of the current offerings in the marketplace, and your organization's approach to differentiating itself from them.[4] Common high-level strategies include cost, quality, and service. Another framework that is commonly used in strategy analysis is a SWOT analysis—systematically reviewing the strengths, weaknesses, opportunities, and threats of a product or organization. Importantly, strategy is as much about what you choose *not* to do as what you affirmatively choose to pursue.

Organizations may offer similar products to the marketplace, but for very different strategic reasons. A common example might be Microsoft, Apple, and Google. All make computer operating systems, but those operating systems play very different roles in their strategies. Microsoft is the simplest and most direct model; it makes money on the operating system itself. Apple makes money on the hardware and includes an operating system as part of an optimized user experience based on that hardware. Google makes money on advertising and offers an operating system as a way to direct as much activity as possible into its suite of ad-supported software offerings. Thus, each makes and offers a product—an operating system—but finds its profits in a different part of its value chain. Understanding the strategic purpose of the various activities and products of your organization will help you design HR strategies that will best help your organization be successful.

Aligning HR strategies to business strategies can be challenging in organizations where HR activities historically have been primarily transactional. Additionally, some HR organizations see themselves as the compassionate heart of an organization and take great pride in designing products and services that make all employees feel heard and valued. In those cases, it can be uncomfortable to, for example, create strategic segmentation of roles or individuals who benefit from an enhanced employee value proposition as a result of their skills or position being more closely aligned to the core profit-generating activities of the organization.

HR operates under constraints that differ from those of the organization as a whole in terms of strategy. While is it very possible to secure HR products and services from consultants and vendors, HR functions have enjoyed a bit of a privileged position in executing HR work. Thus they may not need to invest the same level of energy marketing the differentiation on cost, quality, or service levels that they provide to the customers of their work. However, this privileged position does not exempt HR from the need to be strategic in its own execution. This may include analyzing core segments to address, or determining which HR products and services to buy or rent rather than to build.

If we accept the premise that differentiation is a core attribute of strategy, then, for an action or activity to be strategic, it cannot simply be a copy from some other organization. This suggests that an HR organization should invest its own resources where it can provide a cost, quality, or service advantage, and buy products or services where, for example, scale dramatically reduces cost, or where fairly vanilla offerings are sufficient to meet strategic needs. As examples, consider that new-manager training might be created in-house, to reflect the company's values and culture, but project management training could be sourced most efficiently from a vendor. The same utility and ROI concepts discussed in Chapter 2 can be applied to decisions regarding outsourcing.

Finally, while many of the chapters in this book can be quite pre-scriptive about which formula to use and what specific variables to consider as part of an evaluation of the effectiveness or efficiency of a talent intervention, a strategic analysis, by its very nature, will be a bit looser. In this chapter, you will find some samples and items for your consideration, but you will have to do the heavy lifting to figure out what data elements align to your own differentiated strategy. While it is possible for efficiency to be a source of competitive advan-tage, there are other available strategies for organizations to pursue. A well-crafted talent management strategy will be aligned with and supportive of your organization's overall competitive strategy.

Defining Talent Management

Talent management is a relatively new concept within the field of HR. Definitions range from a suggestion that talent management is simply a new name for HR, to fairly abstract definitions such as "the process through which organizations anticipate and meet their needs for talent in strategic jobs"[5] and deeply specific ones that suggest a "whole range of processes [are] potentially associated with talent management—from planning, searching, locating, attracting, sourcing, assigning and deploying, tasking, coaching, building, developing, retaining, internalizing the learning, and exporting."[6] Collings, Mellahi, and Cascio offer a three-part definition focused on identifying pivotal roles, developing talent pools to fill those roles, and developing a differentiated HR architecture to ensure that pivotal roles are filled with the best available incumbents.[7]

Often, talent management teams and organizations will talk about their charter being to ensure "the right talent, at the right time, in the right place, at the right cost." This simple definition includes four aspects: necessary capabilities, a time horizon, a location geographically or organizationally, and a cost analysis. This simple definition may be the most useful one for practitioners.

Although talent management is a popular topic of discussion, there is little evidence that it is done well, particularly in large, complex, global organizations.[8] However, for talent management to be valuable to organizations, it must be thoughtfully connected to the strategy of the organization.[9] That is, talent management practitioners must carefully diagnose the skills and capabilities required to execute the organization's strategy and take steps to ensure that those skills and capabilities are available through activities such as selection and talent-pipeline development, through training and development activities, through succession planning, and through a thoughtful diagnosis of critical roles and promising talent.

Essential to many implementations of talent management is a discipline around identifying which talent, specifically, is most critical to attaining business objectives. That is, where are the consequences of the talent decisions the greatest? Frequently, talent management will refer to those practices aimed specifically at ensuring an effective talent supply for a critical few roles that most affect the success of the organization. Additionally, there will typically be more attention and investment in the individuals believed most likely to perform at a high level in those pivotal roles.

Segmentation

Efficient use of scarce organizational resources generally requires some analysis of which skills, roles, and individuals are most critical to the organization's success, with some alignment of processes and energy around those that are most critical.[10] These segments then form the basis for talent management activities.

Organizations may elect to build their segments around a variety of criteria and combinations of criteria. Typically, these criteria may include skills, particularly emerging and future skills, or specific roles of disproportionate importance or impact. Other talent management systems focus largely on identifying, developing, and deploying talented individuals.

In the sections below, we will describe three common approaches to segmenting talent. In general, the recommended process for identifying talent priorities and segmenting talent is a qualitative one, although increasingly organizations are using advanced techniques such as organization network analysis to identify particularly influential roles or individuals. As described in Chapter 2, organization network analysis examines patterns of interactions to discover activities and relationships that are particularly strong or that relate particularly well to outcomes of interest.

In the standard qualitative process, subject matter experts, typically business leaders and HR, will conduct in-depth reviews of the current and desired future state for each of the types of talent identified below. That initial evaluation generates the framework that HR professionals can use to identify gaps and opportunity areas.

The three frameworks below discuss segmentation by capabilities, by roles, or by individuals. Each has its own merits, and a talent management system may include a mix of all three. Analytics are relevant both for the original identification and for refining decision-making. In the identification process, data may be used to help identify which roles account for the greatest variability in performance, or which individuals are superstars within the organization. After talent investments are made, analyses can be conducted to identify the most important factors for success, typically using the same processes outlined elsewhere in this volume—for example, in considering selection procedures (Chapter 9).

Capabilities

Core to the definition of talent management is the concept of ensuring that organizations have the capabilities they will need for future success. This is why beginning with a clear understanding of both the strategy of the organization and the strategy for HR is so critical. Typically, talent management processes focus a good deal of their energy on preparing for the future success of the organization. In this preparation, it is important to think about the range of possibilities in the future and to prepare talent in such a way that that the organization can execute multiple different scenarios effectively. That is, it is important to treat future planning like building a portfolio of options.

Effective capability assessment will require the organization to determine what knowledge, skills, abilities, or other characteristics are important for success. For many organizations, this will take the form of competencies that may be assessed through mechanisms such as 360-degree feedback, performance reviews, personal profiles, evaluations during selection, or formal assessments. Increasingly, organizations are using advanced techniques, such as natural language processing, to analyze capabilities from documents such as résumés. Effectively cataloging and maintaining these records can give organizations an advantage in determining what capabilities are available within their existing labor forces, and aid in creating effective segmentation by critical capabilities for future success.

Capability analysis may also include new and emerging skills that will be relevant for a business, such as artificial intelligence for advanced diagnostics in a hospital system. Almost by definition, developing processes to source, hire, deploy, develop, and retain talent in areas that are fundamentally new is a challenge. After all, their very newness means you lack a credible roadmap.

Roles

While individual skills and capabilities can be important for some talent management processes such as selection and training, others, such as succession planning, focus more at the level of the roles. A common framework for analyzing roles segments them into pivotal, critical, and core roles.[11]

Pivotal roles are those where variability in performance has a disproportionate impact on performance. These may not be particularly visible or endowed with high levels of organizational authority, but poor performance can create substantial risk, while high performance can generate significant opportunities.[12] The classic example of a pivotal role is a Disneyland sweeper. These individuals are widely distributed throughout the parks, giving them the opportunity to identify visitors who can be surprised and delighted in unexpected ways, which contributes to the overall magic of Disney. Where roles like the characters are highly constrained to remove risks of error, pivotal roles may be those that require substantial discretion.

Identifying pivotal roles requires an understanding of the nature of the roles, the level of standardization available to control them, and the level of risk or upside potential associated with the roles. In most organizations, there will be relatively few pivotal roles. Because the risk associated with them can be quite high, it is especially important that these roles receive careful consideration across talent management processes.

Critical roles are often confused with pivotal roles. Critical roles are those central to the strategy or main purpose of the organization. However, these roles may be more standardized and thus less variable between incumbents. To continue Boudreau and Ramstad's Disney example from above, Mickey Mouse is a critical role at Disneyland.[13] Mickey is core to the experience, but his role is tightly standardized and controlled. Airline pilots are another example. It is difficult to conceive of an airline without pilots, so they truly are central to the strategic purpose of the firm. However, in part because of their strategic importance, much of the variability and risk have been engineered out of the process—one pilot will fly the aircraft very much like the next one, thanks to rigorous selection, training, engineering, and work processes like checklists. These roles are generally easier to identify within an organization, and, like pivotal roles, should be carefully considered and prioritized within talent management processes.

Core roles are those that are essential to organizational functioning but not intimately connected to strategy. For example, roles that are primarily transactional are often core roles. In some organizations, this might include roles such as accounting, IT staff, HR staff, project managers, and administrative professionals. While the organization cannot function effectively without them, in many cases, their chief contributions are through bottom-line containment of risk rather than differentiated top-line growth or competitive advantage. Talent management processes for pivotal and critical roles should be thoughtful and thorough, which often offers differentiated levels of investment. Investments in core roles, on the other hand, might be aimed at more of a baseline experience, and differentiation may come from efficiency in business process rather than in extraordinary individual performance. For example, processing invoices is typically a standard, though clearly crucial, task for organizations. Efficiency and effectiveness here may be more likely to come from robust, simple tools and business processes, rather than from extraordinary problem solving on the part of individuals. The risk created for the organization from an unfilled core role is generally lower than the risk of an unfilled pivotal role.

While often SME-based (subject matter expert-based) processes are used to identify pivotal, critical, and core roles, it is also possible to use advanced quantitative methods. Notably, it is possible to use organization network analysis to identify consistent patterns across your workforce that can indicate that a specific role has an outsize impact on team or organizational performance.

Individual

While many talent management systems focus on specific skills or categories of roles, others focus on individuals. Traditional high-potential programs generally take this approach, identifying those with the strongest growth potential and providing them with developmental experiences such as job rotations, executive coaching, and formal learning.

Identifying talented individuals is in some ways simpler than focusing on roles or future skills in that it is possible to skip the strategic-alignment step. Additionally, individual identification can be bundled into existing talent processes such as performance reviews. Star performers tend to deliver high levels of value back to their employers, and investing in these top performers can help improve their performance even further and can support retention.[14]

Best practices for individual identification, however, generally include an assessment of individuals against a profile of successful performance. This can help ensure consistency across different organizational units and provide information about development opportunities.

When evaluating individuals as part of a talent-segmentation strategy, it can be helpful to differentiate between, on the one hand, those who are expected to have the capability to perform effectively at higher levels of responsibility (high potentials) from, on the other hand, those who, despite having deep mastery in their current roles, will deliver future differentiated contributions more in the form of coaching others to mastery rather than progressing to higher levels of responsibility themselves (high professionals). This distinction can help HR practitioners identify optimal talent management strategies for each group. For example, high potentials may be promoted quickly, and it is more appropriate for them to be at the lower end of the pay ranges for their jobs since they don't dwell for very long at each progressive step. In fact, high potentials may not even fare particularly well in traditional performance management systems as they may be placed into jobs that are a significant stretch for them. In contrast, high professionals may appropriately be at the top or even above the top of the pay grade for their positions (so-called red-circled pay rates) because of their extraordinary contributions and might consistently fare at the very top of performance management assessments. Thus, even seemingly solid criteria such as performance-review scores and position within a pay grade may be misleading when working to identify individuals in special talent pools.

Typical Talent Management Activities

As we have seen above, talent management can incorporate a wide array of organizational tasks, many of which are covered elsewhere in this volume. Among the typical activities for talent management not elsewhere covered in this volume are talent reviews, succession planning, and high-potential programs. These seek to ensure that organizations have a consistent and reliable bench of future leaders and, in specific types of roles, individual contributors and managers. In this section, we will review briefly each of these three common talent management activities.

Talent Reviews

Often the first step in an active talent management program is to arrange for a review of "top talent" in the organization. While goals and formats will differ, this is an opportunity to increase the familiarity of executives with that top talent, especially with individuals they may not ordinarily meet. Typical talent-review conversations will include consideration of individual development needs and future roles for which they may be suited. Additionally, conducting a large-scale review all at once can surface patterns regarding areas of over- or undersupply in the internal labor market. Thus, the purpose of a talent review is to consider assets and opportunities at an individual level as well as broad patterns of readiness and areas of weakness. Both sets of insights can inform useful action.

Unfortunately, talent reviews are often based on little more than intuition—about what capabilities and roles or which individuals are most important to develop, about what attributes are important to capture, and about what developmental experiences will yield desired improvements. An assessment of potential derailers, such as a pattern of impulsive behavior or an overly cautious approach to problem solving, can also be an important, if frequently neglected, component of a talent review.

Fortunately, from an analytical standpoint, figuring out what attributes to include in an assessment for purposes of a talent review is very similar to examining validity and utility in selection. That is, you have a set of candidates and, in this case, a set of roles that may share common attributes (e.g., they are all leadership roles), and your task is to identify important variations in skills and abilities related to those roles while also identifying whether a new method for identifying skills is sufficiently superior to warrant replacing the previous method. Thus, a high-quality talent review may include fairly detailed data from sources like leadership assessments. It may also consider attributes that may be determined empirically to be important, such as international experience. While the content may be slightly different, the core analyses to determine whether an attribute predicts success accurately and efficiently are essentially the same as those explored in detail in Chapter 9 on staffing and in Chapter 10 on the payoff from staffing programs.

Beyond identifying top talent and pivotal roles, talent reviews often include an additional purpose: identifying or validating development plans. Here again, solid analytics can add value. In this case, the purpose is to look across time to see which types of developmental activities yielded measurable improvement in capabilities, and, as above, the utility of those activities. Fortunately, the same logic and procedures we outline in Chapter 10 apply here.

Thus, talent reviews are a special case where several established practices can come together. Practices around segmentation will identify the targeted set of individuals and roles to review. Practices rooted in selection will identify the key attributes to explore. Finally, practices based on training and development will lay the foundation for prescriptions and action steps coming out of the talent reviews.

Succession Planning

Succession planning is all too frequently a "check-the-box" type of exercise, where organizations complete the plans and then immediately ignore them. However, if done effectively, it can significantly dampen the disruption caused by changes in leadership.

Succession planning offers ample opportunities for analysis. Notably, organizations should take the time to identify how close any given successor is to readiness (e.g., ready now, needs one more job/experience to be ready, needs two more jobs/experiences to be ready) as well as the nature of the gaps (e.g., needs experience in e-business). Capturing this information can directly inform development programming to support each candidate's readiness.

Furthermore, succession planning offers concrete, bounded (that is, not overwhelming) opportunities to engage in strategic workforce planning. Fundamentals of job analysis can be used to group leadership roles to create more stable prediction opportunities—that is, to be able to explore and develop a cohort of potential successors for a group of related roles. From that group of roles, turnover patterns can be identified to inform the size of the necessary succession pool. For example, let's assume an organization has ten senior leadership roles in its sales organization. Assessing the turnover pattern for these roles may reveal that, in a typical year, the organization should plan to fill three of those positions. This is the demand for talent in that group of roles.

At the same time, the candidate pool for these roles can be identified and analyzed. Chapters 9 and 10 provide in-depth discussions of how to think about the quality of a candidate pool and the importance of investing in improved selection under certain conditions. The same logic will apply here, with one twist: rather than investing only in improving selection, organizations can choose to impact materially the overall quality of their candidate pools for certain positions through intentionally designed development activities and experiences. Still, the same logic will apply—HR researchers must consider the cost of improving the likelihood of success in the role (whether through improved selection or improved preparation) against the costs of generating that improvement and the risks of poor performance.

Let's extend our above example of succession planning. We've assumed a group of ten roles, with three positions opening up each year. Let's further assume that the talent pool from which the successors are drawn also experiences some turnover and that not all potential successors will develop sufficiently to perform the job effectively. To extend the example, we might want three potential successors for each of the three roles that are likely to become available. This suggests that the organization should plan to have a pool of nine (three roles times three successors per role) ready-now candidates to ensure business continuity. Talent managers can take that target, analyze their current inventory of ready-now successors, and identify additional candidates for active development to ensure an adequate supply of talent. In highly dynamic business environments where conditions can change rapidly and individuals come and go, having a pool of ready-now or ready-soon talent that can fill any of a number of changing scenarios is known as "workforce readiness."[15]

High-Potential Programs

As noted above, high-potential programs can be a valuable part of an overall talent management strategy. In particular, when they are paired with succession planning or another, larger strategic workforce plan, they can mitigate business risk and ensure a stable bench of future leaders. When constructed well, they can help support the retention of high-performing employees. However, high-potential programs can also have a dark side. Specifically, some organizations experience higher-than-normal attrition among their high-potential program participants who are not selected into more senior roles. That is, these programs can create an expectation of progression, and in cases where that is not delivered, they can stimulate attrition among talented employees. Thus, it is important to be thoughtful regarding the size of your high-potential pool. Carefully balance the supply of high potentials with the demand for available roles for them to take, as outlined above.

A Supply Chain View of Talent Management

A supply chain is a model that balances supply and demand across a system of inputs, throughputs, and ultimately outputs, carefully balancing factors such as time to procure a needed resource against costs to retain that resource in inventory. The modern practice of supply chain management seeks to create balance across the system, rather than optimizing one or more parts of it. For example, it is possible to ensure that you never run out of a particular manufacturing input by ensuring very high inventory levels of that item. However, this creates a good deal of cost that is essentially waste. Good supply chain management is the science of optimizing all elements of the system.

Talent management can be conceptualized as a form of supply chain management.[16] The brief examples we presented earlier regarding succession planning and high potentials are examples of considering talent management practices as part of a system. Below, we explore additional examples.

Talent management is often conceptualized to include many topics that are covered elsewhere in this book, such as selection, learning and development, and performance management. For the remainder of this chapter, we will focus on a few complex talent management issues that are central to strategic workforce planning, framing these issues as a supply chain for talent.

Strategic Workforce Planning

It is important to distinguish the near-term operational plan for talent acquisition, often called a staffing plan, from the larger strategic issue of strategic workforce planning (SWP). Many organizations may use the terms interchangeably, but they are actually quite different. A twelve-month staffing plan is important to ensure that an organization has the necessary number of recruiters and staff to support near-term hiring activity. A staffing plan based on the business plan for an organization translates that into a set of requirements for talent delivery over the next six to twelve months. This is valuable work but is largely operational.

In contrast, SWP is deeply interconnected with the full enterprise plan for achieving strategic objectives. It is the talent component of an organization's strategic plan. Depending on the complexity and sophistication of an organization, implementation of that can vary substantially. Where a staffing plan is often used to make operational decisions about how many recruiters to have available, a strategic workforce plan will instead look at future required capabilities, the current inventory of capabilities, and anticipated changes in the current inventory over the relevant time period—typically three to five years—to determine the best path to ensure that future needs are met. Those paths can include a variety of talent strategies, including development, hiring, and outsourcing. These correspond to the familiar business strategies of make, buy, or rent.

Earlier, we outlined the simplest definition of SWP as ensuring that the organization had the right talent in the right place at the right time and cost. Below, we will address some of the elements that are essential to delivering on that definition. Specifically, we will begin with a discussion of how to ensure that organizations have the right talent through creating a talent inventory and identifying where important risks to that inventory may emerge in the future. Second, to ensure that organizations have talent in the right place, we will explore how to think about location strategy. Finally, to ensure that talent is available at the right time and cost, we will discuss the thoughtful use of regular and contingent workers. While there are many additional factors that one might consider, together these three illustrate the variety of issues that firms typically address in developing an effective talent supply chain as part of a strategic workforce plan.

Talent Inventory

The first step in managing a supply chain is to understand the supply itself—that means assessing what talent is available. While, in practice, this may include assessments of both internal and external talent supply, here we will focus on the internal labor market. It is difficult to conceive of an effective talent management or strategic workforce-planning system that is not grounded in an inventory of current talent. While many organizations will have some core information present in their HR information system (HRIS), that information is generally insufficient for talent management and strategic workforce-planning purposes. Information in an HRIS will likely include information regarding the specific job, location, length of service, and perhaps additional information such as performance-review ratings. Organizations generally also maintain training records for their employees.

Data relevant for talent management purposes, however, will often also include assessment data, information about mobility, and, importantly, information about key skills and capabilities that are relevant to the work of the organization. Some organizations may also track developmental goals, or key experiences, such as international assignments. Thus, many of the items identified in the capabilities and talent-review sections above are relevant for a full talent inventory. Traditionally, talent inventories are completed in one of three ways: they are populated from system information (e.g., job history in an HRIS), they are populated by HR as part of a talent-review process, or they are populated by the target individuals themselves. This is distinct from a talent-review process in that talent reviews are more likely to be managed directly by HR and typically include a fair amount of qualitative, narrative detail regarding the individuals being reviewed. However, advances in natural language processing and machine learning have added efficiency and precision both to the processes for extracting information about skills and capabilities in the first place and also to the processes for matching skills to organizational needs, thus opening the door for greater efficiency in creating profiles and reviews. Naturally, it is most effective for organizations to build a framework of necessary or critical skills and to ensure that their talent inventories accurately capture the skills and capabilities that are most critical for future strategic success. As discussed in the capabilities section above, it is important to determine which attributes of an individual are most relevant to capture and use.

The talent inventory may also include estimates of risk—that is, it should assess whether particular roles (like frontline customer service agents), capabilities (e.g., data analysis), or individuals are at increased risk for exit. Chapter 5, on employee separations, will explore these concepts further. Additionally, we will explore a special type of exit risk as part of a talent inventory in the section on retirements below.

Forecasting

Forecasting future needs for talent is a core and essential part of many talent-analytics functions. While forecasting can be useful for leadership-succession plans or establishing learning and development priorities, the most common application is for staffing plans.

Most organizations will use basic historical information to inform their twelve-month staffing plans. This is an essential and foundational form of forecasting. Where business conditions are stable, this linear approach is fine. If the fundamental nature of the job remains unchanged (and thus the required skills are consistent from one year to the next), if the volume of business anticipated is steady (and thus staffing levels rise or fall to accommodate changes in demand, for example, during seasonal trends), and if the local labor market is stable (and thus external conditions influence neither exits nor competition among employers for hiring), then this straight linear approach is both simple and adequate.

Building a simple forecast is nonetheless more complicated than applying the overall organizational exit rate to all jobs. Table 3.1 below compares the internal labor market movement for two jobs at a fictional organization. Here, we have an imaginary Engineer I position and the related position for engineers functioning with greater autonomy and expertise, Engineer II. Given the movement patterns between these two, the recruiting organization should focus primarily on hiring new graduates for the Engineer I positions rather than focusing on acquiring the limited number of experienced hires required to fill the anticipated Engineer II positions. Instead, the organization should focus on filling Engineer II positions with

Table 3.1. Comparing Internal Labor Market Moves for Related Jobs

	Engineer I	Engineer II
Beginning headcount	621	315
Transfers in (e.g., by promotion)	0	100
Transfers out (e.g., by promotion)	100	75
Exits from the company	90 (14.5%)	30 (9.5%)
Remaining headcount after exchanges	431	310
Gap to be filled by new hiring	190	5

candidates from the Engineer I positions, through investments in development. In the example above, Engineer I requires a strong hiring pipeline to backfill the exits from the company and the promotions out of this role into other roles. Engineer I also does not benefit from internal transfers into the role.

Engineer II, representing about half the total headcount, requires vastly less headcount replacement because of the large number of transfers into the role from other internal jobs. In this case, most of the talent-supply needs are filled through the internal channel. While the organization must recruit externally for nearly one-third of all Engineer I positions in a given year, less than 2 percent of Engineer II positions require external recruitment. As a side note, this brief analysis also illustrates that attrition rates can vary substantially between jobs, thus potentially helping the organization identify key areas where attention to attrition could be beneficial.

This is a simple example, but it clearly displays the benefit of understanding anticipated patterns in talent needs. In this example, the recruiting organization should focus its energy and the development of selection procedures for external candidates on Engineer I, while focusing career development resources on growing individuals from Engineer I into Engineer II as a means of ensuring that Engineer II roles have a sufficient supply of talent.

Wave of Retirements as a Risk
Due in part to population-level demographics of the US workforce, many organizations are concerned about business disruption due to large numbers of retirements. The first step in an SWP approach to addressing this workforce risk is to develop an age profile of the current workforce, as identified in the talent inventory section above. For organizations where demographic risk around retirement is relevant, this requires first analyzing the workforce by current and future retirement eligibility. This analysis will include, at a minimum, an exit analysis by relevant variables, such as age and years of

service with the organization. For example, an organization's overall exit rate might be 10 percent per year but exits among employees over the age of 58 might be 20 percent, or double the baseline rate, and above 65, the rate might go to 40 percent. The first pass at this analysis can be a simple frequency count: how many people in each demographic group exited per year? Simple visualizations to show the overall exit risk for each demographic group can be very helpful at this initial stage.

Other organizations may wish to build more advanced predictive models, incorporating not only age and years of service, but also external factors, such as broader economic indicators or the impact of retention packages on exit decisions. In such an analysis, the outcome variable—exited or not exited—is categorical, so logistic regression is appropriate when analyzing the relative weight of each predictor.

After establishing the likely exit rate for the at-risk population of potential retirees, the next phase in this analysis is to understand the risks created by those anticipated exits. Instead of calculating the exit rates for retirement-age versus nonretirement-age workers, you will calculate the percentage of retirement-eligible workers in each of the important categories in your organization. For many organizations, this will include an analysis by grade level, such as entry-level, mid-level, and senior-level. For others, it might include functional analysis, or even analysis down to the level of specific jobs (especially pivotal jobs). For example, some organizations are still operating information systems that were built on now-obsolete software, such as FORTRAN. The developers who are proficient in those languages tend to be older, and the ability to continue operating such systems is at risk if those employees exit. Replacing the systems can be prohibitively expensive in some cases, creating a significant business incentive to retain these specific workers. In other organizations, the challenge may be that a large percentage of important roles involving leadership or customer relationships are at an unacceptably high risk of disruption due to exits and retirements.

In the first two steps, we established the level of risk and the distribution of risk. SWP is essentially about planning and proactively mitigating risks. Thus, in our third step, we use this risk information to create plans to mitigate the risks. At the broadest level, organizations can respond to these sorts of risks either through talent supply (hiring or retention actions), through training, or by redesigning the nature of the work itself. In the example above regarding obsolete skills, the talent analyst might compare the utility of these four strategies to determine the best one or the optimal combination:

1. Retention packages for the most at-risk employees to incentivize them to remain (using the logistic regression analyses from step 2).

2. Training programs to create new capabilities to complete that work.

3. Hiring or contracting workers to support the legacy systems. In this case, the option to contract the work may include permitting the current workers to retire and then contracting with them for ongoing support.

4. Replacing the legacy systems (i.e., eliminating the retention problem).

The second example includes risks like a high percentage of organizational leaders who have reached retirement age. Here, the options may take a slightly different flavor. Certainly, retention packages can have a place, as can permitting the leaders to retire and then bringing them back as contractors or consultants on specific issues. However, those solutions tend to be shorter-term. In this example, a longer-term solution would likely include building leadership capability, typically in the form of a succession plan and clear learning plans for prospective future leaders. Additionally, hiring externally into leadership roles can be an important strategy, although it is often an expensive one, and externally hired leaders tend to have a higher failure rate than internally developed leaders.[17] Thus, for this scenario, a utility analysis would likely include comparing the development costs to build a cohort of potential future leaders with the talent-acquisition costs of external leaders. While the particulars will vary dramatically with the uniqueness of skill sets, the nature of the industry, and the scope of the role, Table 3.2 is a simple example to illustrate the comparison:

Table 3.2. Comparison of Different Leadership Exit Risk-Mitigation Strategies

Develop Internally	Grow Externally
Develop three successors for the role at a cost of $15k each.	Secure headhunter for job search; fees—30% of $150k starting salary. Signing bonus is 30% of $150k salary.
Total cost for development investments above and beyond normal costs: $45k	Total talent acquisition costs for new leader in this sample: $90k

We can apply the concepts of utility and ROI from Chapter 2 to this analysis. But, in the simplest terms, in this example, it is more cost-efficient to invest in internal talent rather than seeking external talent. This simple financial analysis does not address the benefits and risks to the functioning of the organization, however. Sometimes, it is important as part of a strategic shift to "bring in new blood" (new people, new ideas). It is important to note, however, that seeing familiar and trusted faces pushed aside in favor of unknown new individuals can lead to individuals questioning whether their current employer is a place where they can have fruitful careers. Chapter 7, on employee engagement, will touch on ways to think about issues like these.

Location Strategy
We noted above that good SWP includes ensuring that talent is available in the right place. While the right place can also include internal factors such as business group, deciding where to locate particular capabilities geographically is also an essential component of a good talent management strategy.

This is more than just moving jobs to geographies with lower labor costs, although that is a common strategy. It also includes strategic placement of roles near major customers, major suppliers, major universities generating the necessary talent, major competitors from whom you might wish to hire, or major resources, such as transportation channels or inexpensive electricity. A good location strategy will explicitly consider the availability of the necessary talent with the right skills at the right cost.

Location strategy, however, is devilishly difficult. The set of criteria considered will vary based on the strategic priorities of the organization. For example, it might be critical to place a new location very close to customers or to available natural resources, such as inexpensive hydroelectric power. In many cases, tax and infrastructure considerations will be important also. For highly skilled roles, locating near a top-quality university or near other firms with similar skill sets might be particularly important. At a macroeconomic level, understanding migration patterns might be useful (i.e., whether the locations under consideration are, on average, attracting or losing talent).

While the complexity might seem overwhelming, it is possible to estimate many of the relevant costs for a location strategy. Here, however, a firm's competitive strategy will also come into play (e.g., when strategic choices, such as proximity to a customer, may outweigh pure cost considerations). Thus, location strategy in particular lends itself to a data visualization strategy—where relative strengths or performance on attributes are compared visually—rather than to a purely mathematical comparison. See Table 3.3 for a simplified sample showing the evaluation of several important attributes for each of three cities. This example uses a color-blindness-friendly palette where the darkest boxes are most favorable and the lightest boxes are least favorable. As you can see in this example, any choice will require tradeoffs; while data can inform a choice, ultimately the organization will have to make a strategic choice regarding location.

Table 3.3. Sample Location Visualization

	City 1	City 2	City 3
Availability of needed early career talent (e.g., new college grads)			
Density of similar orgs / availability of mid-managers and leaders			
Prevailing wages and benefits costs			
Attractiveness of location / in-migration patterns			
Risk of weather disruptions			
Infrastructure costs (space, electricitiy)			
Proximity to customers			
Proximity to suppliers			

Worker Types

The final elements in our simple definition of SWP are time and cost. Time considerations can include active talent-pipeline activities, such as supporting programs at a local university or developing and managing high-potential programs, to ensure an adequate supply of leaders when they are required. Cost can include a number of factors beyond the obvious one of prevailing wages. However, for many organizations, a key consideration around cost—and, to a lesser extent, to the on-demand availability of talent—is the use of outsourcing. While, often, people think of SWP as relevant only for "regular" employee types, adding consideration of worker types expands the definition, and the potential for benefit, to the entire body of workers supporting the products and services of the firm, allowing for more effective optimization.

While outsourcing strategies have been popular for decades—or, depending on how you look at it, for millennia—technology has created new opportunities for finding and validating the skills of potential "gig" or nonstandard workers. When considering your workforce strategy, it will be increasingly critical to consider the availability and cost of outsourcing to vendors or to specialized workers who are not regular employees. Fortunately, the logic and calculations we learned in Chapter 2, in particular the concepts of utility and ROI, can also help guide us through decisions regarding worker types.

The broad class of nonemployee workers might include workers provided through a third party or talent platform or workers who contract individually with the primary organization. These nonemployee workers can provide services from the very basic, such as janitorial services, to core skills necessary to run the business, such as IT services, to highly strategic and specialized, such as legal services in support of an acquisition. Additionally, advances in technology have enabled many types of work to be distributed easily around the globe, and new platforms facilitate the process for workers and organizations to readily find each other. Together, these innovations create new, easier possibilities for executing work efficiently and with nontraditional employment structures.

Further, these nonemployee workers may be connected to the primary organization in several ways and for varying durations. For example, they may be connected for many years through contracted services such as those for facilities (janitorial, landscaping, cafeteria), or through long-standing vendor relationships such as the provision of IT services; through episodic, short-term relationships such as video production or legal support for a specific action; or even through "burst capacity" such as contracting for additional staffing support in the case of a specific increase in hiring activity like opening a new facility. In each case, it is possible to estimate the utility of various strategies for getting the work done—comparing the full range of costs to hire for, conduct the work, and then possibly release "regular" employees in comparison to securing those services through an alternative arrangement.

Let's consider, for a moment, only those nonemployee workers who serve interchangeably with "regular" employees. Table 3.4 below includes typical considerations and differences between regular and contracted workers, each of which includes some component of cost. As the table demonstrates, in many cases the hourly rate for contracted workers who possess skills and capabilities comparable to those of regular employees is higher than that for the regular employees. However, the increase in hourly cost is offset by the reduced business risk and cost around the need to recruit, onboard, manage, or potentially exit employees.

Table 3.4. Illustration of Costs Across Regular and Contracted Workers

Attribute	Regular employee	Contracted worker
Per-hour costs	Lower cost for comparable quality	Higher cost for comparable quality
Recruiting costs	Higher cost	Generally included in contract / part contracted cost
Onboarding / training new hires	Higher cost	Generally included in contract / part contracted cost
Ongoing management / performance management / employee engagement activities	Managers must support	Generally included in contract / part contracted cost
Cost and effort to manage poor performance	Managers must support	Generally included in contract / part contracted cost
Exit costs (e.g., severance in case of job elimination, or decrease in need)	Paid by the business	Generally included in contract / part contracted cost

One area where contracted workers can be very cost-effective is where there is a significant variability in the demand for skills and capabilities. In HR, two common examples might be recruiters and trainers. In both of those professions, the demand for delivery can vary dramatically throughout the year or even within a given month. Given that variability of demand, the tradeoff between higher cost for the hours needed against the cost of paying for idle or underused (slack) capability can tilt in favor of the outsourced solution. In many cases, the organization may wish to examine the annual cycle of demand signals to identify the lowest level of demand that is anticipated and then staff the organization to that demand, supplementing with flexible (contracted) capability. This represents another lens on SWP—here, identifying the optimal mix of regular and contracted employees to ensure business continuity and flexibility at the best possible cost.

Conclusion

Throughout this chapter, we have seen how the core analytical concepts of prediction and utility can be applied strategically to manage talent effectively for organizations. We considered different ways to think about segmentation of talent and how to apply strategic workforce planning to ensure that business needs are met efficiently. We also considered some common talent management strategies, such as high-potential programs, succession planning, and outsourcing.

Exercises

1. Build a high-level talent strategy. If working in a group, identify and analyze one member's organization and identify a key strategic differentiator.

   Next, identify a critical role, skill, or ability where differentiations in performance levels create differences in the overall strategic capability.

Next, identify the current and future talent pools for this role, skill, or capability.

Finally, outline a plan for mitigating risks in the current or future talent pools.

2. Identify an individual or role and build a succession plan for your own organization, or, if working in a group, choose one member's organization to analyze. First, identify a specific role or family of roles to plan for.

   What is the typical turnover for this role or family of roles? (This might be one opening every three years for a single role, or two openings each year for a family of related roles.) This gives you a minimum threshold for ready-now successors.

   What are the various strategic capabilities that might be required to execute this role or family of roles successfully in the future? This gives you a multiplier for how many ready-now successors you might need to meet business challenges.

   What is the turnover rate among the successor population for this role or family of roles? If it is high, this means you need to nurture additional ready-now successors.

   List some likely successors, the personal characteristics that they will bring to the role, and any derailers that might impair their ability to be effective.

3. Working with data for one organization, estimate and plan for the organization's risk due to retirements. First, identify

the roles, capabilities, or business units you will analyze for risk. Be sure to be granular enough to identify pockets of risk—for example, by level, for specific skills, or within particular pockets of the organizations such as a business or geography.

Identify the overall rate of exit for these roles.

Identify the proportion of individuals in each role who are retirement eligible.

Identify the rate of exit for retirement-aged or retirement-eligible individuals in these roles.

Identify the rate of exit for the nonretirement-aged or nonretirement-eligible population within these roles.

Examine the table to determine pockets of risk and to estimate future talent needs. Propose talent strategies, such as development, recruitment, retention bonuses, location strategies, or transitions to other worker types, that can mitigate the risks at hand.

References

1. Charles Mitchell, Rebecca L. Ray, and Bart van Ark, "C-Suite Challenge—2018: Reinventing the Organization for the Digital Age" (research report, New York: The Conference Board, 2018), https://www.conference-board.org/c-suite-challenge2018/.
2. Peter Cappelli and J. R. Keller, "The Historical Context of Talent Management," in *The Oxford Handbook of Talent Management*, ed. David G. Collings, Kamel Mellahi, and Wayne F. Cascio (New York: Oxford University Press, 2017), 23–40.

3. John W. Boudreau and Peter M. Ramstad, *Beyond HR: The New Science of Human Capital* (Cambridge, MA: Harvard Business Press, 2007). See also Cappelli and Keller, "Historical Context of Talent Management," 23–40.

4. Michael Porter, "What is Strategy?," *Harvard Business Review*, November-December 1996, 61–78.

5. Cappelli and Keller, "Historical Context of Talent Management," 23–40.

6. Paul Sparrow, Hugh Scullion, and Ibraiz Tarique, "Introduction: Challenges for the Field of Strategic Talent Management," in *Strategic Talent Management: Contemporary Issues in International Context*, ed. Paul Sparrow, Hugh Scullion, and Ibraiz Tarique (Cambridge: Cambridge University Press, 2014), 3–25.

7. David G. Collings, Kamel Mellahi, and Wayne F. Cascio, "Global Talent Management and Performance in Multinational Enterprises: A Multilevel Perspective," *Journal of Management* (forthcoming).

8. Wayne F. Cascio and John W. Boudreau, "The Search for Global Competence: From International HR to Talent Management," *Journal of World Business* 51, no. 1 (January 2016): 103–14.

9. Cliff Bowman and Martin Hird, "A Resource-Based View of Talent Management," in *Strategic Talent Management: Contemporary Issues in International Context*, ed. Paul Sparrow, Hugh Scullion, and Ibraiz Tarique (Cambridge: Cambridge University Press, 2014), 87–116.

10. Günter K. Stahl et al., "Six Principles of Effective Global Talent Management," *MIT Sloan Management Review* 53, no. 2 (2012): 24–32.

11. Boudreau and Ramstad, *Beyond HR*.

12. Mark. A. Huselid, Richard W. Beatty, and Brian E. Becker, "A Players" or "A Positions"?: The Strategic Logic of Workforce Management," *Harvard Business Review*, December 2005, 110–17.

13. Boudreau and Ramstad, *Beyond HR*.

14. Matthew L. Call, Anthony J. Nyberg, and Sherry M. B. Thatcher, "Stargazing: An Integrative Conceptual Review, Theoretical Reconciliation, and Extension for Star Employee Research," *Journal of Applied Psychology* 100, no. 3 (May 2005): 623–40. See also Ernest H. O'Boyle and Sydney Kroska, "Star Employees," in *The Oxford Handbook of Talent Management*, ed. David G. Collings, Kamel Mellahi, and Wayne F. Cascio (New York: Oxford University Press, 2017), 43–65.

15. Wayne F. Cascio, John W. Boudreau, and Allen H. Church, "Using a Risk-Optimization Lens: Maximizing Talent Readiness for an Uncertain Future," in *A Research Agenda for Human Resource Management: HR Strategy, Structure, and Architecture*, ed. Paul Sparrow and Sir Cary Cooper (London: Edward Elgar, 2017), 55–77.

16. Peter Cappelli, *Talent on Demand: Managing Talent in an Uncertain Age* (Boston: Harvard Business School Press, 2008). See also Wayne F. Cascio and John W. Boudreau, "Utility of Selection Systems: Supply-Chain Analysis Applied to Staffing Decisions," in *APA Handbook of Industrial and Organizational Psychology, Vol. 2. Selecting and Developing Members*

for the Organization, ed. Sheldon Zedeck (Washington, DC: American Psychological Association, 2011), 421–44.

17. Matthew Bidwell, "Paying More to Get Less: The Effects of External Hiring Versus Internal Mobility," *Administrative Science Quarterly* 56, no. 3 (September 2011): 369–407.

4

The Hidden Costs of Absenteeism

Call centers (whether in one physical location or a remote configuration of workers from home) are finely tuned operations whose economic outcomes often depend on very precise optimization of staff levels against anticipated call volume.[1] Other similar operations include retail stores and restaurants. When an employee is unexpectedly absent in a call center, it may mean that calls are missed, that other workers must adjust and will do their jobs less effectively, or that a buffer of extra workers must be employed or kept on call to offset the effects of absence. What is it worth to reduce such absences? What costs can be avoided, and what is the likely effect of organizational investments designed to reduce the need or the motivation of employees to be absent?

A first reaction might be: "We should cut absences to zero because we expect employees to show up when they are scheduled." However, as discussed in this chapter, the causes of absence are highly varied, so cutting absence requires a logical approach to understanding why it happens. In fact, an increasing number of jobs have no absenteeism because they have no real work schedule! They are project-based and thus are accountable only for the ultimate results of their work. In such jobs, employees can work whatever schedule they want as long as they produce the needed results on time. For many jobs, however, adhering to the work schedule is an important contribution to successful operations.

Sometimes it is cost-effective just to tolerate the absence level and allow work to be missed or employees to adjust. For example, during flu season, most employers prefer that sick workers stay home rather than come to work and possibly infect others. In other situations, it is very cost-effective to invest in ways to reduce absence (e.g., to deal with chronic absenteeism). It depends on the situation.

Particularly when employees are absent because they are taking unfair advantage of company policies (such as claiming more sick leave than is appropriate), it is tempting to conclude that such absence must be reduced even if it takes a significant investment. It seems unfair to tolerate it. Upon further reflection, however, it's clear that absence is like any other risk factor in business. How we address it should be based on a logical and rational decision about costs and benefits. We need a logical understanding of the consequences of absence to make those decisions. We provide that logic in this chapter.

What Is Employee Absenteeism?

Let us begin our treatment by defining the term absenteeism. *Absenteeism is any failure to report for or remain at work as scheduled, regardless of reason.* The use of the words *as scheduled* is significant, for this automatically excludes vacation, personal leave, jury duty leave, and the like. A great deal of confusion can be avoided simply by recognizing that if an employee is not on the job as scheduled, he or she is absent, regardless of cause. We focus here on unscheduled absence because it tends to be the most disruptive and costly of the situations where an employee is not at work and therefore is not available to perform his or her job as expected. This often means that the work is done less efficiently by another employee or is not done at all. Scheduled or authorized absences (e.g., vacations, holidays) are more predictable. This chapter describes in detail the potential costly consequences of absence.

Although the definition of absenteeism might leave little room for interpretation, the concept itself is undergoing a profound change, largely as a result of the time-flexible work that characterizes more and more jobs in our economy. A hallmark of such work is that workers are measured not by the time they spend, but by the results they achieve. Consider, for example, the job of a computer programmer whose sole job is to write or evaluate computer code. The programmer is judged by whether the program runs efficiently and whether it does what it is supposed to do reliably. It doesn't matter when the programmer works (9 to 5 or from midnight to dawn) or where the programmer works (at the office or at home).

If the work schedule doesn't matter, and workers operate virtually, does the concept of absenteeism still have meaning? Based on a 2018 Swiss survey of 18,000 business professionals across ninety-six international companies, 70 percent of them work remotely—a phenomenon known as telework—at least one day a week, while 53 percent work remotely for at least half of the week.[2] In the US, the Gallup organization reports that the number of people who work from remote locations at least once a week rose to 43 percent in 2016 from 39 percent in 2012.[3]

If workers never report for work, if they are allowed to vary their work time, and if they are accountable only in terms of results, the concept of absenteeism ceases to be relevant. Many teleworkers or "gig" workers fit this category. Many others do not, however, for they are expected to be available during a core time to participate in activities such as chats with coworkers or the boss, conference calls, or webcasts.

In short, absenteeism may still be a relevant concept in a world of telework. Measurement must evolve from traditional absence, where people are co-located, to the concept of being present in a virtual world. If a teleworker is surfing the web during a conference call, is he or she absent?

In fact, many of the effects of traditional absenteeism are still relevant, even if traditional accounting systems would not capture

them. Before attempting to assess the costs of employee absenteeism, therefore, it is important to identify where absenteeism is a relevant concept.

Of course, absenteeism remains relevant for the millions of workers who are scheduled to report to a central location, such as a factory, an office, a retail store, or a call center. In fact, as noted above,
even those who can work from home in a call center, like Jet Blue's
airline reservations agents, have to be at home and on the phone at
certain times to make the scheduling work. More broadly, the growing importance of location-specific or time-specific customer-service
operations, such as the millions of employees who are engaged in
repairs (of cars, appliances, or plumbing systems) or delivery (of
pizzas, newspapers, or mail), makes employee absence a very real
and potent issue for many organizations.

At the outset, let us be clear about what this chapter is and is
not. It is not a detailed literature review of the personal and work-
related causes of absenteeism, such as local unemployment, the
characteristics of jobs, family-to-work conflict, perceived legit-
imacy of absenteeism,[4] gender, age, depression, smoking, heavy
drinking, drug abuse, or lack of exercise.[5] Nor is it a thorough
treatment of the noneconomic consequences of absenteeism, such
as the effects on the individual absentee, coworkers, managers,
the organization, the union, or the family. Instead, the primary
focus in this chapter is on the economic consequences of absenteeism, and on methods for managing absenteeism and abuse of sick
leave—particularly in work settings where those concepts remain
relevant and meaningful.

The Logic of Absenteeism—How Absenteeism Creates Costs

The logic of absenteeism begins by identifying its causes and consequences. To provide some perspective on the issue, we begin

our next section by citing some overall direct costs and data that show the incidence of employee absenteeism in the United States and Europe. Then we focus more specifically on causes and consequences and present a high-level logic diagram that may serve as a mental map for decision-makers to help them understand the logic of employee absenteeism.

Direct and Indirect Costs and the Incidence of Employee Absenteeism

How much does unscheduled employee absenteeism cost? According to one survey of 465 companies, if one excludes planned absences (vacations, holidays), the total direct and indirect costs consume 9 percent of payroll.[6] Direct costs include actual benefits paid to employees (e.g., sick leave, short- and long-term disability), while indirect costs reflect reduced productivity (delays, reduced morale of coworkers, lower productivity of replacement employees).

Thus a one-thousand-employee company that averages $65,000 in salary and benefits per employee would have an annual payroll of $65 million. Of that, 9 percent is $5.85 million, or about $5,850 per employee when direct and indirect costs are both considered.

If we consider the total direct and indirect costs of paid time off as a percentage of payroll, including planned as well as unplanned absences, it ranges from 20.9 percent to 22.1 percent in the United States, 32.8 percent to 34.0 percent in Australia, and 36.3 percent to 38.3 percent in Europe. Now consider productivity losses when a firm has to hire replacement workers to cover unplanned absences. In the US it is 36.6 percent, and that is on top of the average productivity loss from coworkers (29.5 percent) and from supervisors (15.7 percent).[7]

In 2018, the average employee in the United States missed 2.8 percent of scheduled work time, or an average of 5.4 unscheduled absences per year.[8] The percentage of scheduled work time missed was higher in the public sector (3.4 percent) than in the private sector (2.7 percent).[9]

Causes

Typical causes of absenteeism fall into the following major categories: illness, injury, child- and eldercare, burnout/stress, bullying
and harassment, depression, and disengagement.[10] In the private
sector, 28 percent of employees—roughly 45 million individuals—
do not receive sick pay.[11] Sometimes employees are just too tired to
go to work, as *Money* magazine found in a December 2015 poll that
included 1,797 responses.

Table 4.1. How Often *Money* Readers Called in Sick Due to Tiredness

Never	38%
Occasionally	27%
At Least Once a Year	19%
Once	16%

Source: "The Financial Side of Sleep," *Money,*
March 2016, 18.

Consequences

The decision to invest in reducing absence requires a consideration
of the payoff. What consequences of absence will be avoided? We've
noted that absence occurs only in jobs where employees are required
to be at work, or available to be contacted remotely, at specified
times. So the consequences of absence directly relate to the fact that
an employee is unavailable to work as scheduled. Absence is more
economically damaging when the situation has these characteristics:

»   Others have to perform the work of the absent employee,
»   A process must be stopped because of the absence of an
    employee, or
»   Activities must occur at a certain time and are delayed or missed
    because an employee is absent.

It is less economically damaging when these characteristics are
not present.

Categories of Costs

At a general level, four categories of costs are associated with employee absenteeism. We elaborate each of these categories more fully in the sections that follow:

» Costs associated with absent workers (such as employee benefits and wages, if they are paid during absence).

» Costs associated with managing absenteeism (such as supervisors' time spent fixing operational issues, finding replacements, or doing the work themselves).

» The costs of substitute employees (such as overtime pay to substitute employees or temporary help fees).

» The costs of reduced quantity or quality of work (such as machine downtime, lower productivity of replacement workers, and mistakes that cause increased scrap, rework, and poor customer service).

In computing these costs, researchers commonly use the fully loaded cost of wages and benefits as a proxy for the value of employees' time. However, as we cautioned in Chapter 2, "Analytical Foundations of HR Measurement," keep in mind that it is only an approximation and that assuming total pay equals the value of employee time is also not generally valid.

Figure 4.1 presents an illustration of the ideas we have examined thus far.

Analytics and Measures for Employee Absenteeism

In the context of absenteeism, analytics refers to formulas (for instance, those for absence rate, total pay, supervisory time) and to comparisons to industry averages and adjustments for seasonality. Analytics also includes various methodologies used to identify the causes of absenteeism and to estimate variation in absenteeism across

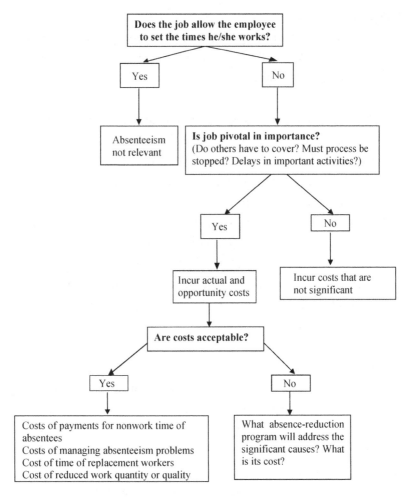

Figure 4.1. The logic of employee absenteeism: how absenteeism creates costs.

different segments of employees or situations. Such methodologies might comprise surveys, interviews with employees and supervisors, and regression analyses.

Measures, on the other hand, focus on specific numbers (for example, finding employee pay-and-benefit numbers, time sampling to determine the lost time associated with managing absenteeism problems, or using the pay and benefits of supervisors as a proxy for the value of their time). Keep these important distinctions in mind as you work through the approach to costing employee absenteeism that is presented next, even though we present both measures and analytics together here because they are so closely intertwined.

Estimating the Cost of Employee Absenteeism

At the outset, it is important to note an important irony—namely, that even in organizations or business units where the concept of absence is relevant, the incidence, and therefore the cost, of employee absenteeism is likely to vary considerably across departments or business units. It is considerably higher in organizations or units with low morale as opposed to those with high morale.[12] It also varies across times of the year. With respect to seasonal variations in absenteeism rates, for example, surveys by the Bureau of National Affairs (BNA) in the United States have shown over many years that the incidence of employee absenteeism is generally higher in the winter months than it is in the summer months.[13] The costs of absenteeism are therefore likely to co-vary with seasonal trends, yet it is paradoxical that such costs are typically reported only as averages.

The following procedure estimates absence cost for a one-year period, but the procedure can be used just as easily to estimate these costs over shorter or longer periods as necessary.[14]

Much of the information required should not be too time-consuming to gather if an organization regularly computes labor cost data and traditional absence statistics. For example, absenteeism rate is generally based on workdays or work hours, as follows:

Absenteeism rate = Days missed / [Average workforce size × working days], or

Absenteeism rate = Hours missed / [Average workforce size × working hours].

In either case, getting the right data will involve discussions with both staff and management representatives. Figure 4.2 shows the overall approach.

1. Compute total employee hours lost to absenteeism for the period.
2. Compute weighted average wage or salary/hour/absent employee.
3. Compute cost of employee benefits/hour/employee.

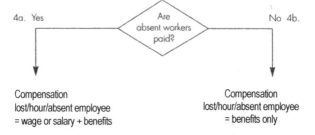

4a. Yes   Are absent workers paid?   No 4b.

Compensation
lost/hour/absent employee
= wage or salary + benefits

Compensation
lost/hour/absent employee
= benefits only

5. Compute total compensation lost to absent employees (item 1 × item 4a or 4b as applicable).
6. Estimate total supervisory hours lost to employee absenteeism.
7. Compare average hourly supervisory salary + benefits.
8. Estimate total supervisory salaries lost to managing absenteeism problems (item 6 × item 7).
9. Compute the costs of substitute employees.
10. Estimate the costs of reduced quantity or quality of work outputs.
11. Estimate total costs of absenteeism (Σ items 5, 8, 9, and 10).
12. Estimate the total cost of absenteeism/employee (item 11 ÷ total number of employees).

Figure 4.2. Overall approach to computing employee absenteeism.

Note that this process should be applied to jobs where the concept of absenteeism is relevant and where absence is most economically damaging, or where its reduction would be most pivotal to unit or organizational success.

To illustrate this approach, we provide examples to accompany each step. The examples use the hypothetical firm Presto Electric, a medium-sized manufacturer of electrical components employing three thousand people. The calculations apply to all employees for whom the concept of absenteeism is relevant and whose jobs are pivotal to the overall success of the organization.

Step 1: Total Hours Lost to Absence
Determine the organization's total employee-hours lost to absenteeism. Include both whole-day and part-day absences in addition to time lost for all reasons except organizationally sanctioned time off,

such as vacations, holidays, or official "bad weather" days. For example, absences for the following reasons should be included: illness, accidents, funerals, emergencies, or doctor appointments (whether excused or unexcused).

In our example, assume that Presto Electric's employee records show that during the prior twelve months there were 158,760 total employee-hours lost to absenteeism for all reasons except vacations and holidays. In most organizations, this number would come from company records. For our example, we took the average absence rate reported in the US in 2018 (2.7 percent) and multiplied it by a typical number of yearly scheduled hours (1,960 per employee) multiplied by the number of employees (3,000).

Step 2: Compensation Paid for Absent Employees' Time
If your organization uses computerized absence reporting, then simply compute the average hourly wage or salary paid to absent employees. If not, compute the average hourly wage or salary for each of the different jobs that experienced absenteeism during the period, and weight them by the proportion of the absences in each job. If absent workers are not paid, skip this step and go directly to step 3.

For Presto Electric, assume that about 60 percent of all absentees are frontline, 30 percent are administrative and support, and 10 percent are management and professional. Estimate the average hourly wage rate per absentee by applying the appropriate percentages to the average hourly wage rate for each major occupational group. Table 4.2 does just that.

Step 3: Benefits Paid for Absent Employees' Time
Estimate the cost of employee benefits per hour per employee. The cost of employee benefits (profit sharing, pensions, health and life insurance, paid vacations and holidays, and so on) currently accounts for about 32 percent of wages.[15] To compute the cost of employee benefits per hour per absent employee, simply multiply the average hourly wage rate per absentee by 0.32. This yields $8.73.

Table 4.2. Determining the Average Hourly Wage Rate per Absentee

Job Group	Average Percent of Total Absenteeism	Average Hourly Wage	Weighted Average Hourly Wage
Frontline	0.60	$26.80	$16.08
Admin./Support	0.30	$21.20	$6.36
Management and professional	0.10	$48.50	$4.85
Total			$27.29

Step 4: Total Compensation Paid for Absent Employees' Time
Compute the total compensation lost per hour per absent employee. This figure is determined simply by adding the weighted average hourly wage or salary per absent employee (item 2 in Figure 4.2) to the cost of employee benefits per hour per employee (item 3 in Figure 4.2). Thus:

$$\$27.29 + \$8.73 = \$36.02$$

Of course, if absent workers are not paid, item 4 in Figure 4.2 is the same as item 3.

Step 5: Total Compensation Cost for All Absent Employees
Compute the total compensation lost to absent employees. Total compensation lost, aggregated over all employee-hours lost, is determined simply by multiplying item 1 by item 4a or 4b, whichever is applicable. In our example:

$$158,760 \times \$36.02 = \$5,718,535.20.$$

Step 6: Supervisory Time Spent on Absence Management
Estimate the total number of supervisory hours lost to employee absenteeism for the period. Supervisors who deal with absenteeism

problems spend an average of 3.4 hours a week managing absences.[16] Management issues include adjusting workflow, locating and instructing replacement employees, checking on the performance of replacements, and counseling and disciplining absentees. Organizations could develop their own in-house estimates by interviewing a representative sample of supervisors or having them keep a diary over several time cycles. Choose the sample time cycles carefully because absenteeism may vary over time. The more experience companies accumulate in making the estimates, the more accurate the estimates become.[17]

After you have estimated the average number of supervisory hours spent per week dealing with employee absenteeism problems, compute the total number of supervisory hours lost to the organization by multiplying the average lost hours per week by the number of supervisors who deal with absence. Then multiply that by the total working weeks.

In our example, we assumed that Presto Electric's data are as follows:

1. Estimated number of supervisory hours lost per week: 3.4 hours.
2. Total number of supervisors who deal with absence problems: 100.
3. Total number of working weeks for the year: 35.

Thus, the total supervisory time spent per year on employee absenteeism is 11,900 hours.

Step 7: Salary and Benefits for Supervisors
Compute the average hourly wage rate for supervisors, including benefits. Include only the salaries of supervisors who deal with employee absenteeism. Typically, first-line supervisors bear the brunt of absenteeism problems.

For Presto Electric, we assume an average hourly supervisory salary of $31.79, and benefits equal to an additional 32 percent of salary, so total compensation per hour per supervisor is $41.96.

Step 8: Total Supervisor Compensation for Time Spent on Absence
Compute total supervisory paid time spent on absenteeism by multiplying total supervisory hours spent on absenteeism (11,900 hours in our example) times the average hourly supervisory compensation ($41.96 in our example). Supervisory paid time is therefore:

$$11,900 \times 41.96 = \$499,357.32$$

Step 9: Costs of Replacement Workers and Overtime
An organization might make up for the lost work of absent employees by some combination of hiring additional temporary workers to replace absentees, or it might have regular workers work overtime. Sometimes, an organization might increase its regular labor pool so that it can draw on regular workers to fill in for absent workers. In the US, replacement workers cost an average of 1.6 percent of payroll,[18] so for our example we will simply multiply the total payroll of Presto Electric (conservatively estimated at $36.02 × 2,080 hours worked per year x 3,000 employees) by 1.6 percent, estimating that substitute employees cost $3,596,237 per year.

Step 10: Costs of Reduced Quantity or Quality of Work Outputs
When fully productive, regularly scheduled employees are absent, chances are good that either their work is not done or, if it is, that there is a reduction in the quantity or quality of the work. The key considerations in this case are how much of a reduction there is in the quantity or quality of work and how much it costs. In terms of a reduction in productivity, survey data indicate that replacement workers hired to replace unplanned absentees are 36.6 percent less productive.[19]

Costs might include items such as the following:

» Machine downtime;
» Increases in defects, scrap, and reworks;
» Production losses; or
» Greater time to learn the job and processes.

The standard level of quality or quantity of work might also be compromised through the reduced productivity and performance of less-experienced replacement workers, such as when customers are served poorly by employees who are stretched thin while trying to cover for their absent coworkers or when potential new business is lost as a result of operating "under capacity."[20] At Presto Electric, let's assume an estimated financial loss of $1,000,000 for the year in productivity losses and inefficient materials usage.

Step 11: Total Absenteeism Costs
Compute the total estimated cost of employee absenteeism. Having computed or estimated all the necessary cost items, we now can determine the total annual cost of employee absenteeism to Presto Electric. Just add the individual costs pertaining to wages and salaries, benefits, supervisory salaries, substitute employees, and the costs of reduced quantity and quality (items 5, 8, 9, and 10). As Table 4.3 demonstrates, this cost exceeds $9 million per year. Dividing that total by the total number of employees may be easier to grasp. At Presto Electric, this figure was about $3,029.97 per year for each of the 3,000 employees.

What About Low Productivity Due to Illness—"Presenteeism"?

Attending work while ill is called "presenteeism."[21] Like absenteeism, presenteeism is a form of withdrawal behavior. It often results

Table 4.3. Total Estimated Cost of Employee Absenteeism (Presto Electric)

1. Total employee-hours lost to absenteeism for the period	158,760
2. Weighted average wage/salary per hour per absent employee	$27.29
3. Cost of employee benefits per hour per absent employee	$9.28
4. Total compensation lost per hour per absent employee	$36.57
a. If absent workers are paid (wage/salary plus benefits)	
b. If absent workers are not paid (benefits only)	
5. Total compensation lost to absent employees (Total employee-hours lost × 4.a or 4.b, whichever applies)	$5,805,853.20
6. Total supervisory hours lost on employee absenteeism	16,660
7. Average hourly supervisory wage, including benefits	$41.96
8. Total supervisory salaries lost to managing problems of absenteeism (Hours lost × Average hourly supervisory wage; Item 6 × Item 7)	$699,053.60
9. Costs of substitute employees	$1,585,000.00
10. Costs of reduced quantity and quality of work	$1,000,000.00
11. Total estimated cost of absenteeism (items 5, 8, 9, 10)	$9,089,906.80
12. Total estimated cost of absenteeism per employee (Total estimated costs / Total number of employees)	$3,029.97

from employees showing up but working at subpar levels due to chronic ailments.[22] Meta-analysis has revealed that the mechanisms that underlie presenteeism are both negative and positive.[23] On the negative side, reasons why employees choose to work while ill include general ill health, constraints on absenteeism (e.g., strict absence policies, job insecurity), job demands and felt stress, lack of job and personal resources (low support and low optimism), and negative experiences relating to others (e.g., perceived discrimination). Positive attitudes, such as high job satisfaction, engagement, and commitment, also motivate workers to come to work while ill.

From an economic perspective, this is not a new category of costs but rather an illustration of our fourth cost category, namely, the costs of reduced quantity or quality of work. In one study, for example, researchers analyzed more than 1.1 million medical and pharmacy claims along with detailed responses from the "Health and Work Performance Questionnaire" in a multiyear analysis. It included ten corporations that employed more than 150,000 workers.[24] The study found that on average, every $1 of medical and pharmacy costs is matched to $2.30 of health-related productivity costs—and that figure is much greater for some conditions. In fact, when health-related productivity costs are measured along with medical and pharmacy costs, the top chronic health conditions driving these overall health costs are depression, obesity, arthritis, back or neck pain, and anxiety.

Because working while sick accounts, in the aggregate, for much more productivity loss than absenteeism, presenteeism may actually be a much costlier problem, with estimates ranging from 1.8 to 10 times that of absence.[25] Yet presenteeism remains difficult to assess in economic or monetary terms because different studies use different measures, worker populations, and methods to convert results into economic terms.[26] Unlike absenteeism, however, presenteeism isn't always apparent. Absenteeism is obvious when someone does not show up for work, but presenteeism is far less obvious when illness or a medical condition is hindering someone's work. Researchers are now starting to link presenteeism as an employee work behavior to worker well-being, team process, and organization strategy.[27] The next sections examine it through the lens of the LAMP model.

» **Logic.** Research on presenteeism focuses on chronic or episodic ailments like seasonal allergies, asthma, migraines, back pain, arthritis, gastrointestinal disorders, and depression.[28] Progressive diseases, such as heart disease and cancer, tend to occur later in life and tend to generate the majority of direct health-related costs for companies. In contrast, the illnesses people take with them to work account for far lower direct costs, but they imply a greater loss in productivity because they are so prevalent, so often go untreated, and typically occur during peak working years. Those indirect costs have largely been invisible to employers.[29]

» **Analytics.** To be sure, methodological problems plague current research in this area.[30] For example, different research methods have yielded quite different estimates of the on-the-job productivity loss—from less than 20 percent of a company's total health-related costs to more than 60 percent.[31] Beyond that, how does one quantify the relative effects of individual ailments on productivity for workers who suffer from more than one problem? The effects of such interactions have not been addressed. Nor has the effect on team performance been studied in cases when one member has a chronic health condition that precludes him or her from contributing fully to the team's mission.

» **Measures.** A key question to address is the link between self-reported presenteeism and actual productivity loss. Some of the strongest evidence of such a link comes from several studies involving credit card call center employees at Bank One, which is now part of J. P. Morgan Chase.[32]

There are a number of objective measures of a service representative's productivity, including the amount of time spent on each call, the amount of time between calls (when the employee is doing paperwork), and the amount of time the person is logged off the system. The study focused on employees with known illnesses (identified from earlier disability claims) and lower productivity scores. One such study, a good example of analytics in action, involved 630 service representatives at a Bank One call center in Illinois. Allergy-related presenteeism was measured with such objective data as the amount of time workers spent on each call. During the peak ragweed pollen season, the allergy sufferers' productivity fell 7 percent below that of coworkers without allergies. Outside of allergy season, the productivity of the two groups was approximately equal.

» **Process.** The next step, of course, is to use this information to work with decision-makers to identify where investments to reduce the costs of presenteeism offer the greatest opportunities to advance organizational objectives. One way to improve productivity is by educating workers about the nature of the conditions that afflict them and about appropriate medications to treat those conditions. Companies such as Comerica Bank, Dow Chemical, and J. P. Morgan Chase are among those that have put programs in place to help employees avoid or treat some seemingly smaller health conditions, or at least to keep productive in spite of them.[33] To ensure employee privacy, for example, Comerica Bank used a third party to survey its employees and found that about 40 percent of them said they suffered from irritable bowel syndrome (IBS), which can involve abdominal discomfort, bloating, or diarrhea. Extrapolating from that, the company estimated its annual cost of lost productivity to be at least $10 million a year (in 2018 dollars). Comerica now provides written materials for its employees about IBS and has sponsored physician seminars to educate workers about how to recognize and deal with it through their living habits, diet, and possible medications.

Education is one thing, but getting workers to take the drugs that their doctors prescribe or recommend is another. The Bank One study found that nearly one-quarter of allergy sufferers did not take any kind of allergy medication. The same study also concluded that covering the cost of nonsedating antihistamines for allergy sufferers (roughly $26 a week for prescription medications, less for generics) was more than offset by the resulting gains in productivity (roughly $52 a week, based on call center employees' wages and benefits, which averaged $720 a week, in 2018 dollars).[34]

These results raise a tantalizing question: might a company's pharmacy costs actually be an investment in workforce productivity? Certainly, companies should monitor and control corporate healthcare expenditures. It is possible, however, that by increasing company payments for medications to treat chronic diseases, the companies might actually realize a net gain in workforce productivity and eliminate the opportunity costs of failing to address the presenteeism issue directly. One obvious example of this is the flu shot. Numerous studies have shown that the cost of offering free flu shots is far outweighed by the savings realized through reductions in both absenteeism and presenteeism.[35] Another simple approach to reducing presenteeism is to offer paid time off, as discussed below. The National Institute for Occupational Safety and Health found that providing paid sick leave to workers who lack it might help decrease the number of workdays lost due to flu and similar illnesses by nearly four to eleven million per year, resulting in an overall cost savings of $1 billion to $2 billion per year.[36] Paid sick leave may help offset the reduced productivity associated with chronic presenteeism.

In the next section, we present a case study that moves beyond the calculation of absenteeism costs to illustrate how awareness of those costs led a healthcare clinic to address a critical operations issue.

Case Study: From High Absenteeism Costs to an Actionable Strategy

A large, multispecialty healthcare clinic was experiencing high absence rates among employees with direct patient-care responsibilities. In terms of costs, the absenteeism problem was impacting the satisfaction of patients with the care they received (and influencing their perceptions of quality). No wonder: fully 25 percent of patient-care work went undone, and 67 percent of non-patient-care work went undone. Remaining workers suffered from burnout and strained relationships with their supervisors. Of course, employee absenteeism was only one of several possible causes of these problems. Focusing only on reducing absenteeism per se might not address important, underlying employee-relations issues. However, let's focus on using this case to illustrate the benefits of reducing absence costs.

With the help of a consultant, the clinic sought to identify the root causes of employee absenteeism for the segment of the workforce that had direct patient-care responsibilities. It found that a majority of the absentees were parents who had young children. In many cases, those parents were unable to find backup childcare for sick children, and this caused last-minute staffing shortages due to unscheduled absences. Moreover, the Family Medical and Leave Act permits employees to use their own sick time to care for ill children (and requires employers to grant employees up to twelve weeks of unpaid annual leave).[37]

Based on this information, management of the clinic made the decision to provide childcare for sick children and backup childcare facilities both for patients using the clinic and for employees to use in emergencies. Doing so yielded payoffs in attraction and in retention of members of this critical segment of the clinic's work force. One year later, the unscheduled absence rate for employees using the backup childcare facility was 70 percent less than that of employees who were eligible but did not use the facility.[38] This case is a good illustration of a concept we discussed in Chapter 2 concerning opportunity savings, or costs not incurred because the hospital provided backup childcare. In terms of the method we illustrated earlier, the dramatic drop in absenteeism among employees using the backup childcare facility enabled the hospital to avoid the costs of salaries and benefits associated with absent employees, the costs of managing absenteeism problems (an opportunity cost for supervisors), and all other incidental costs. For an HR analyst, the next steps would be to calculate the costs avoided—that is, the benefits of backup childcare, together with the cost of implementing backup childcare, to estimate the hospital's ROI over the one-year period.

In the final part of this chapter, we present two research studies describing managing absenteeism and abuse of sick leave. They describe positive incentives and paid time off. We chose these cases primarily because they are rigorously designed, and they contained estimates of economic impact. However, organization-wide absenteeism-control methods (for example, rewards for good attendance, progressive discipline for absenteeism, daily attendance records) may not be effective in dealing with specific individuals or work groups. Special methods (such as flexible work schedules, the redesign of jobs, and improved safety measures) may be necessary for special cases. It is the careful analysis of detailed absenteeism-research data that can facilitate the identification of these problems and suggest possible remedies.[39]

Process—Interpreting Absenteeism Costs

As noted in Chapter 2, the purpose of the process component of the logic, analytics, measurements, and process (LAMP) model is to make the insights gained as a result of costing employee absenteeism actionable. The first step in doing that is to interpret absenteeism costs in a meaningful manner. To do so, begin by evaluating these costs—at least initially—against some predetermined cost standard or financial measure of performance such as an industry-wide average. This is basically the same rationale organizations use when conducting pay surveys to determine whether their salaries and benefits are competitive.

While the US Bureau of Labor Statistics publishes absence rates and lost worktime rates (hours absent as a percentage of hours worked) by industry, absenteeism-cost data are not published regularly, like pay surveys. Very little data are available to help determine whether the economic cost of employee absenteeism is a significant problem. The costs of absenteeism to individual organizations occasionally do appear in the literature, but these estimates are typically case studies of individual firms or survey data from a broad cross-section of firms and industries rather than survey data from specific industries.

Is it worth the effort to analyze the costs of absenteeism to the overall organization—and, more specifically, to strategically critical business units—or is it more appropriate to focus only on costs to individual departments where the concept of absenteeism is relevant? It's better to focus on the costs to the overall organization for at least two compelling reasons. First, such an analysis calls management's attention to the severity of the problem. Translating behavior into economic terms enables managers to grasp the burdens employee absenteeism imposes, particularly in strategically critical business units that are suffering from severe absence problems. A seven- or eight-figure cost is often the spark needed for management to make a concerted effort to combat the problem. Second, an analysis of the problem creates a baseline for evaluating the effectiveness of absence-control programs. Comparing the quarterly, semiannual, and annual costs of absenteeism across strategically critical business units or departments provides a measure of the success, or lack of success, of attempts to reduce the problem.

If we return to the logical elements of absence cost, we can consider the process you can use to relate those costs to ongoing budget and strategy issues in an organization:

» **Cost of payments for nonwork time of absentees.** At the outset, recognize that all lost time is connected. This includes absences due to injuries, accidents, short-term disabilities, and absences that are just a few days in duration. To connect absence to tangible process issues for business leaders, look for benchmarks, such as evidence that levels of paid time off are higher than standard. Managers and other leaders will often signal their interest in reducing the costs paid for nonwork time by noting that sick leave or unscheduled vacation days are higher than they expect. This is an opportunity to take the logic noted above and suggest how much this might change if absence changed.

» **Cost of payments for time of those who manage absence.**
The process signals here will be when supervisors note that
they are spending a great deal of time on nonproductive
workforce management issues. Are statements like these
common when supervisors are setting goals with their managers or during their own performance reviews? Do supervisors
and managers often suggest that they could be more effective
if they spent less time managing around absent employees?
What would they be doing if they did not have to manage
employee absence? Answers to these questions allow you to
connect absence reductions to tangible changes in supervisor behavior.

» **Cost of time of replacement workers.** Signals that this is
an important cost element emerge when business units see
their total labor costs or headcount levels as higher than other
similar units or benchmarks. Leaders may complain that while
they often don't have enough work for all of their employees, they still must keep the extra employees around to fill
in. From a process standpoint, you can use the logic we have
described to engage in a discussion about just how much pay
for lost time would be reduced if some of the extra employees could be deployed elsewhere or even removed from the
work force.

» **Cost of reduced work quantity or quality.** The signals here
will likely not be found in headcount numbers or labor cost
numbers. Instead, the process for unearthing this evidence
will require looking at the performance numbers for operations themselves. Managers and executives might note very
specific connections between the fact that when a particular worker fails to be at work, there are specific things that
don't get done, customers that don't get served, or teams
that have to operate with less-than-full contributions. When
exempt employees have unplanned absences, the Mercer study
on the costs of absenteeism revealed that they make up just

44 percent of their work.[40] You can take these examples and use the logic above to determine how much of the problem is due to absence and how much investing in absence reduction might change them.

Other Ways to Reduce Absence
Controlling Absenteeism through Positive Incentives
This approach focuses exclusively on rewards; that is, it provides incentives for employees to come to work. This positive-incentive absence-control program was evaluated over a five-year period: one year before and one year after a three-year incentive program.[41]

A 3,000-employee nonprofit hospital provided the setting for the study. The experimental group contained 164 employees who received the positive-incentive program, and the control group contained 136 employees who did not receive the program. According to the terms of the hospital's sick-leave program, employees could take up to ninety-six hours—twelve days per year—with pay. Under the positive-incentive program, employees could convert up to twenty-four hours of unused sick leave into additional pay or vacation. To determine the amount of incentive, the number of hours absent was subtracted from twenty-four. For example, twenty-four minus eight hours absent equals sixteen hours of additional pay or vacation. The hospital informed eligible employees both orally and in writing.

During the year before the installation of the positive-incentive program, absence levels for the experimental and control groups did not differ significantly. During the three years in which the program was operative, the frequency of absences in the experimental group was consistently lower, and this difference persisted during the year following the termination of the incentives. The following variables were not related to absence: age, marital status, education, job grade, tenure, or number of hours absent two or three years previously. Two variables were related to absence, although not as strongly as the incentive program itself: gender (women were absent more than men, a trend that appears to be decreasing)[42] and number of hours absent during the previous year.

Had the incentive program been expanded to include all three thousand hospital employees, net savings were estimated at $126,000 (in 2018 dollars). This is an underestimate, however, because indirect costs were not included. Indirect costs include such things as the following:

» Overtime pay,
» Increased supervisory time for managing absenteeism problems,
» Costs of replacement workers, and
» Intentional overstaffing to compensate for anticipated absences.

Cautions: A positive-incentive program may have no effect on employees who view sick leave as an earned right that should be used whether one is sick or not. Moreover, encouraging attendance when a person has a legitimate reason for being absent—for example, hospital employees with contagious illnesses—may be dysfunctional.

In and of itself, absence may simply represent one of many possible symptoms of job dissatisfaction.[43] Attendance incentives may result in "symptom substitution," whereby declining absence is accompanied by increased tardiness and idling (which costs US employers $100 billion annually),[44] decreased productivity, and even turnover. If this is the case, an organization needs to consider more comprehensive interventions that are based, for example, on the results of multiple research methods such as employee focus groups, targeted attitude surveys, and thorough analysis and discussion of the implications of the findings from these methods.

Despite the potential limitations, the study warranted the following conclusions (all monetary figures are expressed in 2018 dollars):

» Absenteeism declined an average of 11.5 hours per employee (32 percent) during the incentive period.

» Net costs to the organization (direct costs only) are based on wage costs of $33.06 per hour (composed of $25.43 in direct wages plus 30 percent more in benefits).

» Savings were $62,351 per year (11.5 hours × average hourly wage [$33.06] × 164 employees).

» Direct costs to the hospital included 2,194 bonus hours, at an average hourly wage of $25.43 per hour = $55,793.

» Net savings were therefore $6,558 per year for an 11.75 percent return on investment ($6,558 / $55,793).

Paid Time Off (PTO)

This approach to controlling absenteeism and the abuse of sick leave is based on the concept of consolidated annual leave. Sick days, vacation time, and holidays are consolidated into one bank to be drawn out at the employee's discretion. The number of PTO days that employees receive varies across employers. For example, at Ikea, employees receive three weeks of PTO at the start of employment, five weeks after five years, and seven weeks after ten years.[45]

Employees manage their own sick and vacation time and are free to take a day off without having to offer an explanation. If the employee uses up all of this time before the end of the year and needs a day off, that time is unpaid. What about unused sick time? Buyback programs allow employees to convert unused time to vacation or to accrue time and be paid for a portion of it.

Employers that have instituted this kind of policy feel that it is a win-win situation for employees and managers. It eliminates the need for lying by employees (that is, abuse of sick leave), and it takes managers out of the role of enforcers. At the same time, to manage a PTO program effectively means making sure it suits a company's culture (one with a high degree of flexibility), it complies with the Americans With Disabilities Act and the Family Medical and Leave

Act, and that it includes clear guidelines (e.g., employees must request PTO in advance except for emergencies; define "emergency"). Finally, it is important to manage the people, not just the PTO. If employees come to work sick, they should be sent home.[46] PTO is certainly a popular benefit, with about 63 percent of employers offering such plans.[47] Employers rate them as the most effective of all absence-control programs.[48]

Exercises

Software that calculates answers to one or more of the following exercises can be found at http://iip.shrm.org.

1. Consolidated Industries, a 2,800-employee firm, is faced with a serious, and growing, absenteeism problem. Last year, total employee-hours lost to absenteeism came to 165,808. Of the total employees absent, 65 percent were frontline (average wage of $27.15 per hour), 25 percent were administrative and support (average wage of $21.80 per hour), and the remainder were management and professional (average salary $47.50 per hour). The firm spends an average of 33 percent more of each employee's salary on benefits, and, as company policy, pays workers even if they are absent. Employees work an average of 40 hours per week. The 45 supervisors (average salary of $29.35 per hour) involved in employee absenteeism problems estimate they lose 40 minutes per day for each of the 245 days per work year just dealing with the extra problems imposed by those who fail to show up for work. Finally, the company estimates it loses $1,270,500 in additional overtime premiums, in extra help that must be hired, and in lost

productivity from the more highly skilled absentees. As HR director for Consolidated Industries, your job is to estimate the cost of employee absenteeism so that management can better understand the dimensions of the problem.

2. Inter-Capital Limited is a 500-employee firm faced with a 3.7 percent annual absenteeism rate over the 1,960 hours that each employee is scheduled to work. About 15 percent of absentees are blue collar (average wage $26.96 per hour), 55 percent are clerical employees (average wage $22.25 per hour), and the remainder are management and professional workers (average salary $44.75 per hour). About 35 percent more of each employee's salary is spent on benefits, but employees are not paid if they are absent from work. In the last six months, supervisors (average salary of $28.90 per hour) estimate that managing absenteeism problems costs them about an hour a day for each of the 245 days per work year. It's a serious problem that must be dealt with since about 20 supervisors are directly involved with absenteeism. On top of that, the firm spends approximately $890,000 more on costs incidental to absenteeism. Temporary help and lost productivity can really cut into profits. Just how much is absenteeism costing Inter-Capital Limited per year per employee? (Use the software available at http://iip.shrm.org.)

3. As a management consultant, you have been retained to develop two alternative programs for reducing employee absenteeism at Consolidated Industries (question 1). Write a proposal that addresses the issue in specific terms. Exactly what should the firm do? (To do this, make whatever assumptions seem reasonable.)

References

1. Adrienne Fox, "The Ins and Outs of Customer-Contact Centers," *HR Magazine*, March 2010, 28–31. See also Martha Frase-Blunt, "Call Centers Come Home," *HR Magazine*, January 2007, 85–89.

2. Ryan Browne, "70% of People Globally Work Remotely at Least Once a Week, Study Says," *CNBC.com*, May 30, 2018, http://www.cnbc.com /2018/05/30/70-percent-of-people-globally-work-remotely-at-least -once-a-week-iwg-study.html.

3. Gallup Inc., *State of the American Workplace*, 2017, https://news.gallup .com/reports/199961/7.aspx.

4. John P. Hausknecht et al., "Work-Unit Absenteeism: Effects of Satisfaction, Commitment, Labor-Market Conditions, and Time," *Academy of Management Journal* 51, no. 6 (December 2008): 1223–45. See also Gary Johns, "Attendance Dynamics at Work: The Antecedents and Correlates of Presenteeism, Absenteeism, and Productivity Loss," *Journal of Occupational Health Psychology* 16, no. 4 (October 2011): 483–500; Joan R. Rentsch and Robert P. Steel, "Testing the Durability of Job Characteristics as Predictors of Absenteeism Over a Six-Year Period," *Personnel Psychology* 51, no. 1 (March 1998): 165–90.

5. David A. Harrison and Joseph J. Martocchio, "Time for Absenteeism: A 20-Year Review of Origins, Offshoots, and Outcomes," *Journal of Management* 24, no. 3 (June 1998): 305–50. See also Gary Johns, "Contemporary Research on Absence from Work: Correlates, Causes and Consequences," in *International Review of Industrial and Organizational Psychology 1997, Vol. 12*, ed. Cary L. Cooper and Ivan T. Robertson (New York: Wiley, 1997), 115–73.

6. Society for Human Resource Management, "Managing Employee Attendance," accessed October 22, 2018, http://www.shrm.org /resourcesandtools/tools-and-samples/toolkits/pages/managingemployee attendance.aspx. See also Michael Klachefsky, *Take Control of Employee Absenteeism and the Associated Costs*, (New York: Mercer, 2008), accessed May 11, 2010, http://www.mercer.com.

7. Society for Human Resource Management, "Total Financial Impact of Employee Absences Across the United States, China, Australia, Europe, India and Mexico" (research report, Alexandria, VA: Society for Human Resource Management, 2014), http://www.shrm.org/hr-today/trends-and-forecasting /research-and-surveys/Documents/Total%20Financial%20Impact%20of%20 Employee%20Absences%20Report.pdf.

8. US Department of Labor, Bureau of Labor Statistics, "Absences from Work of Employed Full-Time Wage and Salary Workers by Occupation and Industry," accessed October 22, 2018, http://www.bls.gov/cps/cpsaat47.htm.

9. US Department of Labor, Bureau of Labor Statistics.

10. Investopedia, "The Causes and Costs of Absenteeism in the Workplace," *Forbes*, July 10, 2013, http://www.forbes.com/sites/investopedia/2013/07/10/the-causes-and-costs-of-absenteeism-in-the-workplace/#2cf2e72b3eb6.

11. Christopher Ingraham, "Employers Who Don't Offer Paid Sick Leave Are Making the Flu Season Worse," *The Denver Post*, February 18, 2018, 7K.

12. Society for Human Resource Management, "Managing Employee Attendance."

13. Bureau of National Affairs, "Job Absence and Turnover, 4th Quarter 2009," accessed May 12, 2010, http://www.bna.com/pdf/jat4q09.pdf.

14. This method is based upon that described by Frank E. Kuzmits in "How Much Is Absenteeism Costing Your Organization?," *Personnel Administrator* 24, no. 6 (June 1979): 29–33.

15. Wayne F. Cascio, *Managing Human Resources: Productivity, Quality of Work Life, Profits*, 11th ed. (New York: McGraw-Hill, 2019).

16. Klachefsky, *Take Control of Employee Absenteeism.*

17. Wayne F. Cascio and Herman Aguinis, *Applied Psychology in Talent Management*, 8th ed. (Thousand Oaks, CA: Sage, 2019).

18. Society for Human Resource Management, "Total Financial Impact of Employee Absences Across the United States, China, Australia, Europe, India and Mexico" (research report, Alexandria, VA: Society for Human Resource Management, 2014), http://www.shrm.org/hr-today/trends-and-forecasting/research-and-surveys/Documents/Total%20Financial%20Impact%20of%20Employee%20Absences%20Report.pdf.

19. Society for Human Resource Management, "Total Financial Impact".

20. S. F. Cyboran, "Absence Management: Costs, Causes, and Cures," workshop presented at Mountain States Employers Council, HR Best Practices Conference, Denver, CO, April 13, 2006.

21. Gary Johns, "Presenteeism in the Workplace: A Review and Workplace Agenda," *Journal of Organizational Behavior* 31, no. 4 (May 2010): 519–42.

22. Cary C. Cooper and Luo Lu, eds., *The Cambridge Companion to Presenteeism at Work* (New York: Cambridge University Press, 2018).

23. Mariella Miraglia and Gary Johns, "Going to Work Ill: A Meta-Analysis of the Correlates of Presenteeism and a Dual-Path Model," *Journal of Occupational Health Psychology* 21, no. 3 (July 2016): 261–83.

24. Ronald Loeppke et al., "Health and Productivity as a Business Strategy: A Multiemployer Study," *Journal of Occupational and Environmental Medicine* 51, no. 4 (April 2009): 411–28.

25. Mariella Miraglia and Gary Johns, "Presenteeism and Wellbeing at Work," in *Presenteeism at Work*, ed. Cary L. Cooper and Luo Lu (New York: Cambridge University Press, 2018), 220–61.

26. Mouna Knani, Caroline Biron, and Pierre-Sébastien Fournier, "Presenteeism: A Critical Review of the Literature," in *The Cambridge Companion to Presenteeism at Work*, ed. Cary L. Cooper and Luo Lu (New York: Cambridge University Press, 2018), 35–68.

27. Cooper and Lu, *Cambridge Companion to Presenteeism*.
28. Paul Hemp, "Presenteeism: At Work—But Out of It," *Harvard Business Review*, October 2004, 1–9.
29. Cooper and Lu, *Cambridge Companion to Presenteeism*.
30. Joachim Gerich, "Sick at Work: Methodological Problems with Research on Workplace Presenteeism," *Health Services and Outcomes Research Methodology* 15, no. 1 (2015): 37–53. See also Daniela Lohaus and Wolfgang Habermann, "Presenteeism: A Review and Research Directions," *Human Resource Management Review*, 29, no. 1 (March 2019): 43–58.
31. Ron Z. Goetzel et al., "Health, Absence, Disability, and Presenteeism Cost Estimates of Certain Physical and Mental Health Conditions Affecting US Employers," *Journal of Occupational and Environmental Medicine*, 46, no. 4 (April 2004): 398–412.
32. Hemp, "Presenteeism at Work," 1–9.
33. Sarah Rubinstein, "Nursing Employees Back to Health," *The Wall Street Journal*, January 18, 2005, D5.
34. Hemp, "Presenteeism at Work," 1–9.
35. Hemp, "Presenteeism at Work," 1–9.
36. US Department of Health and Human Services, National Institute for Occupational Safety and Health, "Paid Sick Leave May Help Employers Reduce Costs," *NIOSH Research Rounds*, October 2017, accessed October 24, 2018, http://www.cdc.gov/niosh/research-rounds/resroundsv3n4.html.
37. US Department of Labor, Wage and Hour Division, "Fact Sheet #28: The Family and Medical Leave Act," accessed October 24, 2018, https://www.dol.gov/whd/regs/compliance/whdfs28.htm.
38. Cyboran, "Absence Management".
39. Society for Human Resource Management, "Managing Employee Attendance." See also Ian A. Miners et al., "Time-Serial Substitution Effects of Absence Control on Employee Time Use," *Human Relations* 48, no. 3 (January 1995): 307–26.
40. Klachefsky, *Take Control of Employee Absenteeism*.
41. Dale L. Schlotzhauer and Joseph G. Rosse, "A Five-Year Study of a Positive Incentive Absence Control Program," *Personnel Psychology* 38, no. 3 (September 1985): 575–85.
42. Dean Enon, "Sex and the Sick List—Women Take More Time Off than Men," *Personnel Today*, July 19, 2017, accessed October 24, 2018, http://www.personneltoday.com/pr/2017/07/sex-and-the-sick-list-women-take-more-time-off-than-men/. See also Gary Johns, "Attendance Dynamics at Work: The Antecedents and Correlates of Presenteeism, Absenteeism, and Productivity Loss," *Journal of Occupational Health Psychology* 16, no. 4 (October 2011): 483–500.
43. Miraglia and Johns, "Going to Work Ill."
44. Andrew Brodsky and Teresa M. Amabile, "The Downside of Downtime: The Prevalence and Work-Pacing Consequences of Idle Time at Work," *Journal of Applied Psychology* 103, no. 5 (May 2018): 496–512.

45. Glassdoor.com, "25 Highest-Rated Companies for Vacation and Paid Time Off," July 7, 2018, accessed October 24, 2018, http://www.glassdoor .com/blog/25-highest-rated-companies-for-vacation-paid-time-off/.

46. F. John Reh, "Vacation Time or PTO?," *The Balance Careers*, September 13, 2018, accessed October 24, 2018, https://www.thebalancecareers.com /sick-leave-vs-paid-time-off-pto-2275775. See also Jennifer Sims, "No-Fault Attendance Policies: Faulty or Faultless?," *HR Professionals Magazine*, December 2018, 40–41.

47. Danielle Braff, "How to Design a 21st Century Time-Off Program," *HR Magazine*, April 2018, accessed October 24, 2018, http://www.shrm.org /hr-today/news/hr-magazine/0418/pages/how-to-design-a-21st-century -time-off-program.aspx.

48. Martha Frase, "Taking Time Off to the Bank," *HR Magazine*, March 2010, 41–46.

5

The High Cost of Employee Separations

Employee separations (often called turnover) occur when an employee permanently leaves an organization. According to the US Department of Labor's Bureau of Labor Statistics, total separations include quits, layoffs and discharges, and other separations. Quits are generally voluntary separations initiated by the employee. Layoffs and discharges are involuntary separations initiated by the employer. Other separations include those due to retirement, death, or disability. Every month, literally millions of employees leave their firms, for cause or not for cause, as employers hire new ones. Figure 5.1 shows a three-year monthly trend of such hires and separations.

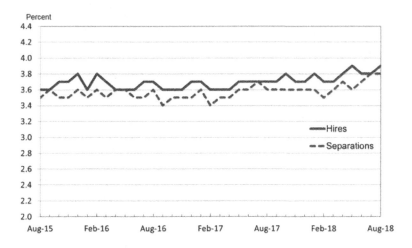

Figure 5.1. Hires and total separations, seasonally adjusted, August 2015–August 2018.

Considering voluntary employee turnover alone, the body of theoretical and empirical research is vast. At least two thousand articles have been published on this topic in the past one hundred years, yet much remains to be studied in terms of time, volitional control, context, and the process of collective turnover.[1] The purpose of this chapter is not to review that literature (see, for example, Hom, Lee, Shaw, and Hausknecht, 2017),[2] but rather to examine the economic consequences of employee separations. Let's begin by considering thirteen research-based signs—or, changes in behavior—that indicate that someone is getting ready to quit:[3]

1. Their work productivity has decreased more than usual.
2. They have acted less like a team player than usual.
3. They have been doing the minimum amount of work more frequently than usual.
4. They have been less interested in pleasing their manager than usual.
5. They have been less willing to commit to long-term timelines than usual.
6. They have exhibited a negative change in attitude.
7. They have exhibited less effort and work motivation than usual.
8. They have exhibited less focus on job-related matters than usual.
9. They have expressed dissatisfaction with their current job more frequently than usual.
10. They have expressed dissatisfaction with their supervisor more frequently than usual.
11. They have left early from work more frequently than usual.
12. They have lost enthusiasm for the mission of the organization.
13. They have shown less interest in working with customers than usual.

If you observed these signs in an employee, what would you do? Is all employee turnover equally costly or damaging to a firm's operations? Is turnover in some jobs more serious than in others? Would you focus on trying to avoid regrettable employee turnover?[4] Should firms discourage all types of turnover? What would be the investment necessary to do that and might it even be desirable? Are there situations where it might actually be desirable to increase turnover? In some cases, might employee turnover actually be healthy for individuals and for employers?

These are complex questions that are often overlooked when organizations adopt simple decision rules, such as "reduce all turnover to below the industry average." In this chapter, we provide frameworks through which organizations can address such questions and thus improve the ways they manage this important aspect of their talent resource.

The Logic of Employee Turnover: Separations, Acquisitions, Cost, and Inventory

Employee turnover is often measured by how many employees leave an organization. A more precise definition is that turnover includes replacing the departed employee (hence the idea of turning over one employee for another). We distinguish employee separations from the employee acquisitions that replace the separated employees. Employee separations and acquisitions are external movements, meaning that they involve moving across the organization's external boundary. (We will discuss movements inside the organization later.)

External movements define situations that include pure growth (acquisitions only), pure reduction (separations only), and all combinations of growth and reduction, including steady state in which the number of acquisitions equals the number of separations.[5] Employee turnover (where each separation is replaced by an acquisition) is one common and important combination, but the frameworks discussed here are helpful when managing any combination of external employee movements. We find it is also very helpful to distinguish employee separations from employee acquisitions, although the term turnover usually refers to separations that are replaced.

Decisions affecting employee movement reflect three basic parameters:

» The quantity of movers,
» The quality of movers (that is, the strategic value of their performance), and
» The costs incurred to produce the movement (that is, the costs of acquisitions or separations).

Decisions affecting the acquisition of new employees (that is, selection decisions) require consideration of the quantity, quality, and cost of those acquisitions. Likewise, decisions affecting the separation of employees (that is, layoffs, retirements, and voluntary quits) require consideration of the quantity, quality, and cost to produce the separations.

The important points to remember are that the results of decisions that affect acquisitions or separations are expressed through quantity, quality, and cost. Second, the consequences of these decisions often depend on the interaction between the effects of acquisitions and separations. Figure 5.2 shows these ideas graphically.

In each period, two processes can change workforce value: employees are added, and employees separate. As time goes on, these same two processes continue, with the beginning workforce value in the new time period being the ending workforce value from the last time period. This diagram is useful to reframe how organization leaders approach employee separations, hiring, shortages, and surpluses. The diagram shows that if leaders consider only turnover rates and costs, they are focusing only on the bottom two boxes shown at the bottom of Figure 5.2. When their only consideration

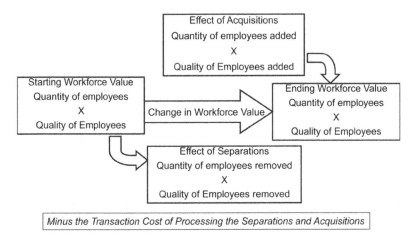

Figure 5.2. Logic of employee turnover.

is filling requisitions quickly, they are focusing on the quantity of employees added (i.e., the top box only).

The figure is intentionally similar to traditional raw-materials or unfinished-goods inventory diagrams, allowing leaders to see that their decisions about workforce inventories are at least as important as their decisions about any other kind of inventory. They can also see the dangers of focusing only on one box, and they can see what additional factors they should consider if they want to optimize workforce quality, cost, shortages, and surpluses. This diagram makes it easier for leaders to see how things like turnover, time-to-fill, and hiring costs are interconnected. The word "turnover" actually originated with inventory management. In a retail store, inventory turns over when it is depleted (sold, stolen, spoiled, etc.) and replaced. The rate of inventory depletion is the turnover rate. Inventory management doesn't just focus solely on whether depletion rates are at benchmark levels or could be reduced. Indeed, if depletion is due to profitable sales, the organization may actually want to increase it!

Instead, inventory optimization integrates the depletion rate into broader questions concerning the optimum level of inventory, the optimum costs of replenishing and depleting inventory, the optimum size, and the frequency of shortages and surpluses. In the same way, employee turnover is best thought of as part of a system that includes the costs and patterns of employee acquisitions, the value and quality of the workforce, and the costs and investments that affect all of them. Boudreau and Berger developed mathematical formulas to express the overall payoff (utility), or net benefits, of workforce acquisitions and separations.[6] In *Retooling HR*, Boudreau shows that the logic of Figure 5.2, combined with the use of inventory-optimization techniques, can retool turnover management from simple turnover reduction to optimization of employee surpluses and shortages.[7] We will return to this idea in Chapter 9, "Staffing Utility: The Concept and Its Measurement."

This chapter focuses on identifying and quantifying the transaction costs associated with external employee separations and the transaction costs of the acquisitions to replace those who left (including the activities to acquire them as well as to train them).

Two popular ways of classifying employee turnover are voluntary versus involuntary and functional versus dysfunctional. We discuss these distinctions next. Then, consistent with the LAMP framework that was introduced in Chapter 1, "Making HR Measurement Strategic," we discuss the analytics, measurements, and processes involved in computing, interpreting, and communicating the actual costs of employee turnover.

Voluntary versus Involuntary Turnover

Turnover may be voluntary on the part of the employee (for example, resignation) or involuntary (for example, firing for cause, requested resignation, permanent layoff, death). Voluntary reasons for leaving—such as another job that offers more responsibility, returning to school full time, or improved salary and benefits—are more controllable than involuntary reasons, such as employee death, chronic illness, or spouse transfer. Most organizations focus on the incidence of voluntary employee turnover precisely because it is more controllable than involuntary turnover. They are also interested in calculating the costs of voluntary turnover because when these costs are known, an organization can begin to focus attention on reducing them, particularly in areas where such costs have significant strategic effects.

Functional versus Dysfunctional Turnover

A common logical distinction focuses on whether voluntary turnover is functional or dysfunctional for the organization. Employee turnover has been defined as functional if the employee's departure produces increased value for the organization. It is dysfunctional if the employee's departure produces reduced value for the organization. Often, this is interpreted to mean that high performers who are difficult to replace represent dysfunctional turnovers, and low performers who are easy to replace represent functional turnovers.[8] Figure 5.2 provides a more precise definition. Turnover is functional when the resulting difference in workforce value is positive and high enough to offset the costs of transacting the turnover. Turnover is dysfunctional when the resulting difference in workforce value is negative, or the positive change in workforce value doesn't offset the costs. The difficulty of replacement is not inconsistent with this idea, but it is a lot less precise. Does "difficult to replace" mean that replacements will be of lower value than the person who left, or that they will be of higher value, but very costly?

Performance, of course, has many aspects associated with it. Some mistakes in selection are unavoidable. However, to the extent that employee turnover is concentrated among those whose abilities and temperaments do not fit the organization's needs, turnover can actually be functional for the organization and good for the long-term prospects of individuals, too. Other employees may have burned out, reached a plateau of substandard performance, or developed such negative attitudes toward the organization that their continued presence is likely to have harmful effects on the motivation and productivity of their coworkers. Here again, turnover can be beneficial, assuming, of course, that replacements add more value than those they replaced.

On the flip side, the loss of hard-working, value-adding contributors is usually not good for the organization. Such high performers often have a deep reservoir of firm-specific knowledge and unique and valuable personal characteristics, such as technical and interpersonal skills. It is unlikely that a new employee would have all of these characteristics, and very likely that he or she would take a long time to develop them. Thus, voluntary turnover among these individuals—and their replacement with others—is very likely to reduce the value of the workforce and to produce costs associated with their separation and replacement. Voluntary turnover is even more dysfunctional, however, when it occurs in talent pools that are pivotal to an organization's strategic success.

Pivotal Talent Pools with High Rates of Voluntary Turnover

As we noted in Chapter 3, companies often divide customers into segments. In a similar fashion, they can divide talent pools into segments that are pivotal versus nonpivotal. Pivotal talent pools are those where a small change in quality or quantity makes a big difference to strategy and value. Instead of asking "What talent is important?," the question becomes "Where do changes in the quantity or quality of talent make the biggest difference in strategically important outcomes?" For example, where salespeople have a lot of discretion in their dealings with customers, and those dealings have big effects on sales, the difference in performance between an average and a superior salesperson is large. Replacements are also likely to be lower performers because the skills needed to execute sales are learned on the job; as a result, workforce value sees a substantial reduction when a high performer leaves and is replaced by a new recruit.

On the other hand, in some jobs, performance differences are smaller, such as in a retail food-service job where there are pictures rather than numbers on the cash register and where meals are generally sold by numbers instead of by individualized orders. Here, the value produced by high performers is much more similar to the value of average performers. The job is also designed so that replacement workers can learn it quickly and perform at an acceptable level. So, in this job, voluntary turnover among high performers and their replacement by average performers does not produce such a large change in workforce value. If the costs of processing departures and acquisitions are low, it may be appropriate not to invest in reducing such turnover.

Even in fast-food retail, deeply understanding the costs and benefits of employee turnover can be enlightening. David Fairhurst, executive vice president and chief people officer for McDonald's restaurants worldwide, invited a university study examining the performance of four hundred McDonald's restaurants in the United Kingdom in 2009. The study found that customer satisfaction levels were 20 percent higher in outlets that employed kitchen staff and managers over age 60 (the oldest was an 83-year-old woman employed in Southampton).[9]

Fairhurst later noted that "sixty percent of McDonald's 75,000-strong workforce are under 21, while just 1,000 are aged over 60. . . . Some 140 people are recruited every day but only 1.0 to 1.5 percent of those are over 60."[10] So turnover among the older employees is much more significant than turnover among the younger ones.

We noted earlier that many analysts and companies refine an overall measure of employee turnover by classifying turnover as controllable or voluntary (an employee leaves of his or her own choice), or as uncontrollable or involuntary (for example, death, dismissal, layoff). After pivotal pools of talent have been identified, it becomes important to measure their voluntary employee turnover rates, assess the cost of that voluntary turnover, understand why employees are leaving, and take steps to reduce voluntary, controllable turnover. Turnover rates in pivotal talent pools need not be high to be extremely costly. Ameriprise Financial provides its leaders with various cuts of turnover data by presenting them with a map that shows where the high performers are least engaged and thus most likely to leave.[11] Departures of high performers receive more attention than departures of middle or low performers, and those with low engagement get more attention because of their greater likelihood of leaving (see Chapter 7, "Employee Attitudes and Engagement").

Voluntary Turnover, Involuntary Turnover, For-Cause Dismissals, and Layoffs

This section shows how to compute the turnover cost elements. However, not all costs apply to all types of turnover. Let's first review which categories of costs apply to which type of employee separations. Table 5.1 provides a guide.

Table 5.1. How Turnover Cost Elements Apply to Different Types of Turnover

Cost Element	Voluntary Quits	For-Cause Dismissals	Involuntary Layoffs
Separation Costs			
Exit interview	X		
Administrative time	X	X	X
Separation pay		X	X
Unemployment tax	X	X	X
Pension and benefit payouts	X	X	X
Supplemental unemployment benefits			X
Severance pay in lieu of bonus			X
Accrued vacation and sick pay	X	X	X
Lawsuits by aggrieved employees		X	X
Replacement Costs			
Communicating job availability	X	X	
Pre-employment administrative time	X	X	
Entrance interview	X	X	
Testing	X	X	
Staff meeting	X	X	
Travel/Moving expenses	X	X	
Post-employment information	X	X	
Medical exam	X	X	

Cost Element	Voluntary Quits	For-Cause Dismissals	Involuntary Layoffs
Rehiring former employees			X
Training Costs			
Informational literature and new-employee orientation	X	X	
Formal training	X	X	
Instruction by experienced employee	X	X	
Lost Productivity			
Performance difference leavers vs. stayers	X		X
Lost business with departing employee	X		X
Lost institutional memory	X		X
Decreased survivor productivity	X	X	X
Lack of staff when business rebounds			X
Risk of labor actions and strikes		X	X
Damage to company reputation	X		X

In the sections that follow, we focus mostly on the costs associated with voluntary quits and for-cause dismissals. Such separations are by far the more prevalent in most companies. Moreover, most of the costs of layoffs are also associated with the other two types of turnover, so the analytic approaches described below can also be used for layoffs.

However, it is worth noting that the costs of layoffs are often much higher than most organizations realize and that some costs are unique to the layoff situation. Cascio, in *Employment Downsizing and Its Alternatives*, notes that direct costs may be as much as $100,000 per layoff, and that in 2008, IBM spent $700 million on employee restructuring.[12] Short-term or one-time costs of layoffs include the range of possible costs, and in the long run, the costs of layoffs can include the rehiring of former employees, pension and severance payouts, and indirect costs of lost productivity. Longer-term concerns include additional lost time of survivors who worry about losing their jobs, potential backlash from clients or customers if the layoffs are perceived as unfair, and increased voluntary separations.

How to Compute Turnover Rates

Conceptually, annual employee turnover is computed by adding up the monthly turnover for a twelve-month period. Monthly turnover is calculated as the number of employee separations during the month divided by the average number of active employees during the same month. More generally, the rate of turnover in percent over any period can be calculated by the following formula:

$$\frac{Number\ of\ turnover\ incidents\ per\ period}{Average\ workforce\ size} \times 100\%$$

In the United States, as shown in Figure 5.1, aggregate monthly turnover rates (for all reasons) between August 2015 and August 2018 averaged about 3.5 percent, or 42 percent per year. The turnover rate in any given year can be misleading, however, because turnover rates are inversely related to unemployment rates (local, regional, national). Over a thirty-six-year period, for example, meta-analysis revealed correlations that ranged from –0.18 to –0.52 between unemployment rates and the magnitude of job satisfaction-turnover relations across studies.[13]

Typically, organizations compute turnover rates by business unit, division, diversity category, or tenure with the company. Then they attempt to benchmark those turnover rates against other organizations to gauge whether their rates are higher, lower, or roughly the same as those of competitors or their own industries. Many HR information systems allow managers to drill down into potential causes of turnover rates in a vast number of ways. Indeed, there are probably hundreds of different turnover rates that might be calculated, tracked, and put into various scorecards.

Logical Costs to Include When Considering Turnover Implications

Turnover can represent a substantial cost of doing business. Indeed, the fully loaded cost of turnover—not just separation and replacement costs, but also the exiting employee's lost leads and contacts, the new employee's depressed productivity while learning, and the time coworkers spend guiding him or her—can easily cost 150 percent or more of the departing person's salary.[14] Merck & Company, the pharmaceutical giant, found that, depending on the job, turnover costs 1.5 to 2.5 times the annual salary paid for it.[15] At Ernst & Young, the cost to fill a position vacated by a young auditor averages 150 percent of the departing employee's annual salary.[16] These results compare quite closely to those reported in the *Journal of Accountancy*, namely, that the cost of turnover per person ranges from 93 percent to 200 percent of an exiting employee's salary, depending on the employee's skill and level of responsibility.[17]

Unfortunately, many organizations are unaware of the actual cost of turnover. Unless this cost is known, management may be unaware of the financial implications of turnover rates, especially among pivotal talent pools. Management also may be unaware of the need for action to prevent controllable turnover and may not develop a basis for choosing among alternative programs designed to reduce turnover.

Organizations need a practical procedure for measuring and analyzing the costs of employee turnover, especially because the costs of hiring, training, and developing employees are now viewed as investments that must be evaluated just like other corporate resources. The objective in costing human resources is not only to measure the relevant costs, but also to develop methods and programs to reduce the more controllable aspects of these costs. Analytics and sound measurement strategies can help address these important issues.

Analytics

Analytics focuses on creating designs and analyses that answer relevant questions. Although computing turnover rates for various subcategories of employees or business units is instructive, our main focus in this chapter is on the financial implications associated with turnover. We use the term "analytics" to refer to formulas (for example, for turnover rates and costs) as well as the research designs and analytical methods that analyze the results of those formulas. Turnover measures are the techniques for actually gathering information—that is, for populating the formulas with relevant numbers. In the following sections, therefore, we describe how to identify and then measure turnover costs. You will see both formulas and examples that include numbers in those formulas. As you work through this information, keep in mind the distinction between analytics and measures.

The general procedure for identifying and measuring turnover costs is founded on three major, separate cost categories: separation costs, replacement costs, and training costs.[18] In addition, the procedure also must consider the difference in dollar-valued performance between leavers and their replacements. Finally, the fully loaded cost of turnover should include the economic value of lost business, to the extent that this is possible.[19] Notice how these elements precisely mirror the categories in Figure 5.2. Costs include those required to complete the separation of the former employee and also those required to acquire and train the replacement. The difference in performance between stayers and leavers is part of the change in workforce value, as is the business that is lost with the leaver.

For each of these categories, we first present the relevant cost elements and formulas (analytics) and then provide numeric examples to illustrate how the formulas are used (measures). The "pay rates" referred to in each category of costs refer to fully loaded compensation costs (that is, direct pay plus the cost of benefits).

Separation Costs

Figure 5.3 presents the key cost elements, together with appropriate formulas for each, that apply to separation costs. These include exit interviews (S_1); administrative functions related to termination, such as deletion of the exiting employee from payroll, employment, and benefits files (S_2); separation pay, if any (S_3); and unemployment tax, if applicable (S_4). The equation thus appears as follows:

$$\text{Total separation costs}(S_T) = S_1 + S_2 + S_3 + S_4$$

Cost Element	Formula				
Exit interview (S_1)	= cost of interviewer's time cost of terminating employee's time	= (time required prior to interview	+ time required for the interview)	x interviewer's pay rate during period	x number of turnovers during period
		= time required for the interview	x weighted average pay for terminated employees	x number of turnovers during period	
Administrative functions related to termination (S_2)	= time required by HR dept. for administrative functions related to termination	x average HR dept. employee's pay rate	x number of turnovers during period		
Separation pay (S_3)	= amount of separation pay per employee termination	x number of turnovers during period			
Unemployment tax (S_4)	= (unemployment tax rate - base rate)	x [($7,000 x number of employees earning at least $7,000) + (weighted average earnings if <$7,000 x (number of employees earning <$7,000)]	+ unemployment tax rate	x ($7,000 or weighted average earnings if <$7,000	x number of turnovers during period)

Figure 5.3. Measuring separation costs.

The cost of exit interviews consists of two factors: the cost of the interviewer's time (preparation plus actual interview time) and the cost of the terminating employee's time (time required for the interview × weighted average pay rate for all terminated employees). This latter figure may be calculated as follows:

» Time a random sample of exit interviews over the course of some period (for instance, three months).

» Interview a representative sample of managers who conduct exit interviews regularly and develop an average or weighted average of their estimated times.

Each organization should specify exactly what administrative functions relate to terminations and the time required for them. Each of those activities costs money, and the costs should be documented and included when measuring separation costs.

Separation pay, for those organizations that offer it, can usually be determined from the existing accounting information system. Key factors affecting the amount of severance pay include length of service, organization level, and the cause of termination. Termination for poor performance generally does not include a severance package. Most lower-level employees receive one or two weeks of pay for each year they worked up to a maximum of about twelve weeks. Mid-level managers typically receive anywhere from three to six months of pay; higher-level executives, six months to one year of pay; and chief executive officers with employment contracts, two to three years of salary in the event of a takeover.[20] Medical benefits typically continue throughout the severance period.

Among organizations that do business in the United States, unemployment tax is relevant. For those doing business elsewhere, this item should not be considered in separation costs. United States employers' unemployment tax rates include federal and state taxes, of which the federal tax equals 6.2 percent of the first $7,000 of each employee's earnings, and states may raise both the percentage and base earnings taxed through legislation.[21] Employers' actual tax rates are based on their history of claims. Those with fewer claims for unemployment benefits are subject to a lower unemployment tax than those with more unemployment claims. This increase in unemployment tax due to an increased incidence of claims is an element that should considered when calculating separation costs.

In practice, high turnover rates lead to high claims for unemployment compensation by former employees and increase the cost of unemployment tax in two ways. First, the state increases the employer's tax rate (called the "penalty" in this instance). Second, the employer must pay additional, regular unemployment tax because of the turnovers. For example, consider a 100-employee firm with a 20 percent annual turnover rate (that is, 20 people) in a state that taxes the first $10,000 of wages. The total increase in unemployment tax is computed in the following example. The penalty:

(New tax rate minus base rate) × [$10,000 × (100 + 20)]
= (5.4%—5.0%) × [$1,200,000]
= $4,800

Additional unemployment tax due to turnover:

(New tax rate) × ($10,000 × Number of turnovers
during period)
= (5.4%) × ($10,000 × 20)
= $10,800

Total additional unemployment tax due to turnover = (Penalty)
+ (Additional tax due to turnover)

= $4,800 + $10,800
= $15,600

What about the incremental costs associated with social security taxes? These costs should be included only if the earnings of those who leave exceed the taxable wage base for the year. Thus, in 2018, the taxable wage base was $128,400, and the employer's share of those taxes was 7.65 percent. For example, if an employee earning $130,000 per year leaves after six months, the employer pays tax only on $65,000. If it takes one month to replace the departing employee, the replacement earns five months' wages or $54,167. Thus, the employer incurs no additional social security tax because the total paid for the position for the year is less than

$128,400. However, if the employee who left after six months was a senior manager earning $250,000 per year, the employer would already have paid the maximum tax due for the year for that employee. If a replacement works five months (earning $104,167), the employer then incurs additional social security tax for the replacement.

A final element of separation costs that should be included, if possible, is the cost of decreased productivity due to employee terminations. This may include the decline in the productivity of an employee before termination or the decrease in productivity of a work group of which the terminating employee was a member. With respect to the effect on productivity as a result of downsizing, evidence to date is mixed. The American Management Association surveyed seven hundred companies that had downsized in the 1990s. In 34 percent of the cases, productivity rose, but it fell in 30 percent of them.[22] One thing we do know, however, is that firms whose training budgets increase following a downsizing are more likely to realize improved productivity.[23]

Example: Separation Costs for Wee Care Children's Hospital

Let us now illustrate the computation of separation costs over one year for Wee Care Children's Hospital, a 200-bed facility that employs 3,000 people. Let's assume that Wee Care's monthly turnover rate is 3 percent. This represents 36 percent of the 3,000-person workforce per year, or about 1,080 employees. From Figure 5.3, we apply the following formulas (all costs are hypothetical):

Exit Interview (S_1)
>   Interviewer's time = (15 min. preparation + 45 min. interview)
>   × $30/hour interviewer's pay + benefits × 1,080 turn-
>   overs during the year
>   = $32,400

Weighted average pay + benefits per terminated employee per
  hour = sum of the products of the hourly pay plus benefits for each employee group times the number of separating employees in that group, all divided by the total
  number of separations, or in this case:

= (19.96 × 281) + (23.44 × 326) + (26.97 × 244) + (29.13 ×
  139) + (34.46 × 53) + (47.17 × 37) divided by 1,080

= $25.42/hour

Terminating employee's time = 45 min. interview time
  (0.75 hour) × $25.42/hour weighted average pay +
  benefits × 1,080 turnovers during the year

= $20,590.20

Total cost of exit interviews = $32,400 + $20,590.20

= $52,990.20

Administrative Functions (S_2)

Time to delete each employee × HR specialist's pay + benefits/
  hour × number of turnovers during the year

= 1 hour × $30 × 1,080

= $32,400

Separation Pay (S_3)

Suppose Wee Care Children's Hospital has a policy of paying two
weeks' separation pay to each terminating employee. Using the
weighted average pay rate of the 1,080 terminating employees as
an example, $25.42/hour × 40 hours/week × 2 = $2,033.60, the
average amount of separation pay per employee terminated.

Total Separation Pay = $2,033.60 × 1,080

= $2,196,288

Unemployment Tax (S_4)

Let us assume that because of Wee Care's poor experience factor
with respect to terminated employees' subsequent claims for

unemployment benefits, the state unemployment tax rate is 5.4 percent, as compared with a base rate of 5.0 percent. Let us further assume that turnovers occur, on the average, after four and a half months (18 weeks). If the weighted average pay + benefits of terminating employees is $25.42 per hour, and Wee Care pays an average of 35 percent of base pay in benefits, the weighted average pay alone is $16.52 per hour ($25.42 minus 35 percent). Over 18 weeks, the direct pay per terminating employee exceeds $7,000.

The dollar increase in unemployment tax incurred because of Wee Care's poor experience factor is therefore as follows:

$$(5.4\% - 5.0\%) \times [\$10,000 \times (3,000 + 1,080)]$$
$$= (0.004) \times [\$10,000 \times 4,080]$$
$$= \$163,200 \ \{\text{Penalty}\} + (5.4\%) \times (\$10,000 \times 1,080)$$
$$= \$583,200 \ \{\text{Additional tax}\}$$
$$\text{Total increase} = \$163,200 + \$583,200$$
$$= \$746,400$$

Now that we have computed all four cost elements in the separation cost category, total separation costs (S_1, S_2, S_3, S_4) can be estimated. This figure is as follows:

$$S_T = S_1 + S_2 + S_3 + S_4$$
$$= \$52,990.20 + \$32,400 + \$2,196,288 + \$746,400$$
$$= \$3,028,078$$

Replacement Costs
As shown in Figure 5.2, employees who replace those who leave are considered acquisitions. The overall value, or payoff, of those acquisitions depends on three parameters: their quantity, quality, and cost. Replacement costs, as described in the following paragraphs, reflect only the quantity and cost of acquisitions, not their quality. We address the issue of staffing quality in Chapter 9, "Staffing Utility: The Concept and Its Measurement."

Replacement costs are incurred by an organization when it replaces a terminated employee. Figure 5.4 shows the cost elements and the formulas for estimating them. As the exhibit indicates, there are eight categories of replacement costs:

1. Communication of job availability,
2. Pre-employment administrative functions,
3. Entrance interviews,
4. Testing,
5. Staff meetings,
6. Travel and moving expenses,
7. Post-employment acquisition and dissemination of information, and
8. Employment medical exams.

The costs of communicating job availability will vary by type of job and targeted labor market. Depending on the methods used

Cost Element	Formula				
Communicating job availability (R_1)	= advertising and employment agency fees per termination	+ (time required for communicating job availability	x HR dept. employee's pay rate)		x number of turnovers replaced during period
Pre-employment administrative functions (R_2)	= time required by HR dept. for pre-employment administrative functions	x average HR dept. employee's pay rate	x number of applicants during period		
Entrance interview (R_3)	= time required for interview	x interviewer's pay rate	x number of interviews during period		
Testing (R_4)	= (cost of materials per person	+ cost of scoring per person)	x number of test given during period		
Staff meeting (R_5)	= [time required for meeting	x (HR dept. employee's pay rate)	+ dept. representative's pay rate]	x number of meetings during period	
Travel/moving expenses (R_6)	= (average travel cost per applicant	x number of applicants)	+ average moving cost per new hire	x number of new hires	
Post-employment acquisition and dissemination of information (R_7)	= time required for acquiring and disseminating information	x average HR dept. employee's pay rate	+ number of turnovers replaced during period		
In-house medical examinations (R_8)	= [(time required for examination	x examiner's pay rate)	+ cost of supplies used]	x number of tunovers replaced during period	
OR Contracted medical examinations (R_9)	= rate per examination	x number of turnovers replaced during period			

Figure 5.4. Measuring replacement costs.

in recruitment, these costs may range from the cost of an online job posting to employment-agency fees borne by the employer.[24] Typically, these costs can be obtained from existing accounting records. However, to the extent that this communication process requires considerable time from HR department employees, the cost of their time should also be included in replacement costs.

Administratively, several tasks are frequently undertaken in selecting and placing each new employee—for example, accepting applications, screening candidates, and checking references. These procedures can be expensive. For example, a simple background investigation that includes verification of last educational degree, a check with the last two employers, a five-year criminal check, and verification of the social security number costs only about $100. However, an extensive check that includes the previous items plus interviews with previous employers, teachers, neighbors, and acquaintances can run $15,000 or more. Unfortunately, the time required to perform these activities is not documented routinely by organizational information systems. However, the methods described earlier for estimating exit interview time requirements may be applied in determining the time necessary for pre-employment administrative functions.

Virtually all organizations use entrance interviews to describe jobs, to communicate employee responsibilities and benefits, and to make some general assessments of candidates. The costs incurred when completing entrance interviews are a function of the length of the interview, pay rates of interviewers involved, and the number of interviews conducted. Valid staffing procedures can reduce future turnover and improve future employee performance. Decision-makers should include both costs and benefits. This chapter focuses on costs; Chapter 9 shows how to calculate the benefits from valid staffing procedures.

Many firms use pre-employment testing of one sort or another, such as aptitude, achievement, drug, and honesty testing. To account properly for the costs of these activities, consider the costs of materials and supplies and the cost of scoring the tests. The costs of materials and scoring for aptitude, achievement, and honesty tests are often less than $25 per candidate. Drug testing typically costs less than $50.[25]

For some classes of employees, especially top-level managers or other professionals, a meeting may be held between the HR department and the department with the vacant position. A measure of this element of replacement costs can be obtained by multiplying the estimated time required for this meeting by the sum of the pay and benefits rates for all attendees. Travel and moving expenses can be extremely costly to organizations. Travel costs for candidates from a local labor market are minimal (carfare, parking, tolls), but travel costs for candidates who must fly in and stay in a hotel can average more than $1,500. Moving expenses can cover a range of cost elements from mortgage differentials, lease-breaking expenses, company purchase of the old house, costs of moving personal effects from the old to the new location, closing costs, hook-up fees for utilities, and more. Fully-loaded moving costs for new hire home-owners average $72,000, versus $86,000 for an existing employee homeowner.[26] Homeowner versus renter status is one basis for placing employees in different mobility tiers that contain different housing subsidies.[27]

The seventh category of replacement costs is post-employment acquisition and dissemination of information. Pertinent information for each new employee must be gathered, recorded, and entered into various subsystems of an HR information system, such as employee records, payroll files, benefits records. If flexible, cafeteria-style benefits are offered by an organization, an HR specialist could spend considerable time in counseling each new employee. The costs of this process can be estimated by calculating the time required for this counseling and multiplying it by the wage rates of employees involved. To compute the total cost of acquiring and disseminating information to new employees, multiply this cost by the number of acquisitions.

Pre-employment medical examinations are the final element of replacement costs. The extent and thoroughness, and therefore the cost, of such examinations varies greatly. Some organizations do not require them at all, while some contract with private physicians or clinics, and others use in-house medical staff. If medical examinations are contracted out, the cost can be determined from existing accounting data. If the exams are done in-house, their cost can be determined based on the supplies used (for example, medical supplies, laboratory supplies) and the staff time required to perform each examination. If the new employee is paid while receiving the medical examination, his or her rate of pay should be added to the examiner's pay rate in determining total cost. The following example estimates replacement costs for a one-year period based on Figure 5.4 for Wee Care Children's Hospital.

Job Availability (R_1)
Assume that fees and advertisements average $350 per turnover; three more hours are required to communicate job availability; the HR specialist's pay and benefits total $30 per hour; and 288 turnovers are replaced during the period. Therefore:

$$R_1 = [\$500 + (3 \times \$30)] \times 1,080$$
$$= \$637,200$$

Pre-Employment Administrative Functions (R_2)
Assume that pre-employment administrative functions to fill the job of each employee who left comprise five hours. Therefore:

$$R_2 = 5 \times \$30 \times 1,080$$
$$= \$162,000$$

Entrance Interview (R$_3$)
Assume that, on the average, three candidates are interviewed for every one hired. Thus, over the one-year period of this study, 3,240 (1,080 × 3) interviews were conducted. Therefore:

$$R_3 = 1 \times \$30 \times 3,240$$
$$= \$97,200$$

Testing (R$_4$)
Assume that aptitude tests cost $15 per applicant for materials, another $15 per applicant to score, and that as a matter of HR policy, Wee Care uses drug tests ($50 per applicant) as part of the pre-employment process. The cost of testing is therefore as follows:

$$R_4 = (\$30 + \$50) \times (1,080 \times 3)$$
$$= \$259,200$$

Staff Meeting (R$_5$)
Assume that each staff meeting lasts one hour, that the average pay plus benefits of the new employee's department representative is $42, and that for administrative convenience such meetings are held, on average, only once for each three new hires (1,080 / 3 = 360). Therefore:

$$R_5 = (\$30 + \$42) \times 360$$
$$= \$25,920$$

Travel/Moving Expenses (R$_6$)
Assume that Wee Care pays travel expenses of $95 for each candidate, plus moving expenses of $50,000 on average, for only one of every twelve new hires. Therefore:

$$R_6 = [\$95 \times (1,080 \times 3)] + (\$50,000 \times 90)$$
$$= \$307,800 + \$4,500,000$$
$$= \$4,807,800$$

Post-Employment Acquisition and Dissemination of Information (R_7)
Assume that two hours are spent on these activities for each new employee. Therefore:

$$R_7 = 2 \times \$30 \times 1,080$$
$$= \$64,800$$

Pre-Employment Medical Examination (R_8 and R_9)
Assume that if the medical examinations are done at the hospital (in-house), each exam will take one hour; the examiner is paid $65 per hour; medical supplies and laboratory analyses cost $335; and 1,080 exams are conducted. Therefore:

$$R_8 = [(1 \times \$65) + \$335] \times 1,080$$
$$= \$432,000$$

If the exams are contracted out, let us assume that Wee Care will pay a flat rate of $450 per examination. Therefore:

$$R_8 = \$450 \times 1,080$$
$$= \$486,000$$

Wee Care therefore decides to provide in-house medical examinations for all new employees. Total costs (R_T) can now be computed as the sum of R_1 through R_8:

$$R_T = \$637,200 + \$162,000 + \$97,200 + \$259,200 + \$25,920$$
$$+ \$4,807,800 + \$64,800 + \$432,000$$
$$R_T = \$6,486,120$$

Training Costs

In virtually all instances, replacement employees must be oriented and trained to a standard level of competence before assuming their regular duties. As discussed in Chapter 10, "The Payoff from Training and Development Programs," this often involves considerable expense to an organization. For the present, however, assume that all replacement employees receive a total of two full days (sixteen hours) of new employee orientation from an HR department representative. After that, they are either placed in a formal training program, assigned to an experienced employee for some period of on-the-job training, or both. The cost elements and computational formulas for this category of turnover costs are shown in Figure 5.5. The three major elements of training costs are equipment (e.g., smartphone, laptop) plus new employee orientation, instruction in a formal training program, and instruction by employee assignment.

The cost of any company-provided equipment furnished to replacement employees should be considered a part of orientation and training costs. Unit costs for those items may be obtained from existing accounting records. Multiplying the unit costs by the number of replacement employees hired during the period yields the first element of training costs. The cost of orientation includes the pay and benefits of the new employees who attend plus the pay and benefits of the HR representative who provides the orientation training times the total number of training hours.

New employees may also be involved in a formal training program. The overall cost of the training program depends on the cost of two major components: costs associated with trainers and costs associated with trainees. Whereas an organization incurs 100 percent of the costs associated with training replacements for employees who leave, the cost associated with trainers depends on the extent to which formal training is attributable to turnover. It is important, therefore, to distinguish between trainees who are replacements for exiting employees and any others who are in training due to other factors, such as new technology or planned expansion of the workforce. For the sake of simplicity, the costs of facilities, food, and other overhead expenses have not been included in these calculations.

Instead of, or in addition to, instruction in a formal training program, new employees may also be assigned to work with more experienced employees for a period of time or until they reach a standard level of competence. The overall cost of this on-the-job training must be determined for all replacement employees hired during the period, for it is an important element of training costs.

Notice that in Figure 5.5, the cost of reduced productivity of new employees while they are learning is not included as an element of overall training costs. This is not because such a cost is unimportant. On the contrary, even if an organization staffs more employees to provide for a specified level of productivity while new employees are training, the cost of a decrease in the quantity and quality of goods or services produced is still very real. Less-experienced employees may also cause an increase in operating expenses because of inefficient use of supplies and equipment. Other elements of lost productivity and lost business include factors such as additional overtime to cover one or more vacancies, cost of temporary help, the offsetting effects of wages and benefits saved due to the vacancy, and the cost of low morale among remaining employees.

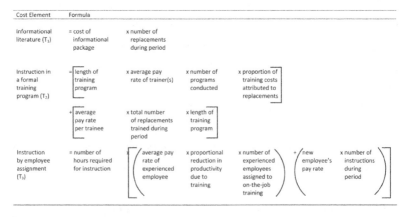

Figure 5.5. Measuring training costs.

At high levels in organizations, and in other jobs where relationships with customers, leads, and contacts are critically important, the economic cost of business lost (that is, opportunities foregone) may be substantial. On top of that, there may also be ripple effects associated with an employee's departure such that other employees follow him or her out the door. Situations such as these are especially prevalent when star employees or A-level players depart and convince others to follow them. Executive recruiters call these situations "lift-outs." As one author noted, "In a way, lift-outs are the iTunes of the merger world: Why buy the whole album when all you really want are its greatest hits?"[28] They can be especially costly, not to mention the huge gaps in staffing that they create. They tend to occur when tight-knit groups or networks of employees (coworkers, former colleagues, classmates, or friends) decide to leave en masse.[29]

All of these costs are important. In the aggregate, they easily could double or triple the costs tallied thus far. When they can be measured reliably and accurately, they certainly should be included as additional elements of training costs. The same is true for potential productivity gains associated with new employees. Such gains serve to offset the costs of training. However, in many organizations, especially those providing services (for example, customer services or patient care in hospitals), the measurement of these costs or gains is simply too complex for practical application. At the same time, they are seldom zero, and it is probably better to include a consensus estimate of their magnitude from a knowledgeable group of individuals than to assume either that they do not exist or that the cost is zero.

Now let us estimate the total cost of training employee replacements at Wee Care. Using the formulas shown in Figure 5.5, Wee Care estimates the following costs over a one-year period.

Equipment and New Employee Orientation (T_1)
Assume that the unit cost of company-provided equipment is $1,700 and that 1,080 employees are replaced. Each of the 1,080

replacements, at an average pay rate plus benefits of $25.42 per hour (see the computation of S_1 above), receives a total of 16 hours (2 full days) of general orientation to the hospital from an HR department representative, who earns $30 per hour in pay and benefits. The total cost of informational literature and new employee orientation is therefore as follows:

$$T_1 = (\$1,700 \times 1,080) + (16 \times \$25.42 \times 1,080) + (16 \times \$30)$$
$$= \$2,275,737.60$$

Instruction in a Formal Training Program (T_2)
New-employee training at Wee Care is conducted 10 times per year, and each training program lasts 40 hours (1 full week). The average pay plus benefits for instructors is $48 per hour, the average pay and benefits rate for trainees is $25.42 per hour, and of the 2,160 employees trained on the average each year, half are replacements for employees who left voluntarily or involuntarily. The total cost of formal training attributed to employee turnover is therefore as follows:

$$T_2 = (40 \times \$48 \times 10 \times 0.50) + (\$25.42 \times 1,080 \times 40)$$
$$= \$9,600 + \$1,098,144$$
$$= \$1,107,744$$

Instruction by Employee Assignment (T_3)
To ensure positive transfer between training program content and job content, Wee Care requires each new employee to be assigned to a more experienced employee for an additional week (40 hours). Experienced employees average $35 per hour in wages and benefits, and their own productivity is cut by 50 percent while they are training others. Each experienced employee supervises two trainees. The total cost of on-the-job training for replacement employees is therefore as follows:

$$T_3 = 40 \times [(\$35 \times 0.50 \times 540) + (\$25.42 \times 1,080)]$$
$$= 40 \times (\$9,450 + \$27,453.60)$$
$$= 40 \times \$36,903.60$$
$$= \$1,476,144$$

Total training costs can now be computed as the sum of T_1, T_2, and T_3:

$$T_T = \$2,275,737.60 + \$1,107,744 + \$1,476,144$$
$$= \$4,859,625.60$$

Performance Differences between Leavers and Their Replacements

A final factor to consider in the tally of net turnover costs is the uncompensated performance differential between employees who leave and their replacements. We will call this difference in performance (DP). DP needs to be included in determining the net cost of turnover because replacements whose performance exceeds that of leavers (as reflected in a higher salary paid to the replacement) reduce turnover costs. Replacements whose performance is worse than that of leavers (as reflected in a lower salary paid to the replacement) increase turnover costs.

To begin measuring DP in conservative, practical terms, compute the difference by position in the salary range between each leaver and his or her replacement. Assume that performance differentials are reflected in terms of deviations from the midpoint of the pay grade of the job class in question. Each employee's position in the salary range is computed as a "compa-ratio"; that is, salary is expressed as a percentage of the midpoint of that employee's pay grade. If the midpoint of a pay grade is $80,000 (annual pay), for example, an employee earning $64,000 is at 80 percent of the midpoint. Therefore, his or her compa-ratio is 0.80. An employee paid $80,000 has a compa-ratio of 1.0 (100 percent of the midpoint rate of pay), and an employee paid \$96,000 has a compa-ratio of 1.2 because he or she is paid 120 percent of the midpoint rate of pay. Compa-ratios generally vary from 0.80 to 1.20 in most pay systems.[30]

To compute DP, use the following formula:

$$DP = \sum_{i=1}^{n} \left(CR_1 - CR_r \right) MP_i$$

Where *DP* is difference in performance between leaver and replacement, $\sum$ is summation over all leavers and their replacements, CR_1 is the compa-ratio of the leaver, CR_r is the compa-ratio of the replacement, and MP_i is the annual rate of pay at the midpoint of the pay grade in question. Consider the following example:

$CR_1 = 0.80$ $CR_r = 1.0$ $MP_i = \$80,000$
$DP = (0.80 - 1.0) \times \$80,000$
$DP = (-0.20) \times \$80,000$
$DP = -\$16,000$

DP is therefore subtracted from total turnover costs because the firm is gaining an employee whose performance, as reflected in the higher salary paid to the replacement, is superior to that of the employee who left.

If the compa-ratio of the leaver is 1.0, that of the replacement is 0.80, and the pay-grade midpoint is \$80,000, then *DP* = \$16,000. These costs are added to total turnover costs because the leaver was replaced by a lesser performer.

Why are differences in performance assumed to covary with differences in pay? Actually, this assumption is true only in a per-fectly competitive labor market.[31] In a perfectly competitive labor market, every worker earns the marginal revenue product accrued to the firm from his or her labor. Thus, the firm is indifferent to workers whose compa-ratios are 0.80, 1.0, or 1.20 because each worker is paid exactly what he or she is worth. Many entry-level jobs (for example, management analysts) approximate conditions where it is reasonable to assume that compa-ratio differences reflect performance differences. Above the entry level, however, labor markets are often imperfect because workers develop what economists call "firm-specific human capital."[32] Workers who have specific job knowledge that is valued by their firms (for example, in banking, automobiles, computers) tend to command higher wages. However, their value is reflected only partly in their higher wages. Wages reflect what economists call "opportunity costs," or the value of a worker's second-best employment opportunity. Competitors are only able to offer a wage that reflects the economic value of a worker to them. Therefore, opportunity costs and the wage rates paid to valued employees tend to reflect only the portion of a worker's economic value that is easily transferable from one employer to another (that is, generic). The portion of an employee's value that is not easily transferable—the firm-specific component—typically is reflected only partially in employee wages, if at all. Thus, the economic value of workers with firm-specific human capital is above their wage (opportunity cost) level but can be assumed to be proportionate to these wages.

If an employee with substantial amounts of firm-specific human capital leaves the firm and is replaced by a worker who lacks such firm-specific human capital, the replacement will receive a lesser wage. However, if a poor performer leaves and is replaced by a worker with more human capital, albeit nonfirm-specific, the replacement will receive a higher wage than the leaver.[33] The difference in pay between leavers and their replacements thus represents an indicator, although an imperfect one, of the uncompensated performance differential due to firm-specific human capital, and it should be considered when determining the net costs of turnover.

It is a conservative assumption that excess value to the firm is a function of wages paid and that excess value and wages covary in a linear (straight line) fashion. In practice, the relationship can be curvilinear (positive or negative); but for our purposes, the conservative assumption of a linear relationship between excess value and wages is appropriate. At the same time, higher (or lower) wages paid to a replacement employee represent additional ongoing costs (or savings) to an organization. It is appropriate to calculate such a pay differential, for it is part of the differential value of the replacement relative to the employee who left. Although an offsetting strategic value may justify paying a replacement more, that is often a subjective estimate by decision makers.

For Wee Care, assume that the net DP = +$450,000. On average, therefore, the firm hired slightly poorer performers than it lost. The following equation, which uses the four major components of employee turnover, represents the total cost of employee turnover:

$$\text{Total cost of turnover} = S_T + R_T + T_T + DP$$

Where S_T is total separation costs, R_T is total replacement costs, T_T is total training costs, and DP is net differential performance between leavers and their replacements. For Wee Care, the total cost of 288 employee turnovers during a one-year period was as follows:

$3,028,078 + $6,486,120 + $4,859,625.60 + $450,000
= $14,823,823.60

This represents a cost of $13,725.76 for each of the 1,080 employees who left the hospital.

The Costs of Lost Productivity and Lost Business

In several places earlier in this chapter, we mentioned that it is useful to include the costs of lost productivity and lost business in the fully loaded cost of employee turnover, if it is possible to tally such costs accurately. The following seven additional cost elements might be included:[34]

» The cost of additional overtime to cover the vacancy (Wages + Benefits × Number of hours of overtime);

» The cost of additional temporary help (Wages + Benefits × Hours paid);

» Wages and benefits saved due to the vacancy (these are subtracted from the overall tally of turnover costs);

» The cost of reduced productivity while the new employee is learning the job (Wages + Benefits × Length of the learning period × Percentage reduction in productivity);

» The cost of lost productive time due to low morale of remaining employees, estimated as ((Aggregate time lost per day of the work group) × (Wages + Benefits of a single employee) × (Number of days));

» The cost of lost customers, sales, and profits due to the departure (Estimated number of customers × Gross profit lost per customer × Profit margin in percent); and

» Cost of additional (related) employee departures (if one additional employee leaves, the cost equals the total per-person cost of turnover).

In terms of analytics, one final caution is in order: avoid being misled by variability across departments or business units that are based on small numbers. After all, if a six-person department loses two employees, that's a 33 percent turnover rate! We noted in Chapter 2, "Analytical Foundations of HR Measurement," the dangers associated with generalizing from small samples that are not representative of the larger population they are designed to represent. In the case of small-sample turnover statistics, to make the sample more representative, it might make sense to segment employee turnover into broader categories that include larger numbers of employees.

Remember, the purpose of measuring turnover costs and using analytical strategies to reveal their implications is to improve managerial decision-making. Here is a brief example of one such analysis.[35] Based on the model shown in Figure 5.2, the researchers developed an analytical model that captured the value associated with employee separations (turnover) and acquisitions (hires) over a four-year period. Their model estimated these three components in each time period:

» Movement costs, or the costs associated with employee separations and acquisitions;
» Service costs, or the pay, benefits, and associated expenses required to support the workforce; and
» Service value, or the value of the goods and service produced by the workforce.

Then, they estimated the dollar-valued implications of three different pay plans (equal pay increases plus two types of pay-for-performance plans) and of the subsequent separation and acquisition patterns over the four years. They did so by subtracting the movement costs and service costs from the service value. In short, they subtracted each pay plan's costs from its benefits.

Traditional compensation cost analysis suggested that a strong link between pay and performance would be unwise, given its extreme cost. When the potential benefits of workforce value were accounted for, however, a different conclusion emerged. That is, by fully incorporating both costs and benefits into their model, the researchers showed that even under the most conservative assumptions, pay-for-performance was a valuable investment, with potentially very high payoffs for the firm. This reinforces a point we made at the beginning of the chapter: turnover is only one part of a family of external moves. Adopting a broader perspective is a wise strategy indeed.

Process

Organizational budgeting practices sometimes provide a natural opportunity to use the costs of employee turnover as part of a broader framework to demonstrate tangible economic payoffs from effective management practices. When line managers complain that they cannot keep positions filled, or that they cannot get enough people to join as new hires, it is a prime opportunity to elevate the conversation.

Revenue at Superior Energy Services in New Orleans is based on billable hours. That fact gave Ray Lieber, the HR vice president, an opportunity to portray every separation as lost revenue. Nearly half of the separations were skilled operators or supervisors with high impact on revenue. Then, he made the case for an investment in statistical modeling to predict how to reduce turnover. He discovered that the most significant factor was not higher pay or benefits, but one-on-one coaching from supervisors. Superior Energy invested in supervisor coaching training and saw turnover drop from 34 percent to about 27 percent.[36]

Thrivent Financial for Lutherans in Minneapolis had always assumed that the more experience a new hire had in the job he or she was hired into, the less likely that new hire was to leave, but it found just the opposite when it analyzed turnover data. That gave HR leaders at Thrivent the chance to get the attention of line management and to invest in studies to discover why those with more experience were more likely to leave. Similarly, at Wawa Inc., a Pennsylvania food service and convenience company, leaders had suspected that hourly wage was the biggest factor in turnover among clerks, but careful analysis found that the most significant turnover predictor was hours worked. Those working more than 30 hours per week were classified as full-time and separated less. This discovery opened the door to moving from 30 percent part-time to 50 percent full-time, reducing turnover rates by 60 percent.[37]

As a final example, consider the SAS Institute of Cary, North Carolina. SAS is renowned for its low voluntary turnover rate among computer programmers. In an industry that routinely experiences 20 percent voluntary turnover per year among programmers, at SAS it runs about 3 percent per year. It does that largely through its enlightened management practices. Those practices are founded on the idea that in an intellectual capital business, attracting and retaining talent is paramount. The way to attract and retain good people is to give them interesting work and interesting people to do it with and to treat them like the responsible adults they are.

SAS is justifiably famous for its pleasant physical work environment and generous, family-friendly benefits. Those benefits include an on-site 7,500-square-foot medical facility and a full-indemnity health plan that includes vision, hearing, and dental care, free physical exams, and free mammography. It also provides on-site Montessori day care, a fitness center, and soccer and softball fields. All of this is free to employees and their families. The company even provides towels and launders exercise clothes—also for free. Finally, it provides eldercare, domestic-partner benefits, and cafeterias with subsidized meals.[38]

Suppose a line leader at SAS addresses the following question to HR leaders: "I'm happy our turnover among programmers is 3 percent, but are we spending too much to keep them, and is it worth it?" In answering that very reasonable question, an HR leader might begin by reviewing the company's business model. In brief, it is as follows.[39]

SAS relies on annual product renewals from its clients, who use its software for deep analysis of their organizational databases. SAS also relies on employees for innovations and services that are tailored to those clients' particular industry requirements and their unique competitive positions in their industries. This means that client relationships with SAS advisers need to be based on a thorough, shared understanding about industry-specific competition and on long-term trust. This may be more important for SAS than for its competitors, whose business models are based more on software purchases than renewable licenses and whose value proposition is not so deeply dependent on close and well-informed relationships with clients.

One way that SAS creates the capability, opportunity, and motivation to achieve this kind of deep, common, client-focused synergy is by creating an employment model that attracts and motivates programmers, designers, and client advisers to join and stay for the long run. This is a distinctive value proposition because a long-term employment deal is unusual in professions where the norm is to move from project to project, often changing employers many times in a few years to find the most interesting work or a higher paycheck.

The HR leader might then present the cost implications of that 17 percent difference in employee turnover between SAS and the software industry. Table 5.2 includes some hypothetical calculations.

Table 5.2. Annual Opportunity Savings from Lower Employee Turnover among Programmers: SAS versus the Software Industry

Annual turnover	3%	20%
Annual salary	$90,000	$90,000
Number per 1,000 programmers who leave	30	200
Cost of turnover per programmer (1.5 × Salary)	$135,000	$135,000
Total cost	$4,050,000	$27,000,000
Annual opportunity savings at SAS	$22,950,000	

Of course, the annual opportunity savings does not include the incremental, yearly cost to SAS of providing such generous benefits and perquisites for its employees. Assume, however, that the annual cost of benefits per SAS employee is as high as 50 percent of salary (compared to a 2018 US average of 32 percent).[40] Its incremental, yearly cost, relative to its competitors, is therefore roughly 18 percent higher. The total annual opportunity savings to SAS as a result of lower employee turnover ($22.95 million − 18% = $18.819 million) may be viewed as an annuity that helps pay for the benefits that keep employee turnover low. Because it takes a long time for a new employee to develop the kind of shared understanding and high level of trust with clients that is central to the SAS business model, retaining talent truly is critical to achieving the company's strategic objectives. The answer to the line leader's original question is that SAS's investments in generous employee benefits are likely to be worth it.

Exercise

Use the software available from http://iip.shrm.org or the worksheet below for all computations.

1. Ups and Downs Inc., a 4,000-employee organization, has a serious turnover problem, and management has decided to estimate its annual cost to the company. Following the formulas presented in Figures 5.3, 5.4, and 5.5, an HR specialist collected the following information. Exit interviews take about 45 minutes (plus 15 minutes preparation); the interviewer, an HR specialist, is paid an average of $33 per hour in wages and benefits; and over the past year, Ups and Downs Inc. experienced a 27 percent turnover rate. Three groups of employees were primarily responsible for this: production employees (40 percent), who make an average of $34.80 per hour in wages and benefits; clerical employees (36 percent), who make an average of $24.50 per hour; and managers and professionals (24 percent), who make an average of $48.75 per hour. The HR department takes about 90 minutes per terminating employee to perform the administrative functions related to terminations, and on top of that, each terminating employee gets two weeks' severance pay. All of this turnover also contributes to increased unemployment tax (old rate = 5.0 percent; new rate = 5.4 percent); and because the average taxable wage per employee is $34.42, this is likely to be a considerable (avoidable) penalty for having a high turnover problem.

It also costs money to replace those terminating. All pre-employment physicals are done by Biometrics Inc., an outside organization that charges $350 per physical. Advertising and employment agency fees run an additional $750, on average, per termination, and HR specialists spend an average of four more hours communicating job availability every time another employee quits. Pre-employment administrative functions take another two and a half hours per terminating employee, and this excludes pre-employment interview time (one hour, on average). Over the past year, Ups and Downs Inc.'s records also show that for every candidate hired, three others had to be interviewed. Testing costs per applicant are $18 for materials and another $18 for scoring. Travel expenses average $125 per applicant, and one in every ten new hires is reimbursed an average of $75,000 in moving expenses. For those management jobs being filled, a 90-minute staff meeting is also required, with a department representative (average pay and benefits of $47.75 per hour) present. In the past year, 17 meetings were held. Finally, post-employment acquisition and dissemination of information takes 75 minutes, on average, for each new employee.

And of course, all these replacements have to be oriented and trained. Equipment furnished to each new employee costs an average of $1,700, and a formal orientation program run by an HR specialist takes 2.5 days (20 hours) spread over the first two months of employment. New employees made an average of $32.50 per hour in wages and benefits. After that, a formal training program (run 12 times last year) takes four 8-hour days, and trainers make an average of $49 per hour in wages and benefits. About 65 percent of all training costs can be attributed to replacements for those who left. Finally, on-the-job training lasted three 8-hour days per new employee, with two new employees assigned to each experienced employee (average pay and benefits = $41.25 per hour). During training, each experienced employee's productivity dropped by 50 percent. Net DP was +$510,000. What did employee turnover cost Ups and Downs Inc. last year? How much per employee who left?

Worksheet

Separation Costs

Exit interview cost of interviewer's time =

Cost of terminating employees' time =

Administrative functions related to terminations =

Separation pay =

Unemployment tax =

Total separation costs =

Replacement Costs

Communicating job availability =

Pre-employment administrative functions =

Testing =

Staff meeting =

Travel/moving expenses =

Post-employment acquisition
and dissemination of information =

Contracted medical examinations =

Total replacement costs =

Training Costs

Equipment and new employee orientation =

Instruction in a formal training program =

Instruction by employee assignment =

Total training costs =

Net differential in performance =

Total turnover costs =

Total cost per terminating employee =

References

1. Thomas Lee et al., "On the Next Decade of Research in Voluntary Employee Turnover," *Academy of Management Perspectives* 31, no. 3 (August 2017): 201–21.
2. Peter W. Hom et al., "One Hundred Years of Employee Turnover Theory and Research," *Journal of Applied Psychology* 102, no. 3 (March 2017): 530–45.
3. Timothy M. Gardner and Peter W. Hom, "13 Signs That Someone Is About to Quit, According to Research," *Harvard Business Review*, October 20, 2016, https://hbr.org/2016/10/13-signs-that-someone-is-about-to-quit-according-to-research.
4. Arlene Hirsch, "Heading Off "Regrettable Resignations," *SHRM Online*, August 28, 2018, http://www.shrm.org/resourcesandtools/hr-topics/employee-relations/pages/heading-off-regrettable-resignations.aspx.
5. John W. Boudreau and Chris J. Berger, "Decision-Theoretic Utility Analysis Applied to Employee Separations and Acquisitions," *Journal of Applied Psychology* 70, no. 3 (August 1985): 581–612.
6. Boudreau and Berger, "Decision-Theoretic Utility Analysis," 581–612.
7. John W. Boudreau, *Retooling HR: How Proven Business Models Can Improve Human Capital Decisions* (Cambridge, MA: Harvard Business Press, 2010), chapter 4.
8. David C. Martin and Kathryn M. Bartol, "Managing Turnover Strategically for Positive Results," *Personnel Administrator*, November 1985, 63–73.
9. Richard Tyler, "Workers Over 60 Are Surprise Key to McDonald's Sales," *Telegraph*, August 13, 2009, http://www.telegraph.co.uk/finance/newsbysector/retailandconsumer/6017391/Workers-over-60-are-surprise-key-to-McDonalds-sales.html.
10. Tyler, "Workers Over 60."
11. Boudreau, *Retooling HR*, chapter 4.
12. Wayne F. Cascio, *Employment Downsizing and Its Alternatives: Strategies for Long-Term Success*, SHRM Foundation's Effective Practice Guidelines Series (Alexandria, VA: SHRM Foundation, December 2009).
13. Jeanne M. Carsten and Paul E. Spector, "Unemployment, Job Satisfaction, and Employee Turnover: A Meta-Analytic Test of the Muchinsky Model," *Journal of Applied Psychology* 72, no. 3 (August 1987): 374–81.
14. Shelly Branch, "You Hired 'Em. But Can You Keep 'Em?," *Fortune*, November 9, 1998, 247–50.
15. J. Solomon, "Companies Try Measuring Cost Savings From New Types of Corporate Benefits," *The Wall Street Journal*, December 29, 1988, B1.
16. Sylvia Ann Hewlett and Carolyn Buck Luce, "Off-Ramps and On-Ramps: Keeping Talented Women on the Road to Success," *Harvard Business Review*, March 2005, 43–54.

17. Arlene A. Johnson, "The Business Case for Work-Family Programs," *Journal of Accountancy* 180, no. 2 (August 1995): 53–58.

18. Howard L. Smith and Larry E. Watkins, "Managing Manpower Turnover Costs," *Personnel Administrator* 23, no. 4 (April 1978): 46–50.

19. John Dooney, *Cost of Turnover* (Alexandria, VA: SHRM, November 2005), http://www.shrm.org/research.

20. Susan M. Heathfield, "Reasons Why an Employer Might Want to Provide Severance Pay," *The Balance Careers*, March 13, 2017, http://www.thebalance.com/severance-pay-1918252. See also Lindsay Olson, "Three Severance Pay Questions Every Employee Should Ask," *US News & World Report*, May 8, 2012, http://money.usnews.com/money/blogs/outside-voices-careers/2012/05/08/3-severance-pay-questions-every-employee-should-ask.

21. Jerry M. Newman, Barry Gerhart, and George T. Milkovich, *Compensation*, 12th ed. (New York: McGraw-Hill, 2017).

22. These data were reported in Rosemary Cravotta and Brian H. Kleiner, "New Developments Concerning Reductions in Force," *Management Research News* 24, no. 3/4, (2001): 90–93.

23. Steven H. Appelbaum et al., "Downsizing: Measuring the Costs of Failure," *Journal of Management Development* 18, no. 5 (July 1999): 436–63.

24. Wayne F. Cascio, *Managing Human Resources: Productivity, Quality of Work Life, Profits*, 11th ed. (New York: McGraw-Hill, 2019), chapter 7.

25. "Think the Cost of Drug Testing Is Too High? Think Again," *HireRight* (blog), accessed April 18, 2017, http://www.hireright.com/blog/2012/02/think-the-cost-of-pre-employment-drug-testing-is-too-high-think-again/. See also Dalia Fahmy, "Aiming for a Drug-Free Workplace," *The New York Times*, May 10, 2007, C6.

26. Dave Zielinski, "Relocation Partners Help HR Move Business Forward," *SHRM Online*, April 6, 2017, https://www.shrm.org/resourcesandtools/hr-topics/talent-acquisition/pages/relocation-partners-help-hr-move-business.aspx.

27. Antonio Franquiz, "Agenda: Relocation All the Right Moves," *HR Magazine*, October 2013, 59–61.

28. Jena McGregor, "I Can't Believe They Took the Whole Team," *BusinessWeek*, December 18, 2006, 120.

29. Bernard Wysocki, Jr., "Yet Another Hazard of the New Economy: The Pied Piper Effect," *The Wall Street Journal*, March 30, 2000, A1.

30. Newman, Gerhart, and Milkovich, *Compensation*.

31. Mark Hirschey, *Fundamentals of Managerial Economics*, 8th ed. (Mason, OH: South-Western Thompson Learning, 2006).

32. Gary S. Becker, *Human Capital*, (New York: National Bureau of Economic Research, 1964).

33. Edward P. Lazear, *Personnel Economics for Managers* (New York: Wiley, 1998).

34. Dooney, *Cost of Turnover.*

35. Michael C. Sturman, "Is It Worth It to Win the Talent War? Evaluating the Utility of Performance-Based Pay," *Personnel Psychology* 56, no. 4 (December 2003): 997–1035.

36. Bill Roberts, "Analyze This," *HR Magazine*, October 2009, 35–41.

37. Roberts, "Analyze This."

38. Charles O'Reilly and Jeffrey Pfeffer, *Hidden Value: How Great Companies Achieve Extraordinary Results with Ordinary People* (Boston: Harvard Business School Press, 2000).

39. John W. Boudreau and Peter M. Ramstad, *Beyond HR: The New Science of Human Capital* (Boston: Harvard Business School Press, 2007).

40. US Department of Labor, Bureau of Labor Statistics, "Employer Costs for Employee Compensation," news release, March 20, 2018, https://www.bls.gov/news.release/ecec.nr0.htm.

6

Employee Health, Wellness, and Welfare

We often think of vital human capital decisions being made by business leaders and their HR colleagues, but some of the most important talent decisions in every organization are those made by employees themselves. Employee decisions that affect their health and wellness have profound effects that are often overlooked. This chapter shows how to capture and evaluate these effects.

In 2009, Steve Burd, CEO of the US supermarket chain Safeway, took eight trips to speak to US politicians about reforming the healthcare system. Safeway's healthcare costs had been rising 10 percent per year for several years before 2004, but since then the company had kept healthcare costs flat, compared to a 40 percent average increase in US companies. How did Safeway do it? The company fully paid for an array of preventative visits and tests, but employees paid in full the next $1,000 in expenses and 20 percent of costs after that, up to a $4,000 maximum. Noting that 75 percent of healthcare costs result from four conditions (cardiovascular disease, cancer, diabetes, and obesity), Safeway had a voluntary program that tests employees for smoking, weight, blood pressure, and cholesterol. Every area they passed resulted in a reduction in their insurance premiums of up to $1,560 per family per year.[1]

How large are the economic effects of healthcare? One study merged physical activity data with healthcare expenditure data for thousands of US adults between 2004 and 2011. The results showed that "overall, 11.1% (95% CI: 7.3, 14.9) of aggregate healthcare expenditures were associated with inadequate physical activity (i.e., inactive and insufficiently active levels)."[2] The US spends more than $3 trillion on healthcare, which suggests that increasing physical activity might save over $300 billion in healthcare costs.

This chapter deals with the economic impacts of employee lifestyle choices on healthcare costs, the return on investment of worksite health promotion programs, and the costs and benefits of employee assistance programs (EAPs). Our objective is not to describe the structure, content, or operational features of such programs, but rather to present methods for estimating their economic impact at the level of the individual firm. To provide some background on this issue, let's begin by considering the relationship of unhealthy lifestyles to healthcare costs. Following that, to provide some perspective on firm-level decisions about healthcare expenditures, we present a logical framework that illustrates how changes in employee health affect financial outcomes.

What Are Health, Wellness, and Worksite Health Promotion?

It is important to note that the concept of health includes more than just the absence of illness. Wellness represents the balance of physical, emotional, social, spiritual, and intellectual health.[3]

The US Centers for Disease Control (CDC) defines workplace health promotion (WHP) as "a coordinated set of programs, policies, benefits, and environmental supports designed to keep all employees healthy and safe. This comprehensive approach addresses multiple risk factors and health conditions at the same time and influences both employees and the overall organization or worksite."[4]

Most WHP interventions focus on educational and skill-building materials and activities. Fewer target organizational practices and policies. Still fewer emphasize both educational/skill-building activities and organizational policies.

Skyrocketing Healthcare Costs Brought Attention to Employee Health

The potential relationships between employee health and organizational productivity are obvious, but the issue is particularly significant in the United States, which is different from many nations because healthcare is largely paid for by corporations and individuals instead of being provided more universally by the government. Even in the United States, organizations did not begin to address the issue of healthcare cost containment seriously until a substantial increase in healthcare costs forced them to look for savings. How large a run-up? From 2012 through 2016, for example, US employers saw premiums for family health coverage increase by 25 percent (to an average of $19,616, of which workers paid $5,547) while workers' earnings increased 14 percent. According to data from the CDC:[5]

» Four of the ten most costly health conditions for US employers—angina pectoris (chest pain), high blood pressure, diabetes, and heart attack—are related to heart disease and stroke.

» Work-related stress is the leading workplace health problem and a major occupational health risk, ranking above physical inactivity and obesity.

» Productivity losses from missed work cost employers $225.8 billion, or $1,685 per employee, each year.

» Full-time workers who are overweight or obese and have other chronic health problems miss about 450 million more days of work each year than healthy workers. The result is an estimated cost of more than $153 billion in lost productivity each year.

» A 1 percent annual reduction in the level of four health risks—weight, blood pressure, glucose, and cholesterol—has been shown to save $83 to $103 annually in medical costs per person.

Rising healthcare costs often translate into less disposable income for employees because wage increases have not kept pace with rising employee healthcare contributions. From 2001 to 2015, the total cost of employer-provided benefits—healthcare, retirement, and postretirement medical—rose from 14.8 percent of pay to 18.3 percent of pay, a jump of 24 percent. Healthcare costs for active employees more than doubled, rising from 5.7 percent to 11.5 percent of pay.[6]

Employers may offset increased healthcare costs by holding down wages.[7] They may also reduce other benefits such as retirement programs. Between 2001 and 2015, retirement benefit costs, which include defined benefit (DB), defined contribution (DC), and postretirement medical plans (PRM), declined by 25 percent, from 9.1 percent to 6.8 percent of pay.[8] Even with such cost shifting, health-related employer costs have risen dramatically. Moreover, no matter who bears the cost, opportunities to reduce such costs can benefit both employers and employees.

One example comes from General Motors in the early 2000s. In analyzing the records of its 1.1 million beneficiaries, GM found that 26 percent were obese under federal guidelines (a body weight that exceeds standard height and weight by 20 percent or more). "Morbid" obesity refers to a body weight more than 100 percent above the norm or more than 100 pounds over the optimal weight.[9] GM also discovered that obese employees cost the company between $1,000 and $3,000 more in health services per year, on average, than beneficiaries who are not obese. That suggests that obesity was costing GM at least $286 million per year.[10] At the level of the individual employee, a longitudinal study of the impact of obesity on worker health and productivity found that obesity was equivalent to adding 20 years of age. Such workers in their mid-20s and 30s had work limitations and cardiovascular risk factors similar to those of normal-weight workers in their 40s and 50s.[11]

As a result of collective bargaining with the United Auto Workers in late 2007, GM changed the way it pays for healthcare among employees and retirees.[12] At the same time, it also is encouraging improved employees' health, such as by installing gymnasiums at manufacturing plants. Installing gymnasiums is supported by some analytical evidence. The World Health Organization reported that workplace physical activity programs in the United States can reduce the use of short-term sick leave by 6 percent to 32 percent, reduce healthcare costs by 20 percent to 55 percent, and increase productivity by 2 percent to 52 percent.[13]

Strategies to Control Healthcare Costs

The CDC lists four key areas to address occupational disease prevention and health promotion, as shown in Figure 6.1.[14]

To control medical costs, organizations can pursue one or both of two broad tactics:

»   Improve workers' health habits, or
»   Reduce employer payments for employee health insurance or healthcare.

Fortune magazine described these five hallmarks of successful corporate wellness programs, based on the research of Laura Linnan, a professor of public health at the University of North Carolina Chapel Hill and head of the CDC-funded Workplace Health Research Network:[15]

1. *Programs Are Practical and Accessible*: Comprehensive wellness initiatives offer a variety of scheduled programs. These might include yoga classes; lunchtime stress management

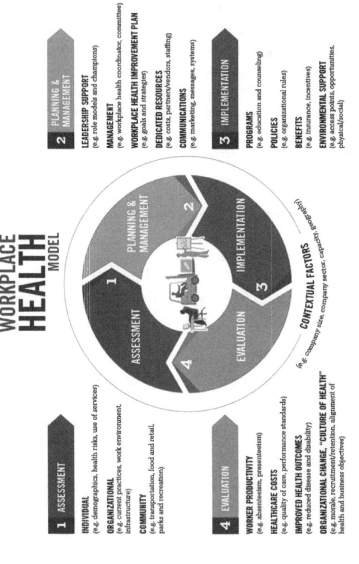

Figure 6.1. Workplace health model.

Source: "Workplace Health Promotion: Using the Workplace to Improve the Nation's Health, at a Glance 2016," US Department of Health and Human Services, Centers for Disease Control and Prevention.

seminars that address everything from sleep to work/life balance to financial health; programs to help employees quit smoking; cooking classes; healthy recipe exchanges; fitness challenges; or weight loss initiatives and competitions.

2. *The Work Environment Is Health-Conscious:* Healthy vending machine and cafeteria offerings often top the list of ways successful wellness programs create workplaces that encourage healthy behaviors on a daily basis. Being mindful of workplace noise, encouraging regular and appropriate breaks, and posting signs informing employees of wellness initiatives are also important ways the corporate environment can foster wellness. Many companies offer in-house workout spaces or marked walking paths on the corporate campus to encourage physical activity. Others institute no-smoking policies or policies requiring seatbelt use in company vehicles.

3. *Wellness Is Integrated into the Company's Structure:* Company leadership needs to see it as a cohesive entity, seamless with workplace safety, benefits, human resources, and other infrastructure elements. "People start to resent when programs are thrown out there, but they're working in hazardous conditions, or their employer is saying they really should lose weight or quit smoking," said Linnan. "They're so stressed, they're smoking because they're stressed." At Draper Inc., full-time safety and wellness director Linda Brinson produces a monthly newsletter featuring "wellness superheroes" who are named by their peers for modeling healthy behaviors in the workplace. "We do things to try to help [employees] create a lifestyle change," she said. "If they make a lifestyle change, that becomes the norm for them."

4. *Wellness Is Linked to Existing Support Programs:* Linkages between a company's wellness program and other company benefits like employee assistance programs (EAPs) are key

to making it easier for employees to get support when they are in a difficult emotional or physical situation that affects both their health and their work. EAPs connect employees to counselors who can advise them confidentially on issues from emotional distress to a difficult medical diagnosis to personal or work relationship issues to life events like marriage or becoming a parent.

5. *Health Screenings and Education Are Offered:* Health screenings are a controversial aspect of the corporate wellness landscape, with some claiming that tracking cholesterol, body mass index, and other figures amounts to de facto discrimination that places a heavier financial burden on workers in less-than-ideal health. In 2014, the US Equal Employment Opportunity Commission filed at least three federal lawsuits against the plastics manufacturing company Flambeau Inc. of Baraboo, WI; Honeywell Corp. of Morristown, NJ; and Orion Energy Systems of Manitowoc, WI, alleging that mandatory medical testing of workers violates the Americans with Disabilities Act. But most companies offer voluntary screenings and often incentivize participation with bonuses like an extra vacation day or a company contribution to a flexible spending account. Researchers recommend these voluntary screenings because they can help educate employees about their own health and empower them to set goals for making improvements; though all employees will receive their screening results from the third-party vendor that typically conducts the tests, high-risk individuals may receive further outreach and counseling to help them set a plan in motion. The data, which companies generally receive in aggregate form without personal identifiers, also helps companies develop programs around the issues that most affect its employees.

The US Office of Health and Human Services, Office of Disease Prevention and Health Promotion offers several examples of the connection between health promotion and economic returns:[16]

1. *Healthy, active employees incur lower health costs.* Companies like Johnson & Johnson saw slower growth in healthcare costs after an employee health promotion program, and "employees saw meaningful reductions in chronic disease risk factors; and average annual savings per employee were $565 (in 2009 dollars), producing a return on investment equal to a range of approximately $2 to $4 saved per dollar spent on the program." In other studies, "total costs were $176 lower for health program participants, and inpatient hospitalization expenses were lower by $182. Over four years, the program produced a return on investment of $1.65 for every dollar spent on the program."

2. *Employees who take advantage of wellness are more productive.* "One study found employees who participated in a health promotion program and improved their healthcare or lifestyle regained an average of 10.3 hours in additional productivity annually and saved their companies an average of $353 per person per year in productivity costs compared to nonparticipants.[17] According to the Centers for Disease Control and Prevention (CDC), productivity losses related to personal and family health problems cost US employers $1,685 per employee per year, or $225.8 billion annually."

3. *Physically active employees are healthier.* "A study found that physical inactivity has become more deadly—and more costly—than smoking.[18] The good news is recent evidence suggests that an hour a day of exercise can help mediate the risks of sedentary lifestyle. Exercise has also been associated with lower risks of multiple chronic diseases and can amplify weight loss efforts."

4. *Wellness programs inspire important behavior changes.* A 2013 research report by the Society for Human Resource Management and Rand Corporation, sponsored by the US Department of Labor, shows that the benefits of employee wellness programs include improvements in physical activity; higher fruit and vegetable consumption; lower fat intake; and a reduction in body weight, cholesterol levels, and blood pressure.[19]

These examples show that wise investments that encourage healthy employee behaviors and reduce employer costs when employees require healthcare can have significant economic effects. Properly designed, investments in such programs can create win-win situations in which both employees and employers benefit. However, not all investments in employee health are appropriate for all companies, and they don't work equally well in all situations or for all employee groups. How can organizations analyze their options and make better choices?

We now turn to the logic that connects investments in employee health and welfare to strategic organizational outcomes.

Logic: How Changes in Employee Health Affect Financial Outcomes

Simply put, the logic of the costs and benefits of employee health and wellness can be traced through the following logical connections:

» Organizations invest in programs that attract, select, develop, or encourage employees to improve their health at the worksite and in their lifestyles.

» Organizations invest in employee assistance programs to address specific employee health issues.

» More and healthier applicants are attracted to the organization and become employees.

» Employees respond by adopting healthier lifestyle behaviors both at and away from work.

» Healthier employees require less treatment for health problems, reducing employer-paid healthcare services or group health insurance premiums.

» Healthier employees are available at work more often because they are absent less (due to both personal health and family health issues), and they separate less frequently.

» Healthier employees perform better at work due to greater physical and mental capacity.

Figure 6.2 shows logical connections between changes in employee health and financial outcomes. The process begins with organizational policies and practices that encourage employees to make healthy lifestyle choices or with assistance with specific issues such as alcoholism or drug abuse. These might include such things as staffing policies, changes in insurance programs, educating employees about health risk factors, health screening, and opportunities to improve personal fitness. It may also extend to such things as serving healthier food in company cafeterias and vending machines and instituting work/life programs to reduce stress levels among employees. We will have more to say about worksite health promotion programs in a later section.

You are probably asking, "Okay, but how much can my company expect to gain from these efforts?" One estimate attributed 15 to 25 percent of corporate healthcare costs to employees' unhealthy lifestyles.[20]

In light of these potential savings, some companies have adopted policies to preempt higher healthcare costs by not hiring those with unhealthy lifestyles in the first place. For example, Rockford Products imposed a $50 per month fee on employees who smoked, were obese, or suffered from hypertension.[21] Weyco Inc., an insurance consulting firm, gave smokers fifteen months to quit—and offered smoking-cessation programs to help them to do so. After

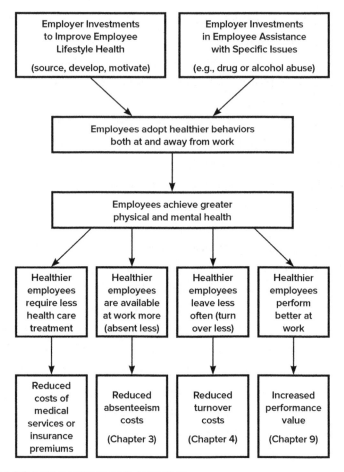

Figure 6.2. Logic of employee health and wellness.

that, it tested employees for evidence of nicotine in their bodies. If they failed the test, they were fired.[22] A study of 251 San Francisco area job hunters between 2013 and 2015, published in the American Medical Association's *JAMA Internal Medicine*, found that after a year 56 percent of nonsmokers found a new job, compared to only 27 percent of smokers. The smokers' hourly income was $5 less than re-employed nonsmokers: $15.10 versus $20.27.[23]

These examples involve creating negative consequences for unhealthy lifestyles, but this should not detract from strategies that *encourage* healthy lifestyles with positive inducements such as onsite gyms, subsidized gym memberships, healthy food choices in company food services, and the like. Continuing with the logic of Figure 6.2, if organizational policies and practices are effective, this should lead to changes in the behavior of employees, and, eventually, in the health of employees. Improved health may be reflected in outcomes such as higher levels of cardiovascular fitness, weight loss, and lower levels of stress. Those changes, in turn, should lead to changes in behaviors, such as reduced absences, accidents, and employee turnover, accompanied by higher levels of employee productivity. Changes in behavior should be reflected eventually in improved financial outcomes: fewer insurance claims; lower overall medical costs; reductions in the costs of employee absence, accidents, and turnover; and higher sales increased value of products and services.

The Typical Logic of Workplace Health Programs

As Figure 6.2 suggests, a useful first step in estimating the savings that accrue from a WHP program is to choose which health-related costs are actually reduced. Some firms establish WHP programs with very specific objectives, such as to reduce the rising costs associated with premature births or to realize cost savings through early cancer detection and treatment. Programs with specific objectives make evaluation more straightforward. Unfortunately, however, the great majority of WHP programs are implemented without such specific objectives.

In a survey of wellness program objectives for selected *Fortune* 500 companies, the top five objectives were the following:

1. To promote better health,
2. To improve cardiovascular fitness,
3. To reduce coronary risk factors,
4. To decrease healthcare costs, and
5. To improve employee relations.[24]

How might one evaluate objectives one and five? Improvements in objectives two and three are important, to be sure, but how do they relate specifically to a firm's healthcare costs? Finally, with respect to objective four, how might one demonstrate the extent to which a reduction in healthcare costs was due to a WHP program and how much to other factors? This is not to diminish the good intentions or employment commitment of firms that instituted wellness programs. However, comparing this list of objectives with the logical approach of Figure 6.2 suggests that setting more specific objectives and carefully analyzing the logical connections can significantly enhance both the effects of such programs and the ability to measure them.

Legal Considerations and Incentives to Modify Lifestyles

At first glance, it might appear that changing employees' unhealthy lifestyles is a win-win for employer and employees. However, some practices would reject applicants with certain lifestyles or even dismiss employees for certain behaviors (for example, smoking, skydiving). If an employer wants to institute such policies, can employees contest them? Federal civil rights laws generally don't protect individuals against such "lifestyle discrimination" because smokers and skydivers aren't named as protected classes. However, more than half of all states prohibit termination for various types of off-duty conduct (for instance, use of tobacco products). US employers also need to beware of violating the Americans with Disabilities Act (ADA). Consider obesity as an example. Obesity per se is generally not considered to be a disability under the ADA.[25] However, in 2009, the US government implemented the Genetic Information Nondiscrimination Act, which restricts employers' and health insurers' ability to collect and disclose genetic information, including family medical history. Some employers say the law stymies wellness promotion efforts by barring them from offering financial incentives to complete health surveys that ask about family history.[26]

Employers must also take care in asking healthcare providers for employee health information, to measure the effects of health programs. The US Department of Health and Human Services says, "Your employer can ask you for a doctor's note or other health information if they need the information for sick leave, workers' compensation, wellness programs, or health insurance. However, if your employer asks your healthcare provider directly for information about you, your provider cannot give your employer the information without your authorization unless other laws require them to do so."[27] When employers pay physicians or other providers to conduct tests to evaluate employees' health, they may make it a condition of employment that the employee authorize releasing the results to the employer.[28]

Regarding bans on hiring smokers, for example, in the United States, there is no federal law that would either prohibit or permit employers to refuse to hire smokers. Instead, state legal frameworks guide these decisions. Increasingly, healthcare and nonhealthcare employers are lawfully prohibiting employees from using tobacco. Contrary to this trend, and for a range of different reasons, approximately half of US states legally protect tobacco users in the employment context.[29]

Analytics for Decisions about WHP Programs

Companies that market services to implement WHP programs provide statistics to support their claims of savings in healthcare costs, but calculating how much any given employer can expect to save is difficult because program sponsors use different methods to measure and report cost-benefit data. When a program's effects are measured and for how long they are measured are crucial considerations. For example, DuPont found that the greatest drop in absenteeism due to illness occurred in the first two or three years; then it leveled off. Other effects, which might not appear for three years or longer, are so-called lagged effects. The greatest savings should accrue over time because of the chronic nature of many illnesses that WHP programs seek to prevent. However, employers should actually expect to see an increase in healthcare claims after initial health assessments are done as employees remedy newly identified problems.[30]

Methodological Considerations in Measuring Health Program Effects

In Chapter 1, "Making HR Measurement Strategic," we noted that analytics relies on rigorous research designs and statistical analyses in order to draw proper conclusions from data. In Chapter 2, "Analytical Foundations of HR Measurement," we emphasized the need to use control groups that did not participate in a treatment (for example, education about healthy lifestyles) in the context of an experimental or quasi-experimental research design to rule out alternative explanations for results.

Unfortunately, many companies use no control groups when evaluating their WHP programs. Without a control group of non-participating employees, there is no way to tell how much of the improved health is due to the WHP program and how much is due to popular trends (for example, the general fitness craze), changes in state or local health policies and regulations, and changes in medical insurance.

The dangers of relying on typical popular accounts of health improvement programs versus studies with control groups was vividly illustrated in data gathered from a large, randomized control-group study of a wellness program at the University of Illinois at Urbana-Champaign.[31] In that data base, more than 1,500 employees were randomly assigned to a control group that received no services, while about 3,300 were invited to receive a biometric health screening and an online health risk assessment. They were then offered a number of wellness activities, including classes on weight loss, exercise, tai chi, smoking cessation, financial wellness, and more. They were even offered financial incentives of various amounts for completing screenings and participating in activities. The researchers followed everyone in both the control and intervention group for a year to see how the program affected their activities, their health, their productivity, and their medical spending.

The study results comparing those offered the program to the control group that was not offered the program suggested no causal effects of the program on health behaviors or medical spending.

Then, as reported in the *New York Times*, the researchers also analyzed the data in the typical way of most popular reports, that is, by looking only at those who were offered the program and comparing those who chose to participate to those that did not participate.[32] This made the results appear more promising. For example, those that didn't use the health program went to the gym 3.8 days per year while those that did participate went 7.4 days per year. However, those in the control group went to the gym 5.9 times per year, and the entire group that was offered the program averaged 5.8 times per year.

When it comes to healthcare spending, comparing those that were offered the program and participated to those that were offered the program and didn't participate, the participants spent significantly less than nonparticipants on healthcare ($525 versus $657) and hospital-related costs ($273 versus $387), which seems promising. However, comparing the control group to the treatment group showed overall spending ($576 versus $568) and hospital spending ($317 versus $297) to be not significantly different.

Other potential methodological problems include biases due to self-selection (those at high risk are less likely to participate) and exclusion from evaluation of employees who drop out of a program. The resulting evaluations have little internal or external validity because they report results only for employees who voluntarily participate in and complete the program.[33]

Researchers also need to address unit-of-analysis issues. Thus, if data are evaluated across worksites at the level of the individual employee, the effect of a WHP program tends to be overstated because the design ignores within-worksite variation. In practice, substantial differences have been found across different worksites receiving the same intervention.[34] Conversely, if the unit of analysis is the plant or worksite, a very large number of sites per intervention is necessary to achieve adequate statistical power to detect effects, if they exist (see Chapter 2 for more on statistical power).

Scholarly Reviews Suggest Health Programs Are Seldom Rigorously Studied and Results Are Mixed

Scholarly reviews of studies evaluating workplace wellness programs reveal patterns in research designs, the prevalence (or lack) of rigorous data, and empirical results of such programs. The overall pattern seems to be that there are very few rigorous studies of health program effects, and the most rigorous studies tend to find mixed effects. Here are a few selected examples:

High-Risk Employees
One review specifically examined studies that recruited high-risk employees to determine what sorts of interventions were used. The study identified 1,131 published studies from 1995 to 2014. Of these, only 27 peer-reviewed articles met the inclusion criteria: reporting data from completed US-based workplace interventions that recruited at-risk employees based on their disease or disease-related risk factors. Selected workplace interventions targeted obesity (n=13), cardiovascular diseases (n=8), and diabetes (n=6). Intervention strategies included instructional education/counseling (n=20), workplace environmental change (n=6), physical activity (n=10), use of technology (n=10), and incentives (n=13). Outcomes were evaluated using self-reported data (n=21), anthropometric measurements (n=17), and laboratory tests (n=14).[35]

Physical Activity

Another review set out to assess the effectiveness of physical activity interventions for improving psychological well-being in working adults. The authors searched English language articles from 2007 to April 2017 in PsycINFO, PubMed, ScienceDirect, Web of Science, Embase, MEDLINE, and the Cochrane library using the following search terms and keywords: "physical activity"; "exercise"; "wellbeing"; "work"; "workplace"; "worksite"; "employees"; and "employee." They found over 33,000 references, but only 5 studies actually measured well-being, included a physical activity intervention, and were conducted at a workplace. Of these, three were randomized controlled trials, one was an experimental design, and one had no control group.[36]

Employee Burnout

Employee burnout refers to a psychological reaction to chronic work stress.[37] The estimated prevalence of severe burnout has ranged from 2 to 13 percent in representative working populations. The resulting cost is mainly due to burnout's association with poor health and work ability. Interventions can be directed at all employees to help prevent burnout from occurring, or they can target those at highest risk. They also can address employees already suffering from burnout to reduce its effects. A review of interventions applied to all employees looked at studies published between 1995 and 2007, finding twenty-five reporting primary interventions, and concluded that 80 percent of programs reduced burnout, with the effects diminishing over time.[38]

Diabetes

A review of interventions to address workplace diabetes found 234 studies published between 2010 and 2016, out of which 22 studies included interventions in the workplace addressing lifestyle changes (exercise, diet, glucose self-monitoring, etc.) and reported outcomes. Of the 22 studies, only 6 involved randomized experimental designs. Five studies used quasi-experimental designs that did not include randomization but did use a control group, and 11 studies focused on a single group with pretest and posttest measurements, generally showing consistent health improvements in biological measures, self-reported behavioral adherence, and psychosocial outcomes.[39]

These reviews were chosen for illustration and are by no means meant to be comprehensive. Still, the patterns they reveal are similar to those from other reviews. There are relatively few studies that actually measure the outcomes of workplace health and welfare programs, and only a handful actually adopt the most rigorous research designs. Evidence of effectiveness is generally encouraging, but mixed. The array of interventions is very large, and the array of outcome measures (biometrics, self-reported behaviors, actual behaviors, workplace outcomes, costs, performance, etc.) is also quite extensive. It is challenging and rare for organizations to study such programs rigorously, but in view of the potential impact, such rigorous research is all the more important.

Measures: Cost-Effectiveness, Cost-Benefit, and Return-on-Investment Analysis

Typically, the evaluation of a WHP program relies on some form of cost-effectiveness, cost-benefit, or return-on-investment (ROI) analysis. We discussed these concepts in Chapter 2, and we apply them here.

Cost-Effectiveness Analysis

Cost-effectiveness (C/E) analysis identifies the cost of producing a unit of effect within a given program. To illustrate, suppose a worksite hypertension-control program incurs an annual cost of $50,000 for a 100-employee population. The average reduction in diastolic blood pressure per treated individual is 8 millimeters of mercury (mm/Hg). The C/E ratio is as follows:

($50,000 / 100) ÷ 8 mm/Hg = $62.50 per mm/Hg reduction per employee

C/E analysis permits comparisons of alternative interventions designed to achieve the same goal. For example, the cost of $62.50 to reduce each mm/Hg achieved by the above program could be compared to alternative programs to reduce diastolic blood pressure that are not offered at the worksite. Unfortunately, from a financial perspective, C/E analysis fails to address the issue of whether the program should have been offered in the first place. Cost-benefit analysis overcomes that problem.

Cost-Benefit and Return-on-Investment Analysis

Cost-benefit (C/B) analysis expresses benefits in monetary terms. One of the most popular forms of C/B analysis, as noted in Chapter 2, is ROI analysis.

Suppose a WHP program costs a firm $250,000 during its first year of operation. The measured savings in that first year are $65,000 from reduced absenteeism, $110,000 from reduced employer healthcare payments (assuming a self-funded plan), and $90,000 from reduced employee turnover. The first-year ROI before interest and taxes would be calculated as shown in Table 6.1.

Table 6.1. ROI of WHP Program

Benefit Type	Benefit Amount
Reduced absenteeism	$65,000
Reduced healthcare payments	$110,000
Reduced employee turnover	$90,000
Total expected benefits	$265,000
ROI = Total expected benefit / Program investment	
ROI = ($265,000–$250,000) / $250,000 = 6%	

The preceding analysis is for a single time period. Data for future time periods (costs and benefits) should be discounted to the present. The numbers provided here are abstract, and firms need to pay careful attention to how they derive them. With respect to absenteeism, for example, savings need to be attributed directly to the WHP program. Employees might take fewer sick days in a given year, and the cost savings from those days not used may be attributed to decreases in employee absenteeism, but how does one know that the savings are due to the WHP program? The same is true for savings attributed to reduced healthcare payments or reduced employee turnover. Measures are blind to the logic and rationale behind the numbers. This is where sound analytics and research design play an important role. To attribute changes in any of the outcomes of interest to a WHP program, a combination of methods may be necessary, such as employee survey data combined with focus groups and structured individual interviews. The research reviews cited earlier can provide good examples of research designs and outcome measurement.

Conclusions Regarding Cost-Effectiveness, Cost-Benefit, and ROI Analyses

Although the logic and techniques of C/E and C/B analysis (including ROI) appear straightforward, there are several unresolved issues, as noted in Chapter 2. Much subjectivity is involved in the choice of variables to include in these models, in attributing savings directly to a WHP program, in estimating the timing and duration of program effects, and in discounting the dollar value of costs and benefits that occur in future time periods. Because of this subjectivity, it is important to conduct sensitivity analyses (to examine the impact of variations in assumptions on C/E and C/B ratios) and break-even analysis (see Chapter 2) to identify the minimum levels of dependent variables (such as early cancer detection or savings in absenteeism) that will allow recovery of investments in the WHP program.

Solving the Analysis and Measurement Dilemmas
to Improve Decisions about WHP Programs

To summarize, these analytical issues can affect decisions about WHP programs:

1. Managers have difficulty identifying the health-related costs that actually decreased.
2. Program sponsors use different methods to measure and report costs and benefits.
3. Program effects may vary depending on when they are measured (immediate versus lagged effects).
4. Program effects may vary depending on how long they are measured.
5. Few studies use control groups.
6. Potential biases exist as a result of self-selection and exclusion of dropouts.
7. Analysis at the level of the individual employee ignores within-site variation. However, analysis at the level of the worksite may produce low statistical power to detect effects.
8. Data on effectiveness are limited in the choice of variables, estimation of the economic value of indirect costs and benefits, estimation of the timing and duration of program effects, and estimation of the present values of future benefits.

A sound experimental design is one that allows cause-and-effect relationships to emerge. The strongest evaluation strategy includes a mix of features that are rarely gathered in actual evaluations but should serve as an ideal toward which organizations should aim. The strategy begins with a determination of the demographics of an organization (age, gender, race, and ethnicity), identification of high-risk employees, expected participation rates, and start-up and maintenance costs required to reach an organization's goals (such as reducing the incidence and costs of undetected cancerous conditions).

The next step is to develop a testing and tracking system to quantify the outcomes of the WHP program for both participants and nonparticipants. Individuals in these two groups should be matched as closely as possible in terms of characteristics such as gender, age, weight category, and lifestyle variables. Pre- and post-comparisons can be made for both groups in terms of behavioral changes, healthcare costs, fitness level, absenteeism, turnover, injury rate and severity, productivity, and job satisfaction. Quantifiable variables (such as healthcare costs and absenteeism) must be analyzed separately by demographic or socioeconomic cohort, for both participants and nonparticipants. Regression, path analysis, or meta-analysis can rule out alternative explanations for observed results. Finally, cost-benefit analyses must include present and future benefits expressed in current dollar values.

Although some studies report favorable C/E or C/B results, it is difficult to evaluate and compare the studies because no uniformly accepted approach currently exists for estimating costs and benefits. Different authors use different assumptions in their estimates of WHP intervention costs and dollar benefits, and small changes in assumptions can have large effects on the interpretation of results. Meta-analyses (that combine research results across studies) and single studies that are based on very large sample sizes can deal with many of these methodological difficulties.[40]

Process—Communicating Effects to Decision-Makers

In communicating the results of WHP programs, it may be helpful to begin by presenting some national-level statistics to serve as benchmarks against which to measure a firm's employees. Here are some examples:

A *chronic condition* is a physical or mental health condition that lasts more than one year and causes functional restrictions or requires ongoing monitoring or treatment. According to a RAND study, 60 percent of Americans had at least one chronic condition in 2014. In addition, about 42 percent had more than one chronic condition and 12 percent had *five or more*. The most prevalent chronic conditions in the US are hypertension (also known as high blood pressure) and high cholesterol. Those with five or more chronic conditions make up 12 percent of the US population but account for 41 percent of total healthcare spending. The annual private insurance healthcare expense for someone with five or more chronic conditions was $18,351, compared to $1,533 for someone with no chronic conditions.[41]

According to the US Centers for Disease Control in 2018:[42]

Eighty-six percent of the US $2.7 trillion annual healthcare expenditures are for people with chronic and mental health conditions.

Nothing kills more Americans than heart disease and stroke. More than 810,000 Americans die of heart disease or stroke every year—that's one-third of all deaths. These diseases take an economic toll, as well, costing our healthcare system $190 billion per year and causing $126 billion in lost productivity on the job.

Each year in the United States, more than 1.7 million people are diagnosed with cancer, and almost 600,000 die from it, making it the second leading cause of death. The cost of cancer care continues to rise and is expected to reach almost $174 billion by 2020. More than twenty-nine million Americans have diabetes, and another eighty-six million adults in the United States have a condition called prediabetes, which puts them at risk for type 2 diabetes. Diabetes can cause heart disease, kidney failure, and blindness, and costs the US healthcare system and employers $245 billion every year.

Obesity affects almost one in five children and one in three adults, putting people at risk for chronic diseases such as diabetes, heart disease, and some cancers. Over a quarter of all Americans 17 to 24 years of age are too heavy to join the military. Obesity costs the US healthcare system $147 billion a year.

Arthritis affects 54.4 million adults in the United States, which is more than one in four adults. It is a leading cause of work disability in the United States, one of the most common chronic conditions, and a common cause of chronic pain. The total cost of arthritis and related conditions was about $304 billion in 2013. Of this amount, nearly $140 billion was for direct medical costs and $164 billion was for indirect costs associated with lost earnings.

Alzheimer's disease, a type of dementia, is an irreversible, progressive brain disease that affects about 5.7 million Americans. It is the sixth leading cause of death among all adults and the fifth leading cause for those aged 65 or older. In 2010, the costs of treating Alzheimer's disease were estimated to be between $159 billion and $215 billion. By 2040, these costs are projected to jump to between $379 billion and $500 billion annually.

In the United States, about three million adults and 470,000 children and teens younger than 18 have active epilepsy— meaning that they have been diagnosed by a doctor, had a recent seizure, or both. Adults with epilepsy report worse mental health, more cognitive impairment, and barriers in social participation compared to adults without epilepsy. The total direct cost of epilepsy in the United States is estimated to be $15.5 billion yearly.

The risk factors most responsible for chronic conditions are these:

Cigarette smoking is the leading cause of preventable death and disease in the United States. More than sixteen million Americans have at least one disease caused by smoking. This amounts to $170 billion in direct medical costs that could be saved every year if we could prevent youth from starting to smoke and help every person who smokes quit.

Not getting enough physical activity comes with high health and financial costs. It can lead to heart disease, type 2 diabetes, some cancers, and obesity. In addition, lack of physical activity costs the nation $117 billion annually for related healthcare.

Excessive alcohol use is responsible for 88,000 deaths in the United States each year, including one in ten deaths among working-age adults. In 2010, excessive alcohol use cost the US economy $249 billion, or $2.05 a drink, and $2 of every $5 of these costs were paid by the public. Binge drinking is responsible for over half the deaths and three-quarters of the costs due to excessive alcohol use.

After you present this sort of general information as background, consider presenting a second, more focused set of information that relates more directly to ROI analyses of WHP programs in your own organization.

ROI Analyses of WHP Programs

Peer-reviewed evaluations and meta-analyses show that ROI is achieved through improved worker health, reduced benefit expense, and enhanced productivity.[43] A review of seventy-two articles concluded that health promotion programs achieve an average ROI of $3.48 per $1 invested when considering healthcare costs alone, $5.82 when considering absenteeism, and $4.30 when both healthcare costs and absenteeism are considered.[44] A one-year study using a pretest and posttest design tracked changes in ten modifiable health risks for 2,458 workers at 121 Colorado businesses that participated in a comprehensive WHP program. Reductions were recorded in ten risk factors examined (reduction for each risk factor presented in parentheses):

1. Poor physical activity (−6.5%),
2. Poor eating habits (−5.8%),
3. High stress (−3.5%),
4. Depression (−2.3%),
5. Obesity (−2.0%),
6. High alcohol consumption (−1.7%),
7. Tobacco use (−1.3%),
8. High total cholesterol (−0.9%),
9. High blood pressure (−0.3%), and
10. High blood glucose (−0.2%).

The ROI model estimated medical and productivity savings of $2.03 for every $1.00 invested. Estimating ROI in cases like this is complex, however, because the ten factors are probably not independent of each other.[45]

Worksite health promotion programs attempt to reduce the health risks of employees at high risk while maintaining the health status of those at low risk. Using an eighteen-year data set composing two million current and former employees, University of Michigan researchers found that increases in costs when groups of employees moved from low risk to high risk were much greater than the decreases in cost when groups moved from high risk to low risk.[46] Programs designed to keep healthy people healthy will likely provide the greatest ROI.

In a study described by the editor of the *American Journal of Health Promotion* as "the most thorough and rigorous systematic review conducted to date," the findings showed that ROI depends on many factors, including the rigor of the study design.[47] According to the editor, their final analysis included 51 studies with 61 intervention arms, 261,901 participants, and 122,242 controls from nine industry types in 12 nations, with studies published between 1984 and 2012. The overall weighted ROI was $2.38 returned for every dollar invested, using the business method common in the United States (ROI = benefits ÷ costs). The 12 studies with randomized controlled trials (RCTs) had mean ROIs of $1.79, whereas the 5 studies with the highest related methodology scores had the lowest ROIs, with a mean weighted value of .78. The 30 studies using quasi-experimental design had a mean weighted ROI of 2.12, whereas those with non-experimental design had a mean weighted ROI of 2.61. The highest mean weighted ROI (3.74) was found in the 25 studies that directly measured claims costs, rather than imputing them based on normal and customary charges or other methods.

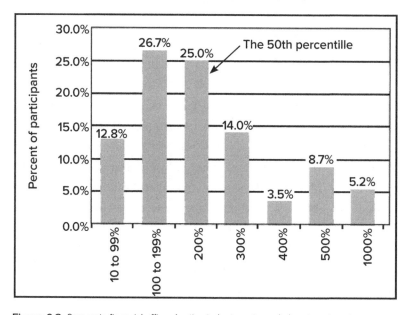

Figure 6.3. Corporate financial officers' estimated returns to workplace investments.

In conclusion, when communicating results to decision-makers in your firm, we suggest that you begin with some broad statistics on healthcare, move on to more focused results that relate to WHP per se, and finish with results from your own firm, based on strong inferences based on a research design such as the one shown in the preceding list. Chief financial officers (CFOs) may be a more receptive audience than one might think. Figure 6.3 shows the perceived percentage returns for each dollar spent improving workplace safety among a sample of 231 corporate financial decision makers. Only 13 percent estimated returns at less than 100 percent, and 68.7 percent estimated returns between 100 percent and 300 percent. These results apply to investments in workplace safety, but they suggest that financial decision-makers may be comfortable with estimated returns that are quite high compared to typical investments.

Improving Employee Welfare at Work: Employee Assistance Programs

Whereas WHP programs focus on prevention, EAPs focus on rehabilitation. An EAP is a system that provides confidential, professional care to employees whose job performance is or may become adversely affected by a variety of personal problems. Supervisors are taught to look for symptoms of declining work performance such as the following and then to refer employees to the EAP for professional help: predictable absenteeism patterns (for example, Mondays, Fridays, or days before or after holidays), unexcused or frequent absences, tardiness, and early departures; arguments with fellow employees; injuries caused to other employees through negligence, poor judgments, and bad decisions; unusual on-the-job accidents; increased spoilage or broken equipment through negligence; involvement with the law; or a deteriorating personal appearance.[48]

The Logic of EAPs

According to the US Office of Personnel Management, "EAPs have a long history in the United States, tracing back to the 1940s. They originally began as occupational alcohol programs to address the negative impact that the misuse of alcohol has on productivity and organizational performance. The focus of these programs expanded as organizations recognized that alcohol was not the only issue affecting employees at work. Current EAPs address a wide range of issues, such as workplace conflicts, family matters, financial challenges, mental health, and so on."[49]

According to the Society for Human Resource Management (SHRM):[50]

» Over 95 percent of companies with more than 5,000 employees have EAPs.

» 80 percent of companies with 1,001 to 5,000 employees have EAPs.

» 75 percent of companies with 251 to 1,000 employees have EAPs.

Modern EAPs are comprehensive management tools that address behavioral risks in the workplace by extending professional counseling and medical services to all "troubled" employees. A troubled employee is an individual who is confronted by unresolved personal or work-related problems. Such problems run the gamut from alcoholism, drug abuse, and high stress to marital, family, and financial problems. Although some of these may originate "outside" the work context, they most certainly will have spillover effects to the work context.

An emerging application of EAPs for critical incident stress response (CISR) is for unexpected, life-threatening, and time-limited events that cause symptoms of post-traumatic stress syndrome. These might include the death of a child, attempted or actual physical assault, break-ins, or a suicide attempt or completed suicide of a patient or prisoner. A 2009 paper by Mark Attridge describes that a CISR program following bank robberies in Australia showed worker absence reduced by 60 percent, and medical benefits and workers' compensation costs reduced by 66 percent. CISR after raids at post office businesses reduced sickness and absence by 50 percent. CISR after traumatic incidents at an Australian prison reduced the costs of assisting stressed employees by 90 percent.[51] Indeed, the economic downturn produced a new sort of "critical incident," the experience of a job loss or impending financial hardship by the employee or a member of the family. Aetna Behavioral Health, part of Aetna Inc., a health insurer, saw a 60 percent increase in EAP members seeking help in the third quarter of 2008 versus the same period in 2007, with financial stress the main source of the increase.[52]

Statistics such as these lead to one inescapable logical conclusion: the personal problems of troubled employees can have substantial negative economic impacts on employers. To help resolve those problems, many employers have adopted employee assistance programs.

Costs and Reported Benefits of EAPs

EAPs are either internal or external. An internal EAP is an in-house service staffed by company employees. An external EAP is a specialty-service provider hired by the employer; it may have multiple locations to make it easy for clients to access. Such arrangements are especially convenient to small employers who do not have the resources to provide internal services. On the other hand, a comparison of the two models found that internal EAPs received 500 percent more referrals from supervisors and 300 percent more employee cases. Perhaps this is because most employees do not seek assistance on their own—they get help only when referred by their supervisors.[53] Costs of the two types of programs were similar: $21.83 per employee per year for internal programs, and $18.09 for external programs.[54]

A large-scale review of the cost-effectiveness of EAPs concluded that "there is no published evidence that EAPs are harmful to corporate economies or to individual employees. All of the published studies indicate that EAPs are cost-effective."[55] By offering assistance to troubled employees, the companies promote positive employee-relations climates, contribute to their employees' well-being, and enhance their ability to function productively at work, at home, and in the community.[56] From a business perspective, well-run programs seem to pay off.

On the other hand, not all programs are equally effective, and anecdotal evidence of the effectiveness of EAPs abounds. Findings do not generalize across studies, however, unless the EAP is implemented in the same way. For example, as noted earlier, in some companies, counselors are available on-site. In other companies, it is possible to access an EAP counselor only through a toll-free telephone number. Evidence indicates that when counselors are available on-site instead of solely through a toll-free number, the programs are more effective.[57] Results of the programs will be more interpretable, to the extent that proper research designs and methods for collecting data are followed. This is the purpose of analytics in the LAMP model, and we consider it further in the next section.

Enhanced Analytical Considerations in EAPs

Actual results may not be quite as rosy as have been reported in the literature or in the media. Evaluation may be ex-ante (estimates computed before implementation of an EAP) or ex-post (measurement of the costs and benefits of actual program operations and impacts after the fact). Evaluation may be expressed in qualitative terms or in quantitative terms.

If evaluation is expressed in quantitative terms—as many operating executives demand—there are two major issues to consider. One is how to establish all program costs and benefits. To establish its costs, an EAP must incorporate an information system that can track factors such as insurance use, absenteeism, performance analysis, accidents, and attendance data. A second issue is how to express and translate the costs and benefits into monetary values. Benefits derived from an EAP may be very difficult to translate into economic terms. In addition, unless proper experimental controls are exercised, cause-effect relations between EAP involvement and one or more dependent variables may be difficult or impossible to identify. As a reminder, these ideas are summarized as follows:

1. Identify all program costs and benefits.
2. Express costs and benefits in economic terms.
3. Demonstrate that implementation of the EAP has caused changes in outcomes of interest.

For example, the International Employee Assistance Professionals Association (EAPA) encourages its members to use a survey called the Workplace Outcomes Suite (WOS) that measures outcomes with these questions to employees:[58]

» **Absenteeism** (looks at the number of hours absent due to a personal problem taking the employee away from work). *"For the period of the past 30 days, please total the number of hours your personal concern caused you to miss work. Include complete eight-hour days and partial days when you came in late or left early."*

» **Presenteeism** (measures decreases in productivity even though the employee is not absent per se but not working at his or her optimum due to unresolved personal problems). *"My personal problems kept me from concentrating on my work."*

» **Workplace Distress** (examines the degree of anxiety or stress at work). *"I dread going in to work."*

» **Work Engagement** (refers to the extent to which the employee is invested in or passionate about his or her job). *"I am often eager to get to the worksite to start the day."*

» **Life Satisfaction** (addresses one's general sense of well-being). *"So far, my life seems to be going very well."*

The 2017 study using this survey reported these results:[59]

Change in Absenteeism: Sample size N = 4,590 EAP cases. Before EAP services, 10.92 hours of work were missed over a 30-day period. At follow-up after EAP services, 5.64 hours of work were missed over a 30-day period. This is a relative improvement of **48%**.

Change in Work Presenteeism: Sample size N = 16,435 EAP cases. Before EAP services, the average rating for level of agreement was 3.29 and at follow-up after EAP services the average rating was 2.42. This is a relative improvement of **26%**.

Change in Work Distress: Sample size N = 16,409 EAP cases. Before EAP services, the average rating for level of agreement was 2.20 and at follow-up after EAP services the average rating was 1.92. This is a relative improvement of **13%**.

Change in Work Engagement: Sample size N = 16,051 EAP cases. Before EAP services, the average rating for level of agreement was 3.21 and at follow-up after EAP services the average rating was 3.42. This is a relative improvement of **7%**.

Change in Life Satisfaction: Sample size N = 16,420 EAP cases. Before EAP services, the average rating for level of agreement was 3.03 and at follow-up after EAP services the average rating was 3.70 This is a relative improvement of **22%**.

A Template for Measuring the Effects of EAPs

In the following sections, we present detailed methods for expressing the returns of EAPs in economic terms for four important outcomes: productivity, employee turnover, unemployment costs, and savings in supervisors' time. These are by no means exhaustive, but they illustrate high-quality analysis elements that are often feasible but overlooked in typical situations.

Productivity
The productivity losses associated with troubled employees can be staggering. Here is one method for determining the productivity cost (ex-ante) attributable to employees who abuse alcohol.[60] To use the method properly, compute the following formula separately for each age-gender cohort. Then sum the costs for all age-gender cohorts.

Equation 1

No. of workers in age-gender cohort in workforce
× Proportion of workers in age-gender cohort with alcohol
  abuse problems
× Annual earnings
× Productivity decrease attributable to alcohol
= Cost of alcohol-related reduced productivity

Two key inputs to this formula might be difficult to acquire:

» The proportion of workers in each age-gender cohort with alcohol abuse problems, and
» The productivity decrease attributable to alcohol.

Over all cohorts, however, national figures suggest that 5 percent to 10 percent of a typical workforce suffers from alcohol abuse,[61] and the figure may be as high as 16 percent across all full-time employees.[62] In well-controlled studies, productivity losses attributable to alcohol abuse have ranged from 14 percent to 21 percent.[63] However, one researcher has estimated that personal problems overall affect 18 percent of the workforce, resulting in an overall productivity loss of 25 percent.[64] It is important to note that the latter figure is an estimate, not a precise number derived on the basis of controlled research. It is used in the calculations shown here simply for illustrative purposes. Keep this in mind in analyzing the example and in applying the formula to actual work situations. For one age-gender cohort in any given workforce, inputs to Equation 1 might be as follows:

100 workers in age-gender cohort in workforce
× 10 percent with alcohol abuse problems
× Annual earnings of $45,000 per worker in cohort
× 20 percent productivity decrease attributable to alcohol
= Cost of alcohol-related reduced productivity of $90,000

At a more general level, the city of Phoenix developed the following formula through its Project Concern to determine the costs due to troubled employees, as well as (ex-ante) the amount of money that could be saved in terms of improved productivity through an EAP:[65]

Equation 2

Compute the average annual wage of employees by dividing the average total number of employees into the annual payroll for employees.

Determine the proportion of the payroll for troubled employees. To do that, multiply the average annual wage by 18 percent of the total number of employees (average percentage of troubled employees identified across many studies).[66]

Determine the present loss in productivity due to troubled employees. To do so, multiply the result of step 2 by 25 percent (average productivity loss across studies).[67]

Identify the potential amount saved per year by an EAP. To do that, multiply the result of step 3 by 50 percent (actual success rate reported by Project Concern).

To illustrate, let us assume that a firm employs 100 workers at an annual payroll cost of $4.5 million, or $45,000 per worker (step 1). To calculate the payroll for troubled employees, let us assume that 18 percent, or 18 workers, are troubled × $45,000 annual earnings/worker = $810,000 (step 2). To determine the present cost of reduced productivity for these troubled workers, multiply $810,000 × 25 percent = $202,500. Finally, to determine the potential amount of money that could be saved per year through an EAP, multiply $202,500 × 50 percent = $101,250.

Note that potential savings in this example reflect only the direct cost of labor (just one component of productivity). To the extent that such savings do not reflect the contribution of improved use of capital and equipment that can be realized by a fully productive employee, they will underestimate the actual level of savings the firm can realize.

Costs of Employee Turnover in EAPs

Turnover savings realized through the implementation of an EAP are "opportunity savings" (see Chapter 2) because they reflect costs that were avoided, but not actually incurred.

In the hypothetical example that follows, let's assume that 10 percent of 2,500 employees (250) can be expected to quit each year. Assume further that of the 250 employees who are expected to quit, 20 percent of them (50 employees) use the firm's EAP. Of those 50, assume that 30 represent production employees, 10 are administrative/technical, and 10 are managerial. Based on the method for calculating the fully loaded cost of turnover that we described in Chapter 5, "The High Cost of Employee Separations" (that is, separation, replacement, and training costs), potential turnover costs may be stated as shown in Table 6.2.

For those employees who use the company's EAP, assume that the actual number who terminate or quit after EAP involvement is as shown in Table 6.3.

Table 6.2. Potential Turnover Costs

	No. of People	No. Using EAP	Individual Cost	Total Cost
Production	150	30	$60,000	$1,800,000
Administrative/ technical	50	10	$82,500	$825,000
Managerial	50	10	$140,000	$1,400,000
Totals	250	50		$4,025,000

Table 6.3. Post-EAP Terminations

	No. of People	Individual Cost	Total Cost
Production	15	$60,000	$900,000
Administrative/ technical	5	$82,500	$412,500
Managerial	5	$140,000	$700,000
Totals	25		$2,012,500

To obtain the overall actual cost to the firm, use the following:

Annual EAP budget $400,000

Terminations/quits $2,012,500

Hospitalization $295,600

Overall actual cost $2,708,100

To compute the ROI, use these numbers:

Potential cost $4,025,000

Minus actual cost $2,708,100

Net benefit = $1,316,900

Compiling this information year after year is particularly useful because numbers can be compared across years and trends can be identified.

Savings in Supervisors' Time in EAPs

If the EAP were not available, supervisors would be forced to deal with employee problems. The hours that supervisors save by not dealing with problems is equal to the total number of hours spent in counseling sessions for the 50 employees who took part in the firm's EAP. Assume that each employee received 20 hours of counseling, on average. Thus, the supervisors had at least 1,000 hours to carry out their duties more effectively. Assuming that the average cost of one hour of supervisory time (wages plus benefits and overhead costs) was $57.50 in 2010 dollars, the economic value of that time was $57.50 × 1,000 = $57,500. Remember, as we cautioned in Chapter 2, the total pay of supervisors does not vary whether they are counseling troubled employees or not. The economic value of their time is simply a proxy, and an imperfect one at that, for the opportunity cost of the lost value that supervisors would have been creating if they had not been using their time to counsel troubled employees.

Future of Lifestyle Modification, WHP, and EAPs

Based on the research reviewed in this chapter, it is clear that workplace health promotion (WHP) programs and EAPs can yield significant payoffs to organizations that adopt them. However, it also is clear that the programs do not work under all circumstances and that the problems associated with assessing relative costs and benefits may be complex. At the very least, we need well-controlled, longitudinal studies to investigate program costs and benefits and the extent to which behavior changes are maintained over time. Moreover, the type and structure of programs should be evaluated for their success and impact on different populations of workers (older/younger; male/female; high, moderate, and low risk; racial or ethnic group), especially in light of the changes in the composition of the workforce that are taking place.[68] We need to understand the factors that affect employee participation or nonparticipation and the factors that promote long-term changes in behavior. If we then build these factors into lifestyle modification, WHP, and EAPs, and if we are successful in attracting troubled or at-risk employees into the programs, the programs will flourish, even in an era of limited resources.

Exercises

Software that calculates answers to one or more of the following exercises can be found at http://iip.shrm.org.

1. Sobriety Inc., a marketer of substance abuse programs, is concerned about the cost of alcohol abuse among its own employees. Based on the following data, what is the productivity cost associated with employees who abuse alcohol? Among all cohorts, the productivity decrease attributable to alcohol abuse is 20 percent.

Age-Gender Cohort	Number	Percentage with Alcohol Abuse	Average Annual Earnings of Cohorts
Males, 25 and under	43	7%	$42,000
Males, 25–44	59	10%	$59,000
Males, 45 and over	38	5%	$74,000
Females, 25 and under	41	5%	$43,000
Females, 25–44	64	10%	$57,000
Females, 45 and over	34	7%	$71,000

2. The following data shows turnover costs for the 4,000 employees of Hulakon Inc., for one year. In any given year, 12 percent of the employees can be expected to quit.

Employee Group	Number of Employees	Individual Cost of Employee Turnover
Production	250	$58,500
Clerical	175	$49,000
Management	55	$84,000

A total of 120 employees participate in the company's EAP (62 production employees, 44 clerical employees, and 14 managers). As a result of that involvement, the following numbers of employees actually quit.

Employee Group	Number of Employees
Production	31
Clerical	22
Management	7

Hospitalization costs are $200,000, or 56 percent of the total amount annually budgeted for the EAP. What is Hulakon's ROI for its employee assistance program for this one year?

3. Your firm is considering establishing an EAP, but it is unsure of which provider to select. Top management has asked you to assess the strengths and weaknesses of possible providers. Make a list of questions to ask each one.

References

1. Kimberley A. Strassel, "Mr. Burd Goes to Washington," *The Wall Street Journal*, June 19, 2009, A13.

2. Susan A. Carlson et al., "Inadequate Physical Activity and Health Care Expenditures in the United States," *Progress in Cardiovascular Diseases* 57, no. 4 (January–February 2015): 315–23.

3. Michael P. O'Donnell, "Definition of Health Promotion: Part III: Expanding the Definition," *American Journal of Health Promotion* 3, no. 3 (December 1988): 5.

4. "Workplace Health Model," US Department of Health and Human Services, Centers for Disease Control and Prevention, last updated May 13, 2016, https://www.cdc.gov/workplacehealthpromotion/model/index.html.

5. "Workplace Health Promotion: Using the Workplace to Improve the Nation's Health, at a Glance 2016," US Department of Health and Human Services, Centers for Disease Control and Prevention, last reviewed February 2, 2017, https://www.cdc.gov/chronicdisease/resources/publications/aag/workplace-health.htm.

6. Willis Towers Watson, "Employers' Cost to Provide Employee Benefits Has Risen 24% Since 2001, Willis Towers Watson Analysis Finds," news release, July 18, 2017, https://www.willistowerswatson.com/en-US/press/2017/07/employers-cost-to-provide-employee-benefits-has-risen-24-percent-since-2001.

7. Wayne F. Cascio, "The Costs—and Benefits—of Human Resources," in Vol. 22, *International Review of Industrial and Organizational Psychology*, ed. Gerard P. Hodgkinson and J. Kevin Ford (Chichester, UK; New York: John Wiley & Sons, 2007), 71–110.

8. Brendan McFarland and Steve Nyce, "Shifts in Benefit Allocations among US Employers," *Willis Towers Watson Insider*, July 14, 2017, https://www.towerswatson.com/en-us/Insights/Newsletters/Americas/insider/2017/07/shifts-in-benefit-allocations-among-us-employers.

9. P. A. Janus, "Weight Discrimination and the Law," 2002, http://www.lexis-nexis.com.

10. Lee Hawkins, Jr. "As GM Battles Surging Costs, Workers' Health Becomes an Issue," *The Wall Street Journal*, April 7, 2005, A1.

11. Robin Hertz et al., "The Impact of Obesity on Work Limitations and Cardiovascular Risk Factors in the US Workforce," *Journal of Occupational and Environmental Medicine* 46, no. 12 (December 2004): 1196–203.

12. "2007 GM-UAW Labor Agreement," The Automotive Lyceum, accessed November 8, 2007, http://www.christonium.com/automotive/ItemID=1193346768436.

13. "Economic Benefits of Physical Activity," World Health Organization, 2003, http://www.who.int/hpr/physactiv/economic-benefits.shtml.

14. "Workplace Health Promotion," US Department of Health and Human Services, Centers for Disease Control and Prevention.

15. Holly Liebowitz Rossi, "Five Hallmarks of Successful Corporate Wellness Programs," *Fortune*, April 13, 2015, http://fortune.com/2015/04/13 /corporate-wellness/.

16. Alexandra Black, "Five Reasons Employee Wellness Is Worth the Investment," US Department of Health and Human Services, Office of Disease Prevention and Health Promotion, May 17, 2017, https://health .gov/news/blog-bayw/2017/05/five-reasons-employee-wellness-is-worth -the-investment/.

17. Rebecca J. Mitchell, Ronald J. Ozminkowski, and Seth Serxner, "Improving Employee Productivity Through Improved Health," *Journal of Occupational and Environmental Medicine* 55, no. 10 (October 2013): 1142–48.

18. I-Min Lee et al., "Effect of Physical Inactivity on Major Non-Communicable Diseases Worldwide: An Analysis of Burden of Disease and Life Expectancy," *The Lancet* 380, no. 9838 (July 21, 2012): 219–29.

19. Soren Mattke et al., *Workplace Wellness Programs Study* (Santa Monica, CA: RAND Corporation, 2013).

20. Carolyn Hirschman, "Off Duty, Out of Work," *HR Magazine*, February 2003, 50–56.

21. Timothy Aeppel, "Ill Will: Skyrocketing Health Costs Start to Pit Worker vs. Worker," *The Wall Street Journal*, June 17, 2003, A1.

22. Morley Safer, "Whose Life Is It Anyway? Are Employers' Lifestyle Policies Discriminatory?," *60 Minutes*, CBS Broadcasting, October 30, 2005, http:// www.cbsnews.com/stories/2005/10/28/60 minutes/main990617.shtml.

23. Judith J. Prochaska, Anne K. Michalek, and Catherine Brown-Johnson, "Likelihood of Unemployed Smokers Attaining Reemployment in a One-Year Observational Study," *JAMA Internal Medicine* 176, no. 5 (May 2016): 662–70.

24. "Planning Wellness: Getting off to a Good Start," *Absolute Advantage* 5, no. 6 (2006), http://www.welcoa.org.

25. Wayne F. Cascio, "Weight-Based Discrimination in Employment: Legal and Psychological Considerations," paper presented at the annual conference of the Society for Industrial and Organizational Psychology, Dallas, TX, May 2006.

26. Cari Tuna, "Wellness Efforts Face Hurdle," *The Wall Street Journal*, February 1, 2010.

27. "Employers and Health Information in the Workplace," US Department of Health and Human Services, https://www.hhs.gov/hipaa/for-individuals /employers-health-information-workplace/index.html.

28. Kim C. Stanger, Patricia Dean, and William W. Mercer, "HIPAA: Disclosing Exam Results to Employers," *The National Law Review*, September 22, 2015, https://www.natlawreview.com/article/hipaa-disclosing-exam -results-to-employers.

29. Rishi R. Patel and Harald Schmidt, "Should Employers Be Permitted Not to Hire Smokers? A Review of US Legal Provisions," *International Journal of Health Policy Management* 6, no. 12 (December 2017): 701–6.
30. Cascio, "The Costs—and Benefits—of Human Resources."
31. Damon Jones, David Molitor, and Julian Reif (2018). "What Do Workplace Wellness Programs Do? Evidence from the Illinois Workplace Wellness Study" (National Bureau of Economic Research Working Paper #24229, January 2018), https://www.nber.org/papers/w24229.
32. Aaron E. Carroll, "Workplace Wellness Programs Don't Work Well. Why Some Studies Show Otherwise," *The New York Times*, August 6, 2018.
33. Russell E. Glasgow et al., "Take Heart: Results from the Initial Phase of a Worksite Wellness Program," *American Journal of Public Health* 85, no. 2 (February 1995): 209–16. See also Robert W Jeffery et al., "The Healthy Worker Project: A Worksite Intervention for Weight Control and Smoking Cessation," *American Journal of Public Health* 83, no. 3 (March 1993): 395–501.
34. See note 33 above.
35. Lu Meng et al., "Strategies for Worksite Health Interventions to Employees with Elevated Risk of Chronic Diseases," *Safety and Health at Work* 8, no. 2 (June 2017): 117–29.
36. Shanara Abdin et al., "The Effectiveness of Physical Activity Interventions in Improving Well-Being Across Office-Based Workplace Settings: A Systematic Review," *Public Health* 160 (July 2018): 70–76.
37. Christina Maslach, William B. Schaufeli, and Michael P. Leiter, "Job Burnout," *Annual Review of Psychology* 52 (February 2001): 397–422.
38. Wendy L. Awa, Martina Plaumann, and Ulla Walter, "Burnout Prevention: A Review of Intervention Programs," *Patient Education and Counseling* 78, no. 2 (February 2010): 184–90.
39. Sharon A. Brown et al., "Effectiveness of Workplace Diabetes Prevention Programs: A Systematic Review of the Evidence," *Patient Education and Counseling* 101, no. 6 (June 2018): 1036–50.
40. Frank L. Schmidt and Nambury S. Raju, "Updating Meta-Analytic Research Findings: Bayesian Approaches Versus the Medical Model," *Journal of Applied Psychology* 92, no. 2 (March 2007): 297–308. See also John H. Hunter and Frank L. Schmidt, *Methods of Meta-Analysis: Correcting Error and Bias in Research Findings*, 2nd ed. (Thousand Oaks, CA: Sage, 2004).
41. Christine Buttorff, Teague Ruder, and Melissa Bauman, *Multiple Chronic Conditions in the United States* (Santa Monica, CA: RAND Corporation, 2017), http://www.fightchronicdisease.org/sites/default/files/TL221_final.pdf.
42. "Health and Economic Costs of Chronic Diseases," US Department of Health and Human Services, National Center for Chronic Disease Prevention and Health Promotion (NCCDPHP), https://www.cdc.gov/chronicdisease/about/costs/index.htm.

43. Julie Britt, "Expert: Disease Management Programs Cut Health Care Costs," *SHRM Online*, May 27, 2004.

44. Steven G. Aldana, "Financial Impact of Health Promotion Programs: A Comprehensive Review of the Literature," *American Journal of Health Promotion* 15, no. 5 (May 2001): 296–320.

45. Ron Z. Goetzel et al., "Estimating the Return on Investment From a Health Risk Management Program Offered to Small Colorado-Based Employers," *Journal of Occupational and Environmental Medicine* 56, no. 5 (May 2014): 554–60.

46. Dee W. Edington, "Emerging Research: A View from One Research Center," *American Journal of Health Promotion* 15, no. 5 (May/June 2001): 341–49.

47. Michael P. O'Donnell, "What is the ROI for Workplace Health Promotion? It Really Does Depend, and That's the Point," *American Journal of Health Promotion* 29, no. 3 (January/February 2015): v-vii. See also Siyan Baxter, Kristy Sanderson, and Alison J. Venn, "The Relationship between Return on Investment and Quality of Study Methodology in Workplace Health Promotion Programs," *American Journal of Health Promotion* 28, no. 6 (July 2014): 347–363.

48. Nancy R. Lockwood, *Employee Assistance Programs: An HR Tool to Address Top Issues in Today's Workplace*, SHRM Briefly Stated Series (Alexandria, VA: SHRM, 2005).

49. "Employee Assistance Programs," US Office of Personnel Management, https://www.opm.gov/policy-data-oversight/worklife/employee-assistance-programs/.

50. Arlene S. Hirsch, "Taking a Fresh Look at EAP Counseling," SHRM, October 12, 2016, https://www.shrm.org/resourcesandtools/hr-topics/employee-relations/pages/taking-a-fresh-look-at-eap-counseling.aspx.

51. Mark Attridge, "The Business Case for Workplace Critical Incident Stress Response: A Literature Review of Clinical and Cost-Effectiveness Research," Crisis Care Network, June 30, 2009, http://www.crisiscare.com/news/news_wp_attridge.pdf.

52. Conrad Deaenille, "A Corporate Perk for a Stressful Time," *The New York Times*, January 18, 2009.

53. Shelly Prochaska, *Employee Assistance Programs: What Does HR Need to Know?*, SHRM White Paper (Alexandria, VA: SHRM, May 2003).

54. "Employee Assistance Programs: Fact Sheet," US Department of Health and Human Services, 2006, http://workplace.samhsa.gov/WPResearch/EAP/FactsEAPfinal.html.

55. Terry C. Blum and Paul M. Roman, *Cost-Effectiveness and Preventive Implications of Employee Assistance Programs* (Washington, DC: US Department of Health and Human Services, 1995).

56. Dianna L. Stone and Debra A. Kotch, "Individuals' Attitudes Toward Organizational Drug Testing Policies and Practices," *Journal of Applied Psychology* 74, no. 3 (June 1989): 518–21.

57. Kenneth R. Collins, *Identifying and Treating Employee Substance Abuse Problems*, SHRM White Paper (Alexandria, VA: SHRM, January 2003).

58. The International Employee Assistance Professionals Association (EAPA) encourages its members to use a survey called the Workplace Outcomes Suite (WOS), http://www.eapassn.org/WOS.

59. Chestnut Global Partners LLC, *Workplace Outcome Suite (WOS) Annual Report 2017: Comparing Improvement After EAP Counseling for Different Outcomes and Clinical Context Factors in Over 16,000 EAP Cases Worldwide*, http://www.eapassn.org/2017WOSReport.

60. David L. Parker et al., "The Social and Economic Costs of Alcohol Abuse in Minnesota, 1983," *American Journal of Public Health* 77, no. 8 (August 1987): 982–86.

61. Lockwood, *Employee Assistance Programs.*

62. National Institute of Alcohol Abuse and Alcoholism, 2006, http://www.niaaa.nih.gov.

63. Parker et al., "The Social and Economic Costs."

64. Dale A. Masi, *Designing Employee Assistance Programs* (New York: American Management Association, 1984).

65. W. G. Wagner, "Assisting Employees with Personal Problems," *Personnel Administrator Reprint Collection Series, Employee Assistance Programs* (Alexandria, VA: American Society for Personnel Administration, 1984).

66. Masi, *Designing Employee Assistance Programs.*

67. Masi, *Designing Employee Assistance Programs.*

68. Edward E. Lawler and James O'Toole, *The New American Workplace* (New York: Palgrave Macmillan, 2006).

7

Employee Attitudes
and Engagement

Every year, a host of organizations publish their lists of best companies to work for. While new players such as GlassDoor, the online job review site, as well as entities like *Working Mother Magazine* and many, many others publish annual "best" lists, the best known and most influential is conducted by *Fortune* magazine. Firms strive to be named to these lists because they receive twice as many applications as firms that are not on the list, and they enjoy employee turnover levels that are less than half those of their competitors.[1] In an environment of fierce competition for talent, high rankings on these lists create a competitive talent advantage. People want to work at places where they are treated well. If engaged employees really do fuel corporate profits, one would expect "100-Best" employers to outperform broad indexes of firms that are publicly traded—and they do.[2]

In one well-controlled study, for example, researchers compared the organizational performance of *Fortune*'s "100 Best Companies to Work For" with two sets of other companies, a matched group and the broad market of publicly traded firms, over a six-year period.[3] They found that organization-level employee attitudes of the "100-Best" firms were both highly positive and stable over time. They also found that the return on assets and market-to-book value of the equity of publicly traded companies included on the "100-Best" list were generally better than those of a matched comparison group.

That finding established an important link between employee attitudes and organization-level financial performance. As for stock returns, the same study found that the "100-Best" companies outperformed the broad market when considering cumulative (longer-term) returns. The authors concluded: "At the very least, our study finds no evidence that positive employee relations comes at the expense of financial performance. Firms can have both."[4] Similar results have been found for the impact of other measures of engagement on financial performance.[5] The accounting and finance literature also reflects this finding, thus making it an unusually robust phenomenon.[6]

Of course, finding a correlation between financial performance and employee attitudes does not necessarily mean that enhancing employee attitudes *caused* the superior financial performance of the organizations in the study. Chapter 2, "Analytical Foundations of HR Measurement," showed that correlation is not the same as causation. For example, people like to work for companies that are financially successful. It is just as plausible that when companies become financially successful, their employees display positive attitudes. This is, in fact, the case for people whose jobs are a "central life interest."[7] For an investor, the link between employee attitudes and financial performance of the firm is a valuable signal, and the direction of causality is irrelevant. From a manager's perspective, however, "what causes what" is extremely important because it affects decisions about talent, including where to focus the organization's limited resources to maximize the desired outcomes.

Given the positive financial results cited earlier for "100-Best" companies, it is perhaps not very surprising that measuring attitudes such as satisfaction, engagement, and commitment has become big business. There are many consulting products and internal organizational processes to define and track employee attitudes and to relate those attitudes to a variety of operational and financial results. Indeed, the very first foray into "HR analytics" for many organizations is to produce a report describing the association between scores on an employee attitude survey and business outcomes.

Yet, the working models of most business leaders are often no more sophisticated than a belief that "happy employees are productive employees" or that "becoming a great place to work will create superior financial results." Of course, a valuable logic and measurement system would do better, by articulating the connections between attitudes and organizational outcomes and directing measures to the areas that best articulate those connections.

Measures like employee surveys are only valuable if they lead to actions or decisions that improve organizational effectiveness and promote long-term, relevant change.[8] This chapter presents key concepts that HR and business leaders can use to collect and interpret relevant measures to make better decisions about programs to improve employee attitudes, and even to make better strategic decisions about where not to invest. Such systems can certainly identify where attitude-assessment or employee-engagement programs are most valuable, but our purpose is not simply to provide tools to justify such investments but rather to enhance decisions based on employee attitudes.

Logic: Defining Employee Attitudes and Their Effects

Researchers define "attitudes" as internal states that are focused on particular features or objects in the environment. Attitudes include three elements: the knowledge or "cognition" that an individual has about the object or employment feature; the emotion an individual feels toward the object or feature; and the action tendency, or readiness to respond to the object or feature.

One reason that it is important to have a clear and logical framework for understanding how attitudes connect to organizational success is that attitudes are often multidimensional. In their simplest form, for example, employee attitudes might be summarized as, "do you like your job?" However, effective strategic decision-making requires more sophistication, because different kinds of attitudes (such as commitment versus satisfaction versus engagement), or about different employment features (such as coworkers versus pay) may have very different implications. In a later section on connecting attitudes to outcomes, we will describe the impact of these distinctions. It is worth noting that the term "employee attitudes" covers a wide range of topics. Most notably, in recent years, the concept of an employee value proposition has become popular.[9] An employee value proposition is generally defined as the relationship between what the organization offers in terms of rewards and experiences, in exchange for the talents and effort brought by the employee. The core attributes captured in an employee value proposition, things like working conditions, manager quality, and rewards, reflect the classic attributes of job satisfaction, organizational commitment, and employee engagement. Thus, we will focus our attention on these core aspects of employee experience.

Distinctions between Satisfaction, Commitment, and Engagement

Satisfaction describes satiation—feelings of contentment.

Engagement describes activation—feelings of energy, enthusiasm, and a positive affective state.[10]

Commitment describes a bond or linking—feelings that make it difficult or easy to leave.[11] It is the emotional engagement that people feel toward their employer.[12] Commitment can be to the job or the organization and can be to contribute, to stay, or both.

Satisfaction and engagement are conceptually distinct, but highly correlated.[13] Commitment is closely related to engagement.[14] Engagement is a positive, fulfilling, work-related state of mind that is characterized by vigor, dedication, and absorption.[15] Vigor refers to high levels of energy and mental resilience while working, the willingness to invest effort in one's work, and persistence even in the face of difficulties. Dedication is characterized by a sense of significance, enthusiasm, inspiration, pride, and challenge at work. Absorption consists of being fully concentrated, happy, and deeply engrossed on one's work whereby time passes quickly, and one has difficulty detaching oneself from work.[16] Engagement fuels discretionary efforts and concern for quality. It is what prompts employees to identify with the success of their companies, to recommend them to others as good places to work, and to follow through to make sure problems get identified and solved.

These three core employee attitudes are strongly related to workplace effectiveness.[17] In a key study, workplace effectiveness included six dimensions: job challenge and learning, autonomy, supervisor task support, climate of respect and trust, work/life fit, and economic security. Each employee attitude type (satisfaction, commitment, and engagement) related somewhat differently to the six criteria, as shown in Table 7.1. This shows why it may be useful to separately measure the three dimensions of employee experience. For example, the top drivers of engagement were job challenge and learning as well as a climate of respect, but the top drivers for

Table 7.1. Effective Workplace Dimensions That Significantly Predicted Work Outcomes, Rank-Ordered by Relative Importance

Greater Engagement	Greater Job Satisfaction	Greater Probability of Retention
1. Job challenge and learning	1. Economic security	1. Economic security
2. Climate of respect	2. Work-life fit	2. Work-life fit
3. Autonomy	3. Climate of respect	3. Job challenge and learning
4. Work-life fit	4. Autonomy	4. Supervisor task support
5. Economic security	5. Supervisor task support	5. Autonomy
6. Supervisor task support	6. Job challenge and learning	

Source: Aumann, K., & Galinsky, E. (2009). Families and Work Institute, 2008 National Study of the Changing Workforce. *The State of Health in the American Workforce: Does Having an Effective Workplace Matter?* Table 13, p. 29. New York, NY: Author.

satisfaction and retention were economic security and work/life fit. The impact of job challenge and learning is particularly interesting; it is the top factor for engagement, but the bottom factor for satisfaction, and solidly in the middle for retention.

Effects of Satisfaction, Commitment, and Engagement

At a general level, employee satisfaction, commitment, and engagement affect organizational performance through employee behaviors. Employees with lower attitudes may be absent, late for work, or quit more often, engage in riskier or less-helpful behaviors, or place less emphasis on customer satisfaction. Figure 7.1 summarizes these evidence-based findings.[18]

Figure 7.1. Logical framework tying workplace attributes to organizational outcomes.

Figure 7.1 shows that enhancing employee attitudes can affect a firm's financial performance. Changing employee attitudes can have direct effects on employee turnover and absence, with the associated effects on the costs of absence and turnover (see Chapters 4 and 5). Having a reputation as a satisfying place to work may enhance the ability to recruit more or higher-quality applicants (see Chapters 9 and 10). In addition, there is some evidence that employee attitudes directly affect employee performance, in particular, the tendency for employees to do tasks that are beyond their formal job description (often called "citizenship behaviors"), and to convey positive emotions to customers. These latter connections show up in productivity or service costs and in sales and revenue.

Measures and Analytics: Quantifying Employee Attitudes and Their Effects

global vs. Facet

Decades of research and practice have produced many valid and useful measures of employee attitudes.[19] Many consulting firms have their own proprietary indices, and industry consortia such as the Mayflower Group share standardized items. The three core attitudes—satisfaction, commitment, and engagement—are multidimensional, so measures typically use multiple questions to assess the entire domain.

You can measure job satisfaction as a "global" attitude toward one's whole job by asking, for example, "Overall, how much enjoyment do you find in your work?," or, more simply "Overall, do you like your job?" While such global questions may give a good sense for the level of satisfaction, they are less helpful in diagnosing the root causes of low satisfaction, and don't offer insight into the mechanisms by which satisfaction relates to important outcomes. Thus, single-item measures can be a helpful, if lightweight, means to identify problem areas and stimulate deeper investigation. A better practice is to measure satisfaction with several questions, each one focused on satisfaction with a single employment feature, such as pay, colleagues, career opportunities, or supervision, and add them up to produce the global satisfaction score. If the purpose is to understand or predict the outcomes of global satisfaction, then global ratings are appropriate. If the purpose is to understand or predict the outcomes of job satisfaction with a particular employment feature, the facet approach is more useful.[20]

Organizational commitment is also multidimensional, with three distinct sub-components: affective, continuance, and normative. Affective commitment refers to how much an employee is emotionally attached to an organization and how much they desire to stay. Continuance commitment refers to how much an employee believes that leaving would be costly or unpleasant. Normative commitment refers to how much an employee feels that staying with the current organization is ethically or morally the right thing to do.[21] There are valid and useful measures of each component of commitment. For example, here is an item from the Organizational Commitment Questionnaire that measures affective commitment: "It would take a lot to get me to leave this organization."[22]

Employee engagement is a positive, fulfilling, work-related state of mind characterized by vigor, dedication, and absorption. Two well-known measures of engagement are the Gallup Organization's Q12 and the Utrecht Work Engagement Scale 9. The Q12 assesses employee perceptions of twelve work characteristics and work-related management practices. Employees respond on a 1–5 Likert-type scale, where "5" is *extremely satisfied*, and "1" is *extremely dissatisfied*. Consider three sample items:[23]

» Do I know what is expected of me at work?
» Does the mission/purpose of my company make me feel my job is important?
» In the last six months, has someone at work talked to me about my progress?

Each item contributes to engagement, and the sum of the items measures engagement as the aggregation of its causes. Each item is designed to suggest actions that relate to important business outcomes, as we will describe in a later section.[24]

The Utrecht Work Engagement Scale 9 (UWES-9) is a nine-item measure of vigor, dedication, and absorption.[25] The three factors are highly correlated, so it is appropriate to use the total score from the UWES-9 as a global measure of engagement. For each item, employees indicate how often they feel this way about their jobs, from *never* (0) to *always* (6). Here are the nine items:

1. At my work, I feel bursting with energy.
2. At my job, I feel strong and vigorous.
3. When I get up in the morning, I feel like going to work.
4. I find the work that I do full of meaning and purpose.
5. I am enthusiastic about my job.
6. My job inspires me.
7. Time flies when I am working.
8. When I am working I forget everything else around me.
9. I feel happy when I am working intensely.

When and How to Measure

The traditional approach to attitude measurement is to conduct a survey of all employees on a one- or two-year cycle. However, the increasing pace of change in organizations has motivated new approaches. Traditional all-employee surveys are major events and consume substantial organizational time and energy. The newer approaches use "pulse" surveys and more passive approaches to employee sensing such as monitoring work performance, email and instant message content, or techniques such as organizational network analysis discussed in Chapter 2. These pulsing and passive approaches are creating their own new controversies, such as concerns over privacy, survey fatigue, and inadequate time or attention to meaningful action.[26]

Pulse surveys, which may take several forms, are designed to reduce the survey time and effort. They might present shorter sets of items or even just one question. They might survey only carefully selected small samples or workgroups rather than all employees. The goal is to optimize the investment by balancing traditional comprehensiveness with greater immediacy and lower cost. Some organizations pursue both strategies: retaining their comprehensive employee surveys for in-depth analytical and organizational-change purposes, and supplementing those with lightweight pulses to identify trends or changes before crises emerge. In the modern work context, workers are potentially generating data constantly. For example, customer-service agents are monitored for how quickly they are able to resolve customer issues, and nearly anyone working a cash register or checkout counter can be measured for speed and accuracy. Delivery and installation drivers can be measured on time to complete and whether their trucks are on the recommended routes between customers. Office workers may generate large volumes of email or instant messages. All of these data are generated in the normal course of executing work tasks, but also present tempting opportunities to measure engagement. However, consider a few cautions before adding passive measures to your employee-engagement measurement strategy. These newer approaches not only create risks around employee privacy, the activities may not be meaningful as measures of engagement, satisfaction, or commitment. Instead, they may be useful as outcome measures.

Before adopting any particular measurement approach, it is important to identify the logical relationships you wish to examine. The descriptions in this section can help you make better choices. Broad, global measures of satisfaction or commitment may be appropriate for examining general employee attitudes, but it may often be appropriate to choose measures that focus on particular work facets that more clearly distinguish the elements of satisfaction, commitment, or engagement. Too often, organizations adopt the most popular or well-known measure without realizing that decades of research have produced many alternatives. Further, it is important to remember that surveys themselves are an intervention. The act of asking a question signals that this is something management considers important and creates an expectation that answers to the questions will result in some sort of change.

Time Lags

The increasing popularity of pulse surveys creates more opportunities to examine variables over time because the survey results are available more frequently, rather than just one snapshot every one or two years. Unfortunately, researchers have not reached a consensus about the most appropriate time lag for collecting survey information either on the same variable at two different times or to assess the relationship between variables (for example, aggregated employee attitudes and organizational performance).

Some pulsing strategies address this by covering an enormous number of items spread across different survey respondents. Each individual is asked only a few of the questions, but different individuals get different questions so that the full array of questions is answered across all individuals. However, for this strategy to be effective, the variables measured and relationships examined must be relatively stable. If they are stable, then carefully designed pulsing strategies can help illuminate patterns across time that might not have been detectable using more conventional strategies.

Different time lags can produce different results.[27] In one study, researchers analyzed employee attitudes from thirty-five companies over eight years and related organizational-level attitudes to financial (return on assets) and market performance (earnings per share). They found consistent and significant positive relationships between aggregated satisfaction with security, pay, and overall job satisfaction (OJS) and financial and market performance.

The researchers examined one-year, two-year, three-year, and four-year lags. They found remarkable stability in employee attitudes aggregated at the organizational level. The correlations between attitudes and organizational outcomes with one-year lags ranged from a low of .66 (satisfaction with work group) to a high of .89 (satisfaction with security). You might expect these correlations to be lower with four-year lags because so many factors can intervene in four years, but in fact, the results revealed substantial similarity, with the four-year lag relationships ranging from a low of

.40 (satisfaction with work facilitation) to a high of .78 (satisfaction with empowerment).

If possible, it is wise to collect data on attitudes and organizational outcomes at multiple times and choose the time-lag that yields the most stable and representative relationships. It is also important to consider the logical connections and strategic decision factors in choosing time lags. In organizations with stable and long-term employment relationships, the correlation between attitudes and financial outcomes spanning several years may be quite relevant and valuable because such organizations reap the rewards of attitude change over many years. In organizations with less stable or more short-term employment relationships, the most useful relationships may be the effect of attitudes on outcomes that occur much sooner.

Levels of Analysis

Organizations that conduct employee surveys frequently overlook an important issue—levels of analysis. Employee attitudes and their effects occur at the individual, team, and organizational levels.[28] So, the level of analysis assumed by the researcher must be consistent with the level of analysis in the measures.[29] For research about attitudes and effects at the individual unit of analysis, items should be framed with an individual perspective (e.g., "My manager supports me"). However, if the objective is to understand relationships at the level of the team, then items should be framed at the team level (e.g., "In my team, our manager supports us"). Finally, if the objective is to understand relationships in a specific business unit (region, store, location, function, etc.), then questions should be framed with that reference (e.g., "Senior leaders at my site support employees"). The same focus, such as "manager support," can generate substantially different results at different levels of analysis, and mixing levels can contribute substantial risk of error in analyses.

It is often best to examine outcomes at multiple levels of analysis. Examining a specific level of analysis can also help guide appropriate action, and diagnosing the specific level of analysis at which an issue is more significant can help guide effective action and reduce waste.

For example, a meta-analysis of 8,000 business units in 36 companies showed a consistent, reliable relationship between twelve employee engagement items and unit-level outcomes such as profits, productivity, employee retention, and customer loyalty. [30] At the level of the work group, groups that had higher levels of employee engagement ere 50 percent more likely to achieve above-average customer loyalty and 44 percent more likely to have above-average profitability. At the level of the business unit (division or plant), those in the top quartile on employee engagement had higher monthly revenues than those in the bottom quartile. There was significant variation among work groups and operating units within single companies, suggesting that even when a company does well overall, there may be significant opportunities to improve individual business units.

In a 2009 study of fifty multinational companies by the London office of Willis Towers Watson, those with high levels of employee engagement outperformed those with low levels on three important financial indicators: twelve-month change in operating income (+19.2% versus −32.7%), twelve-month net income growth rate (+13.7% versus −3.8%), and twelve-month earnings per share growth rate (+27.8% versus −11.2%). [31]

It's important to account for the possibility that the connections between attitudes and organizational outcomes will vary depending on the unit of analysis. One implication is that organizations might be tempted only to measure employee-level attitudes and try to generalize the results to the team, work unit, or organization. It appears that even when relationships at the individual level are weak, there may still be strong relationships between the aggregated employee attitudes and the aggregate performance of work groups or business units. Choosing the appropriate level of analysis requires considering both statistical power and the strategic question of interest. In most organizations, strategic outcomes of interest are business unit or work group performance (e.g., store sales, customer satisfaction, ROI), and work interventions take place at the unit level, not the individual employee level.[32] So, it is encouraging that research suggests that attitude-outcome relationships may be more powerful or stable at the unit level of analysis.

HR analysts and decision-makers must pay close attention to ensure that items are constructed for the specific level of analysis that is most informative and appropriate.

For many strategic decisions and outcomes, what matters is how employee attitudes affect aggregate-level outcomes, not simply individual-level outcomes. Those are the relationships that affect work unit and overall organizational performance. As Macey and Schneider noted, "the unit manager responsible for a work group of 10 frontline employees thinks very differently about the meaning of 8 out of 10 people being engaged than does a division manager who thinks about 8,000 out of 10,000."[33] These proportions have very different implications for the appropriate attitude-enhancement interventions and the likely consequences of those interventions and the managers' change efforts.

At the level of the work unit, performance improves when highly engaged team members devote extra effort to innovation, cooperate with each other, and effectively adapt to change.[34] Having an engaged employee base can facilitate adaptation to change, which is essential to innovation, continuous improvement, and to retaining competitiveness.[35] If one aggregates these kinds of behaviors from highly engaged employees across work units of the organization, this should lead to the kinds of outcomes that speak directly to competitive advantage: improvements in customer satisfaction, profitability, and shareholder value.[36] These are the kinds of outcomes that managers and investors care about. Figure 7.2 shows graphically some relationships among individual, work unit, and organizational levels of engagement and financial outcomes that produce competitive advantage.

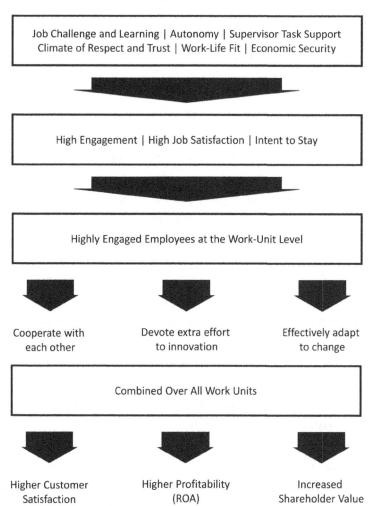

Figure 7.2. Logical framework tying individual level work experience attributes to organizational outcomes.

Causal Ordering

A positive relationship between employee attitudes and individual, unit, or organization-level outcomes might mean two different things. Changes in attitudes might cause changes in outcomes, or better outcomes might cause employee attitudes to increase. If attitudes cause outcomes, then that argues for investments that enhance employee attitudes. However, if outcomes cause attitudes, then such investments will not improve the outcomes. Which is the causal direction or order?

The meta-analysis described above concluded that the causal order runs from employee attitudes to organizational performance, although researchers recognized that multidirectional (reciprocal) relationships might still occur in other settings. In the section on "time lags," recall the study of longitudinal data from 35 companies on employee attitudes and organizational financial and market performance (8 years of data).[37] Those data also suggested that the causal direction runs from attitudes to outcomes.

Organizations may also use techniques such as structural equation modelling (SEM), as described in Chapter 2, to investigate possible causal relationships among variables. Using these types of data and methods, researchers are able to explore questions involving causal ordering and time lags among the two sets of variables. Being able to establish, with some confidence, the causal ordering of variables is important for designing action as a result of research insights; it is important to know which variables influence which other variables, and how strongly.

Keep in mind that relationships between employee attitudes and organizational performance are complex, and typically are multidirectional. HR analysts can be misled if they analyze cross-sectional data and simply assume that employee attitudes predict organizational performance, and if they do not allow for and examine possible reciprocal relationships. The gold standard for avoiding this trap is to measure employee attitudes and organizational performance longitudinally, at multiple points in time. That allows analysts to test forward and backward lags and to draw meaningful inferences about causal direction. Where that is not practical, statistical procedures such as SEM that explicitly analyze multidimensional and reciprocal relationships can be used.

Statistical Techniques for Analyzing Employee Attitude Data

Often it seems that practitioners devote considerable energy to identifying what attitudes they wish to measure and relatively little energy to planning how they will make sense of the data when it is returned to them. In Chapter 2, "Analytical Foundations," we talk in-depth about making sense of data, but there are a few unique issues associated with attitudinal data that bear mentioning here. Specifically, the approach to descriptive statistics, the use of benchmarks, and the use of regression, commonly called "driver analysis" among survey practitioners, are all fairly specific to survey work. Additionally, SEM, while not unique to survey work, can be enormously useful, especially for understanding complex, multidimensional relationships.

In practice, survey results are typically described using "percent favorable" rather than using means and standard deviations. While percent favorable does not convey information about central tendency or variability, it is simple to understand, and translates reasonably well across different scales (e.g., 5-point scales vs. 7-point scales). Benchmark data typically use this format as well. Most survey vendors will have their own benchmark data for key items. However, a word of caution is necessary with respect to benchmark data. Don't pursue benchmark data blindly in an attempt to mimic "best practices." Consider it thoughtfully as part of an overall talent strategy.

Another aspect of survey work is the use of driver analysis. Essentially, this is a statistical technique aimed at determining the relative influence of antecedents (predictors) on consequences (dependent variables). In current practice, this is often accomplished by using a method known as relative weights analysis (RWA), a form of regression that is particularly useful for identifying the unique (orthogonal) percentage of variance in the dependent variable that is attributable to each predictor variable.[38] Where there are several, related variables, using RWA can help focus attention on the most powerful predictors.

We described structural equation modeling (SEM) in Chapter 2, "Analytical Foundations." SEM is by no means unique to survey practice, but it can be especially helpful in examining a complex system. By design, SEM can analyze multiple levels of relationships and is especially good at examining reciprocal relationships, which are quite common in employee attitude work.

Beyond the methods described thus far, several other analytical methods are relevant to analyzing employee surveys. As noted elsewhere in this chapter, correlation, regression, and lagged or cross-lagged designs are all highly useful approaches to making sense of survey findings. Finally, charts and graphs can be incredibly powerful in displaying patterns in attitude and survey data; in particular, comparisons or connections and results over time can be conveyed much more clearly with graphic displays than with tables of tiny numbers.

An especially important consideration in analyzing organizational surveys is the margin of error in attitude surveys.[39] Paradoxically, the most useful results are often the least precise; that is, it is easiest to take compelling action at a fairly low level of granularity, such as a work group, yet measurement in small groups has a larger margin of error, often much larger than people recognize. Thus, for very small groups, the measurement error is so high that measurement should be regarded as more qualitative than quantitative in nature.

The basic formula to calculate error at the 95 percent confidence interval of a simple random sample is quite simple. In essence, the margin of error is a half-width of the confidence interval. For a 95 percent confidence interval, the standard error is 1.96. One half of 1.96 is .98, thus giving us the formula shown in Equation 7.1:

$$0.98 / \sqrt{n} \qquad\qquad (7.1)$$

Applying this formula, we can see that for very small sample sizes, the margin of error is little better than a Magic 8 Ball. Table 7.2 shows the margin of error at various sample sizes that might be relevant to an employee attitude survey. Note that this table applies to the number of respondents, not to the size of the work group or the number of invitees. Thus, if a group of twenty-five (margin of error 20 percent) had a very low response rate of 5, the margin of error would leap to nearly 60 percent! Additionally, this table assumes that the respondents are a random sample representing the population—that they do not vary in any systematic way.

Table 7.2. Margin of Error for Several Survey Sample Sizes.

sample size	margin of error
3	57%
5	44%
8	35%
10	31%
15	25%
25	20%
50	14%
75	11%
100	10%
200	7%
500	4%
1,000	3%
2,000	2%
5,000	1%
10,000	1%

In our experience, nonstatisticians will often unquestioningly accept results for relatively small groups, even down to three respondents in some organizations. In those cases, visualization can be beneficial by displaying error bars on either side of the results.

As a final note regarding margins of error, even for very large sample sizes where the margin of error is very small, researchers may wish to distinguish between what is statistically valid and what is practically meaningful. That is, although a change by two points, from say, 72 percent to 74 percent favorable, might be a statistically reliable finding, it may not be large enough to be meaningful to the organization. Many survey practitioners use a three-point difference as a rule of thumb to indicate meaningful differences over time or between groups.

Linkage Analysis: Describing How Employee Attitudes Affect Outcomes

Organizations may invest in enhancing employee attitudes because it is the right thing to do. Employee attitudes relate to important outcomes that are less tangible or measurable by traditional financial systems, including individual growth and well-being, organizational adaptability, and goodwill. Many organizations measure employee attitudes not only because they provide leading indicators of tangible financial performance, but because they are a signal of subtle nonfinancial outcomes. In other words, improving employee attitudes is seen as a worthy goal in and of itself.

We recognize the nonfinancial outcomes of employee attitudes and their independent value as an organizational goal, but we focus in this chapter on the connections between financial outcomes and employee attitudes. Organizations measure employee attitudes because they believe that doing so will drive some desired outcome. Throughout this chapter, we have described important organizational outcomes that are influenced by employee engagement, commitment, and satisfaction. Almost all organizations measure how attitudes affect employee turnover because there is a clear connection and a tangible consequence. However, focusing only on employee turnover ignores a wild and beautiful universe of important organizational outcomes that can be connected reasonably well to employee experiences and attitudes at work. For example, attitudes show strong and consistent relationships with performance and productivity, organizational citizenship behavior—and its opposite, counterproductive behavior—among many others.[40] The methods used to describe the connection (or link) between employee attitudes and organizational outcomes is called "linkage analysis." Decades of research links employee attitudes to a host of outcomes, although these linkages are not equally direct and powerful.[41] For example, a 2014 study of 100 organizations revealed 40 percent believed that their organization did not do an effective job of connecting business outcomes to employee attitudes.[42] The most interesting and most strategically important linkage analyses will vary with the organization's strategy, the work, and the talent pool. For jobs that depend significantly on customer interactions and conveying positive emotions, the effects of attitudes on service performance will be the pivotal effect. For jobs that seldom encounter a customer, but where teamwork and cooperation are key, the link between attitudes and citizenship behaviors may be the pivotal connection. Where innovation is the raison d'être of a team or organization, attitudes about supervisor support and work autonomy may be most pivotal predictors. Finally, for jobs where absence and turnover costs are significant, the effects of attitudes on these behaviors may be the pivotal measurement question.

Our next section describes a study that empirically linked employee engagement to improved importation outcomes, including service climate, customer loyalty, and financial measures.

Studies Connecting Employee Engagement and Customer Service

A well-controlled field study sampled three employees and ten customers from each of 120 hotel and restaurant units. The results showed that greater organizational resources (such as training, supervisor support, performance feedback) and higher employee engagement associated with more positive service climate, which in turn were associated with higher employee performance, which was associated with increased customer loyalty.[43]

Loyal customers, in turn, tend to do two things:

» Recommend the organization to others, and
» Become repeat customers.

Both of these have been shown to lead to increased revenue growth in the next fiscal quarter.[44] Figure 7.3 illustrates these logical connections.

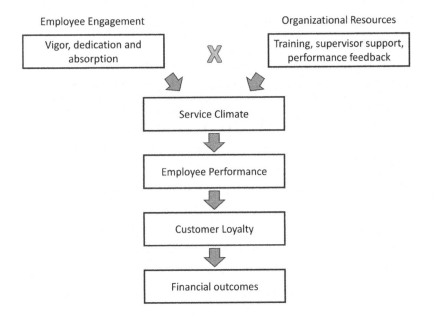

Figure 7.3. Logical framework showing relationship among employee engagement, employee performance, customer loyalty, and financial outcomes.

Note that the effect of employee engagement and organizational resources on service climate is multiplicative, not additive. So, if either resources or engagement is low or zero, the other element cannot compensate and service climate will be low, in turn reducing the remaining elements of the model.

This positive relationship between employee attitudes and organizational outcomes also appears in studies across a wide variety of organizations. The Corporate Leadership Council found that every 10 percent improvement in employee commitment can increase an employee's level of discretionary effort by 6 percent and their performance by 2 percent. In addition, the study found that highly committed employees perform at a 20 percent higher level than noncommitted employees. A similar study by Hewitt Associates reported that double-digit growth companies have 39 percent more highly-engaged employees and 45 percent fewer highly-disengaged employees than single-digit growth companies.[45] These studies provide very useful examples that connect employee attitude measures to intermediate processes and ultimately to customer behaviors and financial results.

Still, these results do not determine causal order as described earlier. Of course, employee engagement may cause double-digit financial growth, but it is equally possible that double-digit-growth companies are fun, exciting places to work and so employees are highly engaged. Academic researchers, consulting firms, and the in-house research departments of large companies conduct studies like these regularly, and their findings are often reported in the popular media. HR analysts and organizational leaders must be savvy consumers of reports of correlations between attitudes and financial performance and be aware of key requirements and limitations of study findings.

Jack in the Box, a fast-food chain, employed a formal employee engagement model that includes alignment (e.g., to brand), capabilities (e.g., competencies and resources), and engagement (e.g., commitment and satisfaction).[46] Researchers carefully assessed these experiences at the store level. The results showed that its stores that were highest on the overall employee-engagement model delivered 10 percent higher sales and 30 percent higher profit than stores with the lowest employee engagement and attitudes.[47] Further, Jack in the Box connected its formal employee experience (engagement) model to specific customer outcomes (e.g., speed, friendliness and food safety/preparation) and to specific financial outcomes over time, noting a $65,000 store-level improvement through focus on these attributes

A vital element of success for Jack in the Box was sharing these results effectively, at a level where those data could be used—in this case, at the store level. Next, we will address how to ensure that employee attitude data can be used to create improvements for the organization.

Process: Using Employee Attitude Measurements as a Lever for Change

Employee surveys are unusual among business data gathering efforts because the mere act of collecting survey data creates an expectation that the organization will share and act on the findings. No matter how rigorous the measures and analytics, little change happens until those data are thoughtfully and effectively analyzed and put into the hands of individuals who can use them to make changes and refine practices.

Organizations will often use employee attitude data at multiple levels, seeking to influence different outcomes at each level. If done poorly, this can create chaos and confusion and do more harm than good. However, done well, organizations can reap significant benefits from examining attitudes and driving action.

Let's consider a fictionalized example. We saw in Table 7.1 that job challenge and learning, followed by climate of respect, were the top drivers of engagement.

Start with the level of the entire organization or enterprise. At the enterprise level, scores on items related to job challenge and learning and climate of respect might be lower than executives would like, compared to benchmark companies. Strategies that an executive team might deploy might include investing in corporate learning and implementing policies that make it easier for employees to change jobs or to pick up developmental opportunities in other groups. To enhance the climate of respect, members of the executive team might work with HR to create community service opportunities where executives and managers work shoulder-to-shoulder with frontline employees, and then share those experiences—and the respect they have for those frontline workers as part of an all-hands communication event.

Now, consider the single-manager level within the organization. Across managers, some will have employees with lower scores than others. Manager-level strategies to enhance employee attitudes would be quite different from the enterprise-level strategies. Low-scoring managers might set up a team meeting to learn what sorts of challenges and learning their team would value most. They might schedule time apart from regular meetings specifically to discuss career goals and create a learning plan together. Or, they might facilitate cross training or job swaps for their employees with employees from different areas. To address the climate of respect, a manager might ask an HR generalist partner or a higher-scoring manager to spend time with his or her team, identifying any behaviors or practices that leave employees feeling dismissed or disrespected—and then publicly commit to changing those behaviors.

When organizations use an outside vendor to deliver and analyze their employee attitude surveys, action plans like these will typically be included as part of the employee survey package. Especially where pulsing strategies are used, those packages will often present real-time data updates, making it possible for managers and leaders to monitor whether their actions are having the desired effect.

A Final Word

Certainly, refinements are needed in the methods described here, but the potential of cost-benefit comparisons of attitude-behavior relationships is enormous. If organizations can develop compelling, logical frameworks that relate employee attitudes and employee engagement to financial outcomes, and if they can use sound analytics and measures to draw meaningful conclusions from their data, they can engage in a more rational decision-making process regarding where they should and should not make investments. As attractive as positive employee attitudes may be in the abstract, it is simply not feasible for organizations to commit to having high positive attitudes for every employee, manager, and business unit. Enhancing employee attitudes, like virtually all HR outcomes, has more value where those attitudes are most pivotal. HR analysts and leaders should better identify the critical decision pivot-points where this kind of information will make the biggest difference.

Exercises

1. Your boss has asked you for evidence that shows the link between employee attitudes such as job satisfaction, commitment, and engagement, and both individual and organizational outcomes. In other words, convince her that attitudes matter. What sort of evidence might you present?

2. Develop a logic diagram that shows the common and unique outcomes that employee satisfaction, commitment, and engagement might be related to.

3. You are a leader in HR for a regional manufacturing organization with several different plants across five states. Despite producing the same goods using the same equipment, some of them are performing very well, while others are struggling to deliver parts on time and according to specifications. The CEO wants to understand what is going on. What do you suggest?

4. You are CEO of a public-relations company. You have been thinking about how to drive productivity in your organization. Based on what you have learned, what strategies might you adopt?

References

1. Wayne F. Cascio and Clifford E. Young, "Work-Family Balance: Does the Market Reward Firms That Respect It?," in *From Work-Family Balance to Work-Family Interaction: Changing the Metaphor* ed. Diane F. Halpern and Susan E. Murphy (Mahwah, NJ: Lawrence Erlbaum Associates, 2005), 49–63.
2. See for example, Alex Edmans, "Does the Stock Market Fully Value Intangibles? Employee Satisfaction and Equity Prices," *Journal of Financial Economics* 101, no. 3 (September 2011): 621–40. See also Peter Cappelli, "The Value of Being a Best Employer," *Human Resource Executive*, accessed June 26, 2008, http://www.hronline.com; Noshua Watson, "Happy Companies Make Happy Investments," *Fortune*, May 27, 2002, 162.
3. Ingrid S. Fulmer, Barry Gerhart, and Kimberly S. Scott, "Are the 100 Best Better? An Empirical Investigation of the Relationship Between Being a 'Great Place to Work' and Firm Performance," *Personnel Psychology* 56, no. 4 (December 2003): 965–93.
4. Fulmer, Gerhart, and Scott, "Are the 100 Best Better?," 987.
5. Benjamin Schneider et al., "Which Comes First: Employee Attitudes or Organizational Financial and Market Performance?," *Journal of Applied Psychology* 88, no. 5 (October 2003): 836–51.
6. Greg Filbeck and Dianna Preece, "*Fortune's* Best 100 Companies to Work for in America: Do They Work for Shareholders?," *Journal of Business Finance & Accounting* 30, no. 5–6 (June 2003): 771–97.
7. Richard M. Vosburgh, "State-Trait Returns! And One Practitioner's Request," *Industrial and Organizational Psychology* 1, no. 1 (March 2008): 72–73.
8. James K. Harter and Frank L. Schmidt, "Conceptual Versus Empirical Distinctions Among Constructs: Implications for Discriminant Validity," *Industrial and Organizational Psychology* 1, no. 1 (March 2008): 36–39. See also William H. Macey and Benjamin Schneider, "Engaged in Engagement: We are Delighted We Did It," *Industrial and Organizational Psychology* 1, no. 1 (March 2008): 76–83.
9. Brett Minchington, "Your Most Important Employer Brand Asset—Your EVP," *Human Resources magazine*, October 2012, 18.

10. William H. Macey and Benjamin Schneider, "The Meaning of Employee Engagement," *Industrial and Organizational Psychology* 1, no. 1 (March 2008): 3–30.
11. Howard J. Klein, Janice C. Molloy, and Joseph T. Cooper, "Conceptual Foundations: Construct Definitions and Theoretical Representations of Workplace Commitments," in *Commitment in Organizations: Accumulated Wisdom and New Directions*, SIOP Organizational Frontiers Series, ed. Howard J. Klein, Thomas E. Becker, and John P. Meyer (New York: Taylor & Francis, 2009), 3–36. See also John E. Mathieu and Dennis M. Zajac, "A Review and Meta-Analysis of the Antecedents, Correlates, and Consequences or Organizational Commitment," *Psychological Bulletin* 108, no. 2 (September 1990): 171–94.
12. Ken Carrig and Patrick M. Wright, *Building Profit through Building People: Making Your Workforce the Strongest Link in the Value-Profit Chain* (Alexandria, VA: Society for Human Resource Management, 2006).
13. Daniel A. Newman and David A. Harrison, "Been There, Bottled That: Are State and Behavioral Work Engagement New and Useful Construct "Wines"?," *Industrial and Organizational Psychology* 1, no. 1 (March 2008): 31–35. See also Harter and Schmidt, "Conceptual Versus Empirical Distinctions," 36–39.
14. Macey and Schneider, "The Meaning of Employee Engagement," 3–30. See also Harter and Schmidt, "Conceptual Versus Empirical Distinctions," 36–39. See also Newman and Harrison, "Been There, Bottled That," 31–35.
15. Wilmar B. Schaufeli, Arnold B. Bakker, and Marisa Salanova, "The Measurement of Work Engagement With a Short Questionnaire: A Cross-National Study," *Educational and Psychological Measurement* 66, no. 4 (August 2006): 701–16. See also Wilmar B. Schaufeli et al., "The Measurement of Engagement and Burnout: A Two-Sample Confirmatory Factor-Analytic Approach," *Journal of Happiness Studies* 3, no. 1 (March 2002): 71–92.
16. Marisa Salanova, Sonia Agut, and José María Peiró, "Linking Organizational Resources and Work Engagement to Employee Performance and Customer Loyalty: The Mediation of Service Climate," *Journal of Applied Psychology* 90, no. 6 (November 2005): 1216–27.
17. Kerstin Aumann and Ellen Galinsky, *The State of Health in the American Workforce: Does Having an Effective Workplace Matter?* (New York: Families and Work Institute, 2009), http://www.familiesandwork.org/site/research/reports/HealthReport.pdf.
18. Scott M. Brooks, Jack W. Wiley, and Emily L. Hause, "Using Employee and Customer Perspectives to Improve Organizational Performance," in *Customer Service Delivery* ed. Lawrence Fogli (San Francisco: Jossey-Bass, 2006), 52–82. See also Aaron Cohen, "Organizational Commitment and Turnover: A Meta-Analysis," *Academy of Management Journal* 36, no. 5 (October 1993): 1140–1157; Cheri Ostroff, "The Relationship Between Satisfaction, Attitudes, and Performance: An Organizational-Level Analysis," *Journal of Applied*

Psychology 77, no. 6 (December 1992): 963–974; Ann Marie Ryan, Mark J. Schmit, and Raymond Johnson, "Attitudes and Effectiveness: Examining Relations at an Organizational Level," *Personnel Psychology* 49, no. 4 (December 1996): 853–83; Kirk L. Rogg et al., "Human Resource Practices, Organizational Climate, and Customer Satisfaction," *Journal of Management* 27, no. 4 (August 2001): 431–49; Wilmar B. Schaufeli and Arnold B. Bakker, "Job Demands, Job Resources, and Their Relationship with Burnout and Engagement: A Multi-Sample Study," *Journal of Organizational Behavior* 25, no. 3 (May 2004): 293–315.

19. Timothy A. Judge et al., "Job Attitudes, Job Satisfaction, and Job Affect: A Century of Continuity and of Change," *Journal of Applied Psychology* 102, no. 3 (March 2017): 356–74.

20. Sharon K. Parker, "Job Satisfaction," in Vol. 1, *Encyclopedia of Industrial and Organizational Psychology*, ed. Steven G. Rogelberg (Thousand Oaks, CA: Sage, 2007), 406–10. See also William K. Balzer and Jennifer Z. Gillespie, "Job Satisfaction Measurement," in Vol. 1, *Encyclopedia of Industrial and Organizational Psychology*, ed. Steven G. Rogelberg (Thousand Oaks, CA: Sage, 2007), 410–13.

21. Natalie J. Allen, "Organizational Commitment," in Vol. 2, *Encyclopedia of Industrial and Organizational Psychology*, ed. Steven G. Rogelberg (Thousand Oaks, CA: Sage, 2007), 548–51.

22. Richard T. Mowday, Richard M. Steers, and Lyman W. Porter, "The Measurement of Organizational Commitment," *Journal of Vocational Behavior* 14, no. 2 (April 1979): 224–47.

23. Gallup Inc., *Gallup Q12 Employee Engagement Survey*, 2018, accessed December 2, 2018, https://q12.gallup.com/Public/en-us/Features.

24. Harter and Schmidt, "Conceptual Versus Empirical Distinctions," 36–39.

25. Schaufeli, Bakker, and Salanova, "The Measurement of Work Engagement," 701–16.

26. Josh Bersin, "It's Time to Rethink the 'Employee Engagement' Issue," *Forbes*, April 10, 2014, accessed November 23, 2018, https://www.forbes.com/sites/joshbersin/2014/04/10/its-time-to-rethink-the-employee-engagement-issue/#9ebfd246cf36

27. Schneider et al., "Which Comes First," 836–51.

28. Macey and Schneider, "Engaged in Engagement," 76–83.

29. David Chan, "Functional Relations among Constructs in the Same Content Domain at Different Levels of Analysis: A Typology of Composition Models," *Journal of Applied Psychology* 83, no. 2 (April 1998): 234–46.

30. James K. Harter, Frank L. Schmidt, and Theodore L. Hayes, "Business-Unit-Level Relationship between Employee Satisfaction, Employee Engagement, and Business Outcomes: A Meta-Analysis," *Journal of Applied Psychology* 87, no. 2 (April 2002): 268–79.

31. Adrienne Fox, "Raising Engagement," *HR Magazine*, May 2010, 35–40.

32. Douglas Pugh and Joerg Dietz, "Employee Engagement at the Organizational Level of Analysis," *Industrial and Organizational Psychology* 1, no. 1 (March 2008): 44–47.

33. Macey and Schneider, "The Meaning of Employee Engagement," 3–30, 78.
34. Mark A. Griffin, Sharon K. Parker, and Andrew Neal, "Is Behavioral Engagement a Distinct and Useful Construct?," *Industrial and Organizational Psychology* 1, no. 1 (March 2008): 48–51.
35. George Graen, "Enriched Engagement Through Assistance to Systems Change: A Proposal," *Industrial and Organizational Psychology* 1, no. 1 (March 2008): 74–75.
36. Macey and Schneider, "The Meaning of Employee Engagement," 3–30.
37. Schneider et al., "Which Comes First," 836–851.
38. Jeff W. Johnson, "A Heuristic Method for Estimating the Relative Weight of Predictor Variables in Multiple Regression," *Multivariate Behavioral Research* 35, no. 1 (2000): 1–19.
39. Sharon L. Lohr, *Sampling: Design and Analysis* (Pacific Grove, CA: Duxbury Press, 1999).
40. Timothy A. Judge et al., "The Job Satisfaction-Job Performance Relationship: A Qualitative and Quantitative Review," *Psychological Bulletin* 127, no. 3 (May 2001): 376–407. See also Thomas S. Bateman and Dennis W. Organ, "Job Satisfaction and the Good Soldier: the Relationship Between Affect and Employee 'Citizenship,'" *Academy of Management Journal* 26, no. 4 (December 1983): 587–95; Jennifer Kish-Gephart, David A. Harrison, and Linda Klebe Trevino, "Bad Apples, Bad Cases, and Bad Barrels: Meta-Analytic Evidence about Sources of Unethical Decisions at Work," *Journal of Applied Psychology* 95, no. 1 (January 2010): 1–31.
41. Timothy A. Judge et al., "Job Attitudes, Job Satisfaction, and Job Affect: A Century of Continuity and of Change," *Journal of Applied Psychology* 102, no. 3 (March 2017): 356–74.
42. The Engagement Institute, "2014 Quarter Four Pulse Survey Results: Engagement Related Measurement Challenges," The Engagement Institute Quarterly Pulse Series, November 20, 2014, https://www.conference -board.org/subsites/index.cfm?id=15136.
43. Benjamin Schneider, Susan S. White, and Michelle C. Paul, "Linking Service Climate and Customer Perceptions of Service Quality: Test of a Causal Model," *Journal of Applied Psychology* 83, no. 2 (April 1998): 150–163. See also Salanova, Agut, and Peiroá, "Linking Organizational Resources," 1216–227.
44. Anthony J. Rucci, Steven P. Kirn, and Richard T. Quinn, "The Employee-Customer-Profit Chain at Sears," *Harvard Business Review*, January-February 1998, 82–97.
45. Corporate Voices for Working Families, "Business Impacts of Flexibility: An Imperative For Expansion," November 2005, accessed June 1, 2010, http:// www.wfd.com/PDFS/Business%20Impacts%20of%20Flexibility.pdf.
46. William A. Schiemann, *The ACE Advantage: How Smart Companies Unleash Talent for Optimal Performance* (Alexandria, VA: Society for Human Resource Management, 2012).

47. Mark Blankenship, "The Engagement Journey at Jack in the Box,"
Presentation, 2017, accessed November 24, 2018, https://ceo.usc.edu
/files/2017/05/The_Engagement_Journey_at_Jack_in_the_Box_Mark
_Blankenship.pdf.

8

Financial Effects of Workplace Flexibility Programs

Jeff Bezos, CEO of Amazon, offers this advice to his staff: "This work-life harmony thing is what I try to teach young employees and actually senior executives at Amazon too. But especially the people coming in," he said. "I get asked about work-life balance all the time. And my view is, that's a debilitating phrase because it implies there's a strict trade-off." Instead of viewing work and life as a balancing act, Bezos said that it's more productive to view them as two integrated parts. "It actually is a circle. It's not a balance. If I am happy at home, I come into the office with tremendous energy. And if I am happy at work, I come home with tremendous energy. You never want to be that guy—and we all have a coworker who's that person—who, as soon as they come into a meeting, they drain all the energy out of the room.... You want to come into the office and give everyone a kick in their step."[1]

A survey of 614 senior HR leaders found that almost half of them said that employee burnout is responsible for 20 to 50 percent of their annual workforce turnover.[2] They believed burnout was caused by unfair compensation, an unreasonable workload, and too much after-hours work.

According to a 2017 study by Technologia, 12 percent of the French workforce—or 3.2 million workers—is at risk of burnout. The study estimated the social cost of work stress to be 2–3 billion euro annually in France.[3] Work creep is such a major issue that the French government introduced legislation that gives

In France
↓

workers "the right to disconnect." Companies with more than fifty workers will be obliged to draw up a charter of good conduct, setting out the hours when staff are not supposed to send or answer emails.[4]

Ernst and Young, a global consultancy, surveyed almost 10,000 full-time workers in the US, UK, India, Japan, China, Germany, Mexico, and Brazil.[5] They found:

» 33 percent say it has gotten more difficult to manage work/family in the last five years.

» 74 percent said it was very important that a potential job provide "being able to work flexibly and still be on track for promotion," and "working with colleagues, including my boss, who support my efforts to work flexibly."

» One in ten US workers say they have "suffered a negative consequence as a result of having a flexible work schedule," and the rate is even higher for millennials, or nearly one in six.

» Full-time employees in Germany and Japan are the most likely to indicate that it has gotten tougher to manage work/life.

» Parents found it more difficult to manage work/life than non-parents in Germany, the UK, India, and the US.

Yet, the desire for work flexibility may not translate into the ability to manage it. One study following German workers over several years found that those who had more control over their work hours actually worked more, not less.[6]

Workplace Flexibility—Growing or Not?

Are workplaces becoming more flexible? The answer is decidedly mixed. A study of 920 US employers with fifty or more employees found significant changes in several forms of workplace flexibility.[7] Between 2005 and 2016, in some areas there was an increase in the percentage of organizations that allow "at least some of their employees" to:

» Periodically change starting/quitting times (+13 to 81 percent in 2016),
» Work at home occasionally (+32 to 66 percent in 2016),
» Work at home regularly (+9 to 40 percent in 2016),
» Control breaks (+13 to 91 percent in 2016), or
» Control overtime (+14 to 42 percent in 2016).

On the other hand, some areas decreased in the percentage of organizations that allow "at least some employees" to:

» Move from full- to part-time and back (–13 percentage points to 41 percent in 2016),
» Take part-year work (–20 percentage points to 18 percent in 2016),
» Phase into retirement (+5 percentage points to 59 percent in 2016),
» Take a sabbatical (–21 percentage points to 28 percent in 2016),
» Take an extended career break (–14 percentage points to 55 percent in 2016), or
» Receive special consideration after extended career break (–15 percentage points to 28 percent in 2016).

Such significant shifts in organizational practices represent substantial changes in the way time, money, and other resources are invested in the workforce. That begs important questions:

» Can organizations enhance both employee productivity and the fit between their work and nonwork lives?
» When do investments in work and nonwork life fit become a recruitment and retention advantage?
» Is the advantage actually enough to offset the costs?

In this chapter we follow the LAMP model of Chapter 1 to offer a logical, analytic, and measurement framework regarding workplace flexibility programs that might facilitate better decisions about investments in them.

Workplace Flexibility Programs: What Are They?

Flexible work arrangements are typically defined as allowing employees to work in different locations or nontraditional working hours.[8] This includes:

» **Flexitime:** where employees can vary their start and finish times provided a certain number of hours are worked. The number of hours may be set weekly or monthly and core working hours, such as 10:00 a.m. to 4:00 p.m., may be set;

» **Part-time or reduced hours:** where the employee works fewer hours than a full-time worker who usually works thirty-five hours or more a week;

» **Term-time working:** where an employee only works during school-term time. This means working around thirteen fewer weeks per year;

» **Homeworking:** where the employee works from home or another location away from the central office one or more days per week;

» **Job sharing:** where two employees share the work of one full-time job;

» **Compressed hours:** where employees work a full week's worth of hours in fewer days (e.g., five days worked over four);

» **Family-leave programs:** where employees get paid or unpaid leave to attend to personal or family responsibilities usually for a temporary period.

A distinction is often made between *time flexibility* in which there is flexibility about *when* work is completed, versus *location flexibility*, in which there is flexibility in *where* work is completed.

Example of a Workplace Flexibility Champion: SAS[9]

SAS Institute, a privately held company that creates business-analytic software, has been on *Fortune*'s list of the 100 Best Places to work for twenty-one years running. *Fortune*'s 2018 review lists these workplace perks:[10]

» Unlimited sick days,
» Telecommuting,
» Job sharing,
» Subsidized childcare,
» Compressed work weeks,
» On-site fitness/subsidized gym,
» On-site medical care facility,
» Nondiscrimination policy includes sexual orientation,
» Health insurance for part-timers,
» Sick days for part-timers, and
» College tuition reimbursement.

This bounty of benefits stems from the company's core beliefs about minimizing distractions and that happy, healthy employees are more productive.

The architect of this culture—based on "trust between our employees and the company"—is Jim Goodnight, its co-founder, and the only CEO in SAS's history. He is famous for his global web-cast in January, 2009, at the depth of the worldwide recession, when he announced that *none* of the 13,000 worldwide employees would lose their jobs. SAS had record profits in 2009, even as other large companies went out of business or were acquired. Some might think that, with all those perks, Goodnight was giving away the store. But, SAS has had an unbroken chain of profitability and growth every year since its founding in 1976. Part of the payoff to investing in workplace inclusion and flexibility is annual turnover of 2–3 percent compared to industry averages of 22 percent. Resources that otherwise would be spent on headhunters, training, and restoring lost productivity are effectively diverted to further enhancing the work/ life experience of employees. Tens of thousands of people apply for the few hundred openings available at SAS every year.[11]

Logical Framework for the Payoff to Workplace Flexibility
The rapidly changing global workforce and workplace are creating new pressures to consider workplace flexibility, and some workers demand and expect more. Figure 8.1 is a logical framework to describe how workplace flexibility programs affect human capital, employee behaviors, and financial outcomes.

As Figure 8.1 shows, there are consequences, both behavioral and financial, to decisions to offer or not to offer one or more workplace flexibility programs. If an organization chooses not to offer such programs, there may be negative consequences with respect to job performance. Some of these potential impacts include heightened stress, more burnout, a higher likelihood of mistakes, and more refusals of promotions by employees already feeling the strain of pressures for better fit between their work and nonwork lives. Under these circumstances, job satisfaction, commitment to the organization, and engagement in one's job (vigor, absorption, dedication—see Chapter 7) are likely to wane. When that happens, people begin to think about quitting, some actually do quit, and customer service may suffer, all of which can lead to significant financial outcomes, as described in Chapters 4 and 5.

If an organization does offer workplace flexibility programs, the financial and nonfinancial effects of those programs depend on several factors. These include the range, scope, cost, and quality of the programs; the extent and quality of communications about the programs to employees; training on how to manage workplace flexibility programs; and support for them from managers and supervisors.

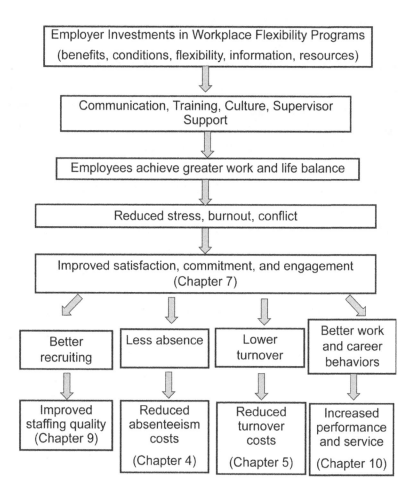

Figure 8.1. Logic of workplace flexibility.

If those conditions are met, employees are more likely to achieve greater work and life fit, which leads to reduced stress, burnout, and conflict, along with increased engagement, satisfaction, and commitment. Those human outcomes lead to improvements in talent management (reductions in withdrawal behaviors and voluntary turnover, and improvements in the ability to attract top talent); motivation to perform well; and financial, operational, and business outcomes. The next sections elaborate on the elements of Figure 8.1 in more detail.

Workplace Flexibility as Total Productive Maintenance for Employees

A fundamental principle of optimal performance in manufacturing, transportation, and production systems is called total productive maintenance (TPM), which aims to increase the productivity of a factory and its equipment with a modest investment in maintenance. The idea is that equipment productivity depends on its "Performance × Availability × Quality." It's often quite possible to achieve short-run cost or productivity improvements by running equipment at excessive speed or for excessive time, but that will eventually cause breakdowns or quality problems. Leaders are well aware of the TPM principle that the optimum approach is to maintain equipment by investing in its continuous maintenance, and not over-strain the equipment. Such maintenance requires investments, and hard decisions to avoid running the equipment at high speed even when that reduces some short-run results. But, leaders know that in the long run the right amount of maintenance enhances performance, availability, and quality more than it costs.

The same logic is depicted in Figure 8.1, and in the examples later in this chapter. Investments in workplace flexibility can be costly, and they can sometimes mean that employees will not be available 24/7. Just as with equipment, it can be tempting to over-strain employees to achieve short-run goals, but that would be just as ill-advised with employees as it is with equipment. The calculations and examples in this chapter are similar to the calculations that engineers would use to determine the optimal amount of maintenance and the optimal level of equipment usage to achieve maximum long-term productivity. This chapter helps you apply such logic to employees.

Impact of Workplace Flexibility on Burnout and Withdrawal

Companies can own tangible assets, such as patents, copyrights, and equipment, but employees are different from such assets.[12] Employees fit their work with other life elements. Conflicts between work and nonwork demands may lead some employees to burn out.

Employees suffering from burnout do the bare minimum, do not show up regularly, leave work early, and quit their jobs at higher rates than less-stressed employees.[13] To reduce such tensions, they may leave the workforce altogether or move to positions in other organizations that generate less stress. For firms that are trying to build valuable human assets that are difficult to copy or to lure away, workplace flexibility programs may provide powerful retention and performance enhancement tools.

AstraZeneca conducted a flexibility survey of the company's Delaware-based headquarters and R&D employees, finding that 96 percent of employees said that flexibility influenced their decision to stay at the company; 73 percent said that flexibility was "very important" in that decision, and an additional 23 percent said that it was "somewhat important."[14]

Other employee withdrawal behaviors, such as reduced effort while at work, lateness, and absenteeism, also diminish the value of human resources to an employer.[15] As shown in Chapter 4, some studies suggest the most frequently cited reason for unscheduled employee absence is personal illness, followed by family-related issues. These two factors account for more than half of all absenteeism. Workplace flexibility programs address precisely these reasons for employee absence and withdrawal. Workplace flexibility initiatives that incorporate flexible work scheduling with family-friendly features can be important to protecting a firm's investment in its human capital.

Workplace Flexibility Programs and Professional Employees
The view of workplace flexibility programs as a strategy for protecting investments in human capital applies particularly well to professional employees. Professional employees are critical resources for organizations because of their expense, their relative scarcity, and the transferability of their skills.[16] In addition, professionals tend to be highly autonomous, substituting self-control for organizational control.

Attracting and retaining professionals is difficult because other employers value their skills. Workplace flexibility programs can be effective for attracting and retaining these employees.[17] Professionals in many countries are delaying the birth of their first child until they have achieved some measure of financial and career security. Given the relatively long years of education and training required of professionals, these people are especially likely to delay starting their families.[18] For this reason, work/family tensions tend to rise for many professionals as they reach their 30s and 40s. If organizations fail to provide assistance in handling this tension, they risk losing these valuable employees to employers that offer more flexibility. Organizations with greater workplace flexibility may be able to retain top-performing professionals more effectively.

Opting Out

Many companies recruit roughly equal numbers of female and male MBA graduates, but they find that a substantial percentage of their female recruits drop out within three to five years. The most vexing problem is not finding female talent but retaining it.[19] How large is the opt-out phenomenon? One survey examined this phenomenon in a sample of 2,443 women and 653 men, all of whom had a graduate degree, a professional degree, or a high-honors undergraduate degree.[20] Thirty-seven percent of the women (43 percent of those with children) took time off from their careers, but only 24 percent of the men did. Among women, the average break lasted 2.2 years, with 44 percent citing child- or eldercare responsibilities, compared with only 12 percent of men, who averaged 1 year off.

Although 93 percent of the women who took time off from work wanted to return, only 74 percent of them were able to do so. Even then, they paid a high price for their career interruptions, with the penalties becoming more severe the longer the break. Among women in business, the average loss in earnings was 28 percent, even though the average break among those women lasted little more than a year. When women spent three or more years out of the work force, they earned only 63 percent of the salaries of those who took no time out. The same survey also found that many women cope with job/family tradeoffs by working part time, by reducing the number of hours they work in full-time jobs, and by declining to accept promotions. Women were less likely to opt out of work if their employers offered flexible career paths that allowed them to ramp up and ramp down their professional responsibilities at different career points.[21] Flexibility is a key retention tool for women as well as for men.

The Toll on Those Who Don't Opt Out

Especially for those who do not or cannot opt out of working, family and personal concerns are a source of stress:[22]

» In professional service firms, well over half the employees can expect to experience some kind of work/family stress in a three-month period.

» Staff members with work/family conflict are three times more likely to consider quitting (43 percent versus 14 percent).

» Staff members who believe that work is causing problems in their personal lives are much more likely to make mistakes at work (30 percent) than those who have few job-related personal problems (19 percent).

» On the other hand, employees with supportive workplaces and supportive supervisors report greater job satisfaction and more commitment to helping their companies succeed.

Organizations want their employees to be highly committed and fully engaged, but in many cases, that is just wishful thinking because of the spillover of workplace issues to employees' personal lives off the job. Research has shown that the impact of work on employees' home lives is balanced between positive, negative, and neutral.[23] A meta-analytic review found that both work and nonwork conflict are negatively related to job and life satisfaction.[24] Negative spillover effects are reflected in high stress, bad moods, poor coping, and insufficient quality and amount of time for family and friends. When employees are worried about personal issues outside of work, they become distracted, and their commitment wanes along with their productivity. Ultimately, both absenteeism and turnover may increase. As we have noted, family/personal issues are widespread sources of stress, and conflicts between work and personal life affect productivity and general well-being.

Perhaps Jeff Bezos's observations in this chapter's introduction are correct because some research suggests a generally positive impact of employees' personal or family lives on work. Half of employees in a large, national study reported that their personal or family lives provide them with more energy for their jobs. Only 12 percent reported that their home life undermines their energy for work, and 38 percent reported a balanced impact of their personal or family lives on their energy levels at work.[25] Organizational programs that support work flexibility reinforce these outcomes. Unfortunately, in many organizations the programs are available but formidable barriers may make it difficult for employees to use them.[26] The next section describes an organization that successfully avoided this problem.

PwC's System of Work/Life Fit

The challenges of optimally engaging professional employees are very significant in professional service industries such as consulting, law, and accounting. Traditionally, such organizations relied on an up-or-out system, whereby young, ambitious (mostly male) associates joined out of college, and then spent years working long hours, traveling most of the time, and being available at virtually any day and hour. In return, after years of good service, some of those associates were promoted to partners, or other senior roles, where they reaped the rewards of higher pay, shares in the company, and a cadre of associates working for them, all of which allowed them to eventually have greater workplace flexibility and control. Because the top managers of such companies had all come through this system, it was perpetuated by each incoming group of partners, who felt that "if we could do it, then so can our younger colleagues." Then, things changed.

Consider the accounting and consulting firm PwC, for example.[27] For decades, fresh graduates had simply accepted they'd be signing away nights, weekends, and any semblance of a normal family life or social calendar in exchange for bragging rights at a big-name firm, a big paycheck at the outset, and the promise of a much bigger one when they made partner later on. It was a deal new recruits were willing to take. As PwC's people innovation leader put it, "We sort of prided ourselves on, 'Ah, we don't need to have lives, we just forge ahead.'" However, by 2013, millennials represented two-thirds of PwC's workforce, and they were no longer willing to put aside their personal lives for the future possibility of a lucrative partnership. PwC experienced a higher attrition among younger employees that was at "crisis" levels—far higher than in the past. The company's recruitment data also revealed greater reluctance among college recruits to join the firm. Was this just "entitled" youngsters who didn't understand reality? No. When PwC analyzed the situation, it realized the concerns of the younger employees were not so different from those of their older colleagues. PwC realized that virtually everything about its business had changed in the prior twenty years, and asked, "why shouldn't our culture change as well?"

The company's response was similar to how it might approach a consulting project with a client. It partnered with the Center for Effective Organizations at the University of Southern California and the London Business School to study the problem using carefully crafted measures and analytics. The company surveyed 44,000 employees around the world. The results were presented to PwC's leaders in a comprehensive report, as well as by means of videos and other tools.[28]

The report noted, "Millennials did not object to long hours outright. They were as committed to their work as older colleagues.

But they were also more willing to question long-held assumptions about how that work should be done. Given the abundance of connectivity, why was it necessary to be in the same physical building for 15 hours (on a good day) to get a job done? Why couldn't they work from home when a project allowed?" One surprise was that "virtually identical percentages of millennial employees and non-millennial workers said they would prefer to be able to shift their work hours to schedules that could accommodate both their personal and professional obligations—heading home early for family dinner, for example, in exchange for an early start or signing back on once the kids were in bed. The only difference was that millennials were willing to speak up about their dissatisfaction, and to opt out when problems couldn't be resolved. Over and over again, the results of the survey made clear: work was important, but a personal life was, too."[29]

PwC initiated workplace flexibility programs under the trademark "Flexibility[2]" that included "everyday" elements such as:[30]

» **Year-round flex days:** Employees can enjoy flex days at any time of the year for additional extended time off. Teams work together to figure out what works for them, taking into consideration the needs of the client and the business.

» **Teaming culture:** A teaming culture in which multiple employees share responsibility for client service and deliverables enables our people to create work schedules that work best for themselves, the team, and the client.

» **Work/life resource and referral:** To help our employees balance personal and work commitments, PwC offers this confidential resource and referral service that can assist PwC employees and their immediate families with financial, educational, career, childcare, eldercare, disability, and stress management, including free articles and publications.

» **Unprescribed sick leave:** To assist employees in maintaining work/life quality, the firm's policy provides an unprescribed

↓ like FMLA

number of sick days for all US full-time and part-time staff scheduled to work at least one thousand hours a year. What's more, PwC's policy allows paid time off not just for one's own illness, but also to care for a sick child, parent, spouse, or same-sex domestic partner.

The program also included "formal flexibility" elements designed to create a workplace "where individual goals are respected as much as professional goals, and contribution is measured by results, not by the number of hours you spend in the office":

» **Reduced Hours:** Reducing hours to fewer than a regular full-time week;
» **Flextime:** Work hours move earlier or later than regular business hours;
» **PwC@Home:** Formal telecommuting, routinely working from home three or more days per week;
» **PwC Offsite:** Telecommuting, routinely working from home one or two days per week;
» **Job-Sharing:** Two people jointly fulfill the responsibilities of one full-time position;
» **Compressed Workweek:** Standard hours compressed into fewer than five work days; and
» **Sabbatical:** Leave of absence while maintaining benefits and a reduced salary.

PwC found that in 2018, 90 percent of its employees incorporated some kind of flexibility into their schedules. January to April is still a busy tax-accounting season when all hands are on deck, but employees can now be creative about getting the heavy workload accomplished. "People could work from home, or leave early on Tuesdays, and the company wouldn't collapse. In fact, people were actually more motivated at work when they knew they had some control over their time."[31]

Not surprisingly, being an accounting firm, PwC studied the impact of the programs. PwC's people innovation leader says "there's been zero [negative] shift in our productivity as a firm."

Enhancing Success through Implementation

The mere presence of a workplace flexibility initiative doesn't guarantee success. As shown in Figure 8.1, one must also consider the range, scope, quality, and cost of workplace flexibility initiatives, along with the quality and care with which they are deployed. Key factors to consider are the careful alignment of the programs with the strategic objectives of the organization, the extent and quality of communications about the programs, training for managers on how to make the programs work for them, and the extent of management and supervisory support for the programs. If implemented properly, workplace flexibility initiatives should reduce employee withdrawal behaviors, increase retention, and increase employees' motivation to perform well. Unfortunately, this is not always the case.

Both employers and employees have reasons for not using workplace flexibility programs. Many supervisors and higher-level managers, for example, think of "workplace flexibility" as "workplace flexibility equals work less." They see such programs benefiting employees only and not their organizations.[32] The Boston College Center for Work and Family summarized managerial concerns: "Manager concerns include that employees will view flexible work arrangements as an entitlement, that they will have trouble supervising their employees, and that there will be a decrease in employee productivity, quality of work, and customer satisfaction. Over half of managers say it is difficult to estimate the productivity of their teleworking employees. While managers in traditional office spaces evaluate employees through face time and observing project developments, remote workers are best assessed through their final products and their behavior. It is necessary to educate managers and team leaders on this type of evaluation before asking them to gauge the effectiveness of remote workers."[33] The challenge, then, is to help managers view workplace flexibility as a new way of working that focuses on fitting work to the employee, not just fitting the employee to the organization's needs. Employees also have their reasons for not using workplace flexibility programs. Researchers in one study used focus groups to investigate why.[34] It revealed six major barriers to more widespread use of the programs:

» **Lack of communication** about the policies (vague or limited knowledge about them);
» **High workloads** (work builds up when employees take time off);
» **Management attitudes** (to some managers, employees who take advantage of the policies show lack of commitment; others are unwilling to accommodate differing needs of employees);
» **Career repercussions** (belief that if employees access workplace flexibility policies, their career progression will suffer);
» **The influence of peers** (fear that employee use of a workplace flexibility program will cause resentment or suggest that the employee is not a team player); and
» **Administrative processes** (excessive paperwork and long approval processes).

In short, not just the policies, but also the environment in which they are implemented, make the biggest difference for employees.[35] Much research supports the critical role that immediate supervisors play in the overall success of workplace flexibility programs.[36]

Yet, the environment remains challenging in most organizations. A survey of US and Canadian HR leaders revealed that:[37]

» Flexibility training for managers and employees remains a rarity in many organizations. Training is not specifically provided for employees or managers about how to be successful with flexible work arrangements.

» 44 percent of organizations do not feature or market flexibility as a key employee benefit when attempting to attract new employees.

» 53 percent of organizations do not have a flexibility strategy or philosophy. However, of those that do, only 19 percent have a formal, written document.

» Access to flexible work arrangements often depends on workforce segments or departments but is not widespread to all employees in 41 percent of organizations.

» Frequently, only a small portion of managers/leaders (42 percent) buy in to the idea that flexibility is an essential element to organizational success.

» When managers are hired or promoted, 76 percent of organizations do not consider their propensity for managing in a flexible work environment.

» 93 percent of managers' stated performance objectives do not typically include goals that encourage consideration and/or use of flexibility options by their employees.

» A majority of organizations have no written flexibility strategy/philosophy, no/few written policies, and no forms, or flexibility is at the discretion of managers for administration.

The 2016 National Study of Employers reported similar findings.[38] As Figure 8.1 illustrates, a more formal approach would include things such as a multichannel communication strategy to promote and publicize the organization's workplace flexibility policies (for example, company intranet, in-house newspaper, email), coupled with training for managers on how to support employees who take advantage of them. For example, that training could be designed around the kinds of behaviors from supervisors that are reflected in just three items from the National Study of the Changing Workforce. Those items are strongly related to employee engagement, job satisfaction, and turnover intentions:[39]

» My supervisor is supportive when I have a work problem.
» My supervisor recognizes me when I do a good job.
» My supervisor keeps me informed of things I need to know to do my job well.

At a broader level, the 2016 National Study of Employers identified seven components of effective workplaces:[40] job challenge and learning opportunities; job autonomy; supervisor task support; climate of respect and trust; satisfaction with earnings, benefits and opportunities for advancement; and work/life fit, including workplace flexibility. The researchers found that employees in more effective and flexible workplaces are more likely than other employees to have:

» Greater engagement in their jobs;
» Higher levels of job satisfaction;
» Stronger intentions to remain with their employers;
» Less negative and stressful spillover from job to home;
» Less negative spillover from home to job; and
» Better mental health.

To break down barriers and to enhance decisions about where investments in workplace flexibility programs are likely to have the most significant strategic value, line managers need a logical framework like Figure 8.1, and economic results. Yet the study of US and Canadian organizations found that only 3 percent even attempt to quantify the ROI of flexibility programs by measuring items such as productivity, employee engagement, and performance rating. Workplace flexibility initiatives are only one determinant of employee behaviors, along with factors such as pay, working conditions, and the work itself, but research indicates that they can have substantial effects on employee decisions to stay with an organization and to produce high-quality work.

Analytics and Measures: Connecting Workplace Flexibility Programs to Outcomes

As we pointed out in earlier chapters, the term *analytics* describes the research designs and statistical models that justify meaningful conclusions from studies of linkages between programs and outcomes. The term *measures* describes the actual data and formulas that populate those models. For workplace flexibility programs, the measures include the investments in the programs, as well as measures of outcomes such as absence and turnover. The analytical challenges include ensuring that program effects are not confused with other factors (controlling for extraneous effects) and determining correlation and causation.

Childcare

A 2017 study by Child Care Aware of America noted that:[41]

» US businesses lose approximately $4.4 billion annually due to employee absenteeism resulting from childcare breakdowns.[42]

» Over a six-month period, 45 percent of parents are absent from work at least once, missing an average of 4.3 days, due to childcare breakdowns.[43]

» 65 percent of parents' work schedules are affected by childcare challenges an average of 7.5 times over a six-month period.[44]

» $28.9 billion in wages is lost annually by working families who do not have access to affordable childcare and paid family and medical leave.[45]

A 2014 study of hospital employees found that employee performance was higher and absenteeism was lower for employees using on-site childcare than employees using an off-site center or who had no children.[46]

Employers considering offering such a benefit should understand childcare service delivery, the cost of care and its availability, what is available in the local market, and any challenges it presents. In addition, employers need to consider the business case for offering childcare.[47] Depending on the nature of the business, the goal may be to improve recruitment and retention, support the advancement of women, reduce absenteeism, retain high performers, or be an employer of choice. Then measure what matters, considering key drivers of the business and the goals established for the program.

Flexible Work Arrangements

To help inform the debate about flexible work arrangements, consider the financial and nonfinancial effects that have been reported for these key outcomes shown in Figure 8.1: *talent management* (specifically, better recruiting and lower turnover) and *human-capital outcomes* (increased satisfaction and commitment, decreased stress), which affect cost and performance, leading to *financial, operational, and business outcomes.*

Talent Management

In 2018, the Australian Victorian Government engaged Nous Group to examine the financial benefits of ten types of flexible work arrangements: part-time work; purchased leave; unplanned leave; parental leave beyond statutory requirements; flexitime; compressed working weeks/hours; time in lieu; job sharing; flexible career management; and working from home/telecommuting. They studied three organizations and found that the economic benefits of improved absence, recruitment, retention, and workforce productivity exceeded the costs in all cases (see Table 8.1).

Human-Capital Outcomes: Employee Satisfaction

Aerospace software manufacturer Orbit Logic was created "with flexibility in mind" when it started doing business, according to its CHRO, Artiana George. Orbit Logic is a "small but growing" business with about twenty employees and has a mix of private-sector and government clients, George said. Flexible schedule and

Table 8.1. Economic Payoffs to Workplace Flexibility in Three Australian Organizations

Economic Impact (per year)	Department of Environment, Land, Water and Planning (3,500 employees)	Mercy Health (7,300 employees)	Wannon Water (220 employees)
Increased Labor Productivity	$29 million	$26 million	$250,000
Reduced Retention Cost	$8.6 million	$17.4 million	$6,000
Reduced Absence Cost	$2.4 million	$420,000	$0
Reduced Recruitment Cost	$643,000	$3.7 million	$33,000
Total Savings	$41 million	$47 million	$288,000
Backfill for Extended Leave	$75,000	$3,000	$1,000
Office Rental	NA	$400,000	NA
Flexible Implementation	$400,000	$490,000	$41,000
Information Technology	$570,000	$4.4 million	$50,000
Onboarding	$790,000	$17.6 million	$3,000
Additional Management	$8 million	$960,000	$50,000
Total Cost	$10 million	$24 million	$138,000
Net Benefit	$31 million	$23 million	$150,000

telework policies were established since the company's founding in 2000, prompted, in part, by notoriously difficult traffic conditions in Washington, DC. But another reason for flexible work arrangements at Orbit Logic was the desire to draw top talent. "To attract the best and brightest software developers and system engineers, we need to give them more flexibility." All employees are eligible for flexible scheduling and telework. George said, "As long as we know where everyone is and what they're working on, we're OK. We do an employee survey every year, and we ask everyone to list their favorite benefit. This company offers profit-sharing as well as 100% paid health benefits. But flexibility is always ranked number one."[48]

At Deloitte & Touche, one employee survey item asked whether employees agreed with the statement "My manager grants me enough flexibility to meet my personal/family responsibilities." Those who agreed that they have access to flexibility scored 32 percent higher in commitment than those who believed they did not have access to flexibility. Likewise, AstraZeneca found that commitment scores were 28 percent higher for employees who said they had the flexibility they needed, compared to employees who did not have the flexibility they needed.

Financial Performance, and Operational and
Business Outcomes: Client Service
Ctrip is an employee-owned Chinese travel agency with 16,000 employees. In a scientific experiment, call-center employees volunteered and were randomly assigned to work at home or in the office for nine months.[49] Home working led to a 13 percent performance increase, of which 9 percent was from working more minutes per shift (fewer breaks and sick days) and 4 percent from more calls per minute (attributed to a quieter and more convenient working environment). Home workers also reported improved work satisfaction, and their attrition rate halved, but their promotion rate conditional on performance fell. Due to the success of the experiment, Ctrip rolled out the option to work from home to the whole firm and allowed the employees who participated in the experiment to reselect between the home and office. Interestingly, more than half of them switched, which led to the gains from working from home almost doubling to 22 percent. Studies such as this one make it

possible to reframe the discussion and to position flexibility not as a "perk," employee-friendly benefit, or advocacy cause, but as a powerful business tool that can enhance talent management, improve important human-capital outcomes, and boost financial and operational performance.[50]

Stock Price Reactions to Work/Life Initiatives

A study examined stock market effects of 130 announcements by *Fortune* 500 companies of work/life initiatives in the *Wall Street Journal*.[51] The study examined changes in share prices the day before, the day of, and the day after such announcements. The average share price reaction over the three-day window was 0.39 percent, and the average dollar value of such changes was approximately $60 million per firm. Apparently, investors anticipate that firms will have access to more resources (such as higher-quality talent) following the adoption of a workplace flexibility initiative. There is a difference, however, between announcements and actual implementation. Only firms that do what they say they will do are likely to reap the benefits of workplace flexibility initiatives.

In another study, researchers used data from 1995 to 2002 to compare the financial and stock market performance of the "100 Best" companies for working mothers, as published each year by *Working Mother* magazine, to that of benchmark indexes of the performance of US equities, the S&P 500, and the Russell 3000.[52] In terms of sales per employee and return on assets, the study found no evidence that *Working Mother* "100 Best" companies were consistently more profitable or consistently more productive than comparable companies. At the same time, however, the total returns on common stock among *Working Mother* "100 Best" companies consistently outperformed the broader market benchmarks in each of the eight years of the study. The researchers found no evidence to indicate that "100 Best" companies are handicapped in the marketplace by offering generous work/life benefits, perhaps because their superior stock returns may lower their cost of capital and, therefore, make it more affordable to invest in such benefits. The point is that these results reflect association, not causation. Nonetheless, the results suggest that at least some of the association is due to work/life investments improving stock market outcomes.

Process

Employees at all levels, both men and women, and the members of different generations, want a new deal at work. To advance this agenda, leaders need to take four actions:[53]

» Stop defining the desire for doable jobs as a women's issue.

» Start viewing efforts to humanize jobs as a competitive advantage and business necessity, not as one-time accommodations for favored employees or executives.

» Realize that progress is actually possible and that many examples show that work at all levels can be retooled.

» Make it safe within your organization to talk about these issues.

Influencing Senior Leaders
Measures and analytics exist to improve decisions about talent and how it is organized. So, a key requirement is that leaders accept the logic and analyses that describe the effects of adopting workplace flexibility programs. Here is a three-pronged strategy to consider in securing that kind of buy-in:[54]

» Make the business case for workplace flexibility initiatives through data, research, and anecdotal evidence.

» Offer to train managers on how to use flexible management approaches—to understand that, for a variety of reasons, some people want to work long hours, way beyond the norm, but that's not for everybody. The objective is to train managers to understand that individual solutions will work better in the future than a one-size-fits-all approach.

» Use surveys and focus groups to demonstrate the importance of workplace flexibility in retaining talent.

» Recognize that no one set of facts and figures applies to all firms. It depends on the unique strategic priorities of each organization.

The Society for Human Resource Management suggests embedding workplace flexibility into organizational strategy:[55]

» Make flex a key part of the organization's employee value proposition.

» Ensure that flex isn't smoke and mirrors, but a key driver of engagement.

» Leverage flex for recruiting untapped talent pools.

» Brand the organization as a provider of flex solutions.

» Leverage flex to redesign work processes.

» Set clear expectations for managers and employees regarding flex arrangements.

» Build the use of flex options into managers' learning and development and embed the effective use of flex practices into career profiles and competencies.

» Evaluate managers on how well they implement flex arrangements, and factor that performance into their compensation decisions.

Figure 8.1 provides a diagnostic logic for conversations about this. Start by discussing whether such initiatives will be part of a recruitment strategy to help the organization become an employer of choice, a diversity strategy to promote the advancement of women and minorities, a total rewards strategy, a strategy to retain top talent, or a health and wellness strategy if the priority is stress reduction.[56] Find out what your organization and its employees care about right now, what the workforce will look like in three to five years, and therefore, what senior leaders will need to care about in the future.[57] Don't rely on isolated facts, because any single study or fact is only one piece of the total picture. Think in terms of a multi-pronged approach:

» External data that describe trends in your organization's own industry;
» Internal data that outline what employees want and how they describe their needs;[58] and
» Internal data, perhaps based on pilot studies, that examine the financial and nonfinancial effects of workplace flexibility programs. As one executive noted, "Nothing beats a within-firm story."[59]

Calculate the costs of absence and turnover. Workplace flexibility often works by reducing employee absence and turnover, so start by describing those costs (see Chapters 4 and 5). For example, many costs associated with employee turnover are not included in financial accounting, so firms often don't track them. As you have seen, when such costs *are* calculated, workplace flexibility initiatives often create attractive payoffs by reducing them.

Add anecdotes to your data. Include stories from your own workers that describe how workplace flexibility programs have helped them. Have quotes from people whom senior leaders know and care about.

Finally, expect that decision-makers may remain skeptical, even after all the facts and costs have been presented. Deeply rooted attitudes and beliefs may underlie the skepticism—such as a belief that allowing employees to attend to personal concerns through time off may erode service to clients or customers, or that people will take unfair advantage of the benefits, or that workplace flexibility issues are just women's issues. To inform that debate, HR leaders need to address attitudes and values, as well as data, on costs and benefits of workplace flexibility programs. As one set of authors noted:

> Every workplace, small or large, can undertake efforts to treat employees with respect, to give them some autonomy over how they do their jobs, to help supervisors support employees to succeed on their jobs, and to help supervisors and coworkers promote work/life fit.[60]

Ultimately, a system of workplace flexibility programs, coupled with an organizational culture that supports that system, will help an organization create and sustain competitive advantage through its people.

Exercises

1. Your boss is skeptical about claims that workplace flexibility is important to managers as well as employees. What evidence can you provide to offset this line of thinking?

2. What is a workplace flexibility program? What are some examples?

3. Describe the wage penalty associated with "opting out" of the workforce.

4. Why is workplace flexibility particularly important to professional employees?

5. Describe some of the key barriers to wider implementation of workplace flexibility programs.

6. Develop a strategy for informing the debate over whether to invest in workplace flexibility programs. What cautions would you build into your game plan?

7. Explain: The concept of "flexibility" reflects a broad spectrum of possible work arrangements.

8. What key features are critical to making decisions about whether to provide options for increased flexibility in work arrangements?

9. How do workplace flexibility programs relate to organizational performance?

10. You are given the following data regarding the costs and payoffs from employer-subsidized childcare arrangements in your 159-person professional services organization. Before offering childcare, employees missed 850 days of work each year. That has been cut by 170 days per year, at a cost savings of $315 per day in direct costs. Likewise, voluntary turnover among high performers has dropped by 22 percent, saving the company $1.1 million each year in costs that were not incurred. The full cost of the childcare program (design and delivery) is $650,000. What is the payoff of this investment?

References

1. Zoë Bernard, "Jeff Bezos Says His Advice to Amazon Interns and Execs is to Stop Aiming for Work-Life 'Balance'—Here's What You Should Strive for Instead," *Business Insider*, November 11, 2018, https://www.businessinsider.com/jeff-bezo-advice-to-amazon-employees-dont-aim-for-work-life-balance-its-a-circle-2018-4.

2. WorkplaceTrends.com, "The Employee Engagement Study," news release, January 9, 2017, https://workplacetrends.com/the-employee-burnout -crisis-study/.

3. Katie Beck, "France's Battle Against the 'Always On' Work Culture," *BBC Capital*, May 8, 2017, http://www.bbc.com/capital /story/20170507-frances-battle-against-always-on-work-culture.

4. "French Workers Get 'Right to Disconnect' from Emails Out of Hours," *BBC News*, December 31, 2016, https://www.bbc.com/news/world -europe-38479439.

5. EYGM Limited, *Global Generations: A Global Study on Work-Life Challenges Across Generations*, EYG no. KK1088 (London: EYGM Ltd. 2015).

6. Yvonne Lott and Heejung Chung, "Gender Discrepancies in the Outcomes of Schedule Control on Overtime Hours and Income in Germany," *European Sociological Review* 32, no. 6 (December 1, 2016): 752–65.

7. Kenneth Matos, Ellen Galinsky, and James T. Bond, *National Study of Employers* (Alexandria, VA: Society for Human Resource Management, 2017), 18–19, https://www.shrm.org/hr-today/trends-and-forecasting /research-and-surveys/Documents/National%20Study%20of%20Employers. pdf.

8. Sharon Clarke and Lynn Holdsworth, *Flexibility in the Workplace: Implications of Flexible Work Arrangements for Individuals, Teams and Organizations*, Ref: 03/17 (Manchester, UK: Alliance Manchester Business School, March 2017), http://www.acas.org.uk/media/pdf/o/7 /Flexibility-in-the-Workplace.pdf.

9. Milton Moskowitz, Robert Levering, and Christopher Tkaczyk, "100 Best Companies," *Fortune*, February 8, 2010, 75–88. See also SAS, "SAS Revenue Jumps 2.2% to Record $2.31 Billion," news release, January 21, 2010, accessed May 28, 2010, http://www.sas.com; SAS, "SAS Ranks No. 1 on *FORTUNE* 'Best Companies to Work For' List in America," news release, January 21, 2010, http://www.sas.com.

10. Fortune.com, "Best Companies 2018," http://fortune.com/best -companies/sas/.

11. Mark C. Crowley, "How SAS Became The World's Best Place To Work," *Fast Company*, January 22, 2013, https://www.fastcompany.com/3004953 /how-sas-became-worlds-best-place-work.

12. Wayne F. Cascio and SHRM Foundation, *Fueling the Talent Engine: Finding and Keeping High Performers: A Case Study of Yahoo!* (Alexandria, VA: Society for Human Resource Management Foundation, 2005), DVD. See also Russell W. Coff, "Human Assets and Management Dilemmas: Coping with Hazards on the Road to Resource-Based Theory," *Academy of Management Review* 22, no. 2 (April 1997): 374–403.

13. Christina Maslach and Michael P. Leiter, "Early Predictors of Job Burnout and Engagement," *Journal of Applied Psychology* 93, no. 3 (May 2008): 498–512. See also Christina Maslach, "Understanding Burnout: Work and Family Issues," in *From Work-Family Balance to Work-Family Interaction: Changing*

the Metaphor, ed. Diane F. Halpern and Susan E. Murphy (Mahwah, NJ: Lawrence Erlbaum, 2005).

14. Corporate Voices for Working Families and WFD Consulting, *Business Impacts of Flexibility: An Imperative for Expansion* (Washington, DC: Corporate Voices for Working Families, 2011).

15. Alison M. Konrad and Robert Mangel, "The Performance Effect of Work-Family Programs," (paper presentation, annual meeting of the Academy of Management, San Diego, CA, August 1998).

16. Konrad and Mangel, "Performance Effect."

17. Nanette Byrnes, "Treating Part-Timers Like Royalty," *BusinessWeek,* October 10, 2005, 78.

18. Konrad and Mangel, "Performance Effect."

19. Laura D. Tyson, "What Larry Summers Got Right," *BusinessWeek,* March 28, 2005, 24.

20. Sylvia Ann Hewlett and Carolyn Buck Luce, "Off-Ramps and On-Ramps: Keeping Talented Women on the Road to Success," *Harvard Business Review,* March 2005, 43–54.

21. Diane Brady, "Hopping Aboard the Daddy Track," *BusinessWeek,* November 8, 2004, 100–101.

22. A. A. Johnson, "Strategic Meal Planning: Work/Life Initiatives for Building Strong Organizations," (paper presentation, conference on Integrated Health, Disability, and Work/Life Initiatives, New York, 25 February 1999).

23. Ellen Galinsky, Kerstin Aumann, and James T. Bond, *The 2008 National Study of the Changing Workforce: Times Are Changing—Gender and Generation at Work and at Home* (New York: Families and Work Institute, 2009).

24. Ellen Ernst Kossek and Cynthia Ozekis, "Work-Family Conflict, Policies, and the Job-Life Satisfaction Relationship: A Review and Directions for Organizational Behavior-Human Resources Research," *Journal of Applied Psychology* 83, no. 2 (April 1998): 139–49.

25. Galinsky, Aumann, and Bond, *2008 National Study,* 2009.

26. Helen De Cieri et al., "Achievements and Challenges for Work/Life Balance Strategies in Australian Organizations," *International Journal of Human Resource Management* 16, no. 1 (2005): 90–103.

27. Corinne Purtill, "PWC's Millennial Employees Led a Rebellion—and Their Demands Are Being Met," *Quartz at Work,* March 10, 2018, https://qz.com/work/1217854/pwcs-millennial-employees-led-a-rebellion-and-their-demands-are-being-met/.

28. Dennis Finn and Anne Donovan, *PwC's Next Gen: A Global Generational Study* (New York: PwC, 2013), https://www.pwc.com/gx/en/hr-management-services/pdf/pwc-nextgen-study-2013.pdf.

29. Purtill, "PWC's Millennial Employees."

30. "Flexibility²,"About Us, PwC United States, https://www.pwc.com/us/en/about-us/diversity/pwc-work-life-balance.html.

31. "Flexibility²,"About Us, PwC United States, https://www.pwc.com/us/en/about-us/diversity/pwc-work-life-balance.html.

32. Kathy Gurchiek, "Expert: Work-Life Initiatives Start at the Top," *HR News*, September 26, 2008, https://www.shrm.org/hr-today/news/hr-news/pages/initiativesstartattop.aspx.
33. Franca Godenzi, *The Future of Flexibility* (Boston, MA: Boston College Center for Work and Family, 2013).
34. Michelle A. Waters and E. Anne Bardoel, "Work-Family Policies in the Context of Higher Education: Useful or Symbolic?," *Asia Pacific Journal of Human Resources* 44, no. 1 (April 2006): 67–82.
35. Mary Blair-Loy and Amy S. Wharton, "Employees' Use of Work-Family Policies and the Workplace Social Context," *Social Forces* 80, no. 3 (March 2002): 813–45.
36. Susan E. Murphy and David A. Zagorski, "Enhancing Work-Family and Work-Life Interaction: The Role of Management," in *From Work-Family Balance to Work-Family Interaction: Changing the Metaphor* ed. Diane F. Halpern and Susan E. Murphy (Mahwah, NJ: Lawrence Erlbaum Associates, 2005), 27–47. See also David A. Zagorski, "Balancing the Scales: The Role of Justice and Organizational Culture in Employees' Search for Work-Life Equilibrium," unpublished doctoral dissertation, Claremont Graduate University, 2005.
37. WorldatWork, *Trends in Workplace Flexibility* (Scottsdale, AZ: WorldatWork, 2015).
38. Kenneth Matos, Ellen Galinsky, and James T. Bond, *2016 National Study of Employers* (Alexandria, VA: Society for Human Resource Management, 2017).
39. Society for Human Resource Management, *2016 National Study of the Changing Workforce* (Alexandria, VA: Society for Human Resource Management, 2017). See also Kerstin Aumann and Ellen Galinsky, *The 2008 National Study of the Changing Workforce: The State of Health of the American Workforce: Does Having an Effective Workplace Matter?* (New York: Families and Work Institute, 2009).
40. Matos, Galinsky, and Bond, *2016 National Study of Employers*.
41. Lynnette Fraga et al., *Parents and the High Cost of Child Care* (Arlington, VA: Child Care Aware of America, 2017), https://usa.childcareaware.org/wp-content/uploads/2017/12/2017_CCA_High_Cost_Report_FINAL.pdf.
42. Maria E. Enchautegui, Marth Johnson, and Julia Gelatt, *Who Minds the Kids When Mom Works a Nonstandard Schedule?* (Washington, DC: Urban Institute, July 2015), http://www.urban.org/sites/default/files/alfresco/publication-pdfs/2000307-Who-Minds-the-Kids-When-Mom-Works-a-Nonstandard-Schedule.pdf.
43. "Why Should Employers Care? Relationship Between Productivity and Working Parents," Early Care & Learning Council, 2014, https://childcarecouncil.com/wp-content/uploads/2014/07/Why-Should-Employers-Care-ECLC.pdf.
44. Early Care & Learning Council, "Why Should Employers Care?"

45. Sarah Jane Glynn and Danielle Corley, *The Cost of Work-Family Policy Inaction: Quantifying the Costs Families Currently Face as a Result of Lacking US Work-Family Policies* (Washington, DC: Center for American Progress, 2016), https://cdn.americanprogress.org/wp-content/uploads/2016/09/22060013/CostOfWorkFamilyPolicyInaction-report.pdf.
46. Nicole L. Gullekson et al., "Vouching for Childcare Assistance with Two Quasi-Experimental Studies," *Journal of Managerial Psychology* 29, no. 8 (2014): 994–1008, https://doi.org/10.1108/JMP-06-2012-0182.
47. Kathy Gurchiek, "Child Care 'Investment' Creates Competitive Advantage," *HR News,* March 5, 2007, accessed May 25, 2010 https://www.shrm.org/hr-today/news/hr-news/pages/cms_020657.aspx.
48. Society for Human Resource Management, *SHRM Research: Flexible Work Arrangements* (Alexandria, VA: Society for Human Resource Management, 2015).
49. Nicholas Bloom et al., "Does Working From Home Work? Evidence From A Chinese Experiment," *The Quarterly Journal of Economics,* 130, no. 1 (February 2015): 165–218.
50. Amy Richman, Arlene Johnson, and Karen Noble, *Business Impacts of Flexibility: An Imperative for Expansion* (Washington, DC: Corporate Voices for Working Families, November 2005), http://www.wfd.com/PDFS/Business%20Impacts%20of%20Flexibility.pdf.
51. Michelle M. Arthur, "Share Price Reactions to Work-Family Initiatives: An Institutional Perspective," *Academy of Management Journal* 46, no. 4 (August 2003): 497–505.
52. Wayne F. Cascio and Clifford E. Young, "Work-Family Balance: Does the Market Reward Firms That Respect It?," in *From Work-Family Balance to Work-Family Interaction: Changing the Metaphor* ed. Diane F. Halpern and Susan E. Murphy (Mahwah, NJ: Lawrence Erlbaum Associates, 2005), 49–63.
53. Jody Miller, "Get a Life!," *Fortune,* November 28, 2005, 110.
54. Gurchiek, "Expert: Work-Life Initiatives."
55. Stephen Miller, "Using Workplace Flexibility as a Talent Strategy," *SHRM Online,* May 4, 2012.
56. Gurchiek, "Expert: Work-Life Initiatives."
57. Betty Purkey et al., "Sitting at the Corporate Table: How Work-Family Policies Are Really Made," in *From Work-Family Balance to Work-Family Interaction: Changing the Metaphor* ed. Diane F. Halpern and Susan E. Murphy (Mahwah, NJ: Lawrence Erlbaum Associates, 2005), 71–82.
58. Susan Caminiti, "Reinventing the Workplace," *Fortune,* September 20, 2004, S12–S15.
59. Bill Roberts, "Analyze This!," *HR Magazine,* October 2009, 35–41.
60. Aumann and Galinsky, *2008 National Study of the Changing Workforce.*

9

Staffing Utility: The Concept and Its Measurement

M anagement ideas and programs often have been adopted and implemented because they were fashionable (for example, Total Quality Management, Quality Circles, re-engineering) or commercially appealing, or because of the entertainment value they offered the target audience.[1] In an era of downsizing, deregulation, and fierce global competition, and as operating executives continue to examine the costs of HR programs, HR executives are under increasing pressure to demonstrate that new or continuing programs add value in more tangible ways. Indeed, an ongoing challenge is to educate managers about the business value of HR programs in areas such as staffing and training. While some of the business value of these programs may be expressed in qualitative terms (such as improvements in customer service, team dynamics, or innovation),[2] our focus in this chapter and the two that follow it is on methods to express the monetary value of HR programs.

This chapter and Chapter 10 describe techniques for calculating the monetary value of HR programs, focusing specifically on the payoff from improved staffing. Chapter 11, "Costs and Benefits of HR Development Programs," focuses on how the logical frameworks for staffing can be adapted to calculate the monetary value of employee training and development. Techniques for estimating monetary value have been particularly well-developed when applied to staffing programs. The combination of analytics based on widely applicable statistical assumptions, plus a logical approach for combining information to connect to the quality of the workforce, and analytical frameworks and tools to understand how workforce quality affects pivotal organizational outcomes, has produced sophisticated frameworks.

We begin this chapter by describing the logic underlying the value of staffing decisions in terms of the conditions that define that value and that, when satisfied, lead to high value. After that, we present a broad overview of utility analysis as a way to improve organizational decisions, especially decisions about human capital. Note that many of the examples in this chapter refer to dollar-valued outcomes because the research was conducted in the United States. However, the same concepts apply to any currency. Recall from Chapter 2, "Analytical Foundations for HR Measurement," that utility analysis generally refers to frameworks that help decision-makers analyze in a systematic manner the subjective value or expected utility of alternative outcomes associated with a decision. The expected utility or usefulness of each outcome is obtained by summing a rating of the outcome's importance or value to the decision maker multiplied by the expectation or probability of achieving that outcome. After summing these values across all outcomes, the decision rule is to choose the option with the highest expected utility. The approach to staffing utility measurement is similar; instead of simple estimates and multiplication, however, the formulas incorporate more nuanced approaches to probabilities, value estimations, and combinations of the individual elements.

A Decision-Based Framework for Staffing Measurement

Measures exist to enhance decisions. With respect to staffing decisions, measures are important to the decisions of applicants, potential applicants, recruiters, hiring managers, and HR professionals. These decisions include how to invest scarce resources (money, time, materials, and so on) in staffing techniques and activities, such as alternative recruiting sources, different selection and screening technologies, recruiter training or incentives, and alternative mixes of pay and benefits to offer desirable candidates. Staffing decisions also include decisions by candidates about whether to entertain or accept offers and decisions by hiring managers about whether to devote time and effort to landing the best talent. Increasingly, such decisions are not made exclusively by HR or staffing professionals, but in conjunction with managers outside of HR and other key constituents.[3]

Effective staffing requires measurements that diagnose the quality of the decisions of managers and applicants. Typical staffing-measurement systems fail to reflect these key decisions, so they end up with significant limitations and decision risks. For example, selection tests may be chosen solely based on their cost and predictive relationships with turnover or performance ratings. Recruitment sources may be chosen solely based on their cost and volume of applicants. Recruiters may be chosen based solely on their availability and evaluated only on the volume of applicants they produce. Staffing is typically treated not as a process, but as a set of isolated activities (recruiting, selecting, offering/closing, and so forth).

Fixing these problems requires a systematic approach to staffing that treats it as a set of decisions and processes that begins with a set of outcomes, identifies key processes, and integrates outcomes with processes. Consider outcomes, for example. We know that the ultimate value of a staffing system is reflected in the quality of talent that is hired or promoted and retained. In fact, a wide variety of measures exists to examine staffing quality, but generally these measures fall into seven categories:

» **Cost:** Cost per hire, cost of assessment activities (tests, interviews, background checks);
» **Time of activities:** Time to fill vacancies, time elapsed from interview to offer;

» **Volume and yield:** Total number of applicants, yield of hires from applicants;
» **Diversity and compliance:** Demographic characteristics of applicants at each stage of the hiring process;
» **Customer/constituent reactions:** Judgments about the quality of the process and impressions about its attractiveness;
» **Quality attributes of the talent:** Pre-hire predictive measures of quality (selection tests, interviewer ratings), as well as post-hire measures of potential and competency; and
» **Value impact of the talent:** Measures of actual job performance and overall contribution to the goals of a unit or organization.

This chapter focuses primarily on two of these measures: the quality attributes and value impact of talent. It focuses on the value of investments in recruiting, screening, and selecting employees. It is important not to lose sight of the broader staffing processes within which screening and selection of talent take place. Figure 9.1 is a graphic illustration of the logic of the staffing process and talent flows.

Groups of individuals (talent pools) flow through the various stages of the staffing process, with each stage serving as a filter that eliminates a subset of the original talent pool. The top row of Figure 9.1 shows the results of the filtering process, beginning with a potential labor pool that is winnowed through recruitment and selection down to a group that receives offers and then is winnowed further as some accept offers and remain with the organization.

The staffing processes in the lower row show the activities that accomplish the filtering sequence, beginning with building and planning (forecasting trends in external and internal labor markets, inducing potential applicants to develop qualifications to satisfy future talent demands) and ending with on-boarding (orientation, mentoring, removing barriers to performance). Integrating measurement categories with the process steps shown in Figure 9.1

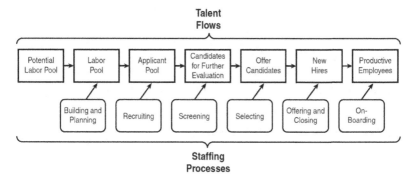

Figure 9.1. Logic of staffing processes and talent flows.

provides a decision-based framework for evaluating where staffing measures are sufficient and where they may be lacking.

Figure 9.1 might usefully be viewed as a supply chain approach to staffing. To appreciate that analogy, consider that the pipeline of talent is very similar to the pipeline of any other resource. At each stage, the candidate pool can be thought of in terms of the quantity of candidates, the average and dispersion of the quality of the candidates, and the cost of processing and employing the candidates. Quantity, quality, and cost considerations determine the monetary value of staffing programs.

Now that we have presented the big picture of the staffing process, let us focus more specifically on one component of that process: employee selection (specifically, on assessing the value of selection by means of utility analysis).

Framing Human Capital Decisions through the Lens of Utility Analysis

Utility analysis is a framework to guide decisions about investments in human capital.[4] It estimates the gain or loss anticipated from various courses of action. When faced with a choice among strategies, management should choose the strategy that maximizes the expected utility for the organization.[5] To make the choice, managers must be able to estimate the utilities associated with various outcomes. Gains and losses may be estimated subjectively or by objective behavioral or accounting procedures, often in monetary terms. This chapter describes models of staffing utility analysis, focusing on the logic and analytics of each one. Then, to build on these ideas, it describes measures and processes and, finally, research on how to communicate results to operating executives to show how staffing can be evaluated from a return-on-investment perspective.

Overview—The Logic of Utility Analysis

Utility analysis considers three important parameters: quantity, quality, and cost. A careful look at Figure 9.1 shows that the top row refers to the characteristics of candidates for employment as they flow through the various stages of the staffing process. For example, the applicant pool might have a quantity of 100 candidates, with an average quality of $100,000 per year, and a quality variation ranging from a low of $50,000 to a high of $170,000. This group of candidates might have an anticipated employment cost (salary, benefits, training, and so on) of 70 percent of their value. Once the applicants have been screened and selected, the resulting group of "offer candidates" might contain 50 candidates, with an average quality of $150,000 per year, ranging from a low of $100,000 to a high of $160,000. Candidates who receive offers might command employment costs of 80 percent of their value because they are more highly qualified and sought-after. Eventually, the organization ends up with a group of new hires (or promoted candidates, in the case of internal staffing) that can also be characterized by quantity, quality, and cost.

Similarly, the bottom row of Figure 9.1 reflects the staffing processes that create the sequential filtering of candidates. Each of these processes can be thought of in terms of the *quantity* of programs and practices used, the *quality* of the programs and practices as reflected in their ability to improve the value of the pool of individuals that survives, and the *cost* of the programs and practices in each process. For example, the quality of selection procedures is often expressed in terms of their validity, or accuracy in forecasting future job performance. Validity is typically expressed in terms of the correlation (see Chapter 2) between scores on a selection procedure and some measure of job performance, such as the dollar volume of sales. Validity may be increased by including a greater quantity of assessments (such as a battery of selection procedures), each of which focuses on an aspect of knowledge, skill, ability, or other characteristic that has been demonstrated to be important to successful performance on a job. Higher levels of validity imply higher levels of future job performance among those selected or promoted, thereby improving the overall payoff to the organization. As a result, those candidates who are predicted to perform poorly never get hired or promoted in the first place. Decision-makers naturally focus on the cost of selection procedures because they are so vividly depicted by standard accounting systems, but the cost of errors in selecting, hiring, or promoting the wrong person is often much greater. The added performance value is often much higher than the added cost of improving the staffing process. In the case of executives, a company often has to pay large fees to headhunters, and poor performance can have serious consequences in terms of projects, products, and customers. That cost can easily be millions of dollars.[6]

In summary, the payoff to the organization (utility) from staffing procedures depends on three broad parameters: quantity, quality, and cost. Each of the staffing utility models that we examine in this chapter addresses two or more of these parameters. The models usually focus on the selection part of the processes shown in Figure 9.1, but they have implications for the other staffing stages too. Each model defines the quality of candidates in a different way, so we start with models that make relatively basic assumptions and move on to those that are increasingly sophisticated.

Utility Models and Staffing Decisions

The usefulness, or utility, of a selection process is simply how much using it, compared with not using it, improves the quality of the selected candidates.[7] Researchers have used two utility models to describe and measure this usefulness:

» The Taylor and Russell[8] model defines usefulness as the increase in the proportion of individuals in the selected group who are successful; and

» The Brogden, Cronbach, and Gleser[9] model defines usefulness as the increase in monetary payoff to the organization.

Taylor-Russell Staffing Utility

Many decision-makers might assume that if candidate ratings on a selection device (such as a test or interview) are highly associated with their later job performance, the selection device must be worth the investment. After all, how could better prediction of future performance not be worth the investment? However, if the pool of candidates contains very few unacceptable candidates, better testing may do little good. Or if the organization generates so few candidates that it must hire almost all of them, again, better testing will be of little use.

Taylor and Russell translated these observations into a system for measuring the tradeoffs, suggesting that the overall utility or practical effectiveness of a selection device depends on more than just the validity coefficient (the correlation between a predictor of job performance and a criterion measure of actual job performance). Rather, it depends on three parameters: the validity coefficient (r), the selection ratio (SR, the proportion of applicants selected), and the base rate (BR, the proportion of applicants who would be successful without the selection procedure).

Taylor and Russell defined the value of the selection system as the "success ratio," which is the ratio of the number of hired candidates who are judged successful on the job divided by the total number of candidates that were hired. They published a series of tables illustrating the interactive effect of different validity coefficients, selection ratios, and base rates on the success ratio. The success ratio indicates the quality of those selected. The difference between the success ratio and the base rate (which reflects the success ratio without any added selection system) is a measure of the added value of the selection system over what would have happened if it had not been used. Let's develop this logic and its implications in more detail.

Analytics
There are three key, underlying assumptions of this model:

1. It assumes fixed-treatment selection: Individuals are chosen for one specified job or other course of action that cannot be modified. For example, if a person is selected for a training program for slow learners, transfer to fast-track instruction is not allowed, regardless of how well the person does in the training program.

2. The Taylor-Russell model does not account for the rejected individuals who would have been successful if hired (erroneous rejections). Because they are not hired, their potential value is not considered.

3. The model classifies those hired as either successful or unsuccessful. That means that being minimally successful is assumed to be equal in value to being highly successful and being just below the acceptable standard is assumed to be equal in value to being extremely unsuccessful.

Of course, these assumptions do not hold in all situations. However, even with these basic assumptions, Taylor and Russell generated useful conclusions about the interplay between testing and the applicant pool. Here are examples of how the selection ratio and base rate reveal insights for investing in selection systems and show decision-makers how the validity of the system is only one key factor:

The selection ratio is simply the number of candidates who must be hired divided by the number of available candidates to choose from. Suppose you have a selection ratio (SR) of 1.0, or 100 percent. That means that you must hire everyone, so even the most valid selection system is of no value because there are no selection decisions to be made. Thus, the closer the SR is to 1.0, the harder it is for better selection to pay off. The opposite is also true because the smaller the SR, the greater the value of better selection. A selection ratio of .10 means the organization will only hire 10 percent of the available applicants. Even selection systems with low validity can be useful if the SR is very low because the organization can choose only the cream of the crop. Conversely, with high selection ratios, almost everyone must be hired, so a selection system must have very high validity in order to increase the success ratio.

It might appear that, because a selection system is always more valuable with a lower selection ratio, organizations should always try to generate more applicants, and thus reduce the selection ratio. However, the optimal strategy is not this simple.[10] Lowering the SR by increasing the number of applicants means greater recruiting and selection effort. In practice, that strategy may be too costly.[11] The Taylor and Russell model also depends on the base rate (the proportion of candidates who would be successful without the selection process). The value of the selection process is the incremental improvement over the base rate. That is, the process must produce more correct decisions than would be made without using it. When the base rate is either very high or very low, it is difficult for a selection measure to improve upon it. For example, with a BR 0.80 and half of the applicants selected, the selection process must have a very high validity of 0.45 to make even a 10 percent improvement. This is also true at very low base rates, when almost no candidates would be successful. At a base rate of 0.20, if the top half of candidates are selected (selection ratio of 50 percent) and the selection process has a validity of 0.45, the success ratio is 0.30, again representing only a 10 percent improvement. Selection measures are most useful when BRs are about 0.50.[12] In short, you can't evaluate the value of a selection system solely by how well it predicts future performance. Situations with markedly different selection ratios and base rates produce quite different outcomes, even with the same selection validity.

Perhaps the major shortcoming of this utility model is that it reflects the quality of the resulting hires only in terms of success or failure. The success ratio tells us that more people are successful, but not *how much more* successful. Sometimes that is appropriate, such as when a production line feeds parts to workers to be inspected at a fixed rate and defects are very similar and easy to spot. The value of performance above the standard (detecting details about the defect) is no greater than the minimum standard (simply detecting the defect). Or, if the definition of minimum value is that the employee remains on the job for some fixed period (such as whether seasonal workers stay for the entire season), then the value of staying longer is no greater than the value of staying the minimum amount.

Still, it's obvious that for most work performance, a very high-quality employee, or one who stays longer, is more valuable than one who just meets the minimum acceptable standard. When this is true, the Taylor-Russell model will underestimate the actual amount of value from the selection system. That observation led to a staffing utility model that could account for the value of better performance—the Brogden-Cronbach-Gleser model.

Brogden-Cronbach-Gleser Staffing Utility

Brogden showed that under certain conditions, the validity coefficient is a direct index of selective efficiency. If both the predictor and the criterion are expressed in standard (Z) score units, then the validity coefficient (r_{xy}) represents the ratio of the average criterion score of those selected using selection predictor scores ($\overline{Z}_y$) to the average score if one had selected them based on their criterion scores ($\overline{Z}_{y'}$). Of course, it is not possible to select applicants based on their criterion scores (because one cannot observe their criterion scores before they are hired), but Brogden's insight means that the validity coefficient is the ratio of how well an actual selection process does compared to perfect prediction, as shown in Equation 9.1:

$$r_{xy} = \frac{\overline{Z}_y}{\overline{Z}_{y'}} \tag{9.1}$$

Recall that our ultimate goal is to identify the monetary payoff to the organization when it uses a selection system to hire employees. Let's assume we could construct a monetary criterion measure. We'll symbolize it as $y_\$$. Examples of this might include the sales made during a week/month/quarter by each of the salespersons on a certain job; the profit obtained from each retail operation managed by each of the store managers across a country; or the outstanding customer debts paid during a week/month/quarter for the customers handled by each of a group of call-center collection agents. If we call that criterion measure $y_\$$, then here is the logic of Brogden's approach.[13]

Step 1: Express the predictor-criterion relationship
as a formula for a straight line
Recall the formula for a straight line that most people learn in their first algebra class, shown here as Equation 9.2.

$$\hat{y}_\$ = a + bx + e \tag{9.2}$$

Where:

$y_\$$ = dependent variable, or criterion (such as a job performance measure), measured in dollars or other monetary units.

x = independent variable or score on a selection system that we hope predicts our criterion (e. g., job performance).

a = "y intercept" or where the line crosses the y axis of a graph when x = 0.

b = slope, or "rise over the run" of the line (for example sales) for every one-unit change in x (score on a sales-aptitude test).

Then, let's substitute the symbol b_0 for a, b_1 for b, and add an e, to reflect the random fluctuation or "error" in any straight-line estimate, and we get Equation 9.3:

$$\hat{y}_s = b_0 + b_1 x + e \tag{9.3}$$

Figure 9.2 shows this idea as a straight line passing through an ellipse. The ellipse represents the cloud of score combinations that might occur in an actual group of people, and the line in the middle is the one that gets as close as possible to as many of the points in the cloud.

In the context of staffing, x would be each employee's score on some selection process, and y would be the same employee's subsequent criterion score (such as performance on the job). If we don't know yet how someone is going to perform on the job (which we can't know before the person is hired), a best guess or estimate of how the employee might perform on the job would be the y_s value obtained from plugging the applicant's x score into Equation 9.3.

Least-squares regression analyses can be used to calculate the best-fitting straight line (that is, Equation 9.3), where *best* means the formula for the straight line that minimizes the sum of all squared errors (e^2).

Step 2: Standardize x
To get to the validity coefficient, we need to convert the actual, or raw, scores on our predictor and criterion to standardized form.

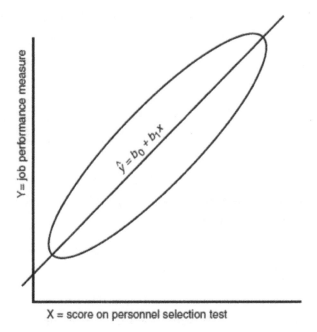

Figure 9.2. Dispersion of actual criterion and predictor scores.

Let's first standardize all the applicants' selection process scores (that is, take their original scores, subtract the average, and divide by the standard deviation), as shown in Equation 9.4:

$$z_i = \frac{x_i - \bar{x}}{SD_x} \tag{9.4}$$

Where:

x_i = selection process score earned by applicant i.

z_i = "standard" or Z score corresponding to the x_i score for applicant i.

$\bar{x}$ = average or mean selection process score, typically of all applicants, obtained in some sample.

SD_x = standard deviation of x_i around $\bar{x}$, or $SD_x = \sqrt{\dfrac{\displaystyle\sum_{i=1}^{n}(x_i - \bar{x})^2}{n-1}}$

When Equation 9.3 is modified to reflect the fact that x is now standardized, it becomes Equation 9.5.

$$\hat{y}_s = b_0 + b_1 z \tag{9.5}$$

Step 3: Express the equations in terms of the validity coefficient
Finally, let's modify Equation 9.4 to show the role of the validity coefficient using this selection process.

The expected value of b_1 can be calculated using multiple-regression software (for example, the regression function in Excel). This is the regression coefficient or beta weight associated with x. By definition, the regression coefficient can also be defined as in Equation 9.6.

$$b_1 = r_{xy} \left(\frac{SD_y}{SD_x} \right) \tag{9.6}$$

Where:

r_{xy} = simple correlation between test scores on the selection measure x and the criterion measure y.

SD_y = standard deviation of the monetary value of the criterion (such as job performance).

SD_x = standard deviation of all applicants' selection-test scores.

The standard deviation of z scores is always 1.0. So, substituting 1 for SD_x, Equation 9.6 becomes $b_1 = r_{xy} SD_y$.

Substituting μ_s (the symbol for the true average dollar criterion value among the applicants) for b_0 and $r_{xy} SD_y$ for b_1 in Equation 9.5, we get Equation 9.7.

$$\bar{y}_s = \mu_s + r_{xy} SD_y \bar{z}_s \tag{9.7}$$

Equation 9.7 describes the expected monetary value of each selected applicant. To calculate the expected average improvement in the monetary value produced by using the staffing system, we subtract the expected value we would get without using the system, symbolized by μ_s, from both sides of the equation.

$$\overline{y}_\$ - \mu_s = r_{xy} SD_y \overline{z}_s \tag{9.8}$$

Finally, the left side of Equation 9.8 is symbolized as ΔU, to stand for the delta, or change in utility, per applicant selected, as shown in Equation 9.9.

$$\Delta U = r_{xy} SD_y \overline{z}_s \tag{9.9}$$

Step 4: Subtract the costs of the selection process
Equation 9.9 tells us how much more monetary value our average selected candidate will generate when using a selection system versus when not using the system. However, that value is not free. Selecting applicants requires resources. Let's use the letter C to stand for the cost of applying the selection process to one applicant and the term N_a to stand for the total number of applicants. The total cost of the selection process is the product of N_a and C. If we divide that by the number of applicants actually selected, that gives us the average cost of the selection process per selected applicant. Finally, if we subtract the average selection process cost per selected applicant from the average value expressed in Equation 9.9, we get Equation 9.10.

$$\Delta U = r_{xy} SD_y \overline{z}_s - \frac{N_a C}{N_s} \tag{9.10}$$

Cronbach and Gleser argued, as did Taylor and Russell, that the value of adding a new selection procedure to an existing process should equal its contribution over and above the existing selection process information. So, the appropriate population for deriving the values in Equation 9.10 would be the candidates produced by the existing process. However, if an organization is considering replacing its old selection process with new ones, then the appropriate population for deriving a validity coefficient, SD_y, and $\bar{Z}_s$, should be the *unscreened* population.[14]

Process: Supply Chain Analysis and Staffing Utility[15]

In this chapter, we have focused exclusively on the utility of staffing decisions, but look carefully again at Figure 9.1. In the conventional approach to staffing, activities like sourcing, recruitment, initial screening, selection, offers, on-boarding of new hires, performance management, and retention tend to be viewed as independent activities, each separate from the others. Such a micro-level, or silo, orientation has dominated the field of HR almost from its inception, and within it, the objective has been to maximize payoffs for each element of the overall staffing process. We believe that there is a rich opportunity for HR professionals to develop and apply an integrative framework whose objective is to optimize investments across the various elements of the staffing process, not simply to maximize payoffs within each element.

To do that, we believe there is much to learn from the field of supply chain analysis. Supply chain analysis pays careful attention to the ultimate quality of materials and components. Reframing utility analysis within that framework makes optimization opportunities more apparent. Perhaps more important, the supply chain framework may help solve one of the thorniest issues in utility analysis: the disturbingly stubborn difficulty in getting key decision-makers to embrace it. How? By relating utility analysis to a framework that is familiar to decision-makers outside of HR, one that they already use.

Essentially, the decision process involves optimizing costs against price and time to achieve levels of expected quality/quantity and risks associated with variations in quality/quantity. If the quality or quantity of acquired resources falls below standard or exhibits excessive variation, decision-makers can evaluate where investments in the process will make the biggest difference.

When a line leader complains that he or she is getting inferior talent, or not enough talent, for a vital position, HR too often devises a solution without full insight into the broader supply chain. HR often responds by enhancing interviews or tests and presenting evidence about the improved validity of the selection process. Yet a more effective solution might be to retain the original selection process with the same validity while recruiting from sources where the average quality of talent is higher.

That is the message of the base rate in the Taylor-Russell utility model.

Or, consider what happens when leaders with too few candidates instruct HR to generate more applicants. HR is often too eager to respond with more recruiting when in fact the number of candidates might already be sufficient, but some leaders are not very effective in getting good candidates to accept their offers. Here, the more effective response may be to help those leaders do a better job of closing the deal.

Leaders are accustomed to a logical approach that optimizes all stages of the supply chain when it comes to raw materials, unfinished goods, and technology. Why not adopt the same approach to talent? Here is an example of one company that did just that.

Valero Energy, a 20,000-employee, $70 billion energy refining and marketing company, developed a new recruitment model out of human-capital metrics based on applying supply chain logic to labor. Valero's manager of employment services said, "Once you run talent acquisition as a supply chain, it allows you to use certain metrics that you couldn't use in a staffing function....We measure every single source of labor by speed, cost, and efficiency."[16] Computer screen dashboards show how components in the labor supply chain, such as ads placed on online job boards, are performing according to those criteria. If the dashboard shows green, performance is fine. If it shows yellow or red, Valero staffing managers can intervene quickly to fix the problem.[17] By doing that, the company can identify where it can recruit the best talent at the most affordable price. From a strategic perspective, it also can identify whether it is better to recruit full-time, part-time, or contract workers, or to outsource the work entirely.

The Economic Value of Improved Work Performance

You may have noticed in Equations 9.9 and 9.10 that the term SD_y refers to the monetary value of a standard deviation difference in job performance. How might you measure that? It's easier when a job produces very clear monetary outcomes such as sales, waste, or profit. We can observe the monetary value of every worker in the job and calculate the standard deviation of those values. Even that value would not be perfect. It would not reflect the variation we would see in the pool of applicants because the workers on the job have already been selected. Also, even in jobs with obvious monetary outcomes, such as sales, there are other performance elements that are not reflected in monetary results (such as when sales people actually sell less because they are training their colleagues).

In short, the question of the value of SD_y is hardly an abstract one. It goes to a fundamental question in all of human resources and talent management: "How much are performance differences worth?" The answer to this fundamental question is necessary to understanding the value of virtually any investment that aims to improve employee performance. Yet, the question remains largely ignored by most HR systems.

Consider this single question: In what jobs or talent pools would a change in the availability or quality of talent have the greatest impact on the success of your organization? Talent pools that meet this standard are known as pivotal talent pools. Alan Eustace, Google's vice president of engineering, told the *Wall Street Journal* that one top-notch engineer is worth three hundred times or more than the average and that he would rather lose an entire incoming class of engineering graduates than one exceptional technologist.[18] This estimate was probably not based on precise numbers, but it still reveals a significant insight where Google puts its emphasis. Recasting performance management to reflect where differences in performance have large impact allows leaders to engage the logic they use for other resources and make educated guesses that can be informative.[19] In defining pivotal talent, an important distinction is often overlooked. That distinction is between average value versus variability in value, something that utility analysis explicitly recognizes. When strategy writers describe critical jobs or roles, they typically emphasize the average level of value (for example, the general importance, customer contact, uniqueness, or power of certain jobs). Yet a key question for managers is not which talent has the greatest average value, but rather, in which talent pools performance variation creates the biggest strategic impact.[20]

Impact identifies the relationship between improvements in organization and talent performance and sustainable strategic success. The pivot point is where differences in performance most affect success. Identifying pivot points often requires digging deeply into organization- or unit-level strategies to unearth specific details about where and how the organization plans to compete, and about the supporting elements that will be most vital to achieving that competitive position. These insights identify the areas of organization and talent that make the biggest difference in the strategy's success.[21]

Logic: Why Does Performance Impact Vary Across Jobs?

Performance is more (or less) pivotal in different jobs for two main reasons: the discretion that the job allows and the strategic value of performance differences.[22]

First, different jobs allow different individual discretion. The work of cooking fries in a fast-food restaurant has preprogrammed virtually all the variables that can affect the finished product (such as the temperature of the oil, the length and width of the fries, and the length of time that the potatoes are fried). So, the performance variability across the cooks (symbolized as SD_y in the earlier equations) will be close to zero. In contrast, the franchisee who manages all the fast-food restaurants in a territory has considerable discretion. Differences in individual abilities and motivation among franchisees produce big differences in store performance, which would imply large values of SD_y. SD_y increases as a function of job complexity.[23]

A second factor is the relative value of performance variations. In some jobs, performance differences are vital to strategic success (for example, creative campaign designers in an advertising agency), but in other jobs, those variations are less vital (such as sending out client bills in the advertising agency). Performance varies in both the creative and the billing jobs, but that variability has very different impact on company strategic success. SD_y is affected by the effect of a job in the value chain of an organization.[24]

Analytics: The Role of SD_y in Selection-Utility Analysis

As earlier equations showed, SD_y translates a one-standard-deviation variation in work performance into economic terms. Without SD_y, the improvement in the quality of those selected (criterion improvement) is expressed only in terms of standard Z-score units. However, when the validity coefficient (r_{xy}) is multiplied by a monetary-valued SD_y, the result puts improvement in monetary terms, which is often more familiar to decision makers. We will often refer to dollar-valued performance or use the dollar sign as a subscript, but the conclusions are valid for any other currency.

No estimate is perfect, but fortunately, utility estimates need not be perfectly accurate, just as with any estimate of business effects. Only errors large enough to lead to incorrect decisions are of any consequence. The key is not how precisely it is measured, but rather that investments in people take account of the fact that the economic value of improved performance can vary greatly across jobs, and the payoff is often greatest in those pivotal jobs. Ironically, the most pivotal jobs (with the largest SD_y values) are often those involving leadership, management, or intellectual capital and have lots of opportunities for individual autonomy and discretion. The value of performance in such jobs is measured least well by standard accounting methods. Subjective estimates, to one degree or another, are virtually unavoidable, but it can be helpful to understand how research has historically tried to make these estimates more objective.

Measures: Estimating the Monetary Value of Variations in Job Performance (SD_y)

Most elements of the utility equations can be obtained from records, such as the number of applicants, the cost of selection procedures, and the selection ratio. This section will describe several methods that researchers historically used to measure SD_y. However, organizations rarely actually calculate this variable. Understanding the historical measurement methods helps you understand the logic and magnitude of SD_y, even if your own estimates are less formal.

Table 9.1 describes three approaches.

Table 9.1. Alternative Approaches for Estimating SD_y

Estimation Approach	Description
Cost accounting	Calculate the accounting value of each person's accounting outcomes such as production or sales, and calculate the standard deviation of those values across individuals.
40 percent rule	Multiply the average total remuneration of the group by 40 percent.

Estimation Approach	Description
Global estimation	Ask experts to estimate the value of performance at the average, 85th percentile and 15th percentile, of the performance distribution, and calculate the differences between their estimates.
CREPID (Cascio-Ramos Estimate of Performance in Dollars)	Identify the individual elements of performance, weight them by contribution to economic value, multiply average remuneration by the importance weight of each element, rate individual performance on each element, multiply performance by monetary value for each dimension for each individual, and sum to get a monetary value for each individual. Calculate the standard deviation of those values across individuals.

Cost Accounting

This method uses information directly from the organization's accounting system. The idea is that such information would already be very credible to managers and other leaders and would be endorsed by the organization's accountants. If that accounting information is used to calculate the economic value of every employee's performance, then you could directly estimate the standard deviation of performance value by calculating the standard deviation of those values. For example, if you assume that the only economic value produced in a job is reflected in sales achieved, then you could estimate each person's performance value by taking his or her sales level and then subtracting the cost of the infrastructure they use and the compensation paid. In one study that applied cost accounting to route salespersons in a Midwestern soft-drink bottling company, SD_y was estimated to be $38,148 per year (all figures in 2018 dollars), with an average performance value of $108,166.[25]

In reality, cost-accounting estimates should consider elements such as:[26]

» Average value of production.
» Quality of objects produced or services accomplished.
» Overhead, including rent, light, heat, cost depreciation, or rental of machines and equipment.
» Errors, accidents, spoilage, wastage, damage to machines or equipment due to unusual wear and tear, and so on.
» The cost of time of other employees and managers.

For that reason, researchers found that cost-accounting estimates required many assumptions and subjective estimates, and so the promise of an objective measure of performance value directly from the accounting system proved unmet.

The 40 Percent Rule

Perhaps the easiest approach to estimating SD_y is simply to assume it is equal to 40 percent of the average salary in the job.[27] Researchers who developed this approach noted that in jobs where work output was easily measured (sales, units produced, etc.), the standard deviation of work output averaged 20 percent of average work output. Also, across the US economy, wages and salaries averaged just over half (57 percent) of the average value of goods and services. So, 40 percent of average salary is approximately the same as 20 percent of the average value of production. This suggested a very easy way to measure SD_y: simply multiply average salary by 40 percent!

Is the standard deviation of output actually about 20 percent of the average value of output? It actually varies. The results of sixty-eight studies that measured work output found that in low-complexity jobs, the standard deviation of output was 15 percent of total output. In medium-complexity jobs, it was 25 percent, and in high-complexity jobs, it was 46 percent. For example, in a study of life-insurance sales jobs, the standard deviation was very large, at 97 percent of average sales.[28] The researchers suggested that this showed that the 40 percent rule was a reasonable middle estimate. However, in actual decisions, leaders should keep in mind that this easy-to-apply rule may significantly underestimate or overestimate the actual value. Still, it is a very easy approach to get an idea about how SD_y might vary across jobs and what might be the rough magnitude of potential people investment payoffs.

Global Estimation

The next approach has the advantage of relying on the insights of experts on the value of job performance. The global estimation procedure reasons that if the monetary value of job performance is distributed as a normal curve, then the difference between the value of a worker performing at the 85th percentile (one standard deviation above average) versus an employee performing at the 50th percentile (average) would equal SD_y.[29] So, this procedure asks experts to estimate the value of performance at the 85th percentile (better than 85 percent of performers) and at the 50th percentile (better than 50 percent of performers) and then estimates SD_y as the difference between them.

One study used supervisors of computer programmers in ten federal agencies.[30] Here is an excerpt of the instructions presented to the supervisors:[31]

> The dollar utility estimates we are asking you to make are critical in estimating the relative dollar value to the government of different selection methods. In answering these questions, you will have to make some very difficult judgments. We realize they are difficult and that they are judgments or estimates. You will have to ponder for some time before giving each estimate, and there is probably no way you can be absolutely certain your estimate is accurate when you do reach a decision. But keep in mind... [that]...your estimates will be averaged in with those of

other supervisors of computer programmers. Thus, errors produced by too high and too low estimates will tend to be averaged out, providing more accurate final estimates.

Based on your experience with agency programmers, we would like for you to estimate the yearly value to your agency of the products and services produced by the average GS 9-11 computer programmer. Consider the quality and quantity of output typical of the average programmer and the value of this output. In placing an overall dollar value on this output, it may help to consider what the cost would be of having an outside firm provide these products and services.

Based on my experience, I estimate the value to my agency of the average GS 9-11 computer programmer at _____ dollars per year.

We would now like for you to consider the "superior" programmer. Let us define a superior performer as a programmer who is at the 85th percentile. That is, his or her performance is better than that of 85% of his or her fellow GS 9-11 programmers, and only 15% turn in better performances. Consider the quality and quantity of the output typical of the superior programmer. Then estimate the value of these products and services. In placing an overall dollar value on this output, it may again help to consider what the cost would be of having an outside firm provide these products and services.

Based on my experience, I estimate the value to my agency of a superior GS 9-11 computer programmer to be _____ dollars per year.

The mean estimated difference in value (in 2018 dollars) of yearly job performance between programmers at the 85th and 50th percentiles in job performance was $134,268.

The global estimation procedure addresses the potential problem that the 40 percent rule might not apply to all jobs, and it offers a way to incorporate the beliefs of leaders and job expert, about the value of performance variation. Still, because the estimation is global, it does not specify what assumptions and work elements might have gone into the estimates.

The Cascio-Ramos Estimate of Performance in Dollars (CREPID)
The methods discussed so far require assuming that the value of job performance follows a bell-curve distribution, and they require experts to estimate the total performance value by subjectively combining many different job performance elements. The next method, called CREPID, does not require the assumption of a normal distribution and identifies the role of individual job elements. While it is more involved and complex than the 40 percent rule or global estimation, it illustrates a way to capture detailed assumptions about how the different elements of a job add value.

CREPID was developed at AT&T and was tested on 602 first-level managers in one operating company.[32] CREPID assumes that employee compensation reflects market rates, and so the economic value of each employee is their annual salary. This is conservative because the value produced by an employee must exceed their average compensation to offset wages, overhead, and profit. CREPID breaks down each employee's job into its principal activities, assigns a proportional amount of the annual salary to each principal activity, and asks supervisors to rate each employee's job performance on each activity. The ratings then are translated into dollar values for each activity. The sum of the dollar values across each activity equals the dollar value of each employee's job performance to the company. This approach is based on the following steps:

1. Identify principal activities. Many job analysis systems identify activities directly. Or, one can identify the activities that comprise at least 10 percent of total work time.

2. Rate each principal activity in terms of time/frequency and importance. Research shows that simple 0–7 Likert-type rating scales are sufficient.[33]

3. Multiply the time/frequency and importance ratings for each activity to calculate an overall weight for each activity. If an activity never is done, or if it is of zero importance, the weight will be zero. After doing all the multiplication, sum the ratings assigned to each principal activity and divide the total rating for each principal activity by the grand total to derive the relative weight for the activity. The relative weight indicates the proportion of the employee's overall salary that should be assigned to the activity. The following illustration assumes there are eight principal activities in a job and shows the calculations.

Calculating Relative Activity Weights

Principal Activity	Time/ Frequency	X Importance	= Total	Relative Weight
1	4.0	4	16.0	16.8
2	5.0	7	35.0	36.8
3	1.0	5	5.0	5.3
4	0.5	3	1.5	1.6
5	2.0	7	14.0	14.7
6	1.0	4	4.0	4.2
7	0.5	3	1.5	1.6
8	3.0	6	18.0	19.0
			95.0	100%

4. Assign dollar values to each principal activity by taking the average pay for all employees in a particular job class and multiplying it by the relative weights for each activity. Continuing our example, we might assume the annual salary for this job is $50,000, producing the following results.

Allocating Pay to Activities

Principal Activity	Relative Weight (%)	Dollar Value ($)
1	16.8	8,400
2	36.8	18,400
3	5.3	2,650
4	1.6	800
5	14.7	7,350
6	4.2	2,100
7	1.6	800
8	19.0	9,500
		50,000

5. Rate performance of every employee on each principal activity on a 0–200 scale. Note that steps 1 through 4 apply to the overall job, but step 5 requires rating how each worker performs each activity. CREPID uses a modified magnitude estimation scale.[34] A value (say 100) is assigned to the average employee, and all comparisons are made relative to this value. Discussions with operating managers indicated that even the very best employee was not more than twice as effective as the average employee, so a 0–200 scale was used to rate each employee on each principal activity.

6. Multiply the performance rating for each employee on each activity by the activity's dollar value.

7. Compute the overall economic value of each employee's job performance by adding the results of step 6 across all the activities. The following table shows the results of steps 5–7 for one hypothetical employee, producing an estimate of his or her total economic value of performance equal to $57,902.50.

Calculating Economic Value of Job Performance

Principal Activity	Performance Rating	Dollar Value of Activity	Dollar Value of Activity Performance
1	1.35	8,400	11,340.00
2	1.00	18,400	18,400.00
3	1.25	2,650	3,312.50
4	2.00	800	1,600.00
5	1.00	7,350	7,350.00
6	0.50	2,100	1,050.00
7	0.75	800	600.00
8	1.50	9,500	14,250.00
Total Dollar Value of Employee's Performance			$57,902.50

8. Compute the mean and standard deviation of the dollar-valued job performance estimates across all the employees.

When CREPID was used with 602 first-level managers at AT&T, the average of dollar-valued job performance was only 3.4 percent more than the average salary. However, the standard deviation (SD_y) was almost ten times the average, and more than three and a half times larger than the standard deviation of salaries. This showed that variations in performance value far exceeded differences in salaries.

CREPID has the advantage of assigning each employee a specific value that can be analyzed explicitly for appropriateness and that may also provide a more understandable or credible estimate for decision makers. However, as noted earlier, CREPID assumes that average wage equals the economic value of a worker's performance. The same value is assigned to both output and wages. This assumption does not hold in pay systems that are based on rank, tenure, or hourly pay rates, so CREPID should not be used in these situations.[35]

Process: How Accurate Are SD_y Estimates, and Does It Matter?

When applying these ideas, it is much more important simply to realize that the value of performance improvements varies between different jobs than it is to fixate on a particular estimate of SD_y. If business leaders ask HR how much a particular program costs, they are typically actually asking if the program's improvement in worker quality is worth it. Clearly distinguishing between the average value of performance and the return on improved performance is extremely helpful to reframe such discussions and improve decisions.

As discussed in Chapter 2, "Analytical Foundations of HR Measurement," one can reframe the question from "How much is this program worth?" to "How certain are we that this investment will produce at least a minimum acceptable return?" In terms of SD_y, this means that often even a wide range of SD_y values will yield the same answer—that what appeared to be a costly HR program is actually quite likely to pay off. The break-even level of SD_y needed for an HR program to meet the minimal acceptable return is typically much less than even the most conservative SD_y estimates. A review of thirty-four studies encompassing more than one hundred SD_y estimates concluded that alternative methods often produce estimates that differ by less than 50 percent.[36] This is what led the authors of a subsequent review to state that "rather than focusing so much attention on the estimation of SD_y, we suggest that utility researchers should focus on understanding exactly what performance represents."[37]

Research suggests that some SD_y techniques are more acceptable to managers. For example, one study found that the 40 percent rule was seen as more credible than CREPID, but the credibility differences explained less than 5 percent of the total variation in credibility.[38] Another study found that managers preferred to see the results of HR programs estimated with numbers rather than anecdotes.[39]

Utility analyses should reflect the context in which decisions are made.[40] All decisions deal with uncertainty, and HR leaders can do that with sensitivity or break-even analysis (see Chapter 2). If an SD_y estimation method suggests that it is very likely that an HR program will pay off above an acceptable financial standard, the decision to invest won't likely change by using other estimation methods. Of course, the broader goal is to focus HR investments where they have the greatest value. That requires answering questions such as "Where would improvements in talent, or how it is organized, most enhance sustainable strategic success?" The key concern is usually not which talent has the greatest average value, but rather for which talent does performance improvement create the biggest strategic impact. SD_y provides one important piece of that puzzle. In the next chapter, we apply SD_y to estimate actual outcomes of employee selection and the role of economic factors, employee flows, and break-even analysis.

Exercises

Software that calculates answers to one or more of the following exercises can be found at http://iip.shrm.org.

1. Use the software to solve these problems by filling in the following table:

Validity	SR	BR	Success Ratio
0.25	0.20	0.30	
0.55	0.70	0.80	
0.20	0.70	0.80	
0.10	0.50	0.50	
0.55	0.50	0.50	

2. Using the Brogden-Cronbach-Gleser continuous variable utility model, what is the net gain over random selection (ΔU overall, and per selectee) given the following information?

Quota for selection: 20

SR: 0.20

SD_y (standard deviation of job performance expressed in dollars): $30,000

r_{xy}: 0.25

C: $35

Hint: To find *N,* the number recruited, divide the quota for selection by the *SR.*

3. Given the following information on two selection procedures, and using the Brogden-Cronbach-Gleser model, what is the relative *difference* in payoff (overall and per selectee) between the two procedures? For both procedures, quota = 50, *SR* = 0.50, and SD_y = $45,000.

Procedure 1: r_{xy} = 0.20 c_1 = $200

Procedure 2: r_{xy} = 0.40 c_2 = $700

4. The Tiny Company manufactures components for aerial drones. Most of the work is done at the 2,000-employee

Tiny plant in the Midwest. Using the instructions provided for the global-estimation procedure, attempt to estimate:

> The value of an assembler at the 50th percentile, and
> The value of an assembler at the 85th percentile in merit.

You are free to make any assumptions you like about the Tiny assemblers, but be prepared to defend your assumptions.

5. Jim Hill is the manager of subscriber accounts for the Prosper Company. The results of a job analysis indicate that Jim's job includes four principal activities. A summary of Jim's superior's ratings of his job activities and Jim's performance of each of them follows.

Principal Activity	Frequency	Importance	Jim's Performance
1	4.5	3	1.00
2	3.0	5	2.00
3	6.0	2	0.50
4	1.0	7	1.00

Assuming that Jim is paid $90,000 per year, use CREPID to estimate the overall economic value of his job performance.

References

1. Stuart Crainer and Des Dearlove, "Whatever Happened to Yesterday's Bright Ideas?," *Across the Board*, May/June, 2006, 34–40.
2. Wayne F. Cascio and John C. Scott, "The Business Value of Employee Selection," in *Handbook of Employee Selection*, 2nd ed., ed. James L. Farr and Nancy T. Tippins (New York: Routledge, 2017), 226–48.
3. Cascio and Scott, "Business Value of Employee Selection," 226–48. See also John W. Boudreau and Peter M. Ramstad, *Beyond Cost-Per-Hire and*

Time to Fill: Supply-Chain Measurement for Staffing (Center for Effective Organizations, University of Southern California, CEO Publication G 04-16 (468), September 2004).

4. John W. Boudreau and Peter M. Ramstad, "Strategic Industrial and Organizational Psychology and the Role of Utility Analysis Models," in Vol. 12, *Handbook of Psychology*, ed. Walter C. Borman, Daniel R. Ilgen, and Richard J. Klimoski (Hoboken, NJ: Wiley, 2004), 193–221.

5. Richard A. Brealey, Stewart C. Myers, and Alan J. Marcus, *Principles of Corporate Finance*, 8th ed. (Burr Ridge, IL: Irwin/McGraw-Hill, 2006).

6. Nanette Byrnes and David Kiley, "Hello, You Must be Going," *BusinessWeek*, February 12, 2007, 30–32. See also Robert Berner, "My Year at Wal-Mart," *BusinessWeek*, February 12, 2007, 70–74.

7. Milton L. Blum and Jack C. Naylor, *Industrial Psychology: Its Theoretical and Social Foundations*, rev. ed. (New York: Harper & Row, 1968).

8. H. C. Taylor and J. T. Russell, "The Relationship of Validity Coefficients to the Practical Effectiveness of Tests in Selection," *Journal of Applied Psychology* 23, no. 5 (October 1939), 565–78.

9. H. E. Brogden, "On the Interpretation of the Correlation Coefficient as a Measure of Predictive Efficiency," *Journal of Educational Psychology* 37, no. 2 (February 1946): 64–76. See also H. E. Brogden, "When Testing Pays Off," *Personnel Psychology* 2, no. 2 (June 1949): 171–85; Lee Cronbach and Goldine C. Gleser, *Psychological Tests and Personnel Decisions*, 2nd ed. (Urbana: University of Illinois Press, 1965).

10. William A. Sands, "A Method for Evaluating Alternative Recruiting-Selection Strategies: The CAPER Model," *Journal of Applied Psychology* 57, no. 3 (June 1973): 222–27.

11. John W. Boudreau and Sara L. Rynes, "Role of Recruitment in Staffing Utility Analyses," *Journal of Applied Psychology* 70, no. 2 (May 1985): 354–66.

12. Taylor and Russell, "The Relationship of Validity Coefficients."

13. The authors would like to thank Professor Craig J. Russell for allowing us to adapt the framework that he developed.

14. John W. Boudreau, "Utility Analysis for Decisions in Human Resource Management," in Vol. 2, *Handbook of Industrial and Organizational Psychology*, 2nd ed., ed. Marvin D. Dunnette and Leaetta M. Hough (Palo Alto, CA: Consulting Psychologists Press, 1991), 621–745.

15. Material in this section comes from Wayne F. Cascio and John W. Boudreau, "Utility of Selection Systems: Supply-Chain Analysis Applied to Staffing Decisions" in Vol. 2, *APA Handbook of Industrial and Organizational Psychology*, ed. Sheldon Zedeck (Washington, DC: American Psychological Association, 2011), 421–44.

16. Hilbert, cited in Craig Schneider, "The New Human-Capital Metrics," *CFO. com*, February 15, 2006, accessed August 5, 2008, http://www.cfo.com.

17. Valero Energy, "2006 Optimas Awards," *Workforce Management*, March 13, 2006, 23.

18. Pui-Wing Tam and Kevin J. Delaney, "Talent Search: Google's Growth Helps Ignite Silicon Valley Hiring Frenzy," *The Wall Street Journal*, November 23, 2005, A1.

19. John W. Boudreau, *Retooling HR: Using Proven Business Tools to Make Better Decisions About Talent* (Boston: Harvard Business Press, 2010).

20. Boudreau, *Retooling HR*. See also Boudreau and Ramstad, "Strategic Industrial and Organizational Psychology."

21. John W. Boudreau and Peter M. Ramstad, *Beyond HR: The New Science of Human Capital* (Boston: Harvard Business School Press, 2007).

22. Elizabeth F. Cabrera and Nambury S. Raju, "Utility Analysis: Current Trends and Future Directions," *International Journal of Selection and Assessment* 9, no. 1–2 (March 2001): 92–102.

23. John E. Hunter, Frank L. Schmidt, and Michael K. Judiesch, "Individual Differences in Output Variability as a Function of Job Complexity," *Journal of Applied Psychology* 75, no. 1 (February 1990): 28–42.

24. Boudreau and Ramstad, *Beyond HR*.

25. Olen L. Greer and Wayne F. Cascio, "Is Cost Accounting the Answer? Comparison of Two Behaviorally Based Methods for Estimating the Standard Deviation of Job Performance in Dollars with a Cost Accounting-Based Approach," *Journal of Applied Psychology* 72, no. 4 (November 1987): 588–95.

26. H. E. Brogden and E. K. Taylor, "The Dollar Criterion—Applying the Cost Accounting Concept to Criterion Construction," *Personnel Psychology* 3, no. 2 (June 1950): 133–54.

27. Frank L. Schmidt and John E. Hunter, "Individual Differences in Productivity: An Empirical Test of Estimates Derived from Studies of Selection Procedure Utility," *Journal of Applied Psychology* 68, no. 3 (August 1983): 407–14.

28. Hunter, Schmidt, and Judiesch, "Individual Differences in Output Variability."

29. Frank L. Schmidt et al., "Impact of Valid Selection Procedures on Workforce Productivity," *Journal of Applied Psychology* 64 (December 1979): 610–26.

30. Schmidt et al., "Impact of Valid Selection Procedures."

31. Schmidt et al., "Impact of Valid Selection Procedures."

32. Wayne F. Cascio and Robert A. Ramos, "Development and Application of a New Method for Assessing Job Performance in Behavioral/Economic Terms," *Journal of Applied Psychology* 71, no. 1 (February 1986): 20–28.

33. Jeff A. Weekley, "A Comparison of Three Methods of Estimating the Standard Deviation of Performance in Dollars," *Journal of Applied Psychology* 70, no. 1 (February 1985): 122–26.

34. S. S. Stevens, "Issues in Psychophysical Measurement," *Psychological Review* 78, no. 5 (September 1971): 426–50.

35. Boudreau, "Utility Analysis for Decisions in Human Resource Management."

36. Boudreau, "Utility Analysis for Decisions in Human Resource Management."

37. Arvey, R. D., and K. R. Murphy, "Performance Evaluation in Work Settings," *Annual Review of Psychology* 49 (1998): 141–68.
38. John T. Hazer and Scott Highhouse, "Factors Influencing Managers' Reactions to Utility Analysis: Effects of SD_y Method, Information Frame, and Focal Intervention," *Journal of Applied Psychology* 82, no. 1 (February 1997): 104–12.
39. Brent W. Mattson, "The Effects of Alternative Reports of Human Resource Development Results on Managerial Support," *Human Resource Development Quarterly* 14, no. 2 (Summer 2003): 127–51.
40. Wayne F. Cascio, "The Role of Utility Analysis in the Strategic Management of Organizations," *Journal of Human Resource Costing and Accounting* 1, no. 2 (1996): 85–95. See also Wayne F. Cascio, "Assessing the Utility of Selection Decisions: Theoretical and Practical Considerations," in *Personnel Selection in Organizations,* ed. Neil Schmitt and Walter C. Borman (San Francisco: Jossey-Bass, 1993), 39–335; Craig J. Russell, Adrienne Colella, and Philip Bobko, "Expanding the Context of Utility: The Strategic Impact of Personnel Selection," *Personnel Psychology* 46, no. 4 (December 1993): 781–801.

10

The Payoff from Improving Employee Selection

The traditional approach to employee selection (one component of the staffing process described in Chapter 9) is as old as employment, and has evolved significantly.[1] Traditionally, it involves defining the work, identifying individual characteristics that might predict work performance, developing systems to score job applicants on those characteristics, and selecting the highest-scoring applicants to receive job offers.

In light of the dynamic, changing nature of work and organizations, this traditional approach to employee selection faces a number of challenges. Cascio and Scott described seven of them:[2]

1. Past behavior may not always predict future behavior (behavioral consistency), particularly if the new job differs in the types of personal characteristics necessary for successful performance. Past behavior that is relevant to future performance may predict that performance effectively.

2. Selection decisions about people and jobs are not independent events in an organization. Indeed, the broader business value of selection is often linked to other HR processes, such as training, promotion, special assignments, staff reductions, career development, and succession planning.

3. Hiring managers do not always hire the best scorers. Validated selection techniques are rarely the only source of information for selection decision-making.

4. Jobs are changing faster than we can do validation studies.
5. Assessing the business value of selection is complex because different constituents—managers, applicants, HR professionals, and those who implement selection systems—value different outcomes.
6. The social context and social psychological processes of selection decisions are often ignored in the traditional approach. Interpersonal processes in group decision-making are extremely important to the implementation of selection systems. For example, a particular decision-maker's position power, influence, and interpersonal attraction to another person may be important to understand in selecting employees.
7. Utility calculations that estimate economic returns on investments for valid selection techniques, as discussed in our last chapter, are not widely accepted or understood by business managers. Managers often do not believe the magnitude of the estimated returns because of their size and also because of the use of complex formulas with many estimates and assumptions. To many, the dollar returns associated with improved performance are not "tangible," and certainly less so than the dollars in one's departmental budget. All of this suggests that few organizations, if any, view the costs related to selection as investments; rather, they consider them as expenses. Beyond that, validity coefficients of equal size, say, 0.35, are not necessarily equally valuable to decision-makers if they reference different criteria. A sales manager, for example, may or may not view a validity of 0.35 for predicting organizational citizenship behaviors as equal in value to a validity of 0.35 for predicting sales volume because the manager believes that sales volume is more pivotal than citizenship.

Although many existing selection methods perform well by focusing on specific job performance criteria, rapid change means that future selection strategies will be more useful if they consider a broader criterion space. That means shifting from the goal of predicting task performance to predicting the broad range of effects—situational, contextual, strategic, and environmental—that may affect individual, team, or organizational performance.[3] Such specification provides a richer, fuller, context-embedded description of the criterion space that we wish to predict.

Organizations legitimately vary in the specific criteria they use to establish the business value of a selection program, but such programs can generally be judged by how well they 1) align with business strategy; 2) adapt to dynamic workforce requirements; 3) integrate with other talent management systems; 4) meet the expectations of multiple constituents (e.g., senior leaders, hiring managers, HR, candidates); 5) conform to operational and minimum legal requirements (e.g., validity, efficiency, lack of bias); and 6) contribute to valued organizational outcomes (e.g., productivity, sales, service, quality, revenue). We won't try to cover all of these requirements in this chapter, but they constitute a general framework for focus in this chapter—how to estimate the economic payoffs of improving employee-selection programs.

Assessing the Economic Value of Valid Staffing Programs

Chapter 9 provided a powerful framework to help leaders understand and estimate the payoffs from improved staffing programs. That framework describes a more integrated decision system than simply focusing on isolated staffing-system attributes such as cost, time-to-fill, number of applicants, or validity.

In this chapter, we tie the ideas from Chapter 9 together to describe research suggesting that more valid selection procedures pay off handsomely. We show how the utility framework of Chapter 9 can incorporate financial considerations (cost of capital, taxes, etc.) to make estimates of the payoff from HR investments comparable to estimates for investments in resources such as technology, R&D, and marketing. Candidly, despite many decades of study, few organizations actually use utility analysis to estimate economic payoffs. However, HR programs continue to receive careful scrutiny and face perpetual budget constraints, so it is increasingly vital that HR leaders offer strong economic justifications for them. This chapter will show you how to make estimates of payoffs from utility analysis more comparable to traditional capital investments. We believe that doing so makes it more likely that HR and business leaders will develop shared mental models and make better decisions.

We start by describing an actual example of economic returns from improved staffing using the Brogden-Cronbach-Gleser model.[4] Then, we expand that example to add five considerations that make the staffing payoffs more realistic and better connected to traditional financial logic:

» Economic factors (variable costs, taxes, and discounting),
» Employee flows,
» Probationary periods,
» The use of multiple selection devices, and
» Departures from top-down hiring.

We then describe how to deal with risk and uncertainty using utility analysis and conclude with some observations about effectively communicating utility analyses results.

Logic: How Staffing Investments Pay Off

Figure 10.1 presents the logic of utility analysis, along with some situational factors that may affect quantity, quality, and cost.

We discussed several of these factors earlier in Chapter 9. Equations 9.9 and 9.10 showed how the Brogden-Cronbach-Gleser model combines the selection ratio (SR), validity of the selection procedure (r), the variability or standard deviation of job performance expressed in monetary terms (SD_y), the average score of those hired on the predictor, and the average cost per selectee of applying the selection process to all applicants $[(N_a \times C)/N_s]$ to estimate the economic utility of improved selection. The other factors shown in Figure 10.1 can increase or decrease this unadjusted utility estimate while making the estimate more compatible with typical financial models.

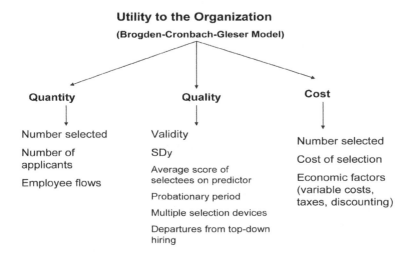

Figure 10.1. The logic of utility analysis and factors that can affect payoffs.

An Illustrative Example: Selecting Computer Programmers with the Programmer Aptitude Test

A 1979 study in the US government examined the payoff from using a more valid selection procedure called the Programmer Aptitude Test (PAT).[5] The PAT had demonstrated consistently high validity (correlation of 0.76) across many organizations. The cost of administering the PAT per examinee was $41 (all figures are adjusted to 2018 dollars). The study focused on the selection of federal government computer programmers at the GS-5 through GS-9 levels. The example will extrapolate the staffing payoff for the US government and also for the US economy.

Measuring the Utility Components:
Quantity, Quality, and Cost

The average quantity of GS-5 through GS-9 programmers selected was 618 per year. The average tenure of government programmers was 9.69 years. So, after estimating the expected payoff in utility per selectee per year, we would multiply by 9.69 years to estimate the total gain over the average tenure of a government programmer.

No data were available to estimate the selection ratio (SR) for computer programmers either in the general economy or in the federal government, so sensitivity analysis allowed the selection ratio to range from 5 percent (very selective) to 80 percent (not very selective).

Regarding validity, the researchers realized that sometimes the PAT would replace a procedure with zero validity, but sometimes the prior procedure would have nonzero validity. So, again, sensitivity analysis varied the assumed previous procedure validities from zero to 0.50.

SD_y was calculated using the global estimation procedure. The estimate was $44,600 per person per year (in 2018 dollars).

Regarding testing costs, when the previous procedure was assumed to have zero validity, its testing cost was assumed to be zero. When the previous procedure was assumed to have a nonzero validity, its associated cost was assumed to be the same as that of the PAT (that is, $41 per applicant) at the time of hiring.

The researchers applied the Brogden-Cronbach-Gleser utility equation in this form:

$$\Delta U = t N_s (r_1 - r_2)(SD_y)(\bar{Z}_x) - N_s(c_1 - c_2)/SR \qquad (10.1)$$

Where:

ΔU = the gain in productivity in dollars from using the new selection procedure for one year

t = the tenure in years of the average selectee (here 9.69)

N_s = the number selected in a given year (this figure was 618 for the federal government and 10,210 for the US economy)

r_1 = the validity of the new PAT (r_1 = 0. 76)

r_2 = the validity of the previous procedure (ranges from 0 to 0.50)

c_1 = the cost per applicant of the new PAT, here $41 (in 2018 dollars)

c_2 = the cost of the previous procedure (zero or $41)

SD_y = the yearly dollar value of a one-standard-deviation difference in performance ($44,600 in 2018 dollars)

SR = the selection ratio (ranges from 5 percent to 80 percent)

$\overline{Z}_x$ = the average Z-score on the predictor of the selected applicants

That Z-score is 0.35 with an SR of 80 percent versus 2.06 with an SR of 5 percent. This estimates the economic value of using the new PAT to hire one group of computer programs whose performance value occurs over the 9.69 years of their tenure.

Note: it is important to think carefully about the meaning of the parameter t in Equation 10.1. Traditionally, and as noted above, t represents the average tenure of individuals in a given job (9.69 years in our example). Perhaps a more nuanced view is to define t as the length of time that the constructs measured by the current selection system remain relevant. The faster that jobs and organizations change, the lower the value of t.[6]

Analytics: Calculating Economic Utility and Its Range

The estimated gains in productivity from one year's use of the PAT in the US government ranges from $24.3 million to $417.6 million (in 2018 dollars). The range reflects different combinations of selection ratios and previous-procedure validity. The $417.6 million estimate assumes the selection ratio (SR) is 5 percent (very selective) and the previous selection procedure had zero validity (so the PAT improves validity by .76), and the total testing cost is $507,000 ($41 times 618 selected times [1/.05]). The $24.3 million estimate assumes the selection ratio (SR) is 80 percent (not very selective) and the previous selection procedure had high validity (so the PAT improves validity by .26), and the total testing cost is zero (the PAT costs the same as the old test). The gain per selectee is the total utility divided by the number selected (618). Remember that those gains are spread out over 9.69 years, the tenure of the hired employees. Gains per year per selectee can be obtained by dividing the total utility by 618 selectees and then by 9.69 years. You can even estimate the payoff per working hour, such as by assuming 2,000 working hours in a year and dividing the total by 618 selectees, then by 9.69 years and then by 2,000 hours. Using the numbers above, this would suggest an economic payoff ranging from $2.02 to $34.86 per employee per hour.

Obviously, this is a very wide range! The utility analysis framework is quite valuable in illustrating when improved selection will and will not pay off. Still, even the lowest utility estimate ($25 million) is still quite high. A financial leader might point out that the estimates have left out several standard financial adjustments, so we will apply those next.

Making Utility Analysis More Comparable to Financial Estimates

Standard financial analysis would account for the costs of improved performance (variable costs), inflation risk (interest rates), and tax increases (tax rates). These are important because taking them into account allows decision-makers to make better comparisons between HR investments and other investments. These adjustments will usually reduce the unadjusted utility estimates under any or all of three conditions:[7]

First, if variable costs (for example, incentive- or commission-based pay, benefits, variable costs of raw materials, variable production overhead) rise with productivity, then a portion (V) of the gain in performance value must pay those costs. Second, organizations pay a portion of their profit as taxes (TAX). Third, when costs and benefits accrue over time, the values of future costs and benefits are worth less than present costs and benefits. Benefits received sooner can be invested to earn returns. With a 10 percent annual return, a dollar received today would be worth $1.21 in two years. So, receiving $1.21 in two years has a "present value" of $1.00. The following utility formula takes these three economic factors into account.[8]

$$\Delta U = (N)\left\{\sum_{t=1}^{T}\left[1/(1+i)^{t}\right]\right\}(SD_{sv})(1+V)(1-TAX)(r_{x,sv})(\bar{Z}_x) - C_t(1-TAX)$$

$$(10.2)$$

Where:

ΔU = the change in overall worth or utility after variable costs, taxes, and discounting

N = the number of employees selected

t = the time period in which an increase in productivity occurs

T = the total number of periods (for example, years) that benefits continue to accrue to an organization

i = the discount rate

SD_{sv} = the standard deviation of the sales value of productivity among the applicant or employee population (similar to SD_y in previous utility models)

V = the proportion of sales value represented by variable costs

TAX = the organization's applicable tax rate

$r_{x,sv}$ = the validity coefficient between predictor (*x*) and sales value (similar to $r_{x,y}$ in previous utility models)

C = the total selection cost for all applicants

Those financial adjustments produce large reductions in unadjusted utility estimates. For example, if variable costs reduce gains by 5 percent (*V* = –0.05), taxes take 45 percent, and the interest (or "discount") rate is 10 percent (which means that a series of benefits received for 9.69 years has a discounted value of 6.34 rather than 9.69), then the total utility values computed earlier now range from a low of $8.31 million ($24.3 million × .95 × .55 × [6.34/9.69]) to a high of $142.76 million ($417.6 million × .95 × .55 × [6.34/9.69]). These values are still substantial, but they are 65.8 percent lower, and they show why leaders must carefully make estimates of HR payoffs compatible to those with other investments.

Next, we apply another idea from financial analysis: the power of compound interest that is created when organizations select multiple groups of employees over several years.

Analyzing Talent Compound Interest: Effects of Employee Flows on Utility Estimates

The value of staffing, or any other HR program, is affected by the way employees flow into, through, and out of an organization.[9] As you have seen, the original utility analysis formulas reflected hiring only one group, and only one year's financial effect of those better-selected employees. Yet, for any investment, the most relevant payoff is the cumulative benefit over time. Applying that idea to HR means recognizing that the benefits of HR programs usually span multiple groups of new hires (or trainees, etc.).

Logic of Employee Flows

In the PAT example, we multiplied the one-year selection benefit by the average tenure of the programmers (9.69 years).[10] This still reflects only the effects of hiring one group that stays for 9.69 years. In practice, selection programs are applied year after year as employees flow into the work force. These are additive cohort effects.[11] Employee flows affect utility through the number of better-selected employees entering the workforce over multiple years. We might call these better-selected employees the treated employees, to refer more generally to employees that are affected by an improved HR program or "treatment," like an improved test, but also including improved training, compensation, and so on. We express the number of treated employees in the workforce k periods in the future (N_k) as shown in Equation 10.3.

$$N_k = \sum_{t=1}^{k} \left(N_{a_t} - N_{s_t} \right) \tag{10.3}$$

Where:

N_{at} = the number of treated employees added to the workforce in period t

N_{st} = the number of treated employees subtracted from the workforce in period t

For example, at the end of the fourth year that a new selection procedure is applied ($k = 4$), suppose that 100 persons were hired in each of the four years, and that 10 of them left in year 2, 15 in year 3, and 20 in year 4. Then, the cumulative flow of benefits from the four years of hiring 100 per year is 355, not 400:

$$N_4 = (100 - 0) + (100 - 10) + (100 - 15) + (100 - 20) = 355$$

Thus, the term N_k reflects both the number of employees treated in previous periods and how many of them leave in each year. The formula for the utility (ΔU_k) occurring in the kth future period that includes these flows plus the economic considerations may be written as shown in Equation 10.4.

$$\Delta U = \left[\sum_{t=1}^{k} \left(N_{a_t} - N_{s_t} \right) \right] \left\{ \left[1/(1+i)^k \right] \left(r_{x,sv} \right) \left(\bar{Z}_x \right) \left(SD_{sv} \right) \left(1+V \right) \left(1-TAX \right) \right\}$$

$$-C_K \left(1-TAX \right) \left[1/(1+i)^{(k-1)} \right] \tag{10.4}$$

This formula modifies the quantity element by keeping track of how many treated employees are in the workforce in each year. Then, after multiplying that number by the increased productive value of the treated employees, the relevant discount rate, cost, tax, and other factors are applied for that particular year.

The utility parameters $r_{x,sv}$, V, SD_{sv}, and TAX are assumed to be constant over time, but this is just for simplicity. Also, the cost (C_k) of selecting the N_{ak} employees added in period k might vary over time because HR programs often have high initial startup costs that are not incurred again as more employees go through the program in later periods. The discount factor for costs carries the exponent $k-1$ because costs are incurred one period prior to receiving benefits.[12]

To express the utility of a program's effects over F periods, the one-period utility estimates (ΔU_k) are summed. Thus, the complete utility model reflecting employee flows through the workforce for a program affecting productivity in F future periods may be written as shown in Equation 10.5.

$$\Delta U = \sum_{k=1}^{F} \left[\sum_{t=1}^{k} \left(N_{a_t} - N_{st} \right) \right] \left\{ \left[1/(1+i)^k \right] \left(r_{x,sv} \right) \times \left(\bar{Z}_x \right) \left(SD_{sv} \right) \left(1+V \right) \left(1-TAX \right) \right\}$$

$$-\sum_{k=1}^{F} \left\{ C_k \left(1-TAX \right) \left[1/(1+i)^{(k-1)} \right] \right\}$$

$$\tag{10.5}$$

The duration parameter *F* in Equation 10.5 is not employee tenure, but rather how long the effects of improved selection last in the workforce, and might be affected by changes in the work, its context, or organization strategy.

Measures: Calculating Effects of Employee Flows for Computer Programmers

If we assume that the PAT is applied to computer programmers for 15 years, and we round up average tenure of 9.69 years to assume that programmers stay for 10 years, then if 618 programmers are added each year, and no one leaves in the first 10 years, N_k will increase by 618 in each year. At the end of year 10, 6,180 programmers selected by the PAT have been added to the work force. Beginning in future period 11, however, one PAT-selected cohort leaves in each period (N_{st} = 618). However, if the PAT is still applied to new cohorts in years 11 through 15, then each year brings 618 new replacements (that is, N_{at} = 618). In future periods 11 through 15, N_{at} and N_{st} offset each other and N_k remains at 6,180. Now, assume that the government stops using the PAT in year 15. Starting in future period 16, the cost and number added (C_k and N_{at}) become zero. But, the treated portion of the workforce does not disappear immediately. Earlier-selected cohorts continue to leave, 618 each year (that is, N_{st} = 618). They are not replaced, so N_k falls by 618 each year until the last-treated cohort (selected in future period 15) separates in future period 25. N_k for each of the 25 periods is shown in Figure 10.2. In Figure 10.2, *F* = 25 periods.

To complete the analysis, we can add dollar values and economic factors. Recall that we assumed that *V* = –0.05, *TAX* = 0.45, and the discount rate is 10 percent. Now, the range of payoffs over the 25-year analysis equals a low of $128.95 million, assuming the selection ratio (*SR*) is 80 percent (not very selective), the previous selection procedure had high validity (so the PAT improves validity by .26), and the total testing cost is zero (PAT costs the same as the old test). It equals a high of $2.214 billion, assuming the selection

Period (k)	N_k
1	618
2	1,236
3	1,854
4	2,472
5	3,090
6	3,708
7	4,326
8	4,944
9	5,562
10	6,180
11	6,180
12	6,180
13	6,180
14	6,180
15	6,180
16	5,562
17	4,944
18	4,326
19	3,708
20	3,090
21	2,472
22	1,854
23	1,236
24	618
25	0

Note: N_k = number of employees receiving a given treatment who remain in the workforce; PAT = programmer aptitude test.

Source: Adapted from Boudreau, J. W. (1983b). Effects of employee flows on utility analysis of human resource productivity improvement programs. *Journal of Applied Psychology 68*, 400. Copyright © 1983 by the American Psychological Association. Reprinted with permission.

Figure 10.2. Example of employee flows over a 25-year period.

ratio (*SR*) is 5 percent (very selective), the previous selection procedure had zero validity (so the PAT improves validity by .76), and the total testing cost is $507,000 per selected cohort ($41 times 618 selected times [1/.05]). Both the low and the high estimates are likely extreme, but the potential for more than $2 billion in benefits from improved selection should not be ignored. Our main point is that it is important to realize that benefits from HR programs often span many future years (much like investments in factories, oil rigs, R&D, and marketing), and estimating the payoffs only for the first cohort hired will usually understate the actual long-term payoff. It's the same idea as evaluating an investment in a new factory over the years of its useful life, and not simply in the first year of operation.

Logic: The Effect of Multiple Selection Devices

So far, our example assumed that the organization implemented one new selection procedure, a test for computer programmers. Most organizations use multiple selection devices, such as application forms, interviews, background checks; aptitude, ability, personality, or work sample tests; medical exams; and assessment centers. Although the validity of some of these devices may be low, each has demonstrated validities greater than zero.[13] When multiple selection devices are combined, the validity of the combination may be higher, assuming that each of them provides unique and valid information. If the costs of adding multiple devices are relatively low and the value of performance variability is high, the higher costs of using more devices are often offset by the increased predictive power. On the other hand, investing in more predictors will be less valuable if they are costly, if they don't add much additional information, or if they are applied where the value of improved performance is low. For example, having executives interview job candidates about their technical skills is very expensive and unlikely to yield better information than a simple skills test.

Logic: The Effects of a Probationary Period

At Whole Foods Market, new employees are selected by a process that looks a lot like reality television. A new employee is hired provisionally, works with his or her prospective future team members, and at the end of four weeks is offered a permanent job only if at least two-thirds of the team votes to hire him or her. A powerful way to increase the validity of staffing is to have candidates actually to do the job for a while and keep only those who do well.[14] This can be expensive. Whole Foods must pay probationary candidates' salaries and benefits and invest the time and effort of the employees who observe and rate the probationary workers. Yet, the added value of the better-screened workforce can easily offset the increased costs, as we saw with the PAT example above. The utility formulas can diagnose when such a probationary period will and won't pay off. Basically, the effect of a probationary period is reflected as the difference in performance value between the employees who begin the probationary period and those who survive.[15] If the probationary period weeds out a lot of poor candidates (resulting in a very low selection ratio), then the average performance of the surviving cohort increases. The actual amount of the improvement depends on the validity of the probationary period to weed out low performers and the proportion of the probationary candidates who are weeded out. The costs would include paying and training employees who are later dismissed and any separation costs.

A probationary period reduces the negative effect of selection errors that occur before probation because those errors are weeded out early instead of getting more permanent positions that take longer before dismissal. Paradoxically, that actually *reduces* the value of the selection procedures used with a probationary period because the selection mistakes such procedures might prevent won't last as long. This reinforces the value of the staffing utility framework in highlighting the integrated effects of different staffing elements such as recruitment, selection, probationary periods, and like this. In essence, the *combination* of selection and a probationary period can yield a higher or lower payoff than either one alone. It depends on their relative validity, the severity of selection errors, and the value of improved performance. The utility framework elegantly reflects this, allowing decision-makers to optimize these factors.

Another way to look at probationary periods is as a special case of the employee movement model that we described in Chapter 5,

"The High Cost of Employee Separations," in Figure 5.1. In essence, the probationary period is a "controlled turnover" process, in which the validity of the dismissal decision determines the economic payoff or cost of turnover.

Finally, when seen this way, it is clear that the combination of selection and probation is much like the supply chain model of Chapter 9, with probation being similar to quality control after raw materials have been accepted and placed into the production process. A combination of screening raw materials when they arrive and then monitoring their quality as they enter the production process may add great value if the cost of errors is quite high and if a lot of valuable information can be gathered after the materials are in the production process. That's the same logic Whole Foods is using. By selecting applicants carefully and then having the team observe them as they enter the workplace, Whole Foods is behaving as if the cost of an error is very high and assumes that the team members can see things that the selection process might miss.

Logic: Effects of Job Offer Rejections

We have assumed that any candidate who receives a job offer accepts it. Does it matter if top-scoring applicants reject offers, forcing the organization to make offers to lower-scoring applicants? Obviously, this lowers the quality of those selected, but how much is the effect? The effect is greatest in a tight labor market, when firms may be forced to lower their minimum hiring requirements in order to fill vacancies.[16]

In the utility model, rejected job offers have the same effect as reduced hiring standards. They increase the selection ratio (SR) and thus reduce the gains from more valid selection. For example, consider a situation in which hiring the top 20 percent (SR of 0.20) would yield the necessary number of new employees, assuming no candidates rejected offers. However, if in practice, candidates reject half of the job offers, then it would be necessary to hire the top 40 percent (SR=0.40) to get enough new hires to fill all the vacancies. The actual economic loss depends on how job offer rejections relate to the quality of the applicants.[17] The more likely that the best applicants reject offers, the greater the economic loss. This may seem obvious, but the staffing utility framework shows how to estimate the effect.

How large are the potential losses? Murphy found that utility results could be reduced by 30 to 80 percent.[18] Utility losses caused by job-offer rejection can be offset by investing in additional recruiting efforts to increase the number of applicants, thereby restoring smaller selection ratios. Or, to increase the probability that the best applicants will accept offers, the organization might invest in its brand or reward package to increase its attractiveness to the better applicants. Both of these investments can be understood better by using the staffing utility model as a decision framework.

Process: How Staffing Processes Are Used

A similar effect to rejected offers occurs when an organization decides to deviate from making job offers top-down, starting with the top-scoring candidates. In one study, researchers compared the utility values for selecting forest rangers under three assumptions:

1. Strict top-down selection,
2. Selecting everyone who scored above the average (the top 50 percent), and
3. Selecting everyone who scored above one standard deviation below average (the top 85 percent).[19]

Top-down selection produced a productivity increase of about 13 percent, which translated into millions of dollars. Selecting randomly from those who scored above the average reduced those gains by 45 percent. Selecting randomly from among those who scored more than one standard deviation below average reduced the gains from top-down selection by 84 percent. Managers who deviate from top-down selection may do so at substantial cost, particularly when the predictor has a high correlation with job performance and where improved performance is very valuable.

The losses may be considerably smaller, however, if the actual test score differences between higher- and lower-scoring candidates are small or if the test scores reflect attributes that are not very pivotal. Ideally, a selection process captures the full range of attributes needed for success in a role. If it doesn't, and instead captures only one or a small subset of pivotal attributes that are critical to effective job performance, then selection of the highest scorers has less impact on productivity or quality improvements.[20] For example, if you were hiring people to repair electrical power lines in a predominantly Spanish-speaking region of a large city, you could certainly test candidates on their technical knowledge of electrical systems and repair procedures. Hiring top-down on those scores would likely obtain the best system repairers. However, if very few of them spoke Spanish, they would be unable to interact effectively with business owners and residents in that neighborhood and could not explain things like the reason for power outages, when the power would be restored, or how to contact the utility company for more information. It might be more effective to expand the pool of hires to include more Spanish speakers, even if that meant including some who scored a bit lower on the technical test.

Cumulative Effects: Putting It All Together

Is it possible to adjust for all of these factors—economic variables, employee flows, probationary periods, multiple selection devices, and rejected job offers? Yes, and computer simulation can be quite helpful. One study used simulated values of 10,000 scenarios, computing the utility value for each scenario that took different values of the five factors described above.[21] The payoffs were compared to a baseline utility of hiring one cohort with no adjustments (see Chapter 9). Results revealed that some adjustments reduced the payoff from the selection system (economic adjustments, deviations from top-down hiring, probationary period) while others increased it (multiple selection devices and employee flows). Economic adjustments had the largest effects, followed by multiple selection devices, departures from top-down hiring, probationary periods, and employee flows. The median effect of the full array of adjustments was to reduce the baseline utility estimates by 91 percent, with a minimum reduction of 71 percent. Sixteen percent of the results actually caused the positive baseline utility estimate to become negative. The lesson is that although valid selection procedures often produce positive payoffs, actual payoffs depend significantly on organizational decisions and situational factors.

Leaders often imagine that "best practices" will invariably improve employee performance. Indeed, meta-analyses of multiple studies often show that test validity is high and consistently positive. Yet, validity is only one factor that affects the value of selection systems. A sound decision science applies a consistent framework to diverse situations and shows how results will change if relevant factors change. Wise organizations will use the utility frameworks presented in this chapter to better understand their own selection situations and to improve their unique decisions, rather than blindly copying the best practices of others.

Dealing with Risk and Uncertainty in Utility Analysis

Many factors might increase or decrease expected payoffs from utility analysis.[22] Considering such factors will increase the realism of utility estimates, but uncertainty always exists when estimating payoffs.

Two techniques can make uncertainty clearer and thus easier to deal with: break-even analysis and Monte Carlo analysis.

Break-Even Analysis

We reviewed break-even analysis in Chapter 2, "Analytical Foundations for HR Measurement." This approach reduces the unnecessary fixation on estimating one precise utility value and focuses on making a good decision even with imperfect information. It also distinguishes areas where disagreements should lead to different decisions, versus where they have little impact. For example, does it matter if estimates of SD_y are not precise? One review of forty-two studies found that there was not a single case where the break-even value of SD_y was more than 60 percent of the estimated value, and in many cases, the break-even value was less than 1 percent of the estimated value.[23] In other words, the SD_y estimates could be on the high side by more than 40 percent and the decision to implement the program would still be the same. Disagreements about the value of SD_y often have little practical effect on the decision to implement a program or not. Of course, even a low break-even value might change when comparing a selection program to other organizational investments, and decision-makers may want to consider parameters other than SD_y.[24] Still, break-even analysis is a powerful tool for producing better decisions and better logic.

Monte Carlo Analysis

Computer-based (Monte Carlo) simulations can estimate variation in utility values.[25] This technique is used for decisions about processes such as manufacturing or in consumer research on the response to new marketing initiatives. Monte Carlo analysis estimates a distribution of values by varying the parameters of a model, like a utility analysis model. In the PAT example earlier, we assumed a range of values for the selection ratio and validity. Monte Carlo analysis might assume those follow a normal distribution. We might similarly examine what would happen if the number of applicants and the number hired vary across a range of values, assuming that the probability of any particular value is normally distributed.

Monte Carlo analysis draws a value for each variable from its assumed distribution, inserts that value into the utility equation, and then calculates utility. This is done repeatedly for up to tens of thousands of combinations of values, which produces a distribution of utility values. The resulting distribution describes the average, range, and likelihood of seeing various utility values. Modeling and analyzing uncertainty with Monte Carlo analysis allows better predictions of the likely outcomes and risks.

Process: Communicating the Impact of Utility Analyses to Decision-Makers

You have seen that utility analysis can produce very large estimates of payoffs, suggesting that investing in HR programs like selection produces very attractive returns. Do business leaders actually believe these estimates? Two provocative studies showed that it makes a big difference how utility results are presented. Presenting utility analysis in some ways reduces managerial support for valid selection procedures, even when the calculated benefits are very large.[26] In one experiment, managers were presented with an unadjusted estimated selection program payoff of more than $121 million (in 2018 dollars), representing a return on investment of 14,000 percent. This result strains belief, and it was no surprise that the managers did not accept it. A fundamental financial principle is that high returns must carry high risks, so even if leaders believed the average estimate, they might well conclude the investment must be highly speculative.[27] There is some controversy about whether leaders will reject high-utility results because two subsequent studies failed to replicate these findings, prompting challenges to the conclusions.[28]

Another study we described earlier took a different tack, adjusting the utility value in the original study for economic variables, multiple selection devices, deviations from top-down hiring, a probationary period, and employee flows.[29] The study used Monte Carlo analysis to generate 10,000 independent scenarios, and the distribution of adjusted utility estimates showed an average payoff of $3,423,736, reducing the original estimate by more than 96 percent. The lowest estimated payoff was a loss of $3,960,104, and the largest predicted gain was $26,371,295 (all figures in 2018 dollars), which was still 71 percent smaller than the unadjusted estimate. The researchers did not test whether leaders would respond better to the adjusted estimate, but this research suggests that utility models offer a framework for being more transparent about how HR payoffs are estimated, expanding what factors are considered, and, ultimately, improving decisions even with imperfect or uncertain information. We know very little about what affects how managers respond to utility analyses. The way to learn more is to share information on how we communicate results, learn where audiences perceive weaknesses, take steps to respond, and repeat the process.[30]

Two hurdles to more widespread use of utility analysis models are their complexity and the lack of knowledge about utility analysis among key decision makers. Few organizational decision-makers are even aware of utility models and the value of their logic and analytics (the elements of the utility formula and adjustments to it), or the measures that populate the formulas (such generating estimates of SD_y). When leaders lack such knowledge, they won't use utility analyses to affect actual decisions about vital investments in talent programs.

Even among those who use utility analysis, there is a need to shift their focus. Too often, analysts ask "How do we construct the best HR measure?" when the better question is: "How do we create change through HR measurement?" HR measurements and utility estimates are not ends in and of themselves, but a decision-support system. The HR field should change its focus from measures per se to the effects of those measures on decisions about talent. If leaders are to take actions based on HR research, then that research must be communicated effectively in language that they understand.

Research suggests that managers are receptive to utility analysis when analysts present conservative estimates, illustrate the tradeoffs involved, do not overload the presentation with technical details, and emphasize the things that operating managers care about (reducing the cycle time of staffing, reducing costs while maintaining validity).[31] The framing of the message is vital to its acceptance.[32] Utility analysis has great potential to improve decision making. To do that, however, it must be seen not as an equation but as a way to clarify and stimulate better thinking about the costs and benefits of HR programs.

Employee Selection and the Talent Supply Chain

In the spirit of connecting selection utility analysis to the mental models that leaders already use, it may be useful to depict the staffing process as a supply chain and retool utility analysis within the language of supply chain optimization, as described in Chapter 3.[33] Table 10.1 shows how the typical questions posed in supply chain management can be translated to apply to employee recruitment, selection, and retention. These questions reflect the logical models in Chapters 9 and 10, combined to reflect a comprehensive logical model for understanding and measuring the talent supply chain.

These questions are illustrative, and many more parallel ideas exist between traditional supply chains and utility analysis for employee staffing. The point of these illustrations is to encourage HR and business leaders to explore how existing and proven business frameworks can be applied to talent and human capital decisions. The utility analysis framework can seem like a foreign language to most business leaders, but it is largely the same language they already apply to other decisions. It's just a matter of translation.

Table 10.1. How Supply-Chain Management and Employee Selection Share Business Logic

	Supply-Chain Management	Employee Selection
Demand Planning and Forecasting	Predicting future resource needs in terms of quality, quantity, cost, and timing, based on business activity and other factors. Planning approaches to better forecast or smooth demand levels for better planning.	Predicting the needed quantity, quality, and timing of future job openings and vacancies. Utility analysis can show where better performance has the highest payoff. Selection data can show where having a longer lead-time can improve selection validity or applicant quality.
Production Planning and Scheduling	Predicting and establishing future production schedules or inventory-acquisition schedules. Optimizing production to fit quality and quantity needs.	Predicting and planning future recruitment and staffing processes. Utility analysis can show the payoff from increased applicant "production" that produces lower selection ratios, and the impact of longer tenure among new hires that reduces turnover and increases the timeframe of the payoff from improved selection.
Distribution and Logistics	Planning how goods will move through space and time, identifying where to place warehouses and transportation channels, and determining how to optimize choices about which sources to use.	Planning whether to recruit locally or more broadly. Locating workplaces near applicant sources. Utility analysis can show the relative quality of applicants from different sources and the relative predictability of applicant quality. Utility analysis can compare the payoffs and costs from different applicant sources.
Inventory Management	Planning how much and where to hold inventory of goods, where shortages and surpluses should be tolerated, and how to optimize the risks of being out of stock, having too much stock, against the costs of ordering and holding inventory.	Planning how far in advance to build inventories of applicants and potential applicants. Planning where to hold a surplus of job-holders and where to allow shortages to occur. Utility analysis captures the ordering costs of improved selection, as well as the potential quality improvements from anticipating job openings to attract better candidates or select more carefully.

Exercises

Software that calculates answers to one or more of the following exercises can be found at http://iip.shrm.org.

1. You are given the following information regarding the CAP test for clerical employees (clerk-2s) at the Berol Corporation:

   Average tenure as a clerk-2: 7.26 years

   Number selected per year: 120

   Validity of the CAP test: 0.61

   Validity of previously used test: 0.18

   Cost per applicant of CAP: $35

   Cost per applicant of old test: $18

   SR: 0.50

   SD, in first year: $34,000

   Use Equation 10.1 to determine (a) the total utility of the CAP test, (b) the utility per selectee, and (c) the per-year gain in utility per selectee.

2. Referring to Exercise 1, suppose that after consulting with the chief financial officer at Berol, you are given the following additional information: variable costs are 0.08, taxes are 40 percent, and the discount rate is 8 percent. Use Equation 10.2 in this chapter to recompute the total utility of the CAP test, the utility per selectee, and the utility per selectee in the first year.

3. The Top Dollar Co. is trying to decide whether to use an assessment center to select middle managers for its consumer products operations. The following information has been determined: variable costs are 0.10, corporate taxes

are 44 percent, the discount rate is 9 percent, the ordinary selection procedure costs $700 per candidate, the assessment center costs $2,800 per candidate, the standard deviation of job performance is $55,000, the validity of the ordinary procedure is 0.30, the validity of the assessment center is 0.40, the selection ratio is 0.20, and the average tenure as a middle manager is 3 years. The program is designed to last 6 years, with 20 managers added each year. Beginning in year 4, however, one cohort separates each year until all hires from the program leave.

Use Equation 10.6 in this chapter to determine whether Top Dollar Co. should adopt the assessment center to select middle managers. What payoffs can be expected in total, per selectee, and per selectee in the first year?

References

1. Wayne F. Cascio and Herman Aguinis, *Applied Psychology in Talent Management*, 8th ed. (Thousand Oaks, CA: Sage, 2019).
2. Wayne F. Cascio and John C. Scott, "The Business Value of Employee Selection," in *Handbook of Employee Selection*, 2nd ed., ed. James L. Farr and Nancy T. Tippins (New York: Routledge, 2017), 226–48.
3. Wayne F. Cascio and Herman Aguinis, "Staffing 21st-Century Organizations," *Academy of Management Annals* 2, no. 1 (January 2008): 133–65.
4. Frank L. Schmidt et al., "Impact of Valid Selection Procedures on Work-Force Productivity," *Journal of Applied Psychology* 64, no. 6 (December 1979): 609–26.
5. Schmidt et al., "Impact of Valid Selection Procedures."
6. Cascio and Scott, "Business Value of Employee Selection."
7. John W. Boudreau, "Economic Considerations in Estimating the Utility of Human Resource Productivity Improvement Programs," *Personnel Psychology* 36, no. 3 (September 1983): 551–76.
8. John W. Boudreau, "Effects of Employee Flows on Utility Analysis of Human Resource Productivity Improvement Programs," *Journal of Applied Psychology* 68, no. 3 (August 1983): 396–406.

9. John W. Boudreau and Chris J. Berger, "Decision-Theoretic Utility Analysis Applied to Employee Separations and Acquisitions," *Journal of Applied Psychology* 70, no. 3 (August 1985): 581–612.

10. Schmidt et al., "Impact of Valid Selection Procedures."

11. Boudreau, "Effects of Employee Flows."

12. Boudreau, "Effects of Employee Flows."

13. Cascio and Aguinis, *Applied Psychology in Talent Management.*

14. "Our Hiring Process," Careers, Whole Foods Market, http://www.wholefoodsmarket.com/careers/hiringprocess.php.

15. Wilfried De Corte, "Utility Analysis for the One-Cohort Selection-Retention Decision with a Probationary Period," *Journal of Applied Psychology* 79, no. 3 (June 1994): 402–11.

16. Brian E. Becker, "The Influence of Labor Markets on Human Resources Utility Estimates," *Personnel Psychology* 42, no. 3 (September 1989): 531–46.

17. Kevin R. Murphy, "When Your Top Choice Turns You Down: Effects of Rejected Offers on the Utility of Selection Tests," *Psychological Bulletin* 99, no. 1 (January 1986): 133–38.

18. Murphy, "When Your Top Choice Turns You Down."

19. Frank L. Schmidt, Murray J. Mack, John E. Hunter, "Selection Utility in the Occupation of US Park Ranger for Three Modes of Test Use," *Journal of Applied Psychology* 69 no. 3 (August 1984): 490–97.

20. Cascio and Scott, "Business Value of Employee Selection."

21. Michael C. Sturman, "Implications of Utility Analysis Adjustments for Estimates of Human Resource Intervention Value," *Journal of Management* 26, no. 2 (April 2000): 281–99.

22. Wayne F. Cascio, "Assessing the Utility of Selection Decisions: Theoretical and Practical Considerations," in *Personnel Selection in Organizations*, ed. Neil Schmitt and Walter C. Borman (San Francisco: Jossey-Bass, 1993), 310–40.

23. John W. Boudreau, "Utility Analysis for Decisions in Human Resource Management," in Vol. 2, *Handbook of Industrial and Organizational Psychology*, 2nd ed., ed. Marvin D. Dunnette and Leaetta M. Hough (Palo Alto, CA: Consulting Psychologists Press, 1991), 621–745.

24. Jeff A. Weekley et al., "A Comparison of Three Methods of Estimating the Standard Deviation of Performance in Dollars," *Journal of Applied Psychology* 70, no. 1 (February 1985): 122–26. See also Calvin C. Hoffman and George C. Thornton III, "Examining Selection Utility Where Competing Predictors Differ in Adverse Impact," *Personnel Psychology* 50, no. 2 (June 1997): 455–70.

25. Sturman, "Implications of Utility Analysis." See also Joseph R. Rich and John W. Boudreau, "The Effects of Variability and Risk on Selection Utility Analysis: An Empirical Simulation and Comparison," *Personnel Psychology* 40, no. 1 (March 1987): 55–84.

26. Gary P. Latham and Glen Whyte, "The Futility of Utility Analysis," Personnel Psychology 47, no. 1 (March 1994): 31–46. See also Glen Whyte

and Gary P. Latham, "The Futility of Utility Analysis Revisited: When Even an Expert Fails," *Personnel Psychology* 50, no. 3 (September 1997): 601–11.

27. John W. Boudreau and Peter M. Ramstad, *Beyond HR: The New Science of Human Capital* (Boston: Harvard Business School Publishing, 2007).

28. Kenneth P. Carson, John S. Becker, and John A. Henderson, "Is Utility Really Futile? A Failure to Replicate and an Extension," *Journal of Applied Psychology* 83, no. 1 (February 1998): 84–96. See also Steven F. Cronshaw, "Lo! The Stimulus Speaks: The Insider's View of Whyte and Latham's 'The Futility of Utility Analysis,'" *Personnel Psychology* 50, no. 3 (September 1997): 611–15; Hoffman and Thornton, "Examining Selection Utility."

29. Sturman, "Implications of Utility Analysis."

30. Wayne F. Cascio, "The Role of Utility Analysis in the Strategic Management of Organizations," *Journal of Human Resource Costing and Accounting* 1, no. 2 (1996): 85–95. See also Beth C. Florin-Thuma and John W. Boudreau, "Performance Feedback Utility in a Small Organization: Effects on Organizational Outcomes and Managerial Decision Processes," *Personnel Psychology* 40, no. 4 (December 1987): 693–713.

31. Calvin C. Hoffman, "Applying Utility Analysis to Guide Decisions on Selection System Content," *Journal of Human Resource Costing and Accounting* 1, no. 2 (1996): 9–17.

32. Carson, Becker, and Henderson, "Is Utility Really Futile?" See also John T. Hazer and Scott Highhouse, "Factors Influencing Managers' Reactions to Utility Analysis: Effects of SD_y Method, Information Frame, and Focal Intervention," *Journal of Applied Psychology* 82, no. 1 (February 1997): 104–12.

33. John W. Boudreau, *Retooling HR: Using Proven Business Tools to Make Better Decisions About Talent* (Boston: Harvard Business Publishing, 2010). See also Wayne F. Cascio and John W. Boudreau, "Supply-Chain Analysis Applied to Staffing Decisions," in *Handbook of Industrial and Organizational Psychology*, ed. Sheldon Zedeck (Washington, DC: American Psychological Association Books, 2010).

11

Costs and Benefits of HR Development Programs

Firms spend billions each year on employee training—between $180 billion and $200 billion in the US alone.[1] On average, employees receive almost 48 hours of training per year, with mid-size companies providing the most hours of training, an average of 54.3 per employee.[2] These outlays reflect the cost of keeping abreast of technological and social changes, the extent of managerial commitment to achieving a competent, productive work force, and the broad array of opportunities available for individuals and teams to improve their technical skills and their social skills. Indeed, the large amount of money spent on training in both public and private organizations is likely to increase in the coming years as organizations strive to meet challenges such as the following:[3]

» *Growing demands for personal and professional development.* Among young adults, the most important feature they look for in a new job is opportunity for continuous learning.[4] In addition to technical skills, employers are looking for people who can interact satisfactorily with customers and who demonstrate responsibility, flexibility, initiative, critical thinking, and a collaborative spirit.

» *The effects of digital technology on work.* To be sure, the digital revolution is changing the manner in which businesses create and capture value, how and where we work, and how we interact and communicate. Technologies such as cloud and mobile computing, big data and machine learning, sensors and intelligent manufacturing, advanced robotics and drones, and clean-energy technologies are transforming the very foundations of global business and the organizations that drive it.[5] In 2018, nearly one in five Americans was working in a job that did not exist in 1980.[6] With respect to training, employees can take a course on nearly any subject online without leaving their desks, or couch, or coffee shop. Indeed, the trend toward consumer-centric learning puts employees, not training departments, in charge.

» *Increased training opportunities for nonstandard workers.* Traditionally, employees received classroom instruction and on-the-job training opportunities as they moved through jobs and hierarchical levels in an organization. Today, more and more workers are operating outside the traditional confines of regular, full-time employment. These nonstandard "gig" workers may be free agents or "e-lancers" (that is, freelancers in the digital world) who work for themselves, or they may be employees of an organization a firm is allied with, employees of an outsourcing or temporary-help firm, or even volunteers.[7] They may be employed for limited periods of time by many organizations as they work on tasks, micro-tasks, and projects. A "career" in the gig economy focuses more on accumulating project and task credits than on progressing through a series of positions in a hierarchy. Ongoing opportunities for professional development are critical to continued employability.

» *Teams.* As more firms move to employee involvement and teams in the workplace, team members need to learn such behaviors as asking for ideas, offering help without being asked, listening and providing feedback, and recognizing and considering the ideas of others. Organizations that provide superior opportunities for learning and growth have a distinct advantage when competing for talented employees.[8]

Indeed, as the demands of the information age spread, companies are coming to regard training expenditures as no less a part of their capital costs than plant and equipment.

Training and development entail the following general properties and characteristics:[9]

» They are learning experiences.
» They are planned by the organization.
» They occur after the individual has joined the organization.
» They are intended to further the organization's goals.

Training and development activities are, therefore, planned programs of organizational improvement undertaken to bring about a relatively permanent change in employee knowledge, skills, attitudes, or social behavior.[10]

The trends noted above suggest that "learning" in organizations has and will continue to evolve to be less formally planned, occurring before or after people join the organization, occurring in worker populations beyond those who actually join the organization (as employees), and will be driven by a balance between furthering the individual's and an organization's goals. The idea of "relatively permanent" will also evolve to reflect shorter time periods, as the useful life of many skills, attitudes, and social behaviors decreases with increasingly rapid change.

Still, the analytical tools that we present here apply to programs as diverse as providing learning through job experiences, coaching, mentoring, formal training, e-learning (online instruction, mobile learning [e.g., podcasts], virtual classrooms), and off-site classes or degrees. We focus our examples on training programs because that is where most of the research and discussion have occurred. In the area of training, topics range from basic skills (technical as well as supervisory skills), to interpersonal skills, team building, and decision-making for individuals or teams. Technologies used run the full gamut from lectures to interactive video, to internet-based training, intranet-based training, social-software applications, Web 2.0 tools (technologies that enable user-generated content, such as blogs and Wikis), and intelligent tutoring systems.[11]

Unfortunately, although billions may be spent providing training and development programs, little is spent assessing the social and financial outcomes of these activities. Consider leadership development programs as an example. One thorough review estimated that only 10 percent of leadership development programs evaluated their impact on the actual behaviors of managers. Most consider only the satisfaction of participants as an indicator of the programs' effectiveness.[12] The most common forms of evaluation are qualitative surveys of participants and the satisfaction of participants. Only 32 percent of firms seek feedback indicating behavior change.[13] The overall result is that little comparative evidence exists by which to generalize or to evaluate the impact of the various technologies. Decision-makers thus remain unguided by systematic evaluations of past experiments and uninformed about the costs and benefits of alternative HRD programs when considering training efforts in their own organizations.

That said, meta-analytic evidence collected across many individual studies and in many different organizations does illustrate the positive benefits of different content, methods, and types of training when designed and implemented properly across different criteria, such as trainee reactions, substantive learning, behavior change, and organizational results.[14] The study we describe next asked a different question, namely, is there a relationship between firm-level investments in training and changes in those firms' stock prices?

The Relationship between Training Expenditures and Stock Prices

At present, firms' investments in human capital—most notably spending on employees' development—are treated as hidden costs that are buried in overhead, specifically in the accounting category "selling, general, and administrative expenses," or SG&A. This treatment makes investments in human capital difficult to obtain.

Using a unique database, one study tested the hypothesis that firms that make unusually large investments in employee development subsequently enjoy higher stock prices than comparable firms that make smaller investments in employee development. To disentangle the effects of training per se from other potentially confounding variables, the authors deployed a variety of multivariate techniques and control variables.[15]

The research revealed that four portfolios of 575 publicly traded companies that invested in employee training and development at roughly twice the industry average outperformed the S&P 500 by 4.6 percentage points over a 25-month period and outperformed it in the year before the study by 17–35 percent.[16] In 2009, the same authors demonstrated in a sample of thirty banks that training expenditures remain a powerful predictor of subsequent stock prices, even through the market turbulence of 2008.[17]

Moreover, some forms of training yield superior benefits relative to others. Specifically, training in technical skills yielded an effect that was 3.5 times higher than the effect for all types of training, and 6 times higher than that for general business skills.

This may be changing, as work automation and other trends create rapid evolution in technical skills, automation takes over an increasing number of technical tasks, and soft skills become the basis for human work contributions. For example, the World Economic Forum's "Future of Jobs" report suggests these as the top ten skills in 2020:[18]

1. Complex Problem Solving,
2. Critical Thinking,
3. Creativity,
4. People Management,
5. Coordinating with Others,
6. Emotional Intelligence,

7. Judgment and Decision-Making,
8. Service Orientation,
9. Negotiation, and
10. Cognitive Flexibility.

The evidence suggests that training expenditures, rather than being the result of past financial performance, actually may predict future stock returns. Researchers found that the one significant relationship was between training expenditures in the year prior to stock returns, with no significant relationship between training expenditures and stock returns in the previous year or the current year. This supports, but does not prove, that training investments help to determine stock-price performance, and not the opposite.

In the absence of a true experimental design, however, it is impossible to rule out the possibility that the training measure is serving, at least in part, as a marker for other unmeasured, firm-level attributes that are correlated with a firm's long-term profitability (and thus equity market valuation). As the authors noted:

> From the perspective of an individual investor, it is far less important whether the correlation between training and stock value represents a causal training effect on firm performance, or whether training is instead simply a leading indicator for other productive firm activities or attributes. In the short run, so long as the underlying relationship between training and whatever firm characteristics that affect productivity continue to hold, investment portfolios that incorporate information about firm training expenditures will yield super-normal rates of return.[19]

Thus, for an investor it may not matter whether training expense serves as a convenient marker for the real factors that drive later financial returns. In contrast, for an organization leader, what matters is whether and how investments in training have a unique effect on those future returns. While the researchers' analyses cannot determine *why* the relationship between training expenditures and stock-price performance exists, three possible explanations seem plausible:

» Training investments have their intended impact; those firms that make greater investments in this area subsequently perform better as a result.

» Training investments may well serve as a proxy for the degree to which a firm is willing and able to take a long-term perspective, rather than focus excessively (and destructively) on quarterly earnings.

» Expenditures on training (and in particular, changes in those expenditures) may serve as a window into an organization's future financial health and prospects (or lack thereof).

Although the tools we describe in this chapter are certainly valuable for increasing the amount and effectiveness of development program evaluation, the issue runs much deeper. Analytical decision tools are not just useful for evaluating programs after they are complete. The lack of evaluation in HR development is a symptom of a more fundamental issue: a lack of systematic logic to plan and refine such programs.

The Logic of Talent Development

This chapter is not advocating that all HRD programs must be evaluated using true experimental or quasi-experimental designs.[20] Rather, it seeks to describe how to express the economic consequences of HRD programs. Let us begin, as we have in other chapters, by presenting the logic of talent development, as shown in Figure 11.1.

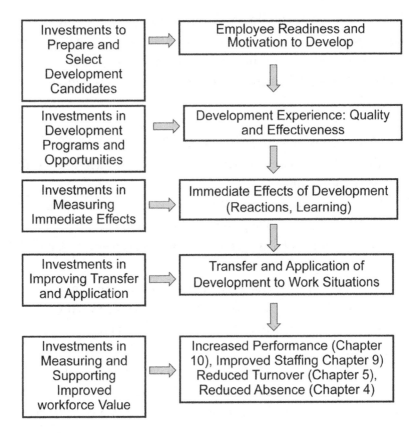

Figure 11.1. Logic of talent-development effects.

As the diagram shows, effectiveness of development is much more than sound design and effective implementation of HRD programs or experiences. These are necessary, but not sufficient by themselves to ensure that what is learned in training is actually applied on the job.[21] For that to occur, other conditions must be satisfied. First, candidates for development must be prepared and motivated both to learn and to apply their learning at work. This requires investments by the organization in both the preparation of development candidates (e.g., through challenging job assignments), as well as in the careful selection of candidates for development experiences, such as jobs or training programs.

Second, after the development experience, there must be an environment that provides the opportunity and motivation for the newly developed individuals to apply or transfer their learning to their work. This second condition requires that supervisors and higher-level managers must support employees' attempts to use on the job what they have learned in training or development. For example, if employees learn all about democratic leadership styles in training but then report back to autocratic leaders on the job, the effects of the training are not likely to have long-term effects. In addition, it is important to offer rewards and incentives to employees when they apply what they learned in training to improve their day-to-day job performance. This means that improved performance will often carry with it increased costs of pay, incentives, or supervisory preparation.

The conditions shown in Figure 11.1 create "line of sight" for development candidates, between their development, their on-the-job behaviors, improved unit performance, and the overall strategic success of the organization. Here are two examples of public-private partnerships designed to produce the kinds of skills that local companies are demanding. Ohio's Tri-Rivers Career Center partnered with robotics companies, local manufacturers, and educators to design a system that is being replicated throughout the state. High school students enroll for free in an automation certification program (RAMTEC—Robotic Advanced Manufacturing Technical Education Collaborative) to learn skills that local businesses are demanding while continuing to earn their traditional diplomas.[22] Most receive job offers before they even complete the program. Similarly, Wichita, Kansas, long a center of aircraft manufacturing, is working with industry, Wichita State University, and the local technical college to train thousands of new workers for companies like Textron, Inc., Airbus SE, and Spirit AeroSystems Holdings, Inc.[23] Company support, coupled with rewards for completing the training program (guaranteed jobs), provides the kind of "line of sight" that links the training needs of companies to educational programs, and for students, the motivation to excel in training.

At the bottom of Figure 11.1, we connect employee development to several other topics covered in this book. Although the vast majority of attention to valuing employee development has focused on its immediate effects or its effects on job performance, it should also be noted that when employees have more tools and opportunities to perform well, they are often more motivated and engaged with their work. This can lead to reduced turnover and absence. In addition, opportunities for development are increasingly an important part of the "total rewards" proposition that employers offer to the labor market.[24] For example, Monster.com reports on companies with "awesome training and development programs," including SAS, Amazon, and Marriott International. Procter & Gamble is known globally for its effective career paths and training programs to develop great marketers.[25] *CEO Magazine* rates companies like GE, EMC, Hitachi Data Systems, IBM, and Johnson Controls best for developing future leaders.[26] Not only do these programs improve the performance of those who directly participate, they also are powerful attractors to external candidates. Thus, enhanced development can also lead to more and better applicants for employment, which, as you saw in Chapter 9, "Staffing Utility: The Concept and Its Measurement," is one element of enhanced workforce value through staffing.

The remainder of the chapter focuses on two broad themes: (1) developing a framework that extends the utility analysis logic we applied to staffing in Chapter 9 to the evaluation of HRD programs; and (2) an illustration of cost analysis, comparing offsite versus web-based meeting costs.

Utility-Analysis Approach to Decisions about HRD Programs

Faced with a bewildering array of alternatives, decision-makers must select the programs that will have the greatest impact on pivotal talent pools—those where investments in HRD will have the largest marginal impact on activities, decisions, and ultimately, on the value created for the firm. Recall that utility analysis specifically incorporates the idea of pivotalness by including the *quantity* of workers affected by an HR program, as well as SD_y, the pivotal value of enhanced worker *quality*. We saw in Chapter 9 that utility analysis is a powerful tool for staffing programs, and now we show how it can be used to evaluate proposed or ongoing HRD programs.[27]

The basic difference is that staffing programs create value through the quality of the choices they support regarding who joins. In contrast, programs such as HRD do not change the membership of the work force. Instead, they change the quality of the existing pool of workers. So, instead of generating changes in quality based on who joins or leaves a work force, training increases the quality of the individuals who already are in it.

Modifying the Brogden-Cronbach-Gleser Model to Apply to Training

In the Brogden-Cronbach-Gleser model, the only difference between the basic equation for calculating staffing utility (Equation 9.9 in Chapter 9, "Staffing Utility: The Concept and Its Measurement") and that for calculating utility from HRD programs is that the term d_t is substituted for the product r_{xy} times $\bar{Z}_s$ (that is, the validity coefficient times the average standard score on the predictor achieved by selectees).[28] The parameter d_t is the effect size. It reflects the difference in job-relevant outcomes between those who participate in the development opportunity and those who do not. It is expressed in standardized units, or Z-scores, just as in the selection utility equation.

The resulting utility formula is as follows:

$$\Delta U = (N)(T)(d_t)(SD_y) - C \qquad (11.1)$$

Where:

ΔU = the monetary gain resulting from the program

N = the number of employees trained

T = the expected duration of the beneficial effects in the trained group

d_t = the difference in job performance between the trained and untrained groups in SD units

SD_y = the standard deviation of dollar-valued job performance among untrained employees

C = the total cost of training N employees

To illustrate that idea graphically, we'll plot the (hypothetical) distribution of job performance outcomes of the trained and untrained groups on the same baseline (expressed in Z-score units, with a mean of 0 and a standard deviation of 1.0), as shown in Figure 11.2.

In Figure 11.2, d represents the size of the effect of the training program. How is d computed? It is simply the difference between the means of the trained and untrained groups in standard Z-score units. This might be the difference in average job performance, time to competency, learning, and so on. Therefore:

$$d = \bar{X}_t - \bar{X}_u / SD_x \qquad (11.2)$$

Where d is the effect size. If the effect is expressed in terms of job performance, $\bar{X}_t$ is the average job performance score of the trained group; $\bar{X}_u$ is the average job performance score of the untrained group; and SD_x is the standard deviation of the job performance scores of the total group, trained and untrained. If the

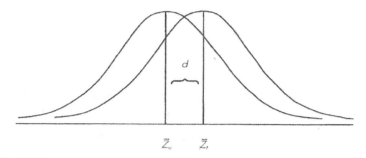

Note: $\bar{Z}_u$ is the average job performance score of the untrained group; $\bar{Z}_t$ is the average job performance score of the trained group; and d is the effect size.

Figure 11.2. Standard-score distributions of job performance outcomes among trained and untrained groups.

SDs of the two groups are unequal, the *SD* of the untrained group should be used because it is more representative of the incumbent employee population. Suppose that we are evaluating the impact of training for quality-control inspectors. Let's say that job performance is evaluated in terms of the number of defects identified in a standard sample of products known to contain ten defects. Suppose the average number of defects detected among trained employees is 7, for those in the untrained group it is 6.5, and the standard deviation of the defects detected is 1.0. The effect size is as shown in Equation 11.3.

$$d = 7 - 6.5 \; / \; 1 = 0.5 \; SD \qquad\qquad (11.3)$$

In other words, the performance of the trained group is half a standard deviation better than that of the untrained group. Because a perfectly reliable, objective measure of job performance was used in this case, the estimate of d need not be corrected for unreliability. In most cases, training evaluation will rely on criteria that are not perfectly reliable, such as supervisory ratings of job performance. In such cases, d must be corrected statistically for unreliability or measurement error in the criterion, or the estimate will be biased (too conservative).

One way to correct for this bias is to use a meta-analysis of performance ratings; one such study reported an average reliability of 0.86.[29] The formula for computing the true difference in job performance between the trained and untrained groups is as shown in Equation 11.4. This equation calculates the corrected effect size by dividing the observed effect size by the square root of the reliability estimate. All terms are as defined earlier and d_t is the square root of the reliability of the job performance measure.

$$d_t = d / \sqrt{r_{yy}} \tag{11.4}$$

Because reliability estimates are always between zero and 1.0, this correction will always produce a corrected effect size larger than the observed effect size.

To express the standard-score difference as a percentage change in output, multiply d_t by the ratio of the pretest standard deviation to the pretest performance average (SD/M) times 100.[30]

Issues in Estimating d_t

If an organization already has conducted a training program and possesses the necessary data, it can compute d_t directly. Pre- and post-measures of job performance in the trained and untrained groups should be collected systematically, with special care taken to prevent the ratings or other measures of job performance from being influenced by knowledge of who has or has not been trained. These are the same kinds of problems that bedevil all HRD evaluation research, not just research on d_t. Several thorough treatments of these issues are available.[31]

If training effects must be estimated for a new HRD program, or where no existing data were collected, d_t is best estimated by the cumulated results of all available studies of comparable training programs, using meta-analysis. As studies accumulate, managers will be able to rely on cumulative knowledge of the expected effect sizes associated with proposed HRD programs. Such a "menu" of effect sizes for HRD programs will allow HR professionals to compute the expected utilities of proposed HRD programs before investing in them. However, presently there are few such studies, and actual training programs may not be precisely comparable to those that are featured in scientific studies. Still, it is often very informative to estimate training effects using scientifically established effect sizes, even if they may not be perfectly comparable. If the results suggest either very high or very low payoffs, then the issue of comparability may not be so important because virtually any reasonable effect size would produce the same decision. See our discussion of break-even analysis below.

What If Training Covers Less Than the Full Range of Job Skills?

Different effect sizes can occur because training is differentially effective in improving its target attributes. Effect sizes can also differ when the attributes used for training evaluations cover different parts of the job. The most methodologically precise evaluations will focus only on training-related outcomes.[32] For example, training evaluations focused on first-level supervisory skills may encompass a large portion of the supervisor's job, but training evaluations focused on sales of a specific product may reflect only small portion of a sales representative's job. Also, not all elements of the job are equally pivotal, so training effects will differ based on the economic impact of the performance elements affected.[33]

Effect sizes measured using specific training outcomes will usually be larger than effects that would be seen using overall job performance. However, there is a trade-off. If the outcomes of training are very narrowly defined, a large effect size must be adjusted to reflect the fact that only part of the work outcomes are considered, so the proportion of total work value affected is smaller. If training evaluations are narrowly focused on esoteric but irrelevant training outcomes, even large training effects may be economically unimportant. The point is that it is vital that the outcomes used to evaluate training are matched to the decision context and vital that training outcomes are comparable to allow meaningful comparisons of effect sizes.[34] The economic value of a measured training effect will vary with the percentage of pivotal tasks measured.

Break-Even Analysis Applied to Proposed HRD Programs

Often, precise estimates of the parameters of the equations (such as d_t or SD_y) will not be available. In such cases, it is often informative to reframe the question away from debate about imprecision in the parameters and instead ask "what value of the parameter(s) would be required to achieve the minimal acceptable return?" If the minimum parameter values needed are extremely high, then it may be a safe decision to not invest in the program because there is a poor chance of an acceptable payoff. Conversely, if the minimum parameter values needed are extremely low, then it may be wise to invest in the program because chances are good that the program will pay off.

For example, suppose that you have determined an expected value of d_t, but there is some debate about the actual value of SD_y. You can use Equation 11.1 to compute a break-even value of SD_y (the value of SD_y at which benefits equal costs and $\Delta U = \$0.00$; see Chapters 2 and 9). For example, suppose 300 employees are trained, the duration of the training effect is expected to be 2 years, $d_t = 0.55$, and the per-person cost of training is $1,500. Setting $\Delta U = \$0.00$ yields the following:

$$\$0.00 = 2(300)(0.55)(SD_y) - 300 \, (\$1,500)$$
$$SD_y = \$1,364$$

Recall from earlier chapters that one rule of thumb is that SD_y is 40 percent of salary. The salary level required to meet this break-even SD_y value would be $1,364 divided by 40 percent, or $3,410 per year. That is quite a low hurdle for the investment to break even.

Or, suppose that there was some doubt about the effect of training (d_t) estimated as 0.55. You could calculate that even if d_t is as low as 0.10, the break-even value of SD_y is still only \$7,500, well below the values of SD_y (for example, \$34,100 to \$47,500 in 2018 dollars) typically reported in the literature. To the extent that precise estimates of d_t and SD_y are unavailable, break-even analysis still allows a decision maker to use the general utility model to make better decisions about investing in HRD programs. The comparison of expected-case and worst-case scenarios thus provides a more complete set of information for purposes of decision making.

Duration of the Effects of an HRD Program

A key parameter in Equation 11.1 is T, the duration of the effect of a training or HRD program. We know that the effects of development will not last forever because the relevance of the learning has a half-life due to changing work situations. Aside from loss of relevance, meta-analysis has found that the longer the interval of nonuse or nonpractice of knowledge and skills, the greater the decay, such that after 365 days the typical individual is performing at only about 8 percent of his or her performance level before the nonpractice interval.[35] The single most important factor in slowing such decay is the amount or degree of overlearning.[36] Overlearning provides additional training beyond that required for initial proficiency. Its actual effect on knowledge retention, however, depends on the amount of overlearning, the type of task, and the length of the retention period.[37]

When knowledge about the duration of training effects is unavailable, researchers conducting the large-scale study described in the previous section computed break-even values of training effect duration: the minimum amount of time that the training effect must be maintained for the value of training to offset the investment. Across 18 training programs (managerial, sales, and technical), they found great variability in results, with break-even periods ranging from a few weeks to several years.

Economic Considerations and Employee Flows Applied to HRD Programs

Because training activities lead to "diminishing returns" over time (that is, training effects dissipate over time), a utility model that incorporates employee flows should be used to assess the net payoff of the program over time.[38] Beyond that, variable costs, taxes, and discounting must be considered to assess correctly the true impact of a proposed or ongoing HRD program. Because we considered these issues in Chapter 9, here we need consider only the summary model that incorporates all of these factors. Then, we present a worked example to demonstrate how the utility analysis proceeds. Equation 11.5 shows the model. It is the same model used in Chapter 9, but here we have substituted the true effect size d_t for the product of the validity coefficient and standardized average predictor score of selectees that we used in Chapter 9.

$$\Delta U = \sum_{k=1}^{F} \left[\sum_{t=1}^{k} \left(N_{a_t} - N_{st} \right) \right] \left\{ [1/(1+i)^k] \times (d_t)(SD_{sv})(1+V)(1-TAX) \right\}$$

$$- \sum_{k=1}^{F} \left\{ C_k (1-TAX) \left[1/(1+i)^{(k-1)} \right] \right\} \tag{11.5}$$

For purposes of illustration let us adopt the d_t value we computed earlier, 0.44. Assume that 100 employees are trained each year for 5 years, and that for each cohort, the training effect dissipates gradually at the rate of 25 percent annually. No employees separate during this period (and therefore $N_{st} = 0$). That information allows us to compute a weighted average d_t value for the trained group each year, as a new cohort of trainees is added. Table 11.1 shows the weighted average d_t values.

To use Equation 11.5, assume that $SD_y = \$30,000$, variable costs $(V) = -0.10$, the tax rate is 45 percent, and the discount rate is 8 percent. Because costs ($1,000 per person) are incurred in the same period that benefits are received, we will use k as the exponent in the

Table 11.1. Diminishing Returns of an HRD Program Over Five Years

Year	Nk	Weighted Average
1	100	$(100(0.44))/100$
2	200	$(100(0.44) + 100(0.44 - 25\%))/200$
3	300	$(100(0.44) + 100(0.44 - 25\%) + 100$ $(0.44-50\%))/300$
4	400	$(100(0.44) + 100(0.44 - 25\%) + 100$ $(0.44-50\%) + 100(0.44 - 75\%))/400$
5	500	$(100(0.44) + 100(0.44 - 25\%) + 100$ $(0.44-50\%) + 100(0.44 - 75\%) + 100$ $(0.44 - 100\%))/500$

Year	Weighted Average d_t Values
1	0.44
2	0.385
3	0.33
4	0.275
5	0.22

Notes: d_t = the true difference in job performance between the trained and untrained groups in standard deviation units; HRD = human resources development; Nk = number of employees receiving training who remain in the workforce.

cost term in Equation 11.5. The total payoff of the HRD program is the sum of the utilities of each of the five periods:

$$\Delta U_1 = 100(0.926)(0.44)(\$30,000)(0.90)(0.55) - \$100,000(0.55)(0.926)$$
$$\Delta U_1 = \$554,118$$
$$\Delta U_2 = 200(0.857)(0.385)(\$30,000)(0.90)(0.55) - \$100,000(0.55)(0.857)$$
$$\Delta U_2 = \$932,802$$
$$\Delta U_3 = 300(0.794)(0.33)(\$30,000)(0.90)(0.55) - \$100,000(0.55)(0.794)$$
$$\Delta U_3 = \$1,123,629$$

$$\Delta U_4 = 400(0.735)(0.275)(\$30,000)(0.90)(0.55) - \$100,000(0.55)(0.735)$$

$$\Delta U_4 = \$1,160,198$$

$$\Delta U_5 = 500(0.681)(0.22)(\$30,000)(0.90)(0.55) - \$100,000(0.55)(0.681)$$

$$\Delta U_5 = \$1,074,959$$

The sum of those one-period utility estimates is \$4,845,706. This is the total expected payoff of the HRD program over the five-year period.

Example: Skills Training for Bankers

The utility analysis concepts discussed thus far were illustrated nicely in a study of the utility of a supervisory-skills training program applied in a large commercial bank.[39] The study incorporated the following features:

» Training costs were tabulated using cost accounting techniques.

» The global estimation procedure was used to estimate SD_y.

» Pre- and post-training ratings of the job performance of (non-randomly assigned) experimental- and control-group subjects were compared in order to determine d_t.

» Utility analysis results that included adjustments for economic factors (discounting, variable costs, and taxes) were compared to unadjusted utility results.

» Break-even analysis was used to assess the minimum change in SD_y required to recoup the costs invested in the program.

» The effect on estimated payoffs of employee flows, decay in training effects, and employee turnover were considered explicitly.

Results showed that the training program paid off handsomely over time, even under highly conservative assumptions. Training 65 bank managers in supervisory skills produced an estimated net payoff (after adjustment for the economic factors noted earlier) of $96,000, and $412,720 by year 5 (all figures in 2018 dollars). Not surprisingly, the reductions in value associated with adjusting for economic factors tended to become greater the further in time they were projected. In general, however, utility figures adjusted for economic factors were 60 percent to 80 percent smaller than unadjusted figures.

When break-even analysis was used, even assuming a 25 percent yearly reduction in the strength of the training effect, break-even values of SD_y were still less than 50 percent of the values used in the utility analysis. Finally, in terms of employee flows, the economic impact of training additional groups was also considerable. For example, the estimate for the tenth year of the utility of training 225 employees in the first five years was more than $1,011,000 (in 2018 dollars) even after adjustment for economic factors. Data such as these are useful to decision makers, whether their focus is on the broad allocation of organizational resources across functional lines or on the choice of specific HR programs from a larger menu of possible programs.

Costs: Off-Site versus Web-Based Meetings

Having illustrated methods and technology for assessing the value of employee-development efforts, this final section of the chapter focuses on identifying costs—specifically, the costs of off-site versus web-based meetings. Given the wide proliferation and continued growth of internet-based technologies, many organizations have opted for a web-based or off-site approach to cut costs. What follows is a general costing framework that can be applied to many types of training and can be used to compare relative costs.

Off-site meetings, those conducted away from organizational property, are useful for a variety of purposes: for conducting HRD programs, for communicating information without the interruptions commonly found at the office, for strategic planning, and for decision making. In many cases, however, the true costs of an off-site meeting remain unknown because indirect attendee costs are not included along with the more obvious direct expenses. The method described here enables planners to compute the actual costs of each type of activity in an off-site meeting.[40] Then we consider web-based meeting costs.

We make the following assumptions about a hypothetical firm, Valco Ltd. The firm has 500 employees, including 100 first-line supervisors and managers. Under the general planning and direction of Valco's training department (one manager and one secretary), Valco holds a total of ten days of off-site meetings per year (either training sessions or various types of meetings for managers). The firm retains outside speakers and consultants to develop and conduct the meetings. On average, 20 managers attend each meeting, and the typical meeting lasts two full days.

Costs shown in Table 11.2 are based on those figures. The estimates we are using here are broad averages intended only to create a model for purposes of comparison. Note that in this example, we make no attempt to place a monetary value on the loss of productive time from the job, although if it is possible to estimate such costs reliably, do include them in the calculations. As with the illustrations in other chapters, we have attempted to make the numbers as realistic as possible, but primary concern should be with the methodology rather than with the numbers.

As you can see in Table 11.2, the per-day, per-person cost of Valco's meeting comes to $3,102.50.

Actually, that figure probably does not represent the true cost of the meeting because no distinction is made between recurring and nonrecurring costs.[41] During the development of a program, organizations absorb nonrecurring costs such as equipment purchases and training designers' salaries. Recurring costs absorbed each time a program is presented include session expenses, such as facilities and trainers' salaries, and costs that correspond to the number of participants in a program, such as training materials and trainees' salaries. Separating costs into categories allows each set of costs to be incorporated into utility calculations for the time period in which each expense is incurred. Thus, the high initial expenses associated with a program may indicate that costs exceed benefits for some period of time or over a certain number of groups of trainees. However, at some point, an organization may begin to derive program benefits that signal the beginning of a payback period. Separating costs from benefits helps decision-makers to clarify information about the utility of HR programs and return on investment.[42] This is as important for off-site meetings as it is for web-based ones.

Web-based meetings incur all the costs shown in Table 11.2, with the exception of sleeping rooms (item 1a), the reception (item 1d), meeting charges (items 2a, b, and c), and transportation to the meeting (item 3). However, for a small-to-medium-sized business, a premises-based license for web-based conferencing typically costs at least $2,400 per year for unlimited usage.[43] Moreover, the emerging generation of unified communications platforms featuring integrated instant messaging, email, video, and audio tools is making it easier for geographically dispersed attendees to exploit the full range of media.[44]

The very highest-level videoconferencing systems, such as the Cisco Telepresence IX5000 Series, Huawei's Immersive Telepresence System, or Polycom's RealPresence Platform, include a set of technologies that allow people to feel as if they are present at a remote location ("being there"), a phenomenon called "telepresence."[45] To achieve the illusion that all attendees are in the same room, each vendor makes its videoconferencing rooms look alike, using the same semicircular conference tables illuminated by the same type of light bulbs and surrounded by identical wall colors. Participants appear as life-size images, and sit at the table facing video displays, which have cameras set just above or around the screen.[46]

Table 11.2. Costs of an Off-Site Management Meeting

Cost Element	Cost per Participant per Day	Total Cost
A. Development of programs (annual) Training dept. overhead + Training staff salaries + Outside consultants + Equipment + meeting materials =	$1,750[a]	$350,000
B. Participant cost (annual) Salaries and benefits (average)	$550[b]	$130,000
C. Delivery of one meeting for 20 people		
1. Facility costs		
a. Sleeping rooms	$220	$4,400
b. Three meals daily	$120[c]	$2,400
c. Coffee breaks	$35[d]	$700
d. Reception	$27.50[e]	$550
2. Meeting charges		
a. Room rental	$100	$2,000
b. Audiovisual equipment rental	$50	$1,000
c. Business services	$250[f]	$500
3. Transportation to the meeting	$225[g]	$9,000
Summary: Total Cost per Participant per Day		
A. Development of programs	$1,750	
B. Participant cost	$550	
C. Delivery of one meeting (hotel + transportation)	$802.50	
Total: $3,102.50		

Notes: Duration of each meeting: 2 full days. Number of meetings: 5. Number of attendees: 20 people. Costs do not reflect an estimate of the value of the lost productive time by the people in the program. Adding it would increase the above costs dramatically.

[a] To determine the per-participant, per-day cost, divide $350,000 by the number of days per meeting (2) divided by the number of managers attending all meetings (100) = $1,750 per day of a meeting.

[b] To determine the per-day cost, divide the total of $130,000 by 236 (average number of work days per year) = $550 per day of the work year.

[c] Assume the following daily costs per person: $20 for breakfast, $30 for lunch, $50 for dinner + 20 percent service fee/gratuity = $120.

[d] Assumes a total cost of $350 per coffee break, one morning + one afternoon = $700/ day, divided by 20 attendees = $35 per person per day.

[e] Assumes a charge of $150 to set up a bar + a $400 minimum total charge = $550 divided by 20 = $27.50 per person per day.

[f] Assumes a daily charge of $500 for internet access, photocopying, and facsimile services.

[g] To determine the per-day cost, divide group total ($9,000) by the number of participants (20); then divide the resulting figure ($450) by the number of meeting days (2) = $225 per day.

Telepresence systems are costly. Cisco's TelePresence IX5000 series costs $299,000, while Polycom's RealPresence Platform, which uses three 84-inch displays to create a giant video wall, starts at $425,000. Those costs will likely limit the use of telepresence systems to large, deep-pocketed organizations.[47]

Why do so many meetings still occur in person all over the globe every year? Perhaps because 64 percent of communication is nonverbal, and most lower-end web-based conferencing systems lose those cues.[48] Hence many organizations feel that there is no substitute for face-to-face contact and the opportunity for interpersonal interaction. The influence of the environment on training cannot be minimized. The task for decision-makers is to consider whether facility costs or web-based conferencing costs will or will not be offset by a corresponding increase in learning value. Only by considering all the factors that have an impact on learning effectiveness—program planning and administration, the quality of the trainer, program delivery, and learning environment—can we derive the greatest return, in time and dollars spent, on this substantial investment in people.

Process: Enhancing Acceptance of Training Cost-Benefit Analyses

The total cost of evaluating 18 training programs in the multinational firm we described earlier in the chapter was approximately $932,000 (in 2018 dollars).[49] That number may seem large, until you consider that during the time of the study, the organization spent more than $448 million on training. Thus, the cost of training evaluation was roughly 0.2 percent of the training budget during this time period. Given expenditures of such magnitude, some sort of accountability is prudent.

To enhance managerial acceptance, the researchers presented the utility model and the procedures that they proposed to use to the CEO as well as to senior strategic planning and HR managers *before* conducting their research. They presented the model and procedures as fallible, but reasonable estimates. The researchers noted that management pre-approval before actual application and consideration of utility results in a decision-making context is particularly important when one considers that nearly any field application of utility analysis will rely on an effect size calculated with an imperfect quasi-experimental design. (See Chapter 2 for more on quasi-experimental designs.)

Conclusion

One of the important lessons to be learned from the material presented in this chapter is that methods are available now for estimating the costs and benefits of HRD programs (proposed, ongoing, or completed). Instead of depending on the power of persuasion to convince decision-makers of the value of HRD programs, HR professionals can, by the use of cost-benefit models, join with the other functional areas of business in justifying the allocation of scarce organizational resources on the basis of evidence rather than on beliefs.

Exercises

Software to calculate answers to one or more exercises below is available at http://iip.shrm.org.

1. Jane Burns, an HR analyst for Standard City, USA, knows that SD_y for firefighters in her city is $31,000. The fire department has asked the city to provide training in team building for 500 of its employees, at a cost of $3,500 per employee. The effects of this organization-development effort are expected to last for two years. Using

Equation 11.1, compute the break-even value for d_t necessary for the city to recoup the costs of the program.

2. Suppose, in Exercise 1, that you have just read a meta-analysis of team-building studies and know that the cumulated estimate of d_t is 0.45. Compute an expected utility for the program and compare it to the break-even value you identified earlier. How might this affect the chances that the project will be funded?

3. With regard to Exercise 2, suppose that the discount rate is 10 percent, and variable costs are –0.10. The city is not taxed. How do these factors affect the estimate of expected utility that you developed in Exercise 2?

4. Pilgrim Industries, a 2,000-employee firm with 400 managers, holds 40 days of off-site meetings per year. Outside consultants develop and conduct the meetings, and, on average, 20 managers attend each meeting. The typical meeting lasts two full days. Last year, total program-development costs consumed $400,000. The average attendee's salary (including benefits) was $91,000. To deliver each two-day meeting for 20 people, sleeping accommodations, food, telephone, and a cocktail reception cost $8,000. In addition, transportation, business services, meeting room, and audiovisual equipment rental totaled another $13,000. Determine the total per-day, per-person cost of one off-site meeting.

5. Pilgrim's CEO has heard about the remarkable quality of "telepresence" web-based conferencing systems, and she has asked you to prepare a per-person, per-day cost comparison of an off-site meeting versus a web-based conference for a two-day meeting. You calculated the per-person per-day cost of an off-site meeting in Exercise 4. What costs must

you consider with respect to a web-based system? Is there any other information you would want to have before recommending one alternative over the other?

References

1. Council of Economic Advisors, *Addressing America's Reskilling Challenge* (July 2018), accessed August 1, 2018, http://www.whitehouse.gov/wp -content/uploads/2018/07/Addressing-Americas-Reskilling-Challenge .pdf.

2. "2017 Training Industry Report," *Training Magazine*, accessed November 4, 2018, https://trainingmag.com/trgmag-article/2017-training-industry -report/.

3. Wayne F. Cascio, "Training Trends: Macro, Micro, and Policy Issues," *Human Resource Management Review* 29, no. 2 (June 2019): 284–97.

4. Arlene S. Hirsch, "What Emerging Adults Want In a Job: 9 Key Requirements," Society for Human Resource Management, January 26, 2016, accessed April 28, 2016, http://www.shrm.org/resourcesandtools /hr-topics/employee-relations/pages/emerging-adults.aspx.

5. Wayne F. Cascio and Ramiro, "How Technology is Changing Work and Organizations," *Annual Review of Organizational Psychology and Organizational Behavior* 3, (2016): 349–75. See also Thomas L. Friedman, *Thank You for Being Late: An Optimist's Guide to Thriving in the Age of Accelerations* (New York: Farrar, Strauss & Giroux, 2016); Ramiro Montealegre and Wayne F. Cascio, "Technology-Driven Changes in Work and Employment," *Communications of the ACM* 60, no. 12 (December 2017): 60–67.

6. Alex Leary, "White House Says Companies Pledge to Create Millions of Job-Training Opportunities," *The Wall Street Journal*, October 31, 2018, accessed October 31, 2018, http://www.wsj.com/articles/white-house-says -companies-pledge-to-create-millions-of-job-training-opportunities -1541001658.

7. Wayne F. Cascio and John W. Boudreau, "Talent Management of Nonstandard Employees," in *The Oxford Handbook of Talent Management*, ed. David G. Collings, Kamel Mellahi, and Wayne F. Cascio (Oxford, UK: Oxford University Press, 2017), 494–519. See also Marion McGovern, *Thriving in the Gig Economy: How to Capitalize and Compete in the New World of Work* (Wayne, NJ: Career Press/New Page Books, 2017).

8. Robert G. Loughery, "Revitalize US Manufacturing Via Training," *The Wall Street Journal*, June 27, 2016, A12. See also Jeffrey Sparshott, "Job Training Ramps Up at Smaller Firms," *The Wall Street Journal*, February 2, 2017, A2.

9. Raymond A. Noe, *Employee Training and Development*, 7th ed. (New York: McGraw-Hill, 2017).

10. Wayne F. Cascio and Herman Aguinis, *Applied Psychology in Talent Management*, 8th ed. (Thousand Oaks, CA: Sage, 2019).

11. Cascio and Aguinis, *Applied Psychology in Talent Management*.

12. Bruce J. Avolio et al., "Leadership Models, Methods, and Applications," in Vol. 12, *Handbook of Psychology*, ed. Walter C. Borman, Daniel R. Ilgen, and Richard J. Klimoski (Hoboken, NJ: Wiley, 2004), 277–307.

13. Rachel Lefkowitz, *2018 Workplace Learning Report: The Rise and Responsibility of Talent Development in the New Labor Market* (LinkedIn Learning, 2018), accessed March 14, 2018, https://learning.linkedin.com/resources/workplace-learning-report-2018.

14. Winfred Arthur, Jr. et al., "Effectiveness of Training in Organizations: A Meta-Analysis of Design and Evaluation Features," *Journal of Applied Psychology* 88, no. 2 (April 2003): 234–45. See also Michael J. Burke and Russell R. Day, "A Cumulative Study of the Effectiveness of Managerial Training," *Journal of Applied Psychology* 71, no. 2 (May 1986): 232–45; Richard A. Guzzo, Richard D. Jette, and Raymond A. Katzell, "The Effects of Psychologically-Based Intervention Programs on Worker Productivity: A Meta-Analysis," *Personnel Psychology* 38, no. 2 (June 1985): 275–91; Charlie C. Morrow, M. Quintin Jarrett, and Melvin T. Rupinski, "An Investigation of the Effect and Economic Utility of Corporate-Wide Training," *Personnel Psychology* 50, no. 1 (March 1997): 91–129.

15. Laura Bassi, "Decision Science: Measuring and Valuing Training Investments," *HR Exchange Network*, August 25, 2011, accessed November 5, 2018, http://www.hrexchangenetwork.com/hr-technology/articles/decision-science-measuring-valuing-training-inve. See also Laura Bassi et al., *The Impact of US Firms' Investments in Human Capital on Stock Prices*, White Paper (Bassi Investments, June 2004), http://www.mcbassi.com.

16. Laura Bassi and Daniel McMurrer, "How's Your Return on People?," *Harvard Business Review*, March 2004.

17. Laura Bassi and Daniel McMurrer, *Training Investments as a Predictor of Banks' Subsequent Stock-Market Performance*, White Paper (McBassi & Company, February 2009), http://www.mcbassi.com.

18. World Economic Forum, *The Future of Jobs: Employment, Skills and Workforce Strategy for the Fourth Industrial Revolution* (Geneva, Switzerland, 2016), accessed February 4, 2016, http://www.weforum.org/agenda/2016/01/the-10-skills-you-need-to-thrive-in-the-fourth-industrial-revolution/.

19. Bassi et al., *Impact of US Firms' Investments*.

20. Wayne F. Cascio and Herman Aguinis, *Applied Psychology in Talent Management*, 8th ed. (Thousand Oaks, CA: Sage, 2019). See also William R. Shadish, Thomas D. Cook, and Donald T. Campbell, *Experimental and Quasi-Experimental Designs for Generalized Causal Inference* (Boston: Houghton Mifflin, 2002).

21. John W. Boudreau and Peter M. Ramstad, *Beyond HR: The New Science of Human Capital* (Boston: Harvard Business School Publishing, 2007).

22. Nathan Bomey, "At Ohio Training Center, Students Embrace Lucrative Future of Automation," Robotics. *USA Today*, February 6, 2017, 1B–2B.

23. Shayndi Raice, "Wichita Aims to Tackle Skills Gap," *The Wall Street Journal*, August 3, 2017, A3.

24. Hirsch, "What Emerging Adults Want In a Job."

25. Isabel Thottam, "Ten Companies with Awesome Training and Development Programs," Monster.com, accessed November 15, 2018, http://www.monster.com/career-advice/article/companies-with-awesome-training-development-programs.

26. Lynn Russo Whylly, "Chief Executive Magazine Announces its 2016 Best Companies for Leaders," *Chief Executive*, January 27, 2016, accessed May 2, 2016, https://chiefexecutive.net/chief-executive-magazine-announces-its-2016-best-companies-for-leaders/.

27. See, for example, Michael C. Sturman et al., "Is It Worth It to Win the Talent War? Evaluating the Utility of Performance-Based Pay," *Personnel Psychology* 56, no. 4 (December 2003): 997–1035. See also Hunter Mabon, "The Cost of Downsizing in an Enterprise with Job Security," *Journal of Human Resource Costing and Accounting* 1, no. 1 (1996): 35–62; Hunter Mabon and Gunnar Westling, "Using Utility Analysis in Downsizing Decisions," *Journal of Human Resource Costing and Accounting* 1, no. 2 (1996): 43–72.

28. Frank L. Schmidt, John E. Hunter, and Kenneth Pearlman, "Assessing the Economic Impact of Personnel Programs on Workforce Productivity," *Personnel Psychology* 35, no. 2 (June 1982): 333–347.

29. Chockalingam Viswesvaran, Deniz S. Ones, and Frank L. Schmidt, "Comparative Analysis of the Reliability of Job Performance Ratings," *Journal of Applied Psychology* 81, no. 5 (October 1996): 557–74.

30. Paul R. Sackett, "On Interpreting Measures of Change Due to Training or Other Interventions: A Comment on Cascio (1989, 1991)," *Journal of Applied Psychology* 76, no. 4 (August 1991): 590, 591.

31. Wayne F. Cascio and Herman Aguinis, *Applied Psychology in Talent Management*, 8th ed. (Thousand Oaks, CA: Sage, 2019). See also William R. Shadish, Thomas D. Cook, and Donald T. Campbell, *Experimental and Quasi-Experimental Designs for Generalized Causal Inference* (Boston: Houghton Mifflin, 2002); Raymond A. Noe, *Employee Training and Development*, 7th ed. (New York: McGraw-Hill, 2017).

32. John P. Campbell, "Training Design for Performance Improvement," in *Productivity in Organizations*, ed. John P. Campbell and Richard J. Campbell (San Francisco: Jossey-Bass, 1988), 177–216.

33. Boudreau and Ramstad, *Beyond HR*.

34. Charlie C. Morrow, M. Quintin Jarrett, and Melvin T. Rupinski, "An Investigation of the Effect and Economic Utility of Corporate-Wide Training," *Personnel Psychology* 50, no. 1 (March 1997): 91–129.

35. Winfred Arthur, Jr. et al., "Factors That Influence Skill Decay and Retention: A Quantitative Review and Analysis," *Human Performance* 11, no. 1 (1998): 57–101.

36. Helen Abadzi, "Training 21-Century Workers: Facts, Fiction, and Memory Illusions," *International Review of Education* 62, no. 3 (June 2016): 253–278. See also Winfred Arthur, Jr. et al., "Factors That Influence Skill Decay and Retention: A Quantitative Review and Analysis," *Human Performance* 11, no. 1 (1998): 57–101; James E. Driskell, Ruth P. Willis, and Carolyn Copper, "Effect of Overlearning on Retention," *Journal of Applied Psychology* 77, no. 5 (October 1992): 615–622.

37. Driskell, Willis, and Copper, "Effect of Overlearning."

38. John W. Boudreau, "Effects of Employee Flows on Utility Analysis of Human Resource Productivity Improvement Programs," *Journal of Applied Psychology* 68, no. 3 (August 1983): 396–406.

39. John E. Mathieu and Russell L. Leonard, Jr. "Applying Utility Concepts to a Training Program in Supervisory Skills: A Time-Based Approach," *Academy of Management Journal* 30, no. 2 (June 1987): 316–335.

40. The method is based on W. J. McKeon, "How to Determine Off-Site Meeting Costs," *Training and Development Journal* 35, no. 5 (May 1981): 122–26.

41. Mathieu and Leonard, "Applying Utility Concepts."

42. Mathieu and Leonard, "Applying Utility Concepts."

43. Martin Feehan, "Skype for Business Licensing – On Premise vs Cloud, OpEx vs CapEx, Common Area Phones, and Piecemeal Approaches," PEI, August 7, 2017, accessed November 7, 2018, http://www.pei.com/2017/08/skype -for-business-licensing-premises-cloud/. See also "Zoom Meeting Plans for Your Business," Zoom, accessed November 7, 2018, https://zoom.us/pricing.

44. Feehan, "Skype for Business Licensing."

45. "Different Types of Telepresence Systems Introduced," ezTalks, accessed November 7, 2018, http://www.eztalks.com/video-conference /different-types-of-telepresence-systems.html. See also Wikipedia, s.v. "Telepresence," last modified November 2, 2018, https://en.wikipedia.org /wiki/Telepresence.

46. V3, "Polycom Unveils Giant Video Conference System to Rival Cisco," February 11, 2014, accessed November 7, 2018, http://www.v3.co.uk /v3-uk/news/2328076/polycom-unveils-giant-video-conference-system -to-rival-cisco.

47. See note 46 above. See also V3, "Cisco Unveils TelePresence IX5000 Video System with Lower Power and Bandwidth Needs," November 18, 2014, accessed November 7, 2018, http://www.v3.co.uk/v3-uk/news/2381978 /cisco-unveils-telepresence-ix5000-video-system-with-lower-power-and -bandwidth-needs.

48. Pearn Kandola, *The Psychology of Effective Business Communications in Geographically Dispersed Teams* (San Jose, CA: Cisco Systems Inc., 2006).

49. Morrow, Jarrett, and Rupinski, "Investigation of the Effect and Economic Utility."

12

Talent-Investment Analysis: Catalyst for Change

Introduction

This book has highlighted the business and financial impact of talent decisions, strategies, and investments. The goal is not simply for HR analysts and professionals to develop logical and strategic models and measures. The true impact of a decision science for investing in people occurs when those models and measurement systems are used by leaders, employees, investors, and other constituents outside the HR profession (see Chapter 1, "Making HR Measurement Strategic"). Finance and marketing frameworks are powerful because every business leader, whatever his or her professional background, is expected to understand basic financial or marketing logic. The ultimate test of any measurement and analysis system is simple: Does it improve decisions about vital resources where they matter most? Regarding investing in people, the vital decisions often occur outside the HR function, or in partnership with HR leaders.

We envision that the ideas in this book will help build a future in which leaders throughout organizations increasingly use data to inform talent decisions and strategies and are held accountable for the quality of those decisions. That requires a sophisticated understanding of the connections between investments in HR programs and their impact on strategic success. Chapter 2, "Analytical

Foundations of HR Measurement," shared evidence-based frameworks and analysis methods to help you design and conduct rigorous analysis and research that can influence actual decisions to improve the sustainable strategic success of organizations. In many organizations, accounting principles and logic are used to evaluate HR practices. This is a good start, but as we have seen, while accounting logic can provide valuable frameworks to track how traditional resources such as cash and time are spent on HR programs and employees, this approach is often inadequate, and can even be dangerous when it is the sole arbiter of HR investments. Chapter 3, "Talent Management as a Source of Competitive Advantage," frames the strategic importance of investing in people and the HR discipline's role in improving those investment decisions. As you have seen, while accounting is often very good at tracking and reducing the costs of such investments, the pivotal factor is often the upside effect on performance, talent quality, retention, and so on. That may not always be apparent using only cost accounting methods. Therefore, useful frameworks will include future upside potential, and not just strict cost avoidance. Indeed, talent management and HR investments can deliver both—a clear ROI detectable with standard costing or accounting approaches, as well as a compelling upside to businesses. For example, leadership succession planning may generate cost savings by retaining executives and avoiding excessive executive recruiting, which is expensive. However, the greater advantages of investments in such planning are typically through enhanced business continuity and performance—factors that are not easily captured by standard accounting practices.

Although this certainly is an important challenge for leaders outside the HR profession, it also holds the HR profession to a high standard. If HR expects its constituents to become more sophisticated, HR must support that by providing the frameworks, opportunities, and systems that enable, indeed that require, more sophistication. That's a key purpose of the frameworks in this book, to create the insights that will improve decisions—and, in turn, to enhance organizational effectiveness.

The evolution of more sophisticated decision frameworks for investing in people is not a simple matter of adopting new calculations, installing a new HR information system, or presenting new and more sophisticated reports to organizational leaders. It requires that HR analysts and leaders accept that not everything that counts can be counted, and not everything that can be counted actually counts.[1] You might divide the effects of investments in people into three categories:

1. Quantifiable effects that can be verified using standard accounting and finance tools (costs or time saved, objective sales or volume, etc.).

2. Nonquantifiable financial effects that cannot be measured precisely, but are still financial in nature, and so can be understood, if not precisely measured, in terms of finance and accounting principles (improved performance, more innovation, higher customer satisfaction, etc.).

3. Nonfinancial effects that can have significant strategic impact but are often not explicitly considered in financial and accounting frameworks (improved employee health and welfare, enhanced image among employees and applicants, more ethical behavior and decisions).

The value of these categories is that they can help make explicit that not everything that matters can be measured precisely, but that it is often possible to make a good decision even with imperfect information. For example, it may not be possible to estimate precisely the number of additional innovations that will occur if the organization can raise the average tenure of R&D scientists from two years to four years. However, leaders will often be able to estimate the effect with enough precision to see that an investment to enhance the retention of R&D scientists is very likely to have a high payoff.

Category 2 in this framework, nonquantifiable financial effects, is especially relevant to strategic interventions. In Chapter 3, we introduced concepts of strategy and walked through several examples of strategic talent management in organizations. While many tasks in HR are operational, bringing a sophisticated strategic lens to talent questions can help drive top-line business value. We explored some of the common opportunities for HR to support strategy execution, through processes like succession planning, high-potential programs, and strategic workforce planning.

Better Answers to Fundamental Questions

Let's recall the questions we posed at the beginning of Chapter 1. Remember that we challenged you to consider how well your organization could address the following questions or requests if they were posed by your CEO or other business leaders outside the HR function. Now that you've read this book, you can see that each question referred to one or more chapters, and that those chapters have given you tools for a more sophisticated, logical, and analytical approach.

Absenteeism Isn't Free

> *"I know that on any given day about 5 percent of our employees are absent. Yet, everyone seems to be able to cover for the absent employees, and the work seems to get done. Should we try to reduce this absence rate, and if we did, what would be the benefit to our organization?"*

Chapter 4, "The Hidden Cost of Absenteeism," described the key direct and indirect costs associated with investments to reduce absence. The direct cost reductions (such as wages paid for time not worked) are easier to estimate, but the indirect effects (such as productivity increases) can be more elusive. The effects of "presenteeism," or reporting to work while ill, can make calculations even more complex. However, estimating the cost efficiency of interventions to reduce absenteeism and presenteeism requires a thorough understanding of the consequences of both.

Using the approach in Chapter 4, you can develop a baseline cost for absenteeism or presenteeism in jobs in your organization. Starting by understanding these costs can help your organization make more rigorous decisions, such as whether it is beneficial to provide sick and emergency childcare options. Such investments typically seem expensive, but using the concepts from Chapter 2, and the absenteeism cost estimates from Chapter 4, it may well be the case that such an investment will pay off.

Layoffs Cut More Than Costs, and Turnover Is Not Always a Bad Thing

> *"Our total employment costs are higher than our competitors, so I need you to lay off 10 percent of our employees. To be fair, let's reduce headcount by 10 percent in every unit to meet that goal."*

> *"Our turnover rate among engineers is 10 percent higher than our competitors. Please institute programs to get it down to industry levels".*

Chapter 5, "The High Cost of Employee Separations," showed that the effects of employee separations, whether dictated by the employer (such as layoffs and dismissals) or by the employee (such as voluntary retirements or quits), incur an array of both costs and benefits. The costs of processing employee separations are typically most obvious and are often the only thing considered. Based on such costs, it is easy to conclude that less turnover is better. The reduction in compensation associated with a layoff is similarly very obvious and so is often the only number considered in deciding how many and where to lay off employees. In both cases, the obvious numbers are merely the tip of the iceberg.

To appreciate the full effects of employee separations requires considering not only the transaction costs of separating employees, but also the costs of acquiring and developing their replacements. More important, instead of considering employee separations solely on the basis of costs, Chapter 5 provided a framework that helps you describe and measure how employee separations affect the quality of the work force. Separations can actually be beneficial when they increase workforce quality if replacements are of higher quality than those who left and if the costs of replacement don't overwhelm the increased quality. We showed that good decisions require seeing beyond simply reducing turnover rates, even when the cost savings are significant. We also showed how organizations can move beyond simply assuming that turnover among high performers is dysfunctional and that turnover among low performers is functional.

The key is to consider employee separations as part of a larger system of processes that increase or decrease workforce quality, depending on how optimally they are managed. In many ways, avoidable employee separations are like to employee selection, except that the organization is selecting which of its current employees will remain. Organizations do this directly through their decisions about layoffs and dismissals, but they also do it more subtly through their decisions regarding how to encourage and reward employees for their decisions to stay or leave.

Layoffs offer a similar opportunity to look beyond simplistic assumptions—such as that they improve profits by reducing the number of employees—and their associated costs. When layoffs are driven solely by labor cost reductions, particularly when they are arbitrarily spread evenly across all departments or business units, the negative consequences can be substantial. The basis of such layoff decisions typically falls far short of the logical and systematic analysis required to optimize workforce quality.

Chapter 5 showed that the right answer to a CEO's request for blanket layoffs or turnover-cost reductions is to step back and consider full array of separation costs and consequences. Organizations that take that approach are likely to discover both hidden costs and potential benefits of employee separations. They are more likely to uncover differences in talent pools that are more pivotal with regard to the effects of separations. Turnover reduction will be directed where it has the greatest net effect on the future quality of the workforce.

If Everyone Else Is Reducing Employee Health Investments, Is It Smart to Invest More?

"In a globally competitive environment, we can't afford to provide high levels of healthcare and health coverage for our employees. Lots of companies are cutting their health coverage and so must we. Please find a cheaper healthcare provision and insurance program to cut our costs by 15 percent."

Chapter 6, "Employee Health, Wellness, and Welfare," showed that investments in employee health and welfare are more than just increased costs. The effects of rising healthcare costs are undeniable, and it is certainly true that for many organizations such costs have a significant effect on profits and financial returns. Investments in employee health and welfare can certainly reduce healthcare costs, but that's not always their most important effect. The less tangible impacts of health and welfare investments on organizational productivity and resilience are equally important. Chapter 6 provided frameworks you can use to estimate the costs of programs that protect and enhance employee health and care for employee injuries and illnesses. It also showed you how you can estimate the effects of improved employee health and welfare on important organizational outcomes such as productivity, innovation, resilience, and image.

Improved employee health affects organizational performance through reductions in the healthcare insurance costs, but more subtly through reductions in absence and turnover, and through increases in productivity. Thus, using techniques we described, organizations can analyze the effects of employee health and welfare investments for their direct impact on costs and medical outcomes, but they can go further to estimate the effects on intermediate outcomes that also affect organizational performance.

Compelling and significant cost reductions are often possible by cutting employee health insurance coverage or increasing employees' health insurance premiums or deductibles. Such analysis must be tempered by being aware of the powerful effects of improved employee health on organizational performance. Greater employer contributions to employee health costs can often result in significant benefits from improved employee health and productivity. Such benefits can be far greater than the more tangible cost savings of less expensive health coverage or premiums. Chapter 6 showed that it is rare for organizations to gather data systematically to fully measure the effects of investments in worker health. Yet, significant research suggests that it is more effective to keep employees healthy than to treat them after they are injured or ill. The rare controlled and rigorous studies that have been conducted suggest significant benefits from improving employee health.

Like so many investments in people, investments in employee health and welfare can be optimized only if decision-makers consider both the tangible cost savings and the less tangible potential benefits. All too often, business leaders frame the questions like we described above and are understandably entranced by the cash flow savings from reducing health insurance coverage and contributions. Organizations that take a more measured and analytical approach may well discover ways not only to achieve greater net productivity, but also to create healthier workplaces in the process.

Positive Employee Attitudes Are Not Soft and Optional

"I read that companies with high employee satisfaction have high financial returns, so I want you to develop an employee engagement measure and hold

our unit managers accountable for raising employ-
ee engagement averages in each of their units."

Should you invest in an enhanced employee experience to improve employee attitudes? Chapter 7, "Employee Attitudes and Engagement," showed that there is tantalizing evidence that organizations with better employee attitudes and higher employee engagement are more likely to be rated as great places to work (and that they provide higher returns to their shareholders). However, before you conclude that investing in employee-attitude enhancement is the path to double-digit growth and stock appreciation, Chapter 7 provides a framework for getting underneath the numbers. Indeed, under the right circumstances, there are logical and research-based reasons to expect that enhanced employee attitudes and higher employee engagement may lead to better customer service, higher customer loyalty, and improved profits. The popular press has provided many examples. The key qualification, however, is *the right circumstances.* We described some of those circumstances in Chapter 7.

Chapter 7 showed that employee attitudes are actually a composite of several different elements, each measured in different ways, and each affecting organizational outcomes differently. Employee job satisfaction is different from employee commitment, which, in turn, is different from employee engagement. Understanding the differences is important to dissecting the logical connections between attitudes and outcomes. Although commitment and satisfaction may drive employee retention, engagement and line of sight may be the key to improving employee work behaviors. Leaders who blindly pursue the goal of being highly rated in the "Best Places to Work" survey may miss more subtle opportunities to enhance attitudes and engagement where they matter most. The pivot-points where enhanced attitudes and engagement make the greatest difference are not revealed by a blanket approach to enhance overall attitudes.

Chapter 7 also showed that the path from employee attitudes to organizational performance may be indirect. Employee attitudes may work because they lead to a more attractive workplace for high-quality applicants. Alternatively, they may produce their effects through the retention of high-performing and hard-to-replace employees. Or, they may have a direct effect on work behaviors when more satisfied or engaged employees demonstrate their attitudes to customers or other key constituents. Consistent with the idea of matching the measurement logic to the strategic situation, Chapter 7 showed how to measure the effects of employee attitudes through a behavioral costing perspective, and through a value profit chain perspective.

In the end, therefore, savvy HR and business leaders will look well beyond the typical focus on overall organizational attitudes, measures of engagement, or the ratings of "Great Places to Work." The tantalizing correlation between those ratings and stock appreciation is just the beginning of a dialogue, one that is guided by principles developed over decades of research and analysis. The danger of equating a correlation with a cause is rarely illustrated more vividly than in the naïve mental models of business leaders who assume that the correlation between employee attitudes and stock performance means that improved attitudes *cause* increased stock performance. There are immense opportunities for improved decisions and organizational performance when the true power of positive employee attitudes and high engagement are understood and when they are approached with more hard science and less soft opinion.

Work/Life Fit Is Not Just a Generational Thing

"I hear a lot about the increasing demand for work and life fit and workplace flexibility, but my generation found a way to work the long hours and have a family. Is this generation really that different, or are they just lazy? Are there really tangible relationships between work/life conflict and organizational productivity? If there are, how would we measure them and track the benefits of workplace flexibility programs?"

Chapter 8, "Financial Effects of Workplace Flexibility Programs," showed that the days when employees will passively accept work demands that require seventy or even one hundred hours per week may be fading. The desire to find a better fit between the demands and rewards of work and the demands and rewards of life outside of work is increasing. And, this is happening not only for those with children or aging parents, but for virtually all workers. A strict accounting approach might make it tempting to hire and induce workers to devote as much time as possible to work. After all, how could more work time be a bad thing? Yet, evidence increasingly suggests that employers that invest in workplace flexibility programs that help workers find better fit between work and life outside of work may reap great benefits.

Chapter 8 showed that workplace flexibility programs can include child and dependent care, flexible work schedules, options for work leave and sabbaticals, remote work, and a supportive organizational culture. The chapter also described how a complete analysis of such programs involves understanding that simply investing in the program is seldom sufficient. Workplace flexibility programs, like other HR programs, require communication, training, and the support of key leaders. The framework of Chapter 8 also showed that the effects of such programs can range from reduced stress to improved attitudes for current employees, which, in turn, lead to greater productivity and reduced turnover and absence. They also can lead to greater workforce quality through becoming attractive to whole new groups of job applicants because increasingly, potential applicants are seeking an approach to work that recognizes that they have important nonwork goals and demands.

To answer the request for specific, tangible measures of the effects of such programs, Chapter 8 showed that it is often possible to estimate how such programs reduce time away from work by providing employees with ways to accomplish child- and eldercare tasks more easily and with greater advance planning. We have seen that some business leaders might see workplace flexibility programs as a nice-to-have perquisite for employees, something that they do only when they can afford it, or something that panders to younger employees who lack sufficient work ethic. The reality is more sophisticated. Workplace flexibility programs can be logical investments that provide powerful business benefits. There is a correlation between enhanced workplace flexibility practices and organizational financial and stock performance. Unearthing whether that correlation means that your organization would benefit from improved workplace flexibility programs requires a deeper analysis within a framework like Chapter 8 provides.

Retooling Staffing as a Supply Chain

"We expect to grow our sales 15 percent per year for the next five years. I need you to hire enough sales candidates to increase the size of our sales force by 15 percent a year and do that without exceeding benchmark cost-per-hire in our industry."

Business leaders typically perceive the elements of employee staffing in silos. They receive cost-benefit analytics on things like recruitment, employment brand, interviews, tests, onboarding, and orientation, but they are presented separately. The staffing elements are seldom presented in a way that is consistent with the supply chain for other resources, where elements such as choosing vendors, procurement, quality control, and inventory are seamlessly linked. Chapters 9 and 10 described the framework to analyze and measure the employee staffing process similarly to an integrated supply chain. The chapters showed that investments in enhanced staffing can be analyzed for their impact on profits and how to take into account standard financial considerations such as variable costs, discount rates, and taxes. Organizations often focus on staffing when they are concerned about potential talent shortages or enhancing their position in the war for talent, but Chapters 9 and 10 showed that savvy organizations will pay attention to staffing throughout the business cycle and go much deeper. It's possible to determine where investments in improved staffing will and will not pay off. The frameworks in Chapters 9 and 10 allow them to do that with greater sophistication, and to consider far more than merely whether positions are filled quickly and at a reasonable cost. Indeed, because many competing organizations manage their staffing processes exclusively in terms of headcount and cost, organizations with a more sophisticated staffing supply chain have an opportunity to emerge victorious in the more subtle game of talent management.

Chapter 9 described how to calculate typical measures such as cost-per-hire and time-to-fill and how to calculate the often substantial cost savings available by managing staffing processes to lower them. However, Chapter 9 also provided an evidence-based framework that shows how a myopic focus on such costs can lead to decisions that create productivity losses far higher than the cost savings. The key is to expand the focus beyond the number and cost of employees hired. Using the framework in Chapter 9, leaders can consider the effects of improved employee sourcing, selection, and retention on workforce quality. Leaders can target improved staffing for the pivotal roles where improved performance has the greatest impact on unit and organization goals. Estimating the relative value of performance differences across different roles and positions opens the door to systematic analysis of pivotal roles, rather than a traditional focus merely on important or critical roles and competencies.

The chapters showed that investments to enhance recruitment, selection, and retention can often pay off handsomely, even when they appear at first to be very costly. They also showed that the idea of simply duplicating the practices of others or setting benchmark cost levels based on what others do is likely to overlook lucrative opportunities for unique competitive success through competing better in the market for talent. The frameworks provided in these chapters allow business leaders to integrate the effects of investments in higher-quality applicant pools with investments in more-valid testing and with investments in enhanced retention of those hired. We saw that greater accuracy in selection does little good without a sufficiently large and high-quality applicant pool and recruiting higher-quality applicants may do little good without a sufficiently valid selection process. Optimization is the key, not maximizing the individual elements.

Just as no organization would manage the supply chain for its raw materials or unfinished goods based only on the cost and volume of goods acquired, organizations should not manage their talent supply chain based only on whether vacancies are filled and whether costs are kept at or below benchmark levels.

Taking HR Development Beyond Training to Learning and Workforce Enhancement

"I know that we can deliver training much more cheaply if we just outsource our internal training group and rely on off-the-shelf training products to build the skills that we need. We could shut down our corporate university and save millions."

Chapter 11, "Costs and Benefits of HR Development Programs," showed that it is dangerous to assume that all training has equal effects, or to assume that low-cost training is always better. As with other HR programs, the most pivotal effects of training are often overlooked by traditional accounting. Leaders who understand how training, development, and learning work together, and what factors enhance their effects, can optimize training investments, avoiding spending too much time and money on development where it is not needed, and too little where it is desperately needed.

Chapter 11 provided a framework that embeds training within a larger concept of employee development. Organizations must consider more than just the development or learning experience. They must also consider whether individuals are sufficiently prepared and ready to develop and whether individuals have opportunities to transfer their learning back to the workplace. A significant implication of this model is that investments that are most pivotal to the effectiveness of development are often in areas beyond the learning or training experience itself. Yet, the vast majority of learning and training analyses fixate on the learning event. Chapter 11 also showed that improved work performance is only one outcome of enhanced development. Job applicants and employees increasingly regard development as a core element of the employment value proposition and experience. This is particularly true in economically developing regions, where the talent competition is often fiercest. Organizations that invest prudently in development have the potential for ancillary benefits through recruitment, retention, and reduced turnover.

As the chapter showed, the value of workforce development investments depend on the costs of that investment, the resulting quality of the workforce, and the impact of that quality improvement on the pivotal elements of the work. Research has found positive relationships, but not necessarily causal ones, between training expenditures and subsequent stock performance. Research also shows that while organizations often focus only on learning or performance as development outcomes, the investments in workforce development can enhance employee attitudes, too.

Finally, Chapter 11 showed how vital it is to consider the value of enhanced job performance in estimating the payoffs from employee development. Essentially, training investments should be targeted to the places where their effects have the most impact on organizational and unit goals. With a few simple modifications, the same formulas that allow you to estimate the economic value of staffing also allow you to project the monetary value of development. Again, a vital factor to consider is the value of performance variability, what we have called the "pivotalness" of performance in a job or role.

Better training is not equally valuable everywhere, and organizations that simply strive to enhance the skills of all employees, or enhance only the lowest skill levels, will fail to optimize their investments. Using the frameworks of Chapter 10, organizations can apply the same rigor and logic to investments in workforce development that they apply to investments in other important resources. This will be increasingly important because accelerated change means that workers must reskill much faster and much more frequently.

Intangible Does Not Mean Unmeasurable

Accounting systems measure important costs, but effective talent decision frameworks will go beyond costs to encompass intangible investments and value. The chapters in this book have shown that intangible elements are not necessarily unmeasurable, even if traditional accounting frameworks frequently overlook them. The first step in improving talent decisions is often just to break the traditional perception that decisions about talent cannot be systematic because talent measures are so soft. Research shows that if managers fail to perceive HR issues as strategic and analytical, they may simply not attend to analytical and numeric analysis. They seem to place HR into a soft category of phenomena that are beyond analysis, and therefore only really addressable through opinions, politics, or other less-analytical approaches.[2]

An initial step in effective measurement is to get managers to accept that HR analysis is possible and informative. The way to do that is often not to present the most sophisticated analysis right away. Instead, the best approach may be to present relatively simple measures that clearly connect to the mental frameworks that managers are familiar with. As you have seen throughout this book, simply calculating and tracking the costs of turnover or absence, for example, reveals that millions of dollars might be saved with even modest improvements in employee retention and attendance. Many organization leaders have told us that such a turnover cost analysis was their first realization that HR issues could be connected to the tangible economic and accounting outcomes they were familiar with.

No one would suggest that measuring only the cost of turnover is sufficient for good decision making. As the frameworks in earlier chapters show, overzealous attempts to cut turnover or absence costs can lead to compromises in workforce quality or flexibility that have negative effects that far outweigh the cost savings. However, the change process toward more enlightened and logical decisions may require starting with costs before presenting leaders with more complete (and complex) analyses. An initial analysis that shows substantial cost reductions can create an awareness among leaders that the same analytical logic they use for financial, technological, and marketing investments can apply to human resources. Recall the framework that we introduced in Chapter 1, with HR measures in all three anchor points (efficiency, effectiveness, and impact). From a change management perspective, efficiency measures may be the appropriate starting point to get broad acceptance of HR analytics and may be the platform from which to build measures of effectiveness and impact.

The belief (or even the reality) that something important can't be measured is simply no excuse for avoiding logical analysis. As you have seen, it is possible to measure many aspects of talent that are seldom recognized by traditional systems. For example, there are several ways to measure the value of differences in performance, changes in employee attitudes, and the responses of employees to investments in employee health and welfare. Organizational leaders remain mostly naïve to these opportunities and therefore naïve to the significant opportunities they provide for enhancing their decisions. Even when perfect measures are unavailable, you have seen that solid logic can enhance decisions, using sensitivity analysis, break-even analysis, and risk assessment to make up for measurement imperfections, just as these tools are used in other areas of management.

Bringing It Together

Throughout this text, we have provided models and techniques for identifying and evaluating human capital interventions. The techniques in this book can equip you to make meaningful improvements for organizations and their constituents. Yet, effective analyses are not the whole story in delivering organizational change. Beyond knowing the correct formulas to use, delivering business results will also depend on approaching problems with a clear logical framework, choosing the right problem to address, gaining buy-in for recommendations, and implementing changes.

The HC BRidge Framework as a Meta Model

Figure 12.1 shows the HC BRidge framework. In Chapter 1, we introduced the anchor points of this framework: efficiency, effectiveness, and impact. Here, we show the linking elements between HR investments and sustainable strategic success. We have not attempted to define measurements for every linking element, and more detail on the linking elements can be found elsewhere.[3] We have suggested that when measuring the effects of HR investments, organization leaders should keep all three anchor points in mind.

Proceeding from the bottom-right side of Figure 12.1, we note that investments and policies and practices are perhaps the most prominent and tangible elements of the measurement frameworks we have described here. The chapters provided detailed frameworks for identifying both the tangible and intangible costs comprising HR investments, and they explained how to measure the frequency and use of HR policies and practices. Relying on those frameworks, HR leaders can estimate more accurately the full costs of programs such as training, healthcare, testing, recruiting, and communication, as well as the activity levels and use of such programs by employees and managers.

A fundamental purpose of this book was to provide logic models that revealed the required conditions that must be achieved for the

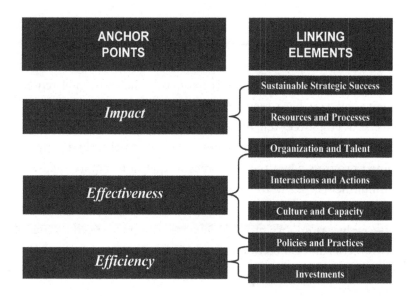

Figure 12.1. HC BRidge Framework.

effects of the programs to offset their costs. These are "necessary and sufficient" conditions.[4] They comprise not only the elements that are necessary, but all the elements that are sufficient, to achieve or explain program success. These conditions not only guide measurement, they also become powerful frameworks for more sophisticated logical discussions about where and how HR programs work. Consider the supply chain framework for staffing, and the logical elements of the staffing utility model. Chapters 9 and 10 showed that by combining powerful statistical assumptions with the concepts of cost, quantity, and quality, we have frameworks that predict when enhanced recruitment, selection, and retention will pay off, and how to optimize the synergy between the three elements. More applicants are not always better, just as more valid testing and higher retention rates are not always optimal. The "necessary and sufficient conditions" depicted in the logic models in each chapter of the book allow leaders to go beyond simply recognizing the idea of optimization and instead actually strive to achieve it.

The role of organizational culture was equally fundamental, but it emerged in a more subtle way. If you look back through the book, virtually every chapter emphasized the importance of a pivotal resource—leadership support and managers, supervisors, and employees who understand and engage with the investments in people. This hidden resource is frequently the most vital requirement, and you have seen examples of its importance in areas as diverse as employee welfare, selection, and training. In addition, you have seen the importance of values, norms, and beliefs in driving sustained progress when the outcomes in question require long-term commitments, as in the case of employee development, health improvement, and better work/life fit and workplace flexibility. Although it is important to understand and track specific program investments and outcomes, it is often contextual factors like leader support and employee motivation that determine the effectiveness of investments in people.

The element of "capacity" in Figure 12.1 has figured prominently in the frameworks we have described. The effectiveness of HR investments almost always includes their effect on the capability (skills and knowledge), opportunity, and motivation of the program participants. We have shown that knowledge and learning are not only measurable, they are also often essential clues to understanding how programs eventually affect organizational performance. You saw how to measure engagement and commitment, which represent important proxies for employee motivation. Measuring the combination of capability, opportunity, and motivation makes it possible to estimate the return on investment from HR programs using logic similar to the ROI calculations that are so familiar in other vital organizational investments. Indeed, you saw that cost-effectiveness analysis frequently provides valuable insights even when outcomes are not translated into monetary values. It is often quite valuable to estimate the cost of a particular increase in knowledge, learning, or engagement, particularly when comparing different programs designed to affect the same outcomes.

In Figure 12.1 the element of "actions and interactions" have figured prominently, because performance is usually observed through the specific actions or behaviors of employees, and their interactions both within and outside the organization. As Chapter 9 showed, deeply analyzing such performance elements often reveals unseen opportunities to create value by improving employee performance. The fundamental distinction between the average value of performance or its importance, and the value of enhanced performance, or pivotalness, is the key to understanding where investments in people have the greatest payoff. You saw that traditional job descriptions often obscure pivot-points, but that estimating the dollar value of performance differences often reveals pivot-points and their associated opportunities. Virtually all leaders recognize the principle of investing where there are large opportunities for gains, but they frequently fail to apply the principle to investments in people. Chapter 9 showed how to find those pivotal opportunities by considering the actions and interactions that make the biggest difference in key performance outcomes.

Resources and processes in the HC BRidge framework (Figure 12.1) provide the connection points between the observable actions and interactions typically measured in performance assessment and their effect on the sustainable strategic success of the organization. This kind of deep strategy analysis is a topic beyond the scope of this book,[5] but the importance of resources and processes in evaluating the effects of improved talent was still apparent. For example, measuring the value of performance relied on understanding how performance affected processes such as sales or production.

As we have seen, although enhanced employee performance, engagement, health, knowledge, retention, and attendance are laudable goals, they are not uniformly valuable. We have seen how important it is to ask questions such as "learning for what purpose?" Often, the answers will require integrating the measurement of HR investments with strategy and planning processes outside the HR function. More precisely measuring the efficiency and effectiveness elements of such programs, which has been the focus of this book, provides a powerful platform for then engaging the question of how these outcomes really affect the business.

Analytics Is a Team Sport

Effective analysis is a necessary but not sufficient component of driving organizational efficiency, effectiveness, and impact. Thus, statistical prowess alone is insufficient for success. Projects such as those identified in this book will be more powerful levers for change to the extent that they are driven by a team of individuals with complementary skills. Different skills are required to identify strategically important opportunities for human capital investment, to identify and curate the data required for analysis, to execute those analyses, make sense of the findings, determine the best course of action, and influence others to pursue that course of action. Loosely, good data work requires at least four major buckets of skills—content expertise to be able to do things like identify relevant questions, data-management expertise to do things like find and manage data, analytical expertise to explore and test those data, and influencing expertise to ensure that results of the work are incorporated.

Taken together, this means that the skills brought by an analyst likely need to be complemented by other skill sets. Common complementary skills include the data-management skills, such as extracting data and managing databases. Each project will bring with it unique demands for content expertise, which may include such things as expertise with the relevant business or a deep understanding of employment law. Finally, expertise in skills such as influencing and change management are essential to making the transition from great idea to implementation and results.

Effectively Communicating Talent-Investment Analyses to Leaders and Decision-Makers

In Chapter 2, we described some key data visualization principles. Effectively using techniques such as storytelling and data visualization can be the difference between a research project that is abandoned and one that is implemented. If "a picture is worth a thousand words," then a compelling story may be worth a thousand pages of graphs and statistics.

Consider the difference between a long PowerPoint presentation that shows detailed descriptions of training programs and costs, post-training learning measures, and turnover patterns of the trained employees, in contrast to a simple assertion: "As a company, we are known as the most effective organization at developing technical talent for our competitors." This simple sentence expresses the essential integration between training and turnover. The power of imagery and exposition in the second approach can be a useful strategy to getting leaders engaged.

A good story has a clear progression, from setting the stage, through rising action and climax, to falling action and eventual resolution.[6] In our example above, the simple opening statement sets a compelling, relatable context and establishes a tension that needs resolution—in this case, that the organization in question is seen as being highly effective at developing talent... for competitors. This particular story can lead to a climax and resolution around several strategic options, depending on the organization's strategy and priorities (see Chapter 3 on strategic talent management). For example, one strategy might involve embracing the role as a training ground for other organizations in the industry and incorporating that as part of an active up-or-out talent strategy. A very different set of strategic investments would follow if the organization chose instead to address this as a retention problem.

Walking decision-makers through a story arc creates an opportunity for those decision-makers to move through six stages:[7]

» **Receive** the analytics at the right time and in the right context;
» **Retrieve** and attend to the analytics;
» **Believe** the analytics are credible and likely to represent their real world;
» **Perceive** a sufficient impact to justify their time and attention;

» **Conceive** that they can use the analytics; and

» **Achieve** improvements in their decisions and actions.

This core list of stages can serve as a handy rubric or checklist in building communications to stakeholders and supporting action.

Lighting the LAMP of Organization Change

William Bryce Cameron famously said, "Not everything that counts can be counted, and not everything that can be counted counts."[8] This quotation reflects some important conclusions and caveats as you apply the frameworks described here. First, it is certainly true that we can't measure everything about talent and HR program effects. Many important elements of such investments remain relatively obscure and cannot be translated precisely into numbers. In particular, they remain outside the domain of traditional business measurement systems. That said, it is also apparent that the frequent failure to make systematic decisions about HR and talent investments is seldom due to the lack of measures. Indeed, advances in technology make it ever more possible to measure vital costs and effects that were once out of reach. Consider the ease with which data from organizational processes, such as supply chains and customer relationship management systems, can be accessed as those processes become more web-enabled. Organizations like Amazon and UPS are experimenting with wearable digital monitors (gloves, goggles, hats, etc.) that automatically track the movement and work in delivery and warehouses. The internet of things promises a digitized array of devices at work and at home that will create a tsunami of data.

HR is no exception. Given the increasing volume, velocity, and variety of HR-related big data, including new technologies to analyze text and other types of unstructured data, there will be no shortage of data available to examine how HR investments relate to organizational outcomes. It is now feasible to connect customer reactions to particular call center or retail encounters with specific employees. Inexpensive and rapidly accessible data storage systems make it possible to archive information about employees at the time they are hired or promoted, and to use that information to determine what factors might be associated with their later success. Indeed, it is now feasible to evaluate business leaders on the accuracy and success of their decisions in hiring, promotion, layoffs, and performance assessment.

However, that brings us to perhaps the core dilemma facing future talent measurement systems: not everything that can be counted necessarily counts. Some things that are easily measured may not be pivotal to decisions. Information overload is a very real danger without logical frameworks that are capable of guiding leaders to the key relationships and measures that matter most to better decisions. That's why in this book we have emphasized logic and analytics over simply lists of measures or examples of scorecards. The examples we have presented are meant to inspire and motivate future leaders to see the potential in evolving digital monitoring and data systems, but the more important purpose of our frameworks is to enhance the logic of decision-based measurement. As you use this book, simple replicating a particular cost calculation, or implementing a particular measure of engagement, attendance, retention, or performance, is not the point. What matters is that you use these examples as templates and develop the most valuable measures for your particular strategic and business situation, while considering the capacities of your measurement systems and decision makers.

You must avoid the temptation to focus only where measures exist today. You may have greater impact using imperfect measures that illuminate more vital factors for improving decisions. Logic and analysis are the tools that help take even imperfect measures and create tangible decision value.

In the end, the true test of talent and HR measurement is not its elegance, or even its acceptance and use by members of the HR profession. These are important factors, but they are merely the intermediate steps to the larger goal: building more effective organizations by making better decisions about talent. We hope that this book will become one important tool in your journey to that important goal.

References

1. William Bryce Cameron, *Informal Sociology: A Casual Introduction to Sociological Thinking* (New York: Random House, 1963).

2. Johns, Gary, "Constraints on the Adoption of Psychology-Based Personnel Practices: Lessons from Organizational Innovation," *Personnel Psychology* 46, no. 3 (September 1993): 569–92.

3. John W. Boudreau and Peter M. Ramstad, *Beyond HR: The New Science of Human Capital* (Boston: Harvard Business School Publishing, 2007).

4. Boudreau and Ramstad, *Beyond HR*.

5. Strategy-analysis frameworks are covered in more detail in Wayne F. Cascio and John W. Boudreau, *Short Introduction to Strategic Human Resource Management* (New York: Cambridge University Press, 2012). See also Arthur A. Thompson et al., *Crafting and Executing Strategy: The Quest for Competitive Advantage*, 20th ed. (New York: McGraw-Hill, 2016).

6. John W. Boudreau, "HR Analysts: Unleash Your Inner Storyteller" Visier, accessed December 3, 2018, https://www.visier.com/clarity/hr-analysts -storyteller/.

7. John W. Boudreau and Wayne F. Cascio, "Human Capital Analytics: Why Are We Not There?," *Journal of Organizational Effectiveness: People and Performance* 4, no. 2 (2017): 119–26.

8. Cameron, *Informal Sociology*.

Index

66216200R00249

Made in the USA
Middletown, DE
05 September 2019